ENVIRONMENTAL CRIME

Law, Policy, Prosecution

ASPEN PUBLISHERS

ENVIRONMENTAL CRIME

Law, Policy, Prosecution

Kathleen F. Brickey

James Carr Professor of Criminal Jurisprudence
Washington University School of Law
St. Louis

Wolters Kluwer
Law & Business

AUSTIN   BOSTON   CHICAGO   NEW YORK   THE NETHERLANDS

Aspen Publishers
Attn: Permissions Department
76 Ninth Avenue, 7th Floor
New York, NY   10011-5201

To contact Customer Care, e-mail customer.care@aspenpublishers.com, call 1-800-234-1660, fax 1-800-901-9075, or mail correspondence to:

Aspen Publishers
Attn: Order Department
PO Box 990
Frederick, MD 21705

Printed in the United States of America.

1 2 3 4 5 6 7 8 9 0

ISBN 978-0-7355-6249-3

Library of Congress Cataloging-in-Publication Data

Brickey, Kathleen F.
  Environmental crime : law, policy, prosecution / Kathleen F. Brickey.
    p. cm.
  "This book...is a law school textbook" — Preface.
  Includes bibliographical references and index.
  ISBN 978-0-7355-6249-3
  1. Environmental law—United States—Criminal provisions. 2. Offenses against the environment—United States. I. Title.

KF3775.B75 2008
344.7304'6—dc22
                          2008022214

About Wolters Kluwer Law & Business

Wolters Kluwer Law & Business is a leading provider of research information and workflow solutions in key specialty areas. The strengths of the individual brands of Aspen Publishers, CCH, Kluwer Law International and Loislaw are aligned within Wolters Kluwer Law & Business to provide comprehensive, in-depth solutions and expert-authored content for the legal, professional and education markets.

CCH was founded in 1913 and has served more than four generations of business professionals and their clients. The CCH products in the Wolters Kluwer Law & Business group are highly regarded electronic and print resources for legal, securities, antitrust and trade regulation, government contracting, banking, pension, payroll, employment and labor, and healthcare reimbursement and compliance professionals.

Aspen Publishers is a leading information provider for attorneys, business professionals and law students. Written by preeminent authorities, Aspen products offer analytical and practical information in a range of specialty practice areas from securities law and intellectual property to mergers and acquisitions and pension/benefits. Aspen's trusted legal education resources provide professors and students with high-quality, up-to-date and effective resources for successful instruction and study in all areas of the law.

Kluwer Law International supplies the global business community with comprehensive English-language international legal information. Legal practitioners, corporate counsel and business executives around the world rely on the Kluwer Law International journals, loose-leafs, books and electronic products for authoritative information in many areas of international legal practice.

Loislaw is a premier provider of digitized legal content to small law firm practitioners of various specializations. Loislaw provides attorneys with the ability to quickly and efficiently find the necessary legal information they need, when and where they need it, by facilitating access to primary law as well as state-specific law, records, forms and treatises.

Wolters Kluwer Law & Business, a unit of Wolters Kluwer, is headquartered in New York and Riverwoods, Illinois. Wolters Kluwer is a leading multinational publisher and information services company.

For
Calico, Cricket, Cupcake,
Newbie, Peekaboo, Pretty Boy,
Pumpkin, Sapphire,
Scarlet, Stardust, Starlight,
Sweet Pea, Twilight,
and all the other little guys and dolls

And for
Dania and Sharon

SUMMARY
OF CONTENTS

CONTENTS

3 *INDIVIDUAL AND ORGANIZATIONAL LIABILITY*   *61*

9   *ENFORCEMENT*   *335*

PREFACE

The term "environmental crime" is a relatively recent addition to the criminal law lexicon. Until the mid-1980s, environmental enforcement was synonymous with civil enforcement. But the advent of modern environmental legislation in the 1970s and 1980s ushered in an era of increased public and congressional support for sending polluters to jail. As Congress began transforming the environmental law landscape by importing criminal law principles into the mix, the Justice Department established a full blown Environmental Crimes Section whose exclusive domain was criminal enforcement of environmental laws; the Environmental Protection Agency (EPA) acquired criminal investigatory tools and created an Office of Criminal Enforcement; and violations of hazardous waste regulations and air and water quality standards became subject to prosecution as felonies. As might have been expected, this succession of events heralded a sea change in environmental enforcement.

This book, which bridges the historical divide between two discrete, specialized fields of law, is the first law school text devoted exclusively to the study of environmental crime. Chapter 1 provides an overview of the environmental regulatory framework and explores key points of contention that are at the core of the criminal enforcement debate. Did Congress overlook dangers inherent in elevating violations of existing environmental standards — originally set at levels designed for *civil* enforcement — into serious crimes? Are the goals of environmental law and criminal law compatible under the current regulatory regime? These are among several recurring conceptual themes that run throughout the book.

Chapters 2 and 3 provide the foundation for integrating fundamental criminal law principles with environmental law concepts in later chapters of the book. Chapter 2 examines the mental states — principally knowledge and negligence — that distinguish criminal violations from their civil counterparts. Are these threshold levels of culpability set too low? Do they unfairly put innocents at risk of criminal prosecution? These, too, are questions that are central to the criminal enforcement debate. Chapter 3 examines principles governing individual and organizational responsibility for criminal conduct. Can corporate officers be held responsible for crimes they did not personally commit? Are subordinate employees criminally liable for environmental violations that occur on the job? When can a corporation or other legal entity be held criminally accountable for environmental crimes, and why? Since most environmental crime prosecutions are based on violations that occur in a business or workplace setting, familiarity with the underlying principles of personal and organizational liability is essential.

Chapters 4 through 7 focus, respectively, on the principal criminal provisions in the Clean Water Act, Clean Air Act, Resource Conservation and Recovery Act (RCRA), and the Comprehensive Environmental Response, Compensation, and Liability Act (CERCLA). Each chapter provides a basic grounding in key environmental law concepts embedded in the relevant criminal enforcement scheme and examines how the applicable environmental and criminal law concepts intersect. Satellite issues such as jurisdiction, double jeopardy, preemption, and immunity are considered in the contexts in which they are most likely to arise.

Although the principal goal of many environmental laws and regulations is prevention of harm to the environment, Chapters 4, 5, and 6 provide insights into environmental laws that have a distinctly different focus. Knowing endangerment provisions in the Clean Water Act, Clean Air Act, and RCRA criminalize environmental violations that cause — or create an unacceptably high risk of causing — death or serious bodily injury. The pending prosecution of W.R. Grace for releasing tons of asbestos into the ambient air in Libby, Montana serves as a focal point for considering the Clean Air Act's knowing endangerment statute.

In Chapter 7, Consolidated Edison's conviction for violating CERCLA's notification requirements after a 1989 steam pipe explosion provides a vehicle for exploring a "worst case scenario" response to an environmental emergency. Although Con Ed knew the explosion had spewed more than 200 pounds of asbestos-contaminated debris into Manhattan's Gramercy Park, Con Ed officials did not notify regulators that the explosion had released asbestos into the environment. Not surprisingly, Con Ed's failure to give the required notice was motivated in part by a desire to avoid the cost of legally required clean-up procedures. The utility's dramatically different response to a similar explosion in 2007 provides a useful object lesson on sentencing and corporate culture.

Chapter 8 turns to conventional criminal statutes — principally conspiracy, mail fraud, false statements, and obstruction of justice — that are often invoked in environmental crime prosecutions. The discussion of liability under the federal false statements statute revisits the Con Ed case to illustrate the interaction between environmental crimes (e.g., failure to notify regulatory authorities of the asbestos release as required by CERCLA) and conventional white collar crimes (e.g., violating the false statements statute by lying to regulators and concealing knowledge of the asbestos release). W.R. Grace also briefly reappears in this chapter. A guilty plea the company entered in connection with the contamination of drinking water wells in Woburn, Massachusetts illustrates how laws like the false statements statute have been used as gap-fillers to augment the coverage of environmental laws. Later, in the obstruction of justice discussion, W.R. Grace makes a second brief appearance in connection with pending cover-up charges in the Libby, Montana prosecution.

And last, Chapter 9 focuses on enforcement issues. How is criminal enforcement authority allocated between environmental regulators and criminal prosecutors? What case selection criteria do EPA and the Justice Department use to determine which violations should be treated as crimes? Are environmental prosecutors "loose cannons," as some critics suggest? Or is the current system of centralized decision making and multi-level review an effective check on prosecutorial discretion? What do we actually know about charging practices in environmental crime prosecutions? While some of these issues were previewed in earlier sections of the book, Chapter 9 explores them more fully in the broader context of the government's criminal enforcement program.

Throughout the book I have tried to make the material accessible to students regardless of their technical or legal background. To further advance that goal, a glossary of acronyms is provided at the end of the book.

For the sake of brevity and clarity, I have omitted a number of footnotes, citations, and parallel citations without specifically flagging their deletion. Remaining footnotes have been renumbered consecutively within each chapter, and explanatory footnotes that I have added to cases and other excerpted material are identified by the legend "— ED."

As of the date of publication, the principal criminal provisions in the Clean Water Act, the Clean Air Act, RCRA, and CERCLA are posted on the website for the book, as are the conventional white collar crime statutes considered in Chapter 8. Several government documents that appear as excerpts in the book have also been posted in full. The website can be accessed at www.aspenlawschool.com/brickey_environment.

There are few occasions for faculty to publicly acknowledge their Dean's positive impact on their productivity. Happily, this is one of them. I am deeply indebted to Kent Syverud for his generous support of my scholarly pursuits. Kent's support has been pivotal in bringing this project to fruition in a relatively short period of time. I am also indebted to the exceptionally talented research assistants who worked on the book. Seth Heller and Edward Lush ably assisted me during the early research phase of the project. Dania Becker and Sharon Palmer, who joined the project at a much later phase, contributed invaluable critiques and superb editorial suggestions. My faculty assistant, Beverly Owens, is a perfectionist's perfectionist. The camera ready manuscript she produced is a testament to her extraordinary skill, patience, and dedication. The book has also benefitted from the assistance of Shelly Henderson, whose eagle eye can spot a typo at 100 paces; from Jane Box's meticulous attention to organization and detail; and from an excellent working relationship with John Devins at Aspen Publishers. I am especially grateful to Annie Smith Piffel for her unique contribution to the book. Annie produced a series of delightful beta sketches, one of which ("Fish F") appears as a watermark on the dedication page. Last but not least, a special word of thanks to my husband, Jim, who so admirably filled the indispensable roles of adviser and confidante, head chef, and remodeler-in-chief. I am grateful for his steadfast support, encouragement, and TLC.

Kathleen F. Brickey

April 2008

ACKNOWLEDGMENTS

I am indebted to the following sources for permission to reprint excerpts from their published works.

Kathleen F. Brickey, *Charging Practices in Hazardous Waste Prosecutions*, 62 Ohio St. L.J. 1077, 1091-1093 (2001). Reprinted with permission.

Kathleen F. Brickey, *Environmental Crime at the Crossroads: The Intersection of Environmental and Criminal Law Theory*, 71 Tul. L. Rev. 487, 494-497, 498-504 (1997). Reprinted with permission.

Kathleen F. Brickey, *The Rhetoric of Environmental Crime: Culpability, Discretion, and Structural Reform*, 84 Iowa L. Rev. 115, 120-121, 126-131, 133-135 (1998). Reprinted with permission.

Kathleen F. Brickey, *Wetlands Reform and the Criminal Enforcement Record: A Cautionary Tale*, 76 Wash. U. L.Q. 71, 76-84 (1998). Reprinted with permission.

John C. Coffee, Jr., *Does "Unlawful" Mean "Criminal"?: Reflections on the Disappearing Crime/Tort Distinction in American Law*, 71 B.U. L. Rev. 193, 219-220 (1991). Reprinted with permission.

Francis T. Cullen, Gray Cavendar, William J. Maakestad & Michael L. Benson, Corporate Crime Under Attack: The Fight to Criminalize Business Violence 362-364 (2006). Reprinted from Corporate Crime Under Attack: The Fight Against Corporate Violence with permission. Copyright 2006 Matthew Bender & Company, Inc., a member of the LexisNexis Group. All rights reserved.

Richard J. Lazarus, *Assimilating Environmental Protection into Legal Rules and the Problem with Environmental Crime*, 27 Loy. L.A. L. Rev. 867, 881-883 (1994). Reprinted with permission of the Loyola of Los Angeles Law Review and Richard J. Lazarus.

Richard J. Lazarus, *Meeting the Demands of Integration in the Evolution of Environmental Law: Reforming Criminal Law*, 83 Geo. L.J. 2407, 2487-2490 (1995). Reprinted with permission of the publisher, Georgetown Law Journal © 1995.

Andrew Schneider & David McCumber, An Air That Kills 66-68, 73-75, 85-87 (2004). Reprinted by permission.

ENVIRONMENTAL CRIME

Law, Policy, Prosecution

1

ENVIRONMENTAL CRIME

Public concern about a newly perceived social problem — the environment, worker safety, child neglect, etc. — seems to trigger a recurring social response: namely, an almost reflexive resort to criminal prosecution.[†]

Just because the wrongdoer has [caused harm] by way of an environmental medium — such as air or water — does not make that conduct any less deserving of criminal sanction.[††]

The concepts of environmental crime and criminal enforcement of environmental laws are relatively recent phenomena. Although surveys conducted in the 1970s and 1980s showed strong public support for sending polluters to jail, the legislative process and the development of effective criminal enforcement tools within the executive branch lagged behind the

---

[†]Professor John C. Coffee, Jr.
[††]Professor Richard J. Lazarus.

public perception that egregious violations of environmental standards warrant treatment as serious crimes.

A. SUPPORT FOR CRIMINAL SANCTIONS

Public opinion polls conducted during the period when Congress and executive agencies were developing criminal enforcement mechanisms suggested (perhaps surprisingly) a "get tough" attitude toward environmental crime. More than two-thirds of survey respondents favored incarceration for deliberate violations of environmental laws, and environmental crime ranked seventh in importance in a survey on public attitudes toward crime.[1]

Since environmental crime was not yet a well-established concept in theory or in law when these polls were conducted, what prompted a substantial segment of the public to rank pollution of a city's drinking water supply as more serious than arson or giving a bank robber a floor plan of the bank? What comes to mind when we think of "environmental crime" and why?

First and foremost, many members of the public associate environmental contamination with catastrophic harm to human health and the environment. One example that readily comes to mind is Love Canal, a New York community that was destroyed by toxic waste.

After disposing of hazardous chemicals contaminated with dioxin and pesticides in Love Canal over a substantial period of time, Hooker Chemical gave the contaminated property to the Niagra Falls Board of Education in the early 1950s. The city later built a public school on the site and permitted residential development in adjacent areas.

Twenty-five years later, the New York State Health Department declared a public health emergency and relocated more than 200 families after it was confirmed that women living closest to the canal experienced unusually high rates of miscarriages. Although the Health Department did not believe the remaining families were at risk, a private health survey revealed geographic clusters of more serious health problems associated with the

---

[1]*See* U.S. Dept. of Justice Bureau of Justice Statistics, The National Survey of Crime Severity, vii-viii (1985); Robert Deeb, *Environmental Criminal Liability*, 2 S.C. ENVTL. L.J. 159, 160-161 (1993); F. Henry Habicht, II, *The Federal Perspective on Environmental Criminal Enforcement: How to Remain on the Civil Side*, 17 Envtl. L. Rep. (Envtl. L. Inst.) 10,478, 10,484 & n. 64 (1987); Susan Hedman, *Expressive Functions in Environmental Law*, 59 GEO. WASH. L. REV. 889, 889 & n.1 (1991).

contamination, including diseases of the central nervous system. Before all was said and done, more than 1,000 households were declared uninhabitable because of the contamination.

But environmental contamination not only poses serious public health risks. It can also adversely affect local economies and ways of life. In 1989, the tanker *Exxon Valdez* ran aground on Bligh Reef in Prince William Sound, Alaska, spilling more than 10 million gallons of oil into the Sound. The spill fouled hundreds of miles of pristine Alaskan coastline, devastated marine and waterfowl populations, destroyed vast amounts of wildlife habitat, seriously damaged fragile ecosystems, and wreaked long-term havoc on the economic and social fabric of indigenous populations.

The examples are legion, but Love Canal and Exxon Valdez suggest why a significant percentage of the public would favor criminal prosecution of egregious environmental violations.

But while environmental crime immediately brings to mind highly visible cases like these, environmental crime also encompasses clandestine activity like midnight dumping of hazardous waste, moving hazardous chemicals from one location to another pending government inspections, burying toxic contaminants, and other similar efforts to conceal hazards to human health and the environment.

Because the harm flowing from environmental violations ignores political and geographic boundaries, it is not surprising that the public would support the use of criminal sanctions against those who cause or create the risk of such harm.

B. THE REGULATORY FRAMEWORK

Although federal environmental regulations have been on the books for years, it was not until the 1970s that Congress acknowledged the need to address environmental concerns with comprehensive legislation. As Congress began to address them, however, it was against a historical backdrop of civil rather than criminal enforcement. While criminal prosecutions were not unprecedented, "there was no systematic effort by either federal or state governments to utilize criminal sanctions on behalf of environmental protection goals."[2]

---

[2]Richard J. Lazarus, *Assimilating Environmental Protection into Legal Rules and the Problem with Environmental Crime*, 27 Loy. L.A. L. Rev. 867, 868-869 (1994) [hereinafter Lazarus, *Assimilating Environmental Protection*].

1. FEDERAL LEGISLATION

Congress marked the beginning of modern environmental law with the enactment of the Clean Air Act Amendments of 1970 (the Clean Air Act) and the Federal Water Pollution Control Act Amendments of 1972 (the Clean Water Act). These landmark legislative achievements were followed by the Resource Conservation and Recovery Act (RCRA) in 1976, which provides cradle to grave regulation of hazardous waste, and the Comprehensive Environmental Response, Conservation and Liability Act (CERCLA) in 1980, also known as the Superfund law, which provides a mechanism for financing cleanup of the worst hazardous waste sites in the country.

Although these four major environmental acts created a comprehensive regulatory framework, they did little to encourage criminal enforcement. The criminal provisions carried only misdemeanor penalties, which had little deterrent value and provided little incentive for prosecutors to invest scarce resources in criminal enforcement.

It was not until 1980 that Congress authorized the first felony penalties for environmental violations in federal law by amending RCRA's criminal provisions. The 1980 amendments also created a new RCRA crime, knowing endangerment, which also carried felony penalties.[3] But it took another four years for Congress to revamp the definition of the endangerment crime to make it an effective enforcement tool.[4]

Congress continued the trend toward criminalizing environmental law when it enacted the Clean Air Act Amendments of 1990, which expanded the scope of the criminal provisions to include, among others, a knowing endangerment offense, and increased the maximum fines and prison terms for criminal violations of the Clean Air Act.

Thus, the principal statutory and enforcement tools that marked official recognition of the concept of environmental crime have evolved on an incremental basis over time.

---

[3]The knowing endangerment provision is considered in Chapter 6.

[4]As originally enacted, the knowing endangerment provision required proof that the defendant's conduct showed "unjustified and inexcusable disregard for human life" or "extreme indifference to human life." Congress repealed the "inexcusable disregard" and "extreme indifference" requirements in 1984.

2. REGULATION

The principal environmental statutes, which are both proactive and reactive, are not self-implementing. The enactment of these four large and highly complex environmental acts over a period of just ten years gave the Environmental Protection Agency (EPA), the fledgling administrative agency charged with responsibility for implementing them,[5] an enormous regulatory task. The difficulty of its task was compounded by often unrealistic congressional deadlines for promulgating thousands of pages of regulations and setting up workable mechanisms for implementing them.

Moreover, the EPA was often diverted from performing these tasks by overly zealous congressional oversight of the agency's performance and by the necessity of defending hundreds of lawsuits challenging EPA's exercise of its regulatory authority.[6] These diversions, in turn, strained EPA's human and budgetary resources, further hampering its ability to fulfill its primary mission.

3. ENFORCEMENT

The EPA's struggle to simultaneously implement the Clean Water Act, the Clean Air Act, RCRA, and CERCLA meant that it could give little time and attention to enforcing recently promulgated regulatory requirements, much less give priority to criminal enforcement.

More importantly, the EPA has limited enforcement capabilities. It has only civil enforcement authority, which includes the power to investigate potential violations.[7] If, during the exercise of its investigative power, EPA discovers conduct that might warrant filing criminal charges, it may refer the

---

[5]Congress created the EPA in 1970 to consolidate enforcement powers that had been shared by the Department of the Interior, the Army Corps of Engineers, and the Department of Health, Education and Welfare.

[6]Lazarus, *Assimilating Environmental Protection, supra* note 2, at 869-879; Richard J. Lazarus, *The Tragedy of Distrust in the Implementation of Federal Environmental Law*, 54 LAW & CONTEMP. PROBS. 311, 355-358 (1991) [hereinafter Lazarus, *Tragedy of Distrust*]. *See also* Robert Glicksman & Christopher H. Schroeder, *EPA and the Courts: Twenty Years of Law and Politics*, 54 LAW & CONTEMP. PROBS. 249, 256-276 (1991).

[7]The principal environmental laws grant the EPA authority to issue administrative compliance orders that include timetables for the violator to correct violations, to impose administrative civil penalties, and to file civil suits seeking injunctive relief and/or civil penalties. *See* FREDERICK R. ANDERSON, ROBERT L. GLICKSMAN, DANIEL R. MANDELKER, A. DAN TARLOCK, ENVIRONMENTAL PROTECTION: LAW AND POLICY 1079-1082 (3d ed. 1999).

matter to the Justice Department for further investigation and possible prosecution.[8]

But structural problems in the EPA's enforcement powers, limited human resources, and tensions between the EPA and the Justice Department further hindered development of an effective criminal enforcement program.

KATHLEEN F. BRICKEY, ENVIRONMENTAL CRIME AT THE CROSSROADS: THE INTERSECTION OF ENVIRONMENTAL AND CRIMINAL LAW THEORY

71 TUL. L. REV. 487, 494-497 (1997)

The EPA's early efforts were necessarily directed at trying to bring industry into compliance. Implementation of recently enacted and highly complex environmental statutes entailed promulgating thousands of pages of technical regulations, putting into place vast regulatory regimes, and defending hundreds of legal challenges to the EPA's administration of the laws.

Laying those administrative burdens aside, criminal enforcement of environmental laws remained a low priority because the EPA lacked personnel trained or experienced in criminal investigation techniques, lacked authority to use customary criminal investigative tools (including search warrants), had a legal staff that often misunderstood the rules of criminal procedure and the differences between civil and criminal cases, and, more fundamentally, lacked consensus about the role of criminal enforcement.

... In 1982, ... the EPA General Counsel issued a policy statement signaling that criminal enforcement would play an important role in the overall enforcement effort.[9]

But the EPA's efforts were severely constrained by its lack of real law-enforcement authority and its inability to gain needed cooperation and assistance from the Justice Department, the United States Marshal's Service, the FBI, and other federal law-enforcement agencies. After a period of

---

[8]The respective enforcement roles of EPA and the Justice Department are considered in Chapter 9.

[9]*See* Daniel Riesel, *Criminal Prosecution and Defense of Environmental Wrongs*, 15 Envtl. L. Rep. (Envtl. L. Inst.) 10,065, 10,067 (1985). For a fuller discussion of the development of the EPA criminal-enforcement program, *see* Judson W. Starr, *Turbulent Times at Justice and EPA: The Origins of Environmental Criminal Prosecutions and the Work that Remains*, 59 GEO. WASH. L. REV. 900, 907-12 (1991).

apparent foot-dragging, the Justice Department authorized the EPA to deputize its agents in 1984, and in 1988 Congress granted EPA investigators full, permanent law-enforcement authority.

In the meantime, the Justice Department was on a parallel track in developing its own criminal-enforcement program. In 1983 the Department created an Environmental Crimes Unit whose exclusive domain was criminal enforcement of environmental laws, and by 1988 the Unit had been elevated to full Section status. In its first ten years of operation, the Department's criminal-enforcement program obtained more than nine hundred environmental crime indictments that resulted in nearly seven hundred guilty pleas and convictions.

Despite its apparent numerical success, the Justice Department's criminal-enforcement record is plagued by political controversy. Spearheaded by Representative John Dingell, whose Subcommittee on Investigations and Oversight of the House Energy and Commerce Committee held extensive hearings in 1992 and 1993, critics challenged the rigor of the criminal-enforcement program by questioning the Department's judgment in declining to prosecute seemingly strong cases (sometimes over strenuous objections from line prosecutors); its apparently deferential treatment of powerful corporations and their executives; its holding of closed-door meetings with defense lawyers without informing EPA officials or the United States Attorney's office; and its "ready agreement to trivial financial penalties in cases involving serious and long-standing environmental violations."[10]

The hearings prompted the Department to appoint an Internal Review Committee to examine the environmental-crimes program in 1993. The following year, the Committee issued a report that defended the Environmental Crimes Section's record. While acknowledging that the Section had experienced some managerial problems,[11] the report concluded that the Section's decisions to decline prosecution in cases targeted by critics were appropriate exercises of prosecutorial discretion and insisted that the Department pursues difficult environmental cases just as it prosecutes complex cases in other statutory contexts.[12]

---

[10]Lazarus, *Assimilating Environmental Protection, supra* note 2, at 874-75.

[11]*See* WILLIAM J. CORCORAN ET AL., INTERNAL REVIEW OF THE DEPARTMENT OF JUSTICE ENVIRONMENTAL CRIMES PROGRAM: REPORT TO THE ATTORNEY GENERAL 162-67 (1994).

[12]*See id.* at 105 & n.143. Notably, the report reveals striking ambivalence about the desirability of environmental criminal enforcement.

This political and very public controversy was not the only signal that Congress favored aggressive prosecution of environmental crimes. During the decade when the EPA and Justice Department criminal-enforcement programs began to evolve, Congress continued to strengthen enforcement tools by adding new criminal provisions to the major environmental statutes, elevating most misdemeanor violations to felonies, and generally increasing the severity of environmental criminal penalties.

———————

The congressional oversight hearings culminated in a report that was strongly critical of the Justice Department's performance in several notable respects. They included:

(1) "a pronounced failure to prosecute environmental crimes to the same degree as conventional crimes . . . [and] to prosecute individuals"; (2) "deep divisions and mistrust between the Environmental Crimes Section and various United States Attorneys' offices"; (3) "chronic case mismanagement"; and (4) "possible political influence in both individual cases and general policies within the Environmental Crimes Section."[13]

Thus, turmoil within the Justice Department was partly responsible for what some regarded as foot dragging in the development of a coherent criminal enforcement program.

C. FRAMING THE CRIMINAL ENFORCEMENT DEBATE

As the rocky relationship between the EPA and the Justice Department in the 1980s suggests, the blending of environmental law principals and criminal law theory is often an uneasy alliance. Some critics of environmental crime prosecutions maintain that environmental law has distinguishing attributes that set it apart from other legal regimes. That, in turn, raises the question whether it is desirable or appropriate to simply incorporate general principles of criminal law into environmental law, or whether a different approach is needed.

———————————

[13]Lazarus, *Assimilating Environmental Protection, supra* note 2, at 875 (quoting Jonathon Turley, The George Washington Univ. Nat'l Law Ctr., Preliminary Report on Criminal Environmental Prosecution by the United States Department of Justice (Oct. 19, 1992)).

1. THE NATURE OF ENVIRONMENTAL LAW

Environmental law scholars maintain that three characteristics make environmental law distinctive: its aspirational qualities, evolutionary nature, and high degree of complexity. Some environmental law scholars maintain that consideration of these features is essential to understanding the dynamics of criminal enforcement in the environmental context and are the core of any fair and sensible criminal enforcement policy.[14]

KATHLEEN F. BRICKEY, ENVIRONMENTAL CRIME AT THE CROSSROADS: THE INTERSECTION OF ENVIRONMENTAL AND CRIMINAL LAW THEORY

71 TUL. L. REV. 487, 498-504 (1997)

A. Aspirational Qualities

Environmental law is "aspirational" or "inspirational" in the sense that it seeks to bring about radical change in human behavior to minimize environmental degradation and hazards to public health. It invokes technology-forcing mandates that are often unrealistic or flatly unobtainable — typically under scientifically or administratively infeasible deadlines.[15]

The earliest notable example of aspirational environmental legislation, the Clean Air Act of 1970, directed states to achieve national ambient air-quality standards commensurate with the protection of public health and

---

[14]*See, e.g.*, Richard J. Lazarus, *Meeting the Demands of Integration in the Evolution of Environmental Law: Reforming Environmental Criminal Law*, 83 GEO. L.J. 2407, 2423-2424, 2453-2454 (1995) [hereinafter Lazarus, *Meeting the Demands*]; Christopher H. Schroeder, *Cool Analysis Versus Moral Outrage in the Development of Federal Environmental Criminal Law*, 35 WM. & MARY L. REV. 251, 252-253 (1993).

[15]*See, e.g.*, Ozone and Carbon Monoxide Plans, 53 Fed. Reg. 49,494, 49,495 (1988) (stating that immediate attainment of the applicable ozone standard in the Los Angeles area is impossible, and attainment within five years would require such draconian measures that it would "remake life" in the region); J. QUARLES, FEDERAL REGULATION OF HAZARDOUS WASTES: A GUIDE TO RCRA 93 (1982) (suggesting that since processing all RCRA permit applications would probably take a decade or more, creation of "interim status" for entities while permanent RCRA permit applications were pending was essential to enable existing facilities to continue to operate; enforcement of RCRA's general prohibition would have caused an "intolerable situation" and "completely disrupt[ed]" ongoing operations).

welfare within three years. That mandate was issued notwithstanding that these standards could only be achieved by radical changes not only in the pollution-control technology and industrial processes of tens of thousands of major stationary sources of air pollution, but in automobile emission-control technology as well. Attaining the necessary air-quality standards for ozone in the South Coast Basin that surrounds Los Angeles, for example, would have required prohibiting almost all traffic, shutting down major business activity, and imposing other draconian constraints on the region's social and economic life.

No less ambitious in its sweep, the Clean Water Act of 1972 adopted the goal of eliminating *all* discharges of pollutants into the nation's waters by 1985, an objective we are nowhere close to attaining more than a decade after the compliance date expired.[16] Nor have we met the (somewhat) more modest goal that all of the nation's waters be fishable and swimmable by 1983, a date that preceded extensive contamination of the New Jersey shoreline with medical wastes[17] and the accidental release of more than ten million gallons of oil into Alaska's Prince William Sound. Although the examples are legion, the air- and water-pollution statutes amply illustrate the point. By mandating unattainable goals, environmental laws impose extraordinarily high standards and simultaneously assure the inability of the regulated community to comply.

To be sure, some commentators credit much of the success of the nation's environmental-enforcement program to the aspirational qualities of environmental law,[18] while others regard this phenomenon as "unrealistic and

---

[16]A Council on Environmental Quality study concluded that during the decade from 1970 to 1980, water quality in the nation's rivers and streams had changed little. *See* COUNCIL ON ENVIRONMENTAL QUALITY 1980, THE ELEVENTH ANNUAL REPORT OF THE COUNCIL ON ENVIRONMENTAL QUALITY 108 (1981). According to EPA estimates, more than 60% of major municipal treatment facilities failed to comply with 1977 statutory deadlines that required secondary or more demanding treatment to meet water quality standards. *See id.* at 131.

[17]Medical waste washed up on the Eastern seaboard in the summer of 1988. Beaches in New York and New Jersey were closed because of high levels of bacteria and the presence of hypodermic needles, blood vials (some of which tested positive for the hepatitis antigen and/or the AIDS antibody), surgical tubing, gauze, gloves, and other medical items. *See* Bob Liff, *Who's Responsible? Investigators Struggle to Pin Down Sources of Waste*, NEWSDAY, Aug. 29, 1988, at 7.

[18]*See* Lazarus, *Meeting the Demands, supra* note 14, at 2426.

even irrational."[19] But, apart from the merits of this mode of environmental policymaking, one might well postulate that environmental law's aspirational qualities make criminal enforcement less appropriate.[20]

B. Evolutionary Nature

Environmental law is in a constant state of flux. Continual change in environmental regulation is all but inevitable. Setting environmental standards requires making "scientifically informed value judgments"[21] based on evolving and often tentative scientific principles.

Environmental policymaking also reflects the volatile forces of public opinion and political conflict over a hierarchy of competing values and interests. Stated simply, environmental policymaking occurs in a rough-and-tumble world. In contrast with the stability normally associated with traditional criminal law, environmental law must perpetually respond to prevailing scientific, political, and social norms.

The evolutionary nature of environmental law creates uncertainty about what the law is or is likely to be, including what conduct will be considered criminal. The unpredictability of the governing legal standards thus may implicate questions of fairness in the context of criminal enforcement and reinforce the belief that the distinctive features of environmental law should not only inform criminal-enforcement policymaking, but should also prescribe its bounds.

C. High Degree of Complexity

No one would argue with the premise that environmental law is highly complex. It is fraught with highly technical scientific, engineering, and economic jargon that, even to one schooled in the intricacies of environmental science and economics, can be truly mind-boggling.

---

[19]Schroeder, *supra* note 14, at 254-55 (articulating cool analysts' argument that in response to "emotional, ill-informed, and irrational public opinion," the EPA spent its first 20 years working on problems the public found important rather than on issues involving the greatest public-health risks).

[20]*See* Lazarus, *Meeting the Demands, supra* note 14, at 2426 ("[I]t does not inexorably follow that such aspirational laws are equally well-suited to civil and criminal enforcement.").

[21]A. Dan Tarlock, *The Nonequilibrium Paradigm in Ecology and the Partial Unraveling of Environmental Law*, 27 LOY. L.A. L. REV. 1121, 1133 (1994).

Apart from the special expertise needed to penetrate the technical facets of environmental law, the draftsmanship in the statutes and regulations is notoriously flawed. The Clean Water Act has been variously described as a "poorly drafted and astonishingly imprecise statute"[22] that is "difficult to understand, construe and apply"[23] and (needless to say) "devoid of plain meaning."[24] Hazardous waste regulations are so complex that they "defy the comprehension of any one person."[25] The Oil Pollution Act of 1990 contains only "[p]ockets of certainty" amidst its "broad mixtures of complex and ambiguous provisions."[26] And so it goes down the line.

In addition to these barriers to understanding environmental law, much of the law itself is obscure. The Oil Pollution Act of 1990, for example, "buries laws within laws and jumbles concepts within a huge legal stew."[27] And as environmental regulations consume literally thousands of pages in the Code of Federal Regulations,[28] "the quantity of minutely detailed language . . . beggars description."[29]   To complicate this overlay of complexity, much of environmental law is hidden in detailed preambles that are not published in the Code of Federal Regulations with the regulations they explain, and in private informal guidance memoranda and letters — hence, the problem of "underground" environmental law.[30]

---

[22]E.I. DuPont de Nemours & Co. v. Train, 541 F.2d 1018, 1026 (4th Cir. 1976), *aff'd in part and rev'd in part*, 430 U.S. 112 (1977).

[23]American Petroleum Inst. v. EPA, 540 F.2d 1023, 1027 (10th Cir. 1976).

[24]Hooker Chems. & Plastic Corp. v. Train, 537 F.2d 620, 627 (2d Cir. 1976).

[25]John-Mark Stensvaag, *The Not So Fine Print of Environmental Law*, 27 LOY. L.A. L. REV. 1093, 1093 (1994). Indeed, the EPA official with oversight responsibility for the hazardous-waste programs asserted that only " 'five people in the agency . . . understand what 'hazardous waste' is' " because the rules change so often. United States v. White, 766 F. Supp. 873, 882 (E.D. Wash. 1991) (quoting Don R. Clay, EPA Assistant Administrator for the Office of Solid Waste and Emergency Response).

[26]WILLIAM H. RODGERS, JR., ENVIRONMENTAL LAW § 4.9, at 379 (2d ed. 1994).

[27]*Id.*

[28]*See* Lazarus, *Meeting the Demands*, *supra* note 14, at 2436. That is also true of Internal Revenue regulations, which are supplemented by scores of volumes of Revenue Rulings (sometimes called "junior regulations"), which are substantive rulings published to promote uniform application of the tax laws, and of Revenue Procedures, which announce IRS practices and procedures that may affect the public or are otherwise of interest to the public.

[29]Stensvaag, *supra* note 25, at 1093.

[30]*See* Lazarus, *Meeting the Demands*, *supra* note 14, at 2437; Lazarus, *The Tragedy of Distrust*, *supra* note 6, at 356. The "underground law" phenomenon appears elsewhere as well. Federal regulatory law is teeming with practices and procedures through which

As is true of its evolutionary nature then, the complexity of environmental law contributes to uncertainty about what conduct will be deemed to be in compliance, and raises concerns among environmental scholars about the appropriateness of criminal enforcement in the midst of such uncertainty.

―――――――――

If environmental law's aspirational qualitites, evolutionary nature, and complexity are truly distinctive and set it apart from other fields of law, then the question becomes whether and to what extent it is appropriate to criminalize environmental violations. Did Congress adequately take these factors into account when deciding which environmental violations to criminalize? That is a subject to which we will turn after briefly considering three key criminal law principles.

2. CORE CRIMINAL LAW CONCEPTS

Traditional criminal law theory is rooted in the core concepts of harm, culpability, and deterrence.

a. Harm

Harm is a central value in the criminal law. It is "the fulcrum between criminal conduct . . . and the punitive sanction."[31] Yet despite the centrality of harm in criminal law theory, conduct that falls short of causing actual harm may constitute a punishable crime. That is particularly true of conduct that creates an unjustifiable risk of harm, and this principle is embedded in the law of inchoate crimes like attempt and conspiracy. It is also embedded in specialized criminal statutes such as laws punishing the crime of reckless endangerment,[32] which has close parallels in the Clean Water Act, the Clean Air Act, and the Resource Conservation and Recovery Act.

Even when harm or a serious risk of harm is not an explicit element of a crime, if the actor's conduct actually causes a tangible harm, the presence (and, perhaps, extent) of the harm may be relevant in determining the seriousness of the violation or the applicable range of punishment.

―――――――――――――――――

regulatory agencies provide private interpretations and advice. [This phenomenon is found in tax and securities law and in the implementation of the Foreign Corrupt Practices Act.]

[31] JEROME HALL, GENERAL PRINCIPLES OF CRIMINAL LAW 213 (2d ed. 1960).

[32] *See, e.g.,* MODEL PENAL CODE § 211.2 (Official Draft and Revised Comments, 1985).

Simply put, one of the principal purposes of the criminal law is prevention of unjustifiable harm, however proximate the actor is to actually causing it.

> **Illustration A:** An environmental engineer who works for a chemical manufacturer decides to discharge treated chemical waste into a nearby river. The engineer knows it is illegal to discharge the waste without a permit, but he does not apply for one because he doesn't want to bother with the paperwork. Since the waste has been pretreated and there is only a minuscule amount of chemicals in the wastewater, the discharges do not affect water quality and pose no risk of harm to human health or the environment. Had the engineer applied for a permit to discharge the wastewater as required by law, the permit would have been issued and the discharges would be legal.

Here there is no tangible environmental harm, yet the engineer could be criminally charged for discharging the wastewater into the river. Why would his conduct be punishable if, but for the lack of a permit, the discharges would otherwise be legal? Where is the harm in this scenario?

> **Illustration B:** The owner of a small business illegally dumps hazardous industrial sludge in a gravel pit over a long period of time. The pit is located on property near a small town whose residents rely on town wells for their drinking water. Scientists agree that the sludge could eventually contaminate the wells but disagree on how long it would take the contaminants to traverse the distance between the pit and the wells. Scientists are also uncertain about what health risks the town residents would be exposed to if they drank the water after small amounts of the contaminants entered the wells.

In Illustration B, there is a strong possibility that the town's drinking water supply would be contaminated, but no time line for how long it would take before that occurred. And, as in Illustration A, there is as yet no tangible harm to human health or the environment and no certainty that it will occur.

If prosecutors in Illustration B were required to wait until actual harm occurred before they could charge the business owner for the illegal dumping, there could be serious complications. It might take years for the contaminants to reach the wells, for example, and by that time the statute of limitations for the act of dumping might well have expired, making the prosecution time-barred.

Or suppose the owner of a different business located a few miles on the other side of the town wells illegally buried the same or similar hazardous contaminants on the premises. Assuming that the wells eventually became contaminated and that it took a period of years, establishing a causal link between the offending company and the harm done could be an extremely difficult and complex task.

And the more time that elapses between the prohibited act and an investigation and trial, the more likely it is that witnesses will be gone and other crucial evidence will be stale.

> **Illustration C:** A chemical manufacturer illegally releases flammable waste into a city sewer system, causing a series of underground explosions in the sewer. The explosions injure four people, cause millions of dollars of damage, and require the evacuation of an entire neighborhood. Because much of the sewer was damaged or destroyed, the city had to divert untreated sewage into a river that was the source of drinking water for communities located downstream.

Illustration C poses a case in which there is clearly significant harm. But as in Illustration B, the discharge of flammable waste into the sewer would have been illegal regardless of whether it caused explosions or polluted the river. In what sense is the actual harm caused relevant in a prosecution for the illegal discharge?

b. Culpability

Responsibility for causing harm is not, standing alone, a sufficient predicate for imposing criminal liability. Instead, the criminal law requires a measure of blameworthiness, and blameworthiness depends in large measure on the actor's state of mind. One who undertakes a socially undesirable course of action with the prescribed state of mind — which could run the gamut from willfulness to negligence — is deemed morally blameworthy for exposing another person to an unreasonable risk of serious harm. One who lacks the required state of mind is not.

> **Illustration D:** Assume the facts in Illustration C with the following variation. The employee responsible for the release of flammable waste intended to discharge rinse water, a harmless substance that the manufacturer could legally introduce into the sewer. The employee mistakenly turned the wrong valve, accidentally discharging flammable waste instead.

Is the employee's conduct blameworthy? As we will see in Chapter 2, it depends on what level of culpability the statute prescribes. If the required mental state is intent or knowledge, then the employee likely would not be criminally responsible since the release was accidental. If the statute requires negligence, then the question of blameworthiness would turn on whether he should have known the valve he turned was the wrong one.

c. Deterrence

The decision to criminalize or criminally enforce legal norms invokes the moral force of the law in its most powerful form — the power to punish. The power of the state to impose punishment for blameworthy conduct provides, at least in theory, strong incentives for those in the regulated community to comply with the law.

For individuals, the prospect of jail time and the stigma of criminal conviction will deter wrongdoing if the expected punishment outweighs the anticipated gains. For organizations, the punishment must be sufficiently severe that it cannot reasonably be considered another cost of doing business. That is especially true in the context of environmental regulation, where the costs of compliance can easily exceed an ordinary criminal fine. Stated differently, only when the maximum authorized fine is greater than the cost of compliance can the threat of a fine realistically serve as a deterrent to noncompliance.

> **Illustration E:** The manager of an industrial plant knows that fluorides and fluoride particulates emitted from the plant have harmed the neighboring property every year for at least 15 years. The contamination was largely preventable through installation of proper fluoride controls, which would reduce the quantity of fluoride particulates released into the air by at least 90 percent. When asked by the neighboring property owner why he had not used more effective controls, the manager replied: "It is cheaper to pay claims than it is to control fluorides."[33]

Even if the claims paid to neighboring businesses were commensurate to the harm, they were clearly not sufficiently large or bothersome to deter the manager from continuing to pollute the surrounding air. A credible threat of

---

[33]Reynolds Metals Co. v. Lampert, 324 F.2d 465, 466 (9th Cir. 1963).

criminal prosecution accompanied by potentially large fines and remediation costs would have been more likely to command the manager's attention.

3. THE MERITS OF CRIMINAL ENFORCEMENT

The theoretical and policy underpinnings of environmental law and criminal law have marked similarities and dissimilarities. But critics of environmental criminal enforcement believe the dissimilarities are sufficiently great that criminal prosecution should be the enforcement tool of last resort. From a criminal law perspective, the similarities are sufficiently great that potential criminal violations of environmental standards should not be treated as significantly different from criminal violations of other complex regulatory statutes like tax and securities laws.[34]

a. Criminal Law Perspective

As we have already seen, both environmental crimes and traditional common law crimes have the potential to cause enormous harm. Whether a sewer system is blown up by a terrorist or by a company's discharge of flammable waste into the system, as in Illustration C, the resulting harm is precisely the same. Similarly, a town resident who contracts a fatal form of cancer after drinking contaminated water from the town well, as might happen in Illustration B, is no less dead than a robbery victim who is shot and killed by the robber.

As we have also seen, environmental crimes also require, with one minor exception, proof of a culpable mental state. If the president of the chemical company in Illustration C had ordered a subordinate to discharge flammable waste into the sewer system to cut costs and maximize profits, would his conduct be less blameworthy simply because it was economically motivated?[35] From a criminal law perspective, the answer would clearly be no. The measure of culpability in criminal law is knowledge and intent, not motive.

And, from a criminal law perspective, the threat of criminal prosecution and punishment is needed to preserve the integrity of the environmental regulatory regime. The high costs of compliance provide a strong temptation

---

[34]*See* Kathleen F. Brickey, *Environmental Crime at the Crossroads: The Intersection of Environmental and Criminal Law Theory*, 71 TUL. L. REV. 487, 503 n.86 (1996) [hereinafter Brickey, *Environmental Crime at the Crossroads*].

[35]*Cf.* Lazarus, *Assimilating Environmental Protection*, *supra* note 2, at 879.

to cut corners, particularly in the hazardous waste industry, where many businesses are undercapitalized and thus "are financially weak to begin with."[36]

KATHLEEN F. BRICKEY, CHARGING PRACTICES
IN HAZARDOUS WASTE PROSECUTIONS

---

62 OHIO ST. L.J. 1077, 1091-1093 (2001)

. . . That point is nowhere better illustrated than by the frantic pace at which companies dumped and abandoned hazardous and toxic waste in the months before RCRA's regulatory scheme came into effect. Aided by a multitude of cut-rate disposal services run by unscrupulous owners, companies hurriedly disposed [of] thousands of tons of chemical waste before the regulatory deadline. They dumped hazardous waste in city sewers, intentionally spilled it from moving trucks onto roads, abandoned it in shopping center parking lots and rented warehouses, and shipped it hundreds of miles by rail to fictitious addresses — all to avoid responsibility under the new rules.

* * *

Because proper transportation and disposal of hazardous waste is so costly, illegal hazardous waste management practices are almost invariably driven by economic considerations. The problem may be especially acute for some small businesses, whose disposal costs could consume a high percentage of their modest net revenue. . . .

Thus, a subculture of unscrupulous hazardous waste haulers (called "sludge runners") employs expedient disposal practices like driving tank trucks with open spigots down highways on rainy days and mixing hazardous waste with diesel fuel for sale as home heating oil. Similarly, dishonest haulers participate in the widespread practice of "cocktailing" toxic liquids by pouring them over construction and demolition materials, which an unsuspecting landowner may accept as "clean fill." Examples like these underscore how bottom-line business decisions can and do affect environmental compliance policies. Indeed, one explanation for the frenzied pace of toxic dumping in the Northeast in the months before RCRA's

---

[36]Brickey, *Environmental Crime at the Crossroads, supra* note 34, at 509.

regulatory deadline is that New England was the only region in the country that had no major approved disposal sites. That being true, New England industries that produced or used hazardous materials would have had to transport the waste to disposal sites as far away as North Carolina.

The scarcity of approved sites created similar problems in other parts of the country as well. Thus, when Kentucky began the cleanup of the Valley of the Drums[37] — an illegal dumpsite that contained 17 thousand partially buried barrels of hazardous waste — officials had difficulty locating a safe place to dispose of it. Only a handful of sites nationwide were certified to accept that type of waste, and only one of them was less than 1,000 miles away. In consequence, state officials estimated that transportation costs could reach several million dollars.

The resourcefulness of businesses seeking to skirt costly regulatory requirements and gain a competitive edge highlights the need for strong deterrent measures to override powerful economic incentives to cut corners. While the problem may be more pronounced among hazardous waste generators, this is by no means an isolated phenomenon when it comes to environmental compliance issues. That, in turn, makes the argument favoring prosecutors' use of credible threats of criminal prosecution as a deterrent far more potent.

b. Environmental Law Perspective

Although some critics of environmental criminal enforcement concede that the argument supporting the use of criminal sanctions is "fairly straightforward and compelling," it is said to be "deceptively so."[38]

---

[37] *See infra* Chapter 6, at text accompanying n.5. — ED.

[38] Lazarus, *Assimilating Environmental Protection, supra* note 2, at 879.

RICHARD J. LAZARUS, ASSIMILATING ENVIRONMENTAL PROTECTION INTO LEGAL RULES AND THE PROBLEM WITH ENVIRONMENTAL CRIME

27 LOY. L.A. L. REV. 867, 881-883 (1994)

. . . Congress made virtually *all* "knowing" and some "negligent" violations of environmental pollution control standards, limitations, permits, and licenses subject to criminal as well as to civil sanctions. Congress made relatively little effort to define thresholds for when a defendant's conduct justified adding the possibility of criminal sanctions to civil penalties. Except for the knowing and negligent mens rea requirements, Congress just assumed that the civil and criminal thresholds should be precisely the same. The problems with such an assumption are several.

First, the environmental standards are not set based on the existence of traditional notions of criminal culpability. . . . They are instead set at far more precautionary, risk-averse levels of protection against risks to human health and the environment. The public — this Author included — may believe that such precautionary levels are wise and appropriate, but that presents a far different public policy issue than whether all such violations rise to a level justifying severe criminal as well as civil sanctions. . . .

Congress, for the most part, has not been especially discriminating in defining the mens rea requirements for environmental crimes. . . . Hence, although the environmental statutes generally require some mens rea for criminal prosecution — they are not simply strict liability offenses — they do not require much at all in terms of the defendant's knowledge of the actual risks of his or her activity. . . .

What makes such an approach to mens rea particularly problematic in the environmental law context is that environmental standards, unlike most traditional crimes, present questions of degree rather than of kind. Murder, burglary, assault, and embezzlement are simply unlawful. There is no threshold level below which such conduct is acceptable. In contrast, pollution is not unlawful per se: In many circumstances, some pollution is acceptable. It is only pollution that exceeds certain prescribed levels that is unlawful. But, for that very reason, the mens rea element should arguably be a more, not less, critical element in the prosecution of an environmental offense.

Finally, Congress failed to adequately account for the fact that the civil standards are often set at an action-forcing level and are anything but static. The standards do not necessarily reflect standards of performance that are either economically or technologically feasible. They do not reflect existing conduct or long-settled cultural norms. They instead are more likely to reflect policy makers' predictions of what will be possible and the public's aspirations for a cleaner environment. The underlying science is often very uncertain, and the regulations constantly change in response to new information, court challenges, and sweeping statutory amendments.

Full compliance with all applicable environmental laws is consequently the exception rather than the norm. Just as the EPA rarely meets congressional aspirations in meeting all of the deadlines in environmental laws — it meets roughly fourteen percent of all congressional deadlines — industry rarely meets all of those aspirations as reflected in the statutory and regulatory requirements themselves. Nor does government itself or its contractors . . . strictly comply with environmental requirements. In a recent survey, two-thirds of all corporate counsel reported that their companies have recently been in violation of applicable environmental laws.

For that reason, however, there is a danger, indeed a potential impropriety, in Congress's approach to environmental criminal liability. The question whether certain conduct warrants a criminal sanction is far different than whether a civil sanction may be warranted, precisely because the latter is susceptible to being no more than an economic disincentive. Criminal liability standards should be more settled and less dynamic. They should be more reflective of what in fact can be accomplished rather than of the public's aspirations of how, if pushed, the world can change in the future.

Perhaps most importantly, criminal sanctions should also be tempered by the gravity of the decision that certain conduct warrants the most severe of sanctions. Criminal sanctions are not simply another enforcement tool in the regulator's arsenal to promote public policy objectives. A criminal sanction is fundamentally different in character. The reason why criminal sanctions have greater deterrent value is also the reason why they must be used more selectively. Criminal sanctions should be reserved for the more culpable subset of offenses and not used solely for their ability to deter.

4. THE CIVIL/CRIMINAL WRONG DISTINCTION

As Professor Lazarus observes, the respective roles that civil and criminal penalties should play in environmental enforcement is the subject of considerable debate. While it once may have been true that "there is no distinction better known, than the distinction between civil and criminal law,"[39] that seemingly clear line is now considerably blurred. As Professor John Coffee observed in 1991, "the dominant development in substantive federal criminal law over the last decade has been the disappearance of any clearly definable line between civil and criminal law."[40]

Some early commentators differentiated civil and criminal law by drawing the line between private (civil) and public (criminal) wrongs. That approach gradually became unworkable as Congress increasingly began to attach criminal penalties to laws defining broader civil obligations. As Professor Lazarus puts it, "at the federal level, Congress has virtually criminalized civil law by making criminal sanctions available for violations of otherwise civil federal regulatory programs."[41] Finding this particularly troubling in the context of environmental law, he faults Congress for failing to make a "meaningful or systematic effort to consider criminal sanctions as presenting an issue distinct from that presented by civil sanctions"[42] and for failing to give meaningful consideration to which levels of culpability and which types of environmental standards are the most appropriate subjects of criminal enforcement. In consequence, the substantive standards for civil and criminal violations may well be the same.

Under the Clean Water Act, for example, it is unlawful to discharge pollutants into navigable waters without first obtaining a permit. Discharging pollutants without a permit will subject the actor to a civil fine and, perhaps, other civil or administrative sanctions. In the context of environmental law, the remedy (or sanction) is sought (or imposed) by the Environmental Protection Agency, the administrative agency charged with the responsibility of implementing and enforcing federal environmental laws.[43] If the actor *knowingly* discharged the pollutants into the water

---

[39]Jerome Hall, *Interrelations of Criminal Law and Torts*, 43 COLUM. L. REV. 753, 757 (1943) (quoting Lord Mansfield's dictum in Atcheson v. Everitt, 1 Cowp. 382, 391 (1775)).

[40]John C. Coffee, Jr., *Does "Unlawful" Mean "Criminal"?: Reflections on the Disappearing Tort/Crime Distinction in American Law*, 71 B.U. L. REV. 193, 193 (1991).

[41]Lazarus, *Meeting the Demands, supra* note 14, at 2441. According to one estimate, in the early 1990's more than 300,000 federal regulations were subject to criminal enforcement. Coffee, *supra* note 40, at 216 (citing an estimate made by a prominent white collar crime practitioner).

[42]Lazarus, *Assimilating Environmental Protection, supra* note 2, at 883.

[43]The Environment and Natural Resources Division of the Justice Department often assists the EPA in civil enforcement actions.

The environmental statutes also contemplate supplemental enforcement actions by state agencies, particularly under the Clean Air Act. Citizen suits may serve as ancillary enforcement tools as well.

without a permit, the overlay of "knowledge" transforms what would otherwise be a civil violation into a crime, and the enforcement action would be in the form of a prosecution brought by a United States Attorney's office and/or the Environmental Crimes Section of the Justice Department.

Whether the violation is treated by enforcement authorities as civil or criminal, the violation is in the nature of a public wrong. It causes a social harm that interferes with the public's right to use and enjoy a public waterway for recreational (e.g., swimming and boating) or utilitarian (e.g., drinking water) purposes — even though it may also coincidentally cause private harm of a different sort (e.g., damaging a private dock). Similarly, regardless of whether a sanction is labeled civil or criminal, it may have a punitive purpose or may be intended to deter or prevent future violations. Simply put, "[c]ivil sanctions seem more and more like criminal sanctions in their severity and harshness."[44]

Even though it is not always crystal clear whether a penalty is civil or criminal,[45] the distinction between civil and criminal enforcement can have important practical consequences. Criminal enforcement may trigger constitutional rights — including the Fifth Amendment privilege against self-incrimination, the Sixth Amendment right to counsel, the Eighth Amendment protection against double jeopardy, and the Due Process right to have criminal charges proved beyond a reasonable doubt — that civil enforcement actions may not. And, of course, the environmental criminal provisions differ from their civil counterparts in that they authorize imprisonment in addition to a fine.[46]

JOHN C. COFFEE, JR., DOES "UNLAWFUL" MEAN "CRIMINAL"?: REFLECTIONS ON THE DISAPPEARING TORT/CRIME DISTINCTION IN AMERICAN LAW

71 B.U. L. REV. 193, 219-220 (1991)

Public concern about a newly perceived social problem — the environment, worker safety, child neglect, etc. — seems to trigger a recurring

---

[44]Lazarus, *Meeting the Demands, supra* note 14, at 2441.

[45]*Cf.* United States v. Ward, 448 U.S. 242, 249-251 (1980) (rejecting the argument that a civil penalty imposed for defendant's Clean Water Act violation was sufficiently punitive to trigger his Fifth Amendment privilege against self-incrimination).

[46]Like some of their civil counterparts, several of the criminal provisions also debar the defendant from bidding on or performing government contracts upon conviction.

social response: namely, an almost reflexive resort to criminal prosecution, either through the enactment of new legislation or the use of old standby theories that have great elasticity. . . . [O]ne aspect of this problem deserves special mention in view of the apparent escalation of public welfare offenses into felonies.

If the disposal of toxic wastes, securities fraud, the filling-in of wetlands, the failure to conduct aircraft maintenance, and the causing of workplace injuries become crimes that can be regularly indicted on the basis of negligence or less, society as a whole may be made safer, but a substantial population of the American workforce (both at white collar and blue collar levels) becomes potentially entangled with the criminal law. Today, most individuals can plan their affairs so as to avoid any realistic risk of coming within a zone where criminal sanctions might apply to their conduct. Few individuals have reason to fear prosecution for murder, robbery, rape, extortion or any of the other traditional common law crimes. Even the more contemporary, white collar crimes — price fixing, bribery, insider trading, etc. — can be easily avoided by those who wish to minimize their risk of criminal liability. At most, these statutes pose problems for individuals who wish to approach the line but who find that no bright line exists. In contrast, modern industrial society inevitably creates toxic wastes that must be disposed of by someone. Similarly, workplace injuries are, to a degree, inevitable. As a result, some individuals must engage in legitimate professional activities that are regulated by criminal sanctions; to this extent, they become unavoidably "entangled" with the criminal law. That is, they cannot plan their affairs so as to be free from the risk that a retrospective evaluation of their conduct, often under the uncertain standard of negligence, will find that they fell short of the legally mandated standard. Ultimately, if the new trend toward greater use of public welfare offenses continues, it will mean a more pervasive use of the criminal sanction, a use that intrudes further into the mainstream of American life and into the everyday life of its citizens than has ever been attempted before.

———————

Since the distinction between civil and criminal law has traditionally revolved around mens rea, it is to that concept that we now turn in Chapter 2.

2

MENS REA

I know nothing, I hear nothing.[†]

Well, if I don't get caught, what then?[††]

A. OVERVIEW OF MENTAL STATES

Mens rea plays a pivotal role in defining the boundary between tort and crime. In criminal law, mens rea ("guilty mind") imports a measure of moral blameworthiness into the equation. While a few environmental criminal statutes require proof of willfulness[1] and several others provide that negligence will suffice,[2] the most commonly required mental state for environmental crimes is knowledge. The actor must be shown to have "knowingly" engaged in prohibited conduct.

To provide a framework for the materials in this chapter, consider the following illustrative fact patterns.

[†]Robert Hopkins, vice president of Spiro International Corporation.

[††]Attique Ahmad, owner of Spin-N-Market convenience store and gas station.

[1]*See, e.g.*, 15 U.S.C. § 2615(b) (Toxic Substances Control Act); 33 U.S.C. § 1232(b)(1)-(2) (Ports and Waterways Safety Act); 42 U.S.C. § 300h-2(b)(2) (Safe Drinking Water Act).

[2]*See, e.g.*, 33 U.S.C. § 1319(c)(1), (c)(1)(B) (Clean Water Act); 42 U.S.C. § 7413(c)(4) (Clean Air Act).

Illustration A: Burton Oil Company owns a pipeline that runs along a canal. Burton Oil performs regular pipeline maintenance and conducts periodic pipeline inspections. Despite these precautions, the pipeline unexpectedly bursts, causing a massive oil spill into the canal.

Illustration B: Chemtron Petroleum operates a petroleum refinery on property located next to a bay. Chemtron stores diesel fuel produced at the refinery in a large steel tank. The tank, which has been in use for nearly 50 years, does not meet current industry standards. Nor do refinery workers who are responsibile for maintaining the tank perform routine tests that could detect major structural defects. As it turns out, the tank is not structurally sound and it collapses and spills 500,000 gallons of diesel fuel into the bay.

Illustration C: A tugboat owned by Dime Transport Service pulls into a cove on the river for the night. A member of the crew opens a valve to dispose of oil that has accumulated in the boat's bilge. The open valve releases the oil directly into the river.

As you read through the materials in this chapter, consider how these illustrations fit within the hierarchy of mental states found in environmental criminal statutes and the extent to which it is appropriate to assign individual fault for each of the spills in Illustrations A-C.

B. KNOWLEDGE

The principal criminal provisions in the environmental statutes require proof that the actor "knowingly" engaged in prohibited conduct. But knowledge is a term of different meanings, and most environmental criminal laws do not define it. A person "knows" something if he has actual knowledge (or awareness) of it.

Illustration D: An automobile mechanic pours a barrel of waste oil that is a byproduct of oil changes into a nearby stream. Has he acted knowingly?

The mechanic acted knowingly in the sense that he was aware of the nature of his conduct (i.e., that he was disposing of the contents of the barrel), aware of the nature of the substance (i.e., that it was liquid waste), and the circumstances that made the disposal illegal (i.e., that he was dumping it into a stream). He may or may not have known that pouring waste into the stream is illegal.

> **Illustration E:** The mechanic in Illustration D leaves a badly punctured barrel of waste oil on the bank of the stream. By the time a week has gone by, all of the oil has leaked out and spilled into the water. Has he knowingly discharged the oil into the stream?

Here, he does not actually know the oil has leaked into the water. But common experience would suggest that if he knew the barrel was punctured, he knew its contents would leak out. In view of where he left the barrel in that condition, it could be argued that he knew it was practically certain that oil would spill into the stream. And if he was aware of the high probability that it would, he knowingly introduced oil into the stream. Thus, one may be charged with knowledge when he was aware that his conduct (leaving the leaking barrel on the bank) was almost certain to cause a particular result (oil spilling into the stream).

1. FACTS VERSUS LAW

One of the difficulties courts have confronted in the environmental crime context is what the term "knowingly" modifies. In the preceding examples, the mechanic was aware of the nature of his conduct and of the relevant attendant circumstances. But for his conduct to violate the Clean Water Act, the stream would have to be classified as a navigable water of the United States.[3] Assuming that it was, the question then becomes whether the statute requires knowledge that the stream is navigable, that the used oil is considered a "pollutant," and that introducing pollutants into navigable waters is illegal.

---

[3]We will examine this issue at a later point in Chapter 4.

a. Factual Elements

UNITED STATES V. AHMAD

101 F.3d 386 (5th Cir. 1996)

SMITH, Circuit Judge.

Attique Ahmad appeals his conviction of, and sentence for, criminal violations of the Clean Water Act ("CWA"). Concluding that the district court erred in its instructions to the jury, we reverse and remand.

I

This case arises from the discharge of a large quantity of gasoline into the sewers of Conroe, Texas, in January 1994. In 1992, Ahmad purchased the "Spin-N-Market No. 12," a combination convenience store and gas station located at the intersection of Second and Lewis Streets in Conroe. The Spin-N-Market has two gasoline pumps, each of which is fed by an 8000-gallon underground gasoline tank. Some time after Ahmad bought the station, he discovered that one of the tanks, which held high-octane gasoline, was leaking. This did not pose an immediate hazard, because the leak was at the top of the tank; gasoline could not seep out. The leak did, however, allow water to enter into the tank and contaminate the gas. Because water is heavier than gas, the water sank to the bottom of the tank, and because the tank was pumped from the bottom, Ahmad was unable to sell from it.

In October 1993, Ahmad hired CTT Environmental Services ("CTT"), a tank testing company, to examine the tank. CTT determined that it contained approximately 800 gallons of water, and the rest mostly gasoline. Jewel McCoy, a CTT employee, testified that she told Ahmad that the leak could not be repaired until the tank was completely emptied, which CTT offered to do for 65 cents per gallon plus $65 per hour of labor. After McCoy gave Ahmad this estimate, he inquired whether he could empty the tank himself. She replied that it would be dangerous and illegal to do so. On her testimony, he responded, "Well, if I don't get caught, what then?"

On January 25, 1994, Ahmad rented a hand-held motorized water pump from a local hardware store, telling a hardware store employee that he was planning to use it to remove water from his backyard. Victor Fonseca, however, identified Ahmad and the pump and testified that he had seen Ahmad pumping gasoline into the street. Oscar Alvarez stated that he had seen Ahmad and another person discharging gasoline into a manhole. Tereso

Uribe testified that he had confronted Ahmad and asked him what was going on, to which Ahmad responded that he was simply removing the water from the tank.

In all, 5,220 gallons of fluid were pumped from the leaky tank, of which approximately 4,690 gallons were gasoline. Some of the gas-water mixture ran down Lewis Street and some into the manhole in front of the store.

The gasoline discharged onto Lewis Street went a few hundred feet along the curb to Third Street, where it entered a storm drain and the storm sewer system and flowed through a pipe that eventually empties into Possum Creek. When city officials discovered the next day that there was gasoline in Possum Creek, several vacuum trucks were required to decontaminate it. Possum Creek feeds into the San Jacinto River, which eventually flows into Lake Houston.

The gasoline that Ahmad discharged into the manhole went a different route: It flowed through the sanitary sewer system and eventually entered the city sewage treatment plant.[12] On January 26, employees at the treatment plant discovered a 1,000-gallon pool of gasoline in one of the intake ponds. To avoid shutting down the plant altogether, they diverted the pool of gasoline and all incoming liquid into a 5,000,000-gallon emergency lagoon.

The plant supervisor ordered that non-essential personnel be evacuated from the plant and called firefighters and a hazardous materials crew to the scene. The Conroe fire department determined the gasoline was creating a risk of explosion and ordered that two nearby schools be evacuated. Although no one was injured as a result of the discharge, fire officials testified at trial that Ahmad had created a "tremendous explosion hazard" that could have led to "hundreds, if not thousands, of deaths and injuries" and millions of dollars of property damage.

By 9:00 A.M. on January 26, investigators had traced the source of the gasoline back to the manhole directly in front of the Spin-N-Market. Their suspicions were confirmed when they noticed a strong odor of gasoline and saw signs of corrosion on the asphalt surrounding the manhole. The investigators questioned Ahmad, who at first denied having operated a pump the previous night. Soon, however, his story changed: He admitted to having used a pump but denied having pumped anything from his tanks.

Ahmad was indicted for three violations of the CWA: knowingly discharging a pollutant from a point source into a navigable water of the United States without a permit, in violation of 33 U.S.C. §§ 1311(a) and 1319(c)(2)(A) (count one); knowingly operating a source in violation of a pretreatment standard, in violation of 33 U.S.C. §§ 1317(d) and 1319(c)(2)(A) (count two); and knowingly placing another person in imminent danger of death or serious bodily injury by discharging a pollutant, in violation of 33 U.S.C. § 1319(c)(3) (count three). At trial, Ahmad did not dispute that he had discharged gasoline from the tank or that eventually it had found its way to Possum Creek and the sewage treatment plant. Instead, he contended that his discharge of the gasoline was not "knowing," because he had believed he was discharging water.

. . . The jury found Ahmad guilty on counts one and two and deadlocked on count three.

II

Ahmad argues that the district court improperly instructed the jury on the mens rea required for counts one and two. The instruction on count one stated in relevant part:

> For you to find Mr. Ahmad guilty of this crime, you must be convinced that the government has proved each of the following beyond a reasonable doubt:
>
> (1) That on or about the date set forth in the indictment,
> (2) the defendant knowingly discharged
> (3) a pollutant
> (4) from a point source
> (5) into the navigable waters of the United States
> (6) without a permit to do so.

On count two, the court instructed the jury:

> In order to prove the defendant guilty of the offense charged in Count 2 of the indictment, the government must prove beyond a reasonable doubt each of the following elements:
>
> (1) That on or about the date set forth in the indictment
> (2) the defendant,
> (3) who was the owner or operator of a source,
> (4) knowingly operated that source by discharging into a public sewer system or publicly owned treatment works
> (5) a pollutant that created a fire or explosion hazard in that public sewer system or publicly owned treatment works.

Ahmad contends that the jury should have been instructed that the statutory mens rea — knowledge — was required as to each element of the offenses, rather than only with regard to discharge or the operation of a source. . . .

The principal issue is to which elements of the offense the modifier "knowingly" applies. The matter is complicated somewhat by the fact that the phrase "knowingly violates" appears in a different section of the CWA from the language defining the elements of the offenses. Ahmad argues that within this context, "knowingly violates" should be read to require him knowingly to have acted with regard to each element of the offenses. The government, in contrast, contends that "knowingly violates" requires it to prove only that Ahmad knew the nature of his acts and that he performed them intentionally. Particularly at issue is whether "knowingly" applies to the element of the discharge's being a pollutant, for Ahmad's main theory at trial was that he thought he was discharging water, not gasoline.

The Supreme Court has spoken to this issue in broad terms. In United States v. X-Citement Video, Inc., 115 S. Ct. 464, 467 (1994), the Court read "knowingly" to apply to each element of a child pornography offense, notwithstanding its conclusion that under the "most natural grammatical reading" of the statute it should apply only to the element of having transported, shipped, received, distributed, or reproduced the material at issue. The Court also reaffirmed the long-held view that "the presumption in favor of a scienter requirement should apply to each of the statutory elements which criminalize otherwise innocent conduct." *Id.* at 469.

Although *X-Citement Video* is the Court's most recent pronouncement on this subject, it is not the first. In Staples v. United States, 511 U.S. 600, 619-20 (1994), the Court found that the statutes criminalizing knowing possession of a machinegun require that defendants know not only that they possess a firearm but that it actually is a machinegun. Thus, an awareness of the features of the gun — specifically, the features that make it an automatic weapon — is a necessary element of the offense. More generally, the Court also made plain that statutory crimes carrying severe penalties are presumed to require that a defendant know the facts that make his conduct illegal.

Our own precedents are in the same vein. In United States v. Baytank (Houston), Inc., 934 F.2d 599, 613 (5th Cir. 1991), we concluded that a conviction for knowing and improper storage of hazardous wastes under 42 U.S.C. § 6928(d)(2)(A) requires "that the defendant know[] factually what he is doing — storing, what is being stored, and that what is being stored factually has the potential for harm to others or the environment, and that he has no permit. . . ." This is directly analogous to the interpretation of the

CWA that Ahmad urges upon us. Indeed, we find it eminently sensible that the phrase "knowingly violates" in § 1319(c)(2)(A), when referring to other provisions that define the elements of the offenses § 1319 creates, should uniformly require knowledge as to each of those elements rather than only one or two. To hold otherwise would require an explanation as to why some elements should be treated differently from others, which neither the parties nor the caselaw seems able to provide.

In support of its interpretation of the CWA, the government cites cases from other circuits. We find these decisions both inapposite and unpersuasive on the point for which they are cited. In United States v. Hopkins, 53 F.3d 533, 537-41 (2d Cir. 1995), the court held that the government need not demonstrate that a § 1319(c)(2)(A) defendant knew his acts were illegal. The illegality of the defendant's actions is not an element of the offense, however. In United States v. Weitzenhoff, 35 F.3d 1275 (9th Cir. 1994), the court similarly was concerned almost exclusively with whether the language of the CWA creates a mistake-of-law defense. Both cases are easily distinguishable, for neither directly addresses mistake of fact or the statutory construction issues raised by Ahmad. . . .

IV

. . . The convictions are reversed and the case remanded.

DISCUSSION QUESTIONS

1. Does *Ahmad*'s holding that the scienter requirement applies to each element of the offense require proof that the defendant knew he needed a permit to pump the tank's contents into the sewer system? Would it make sense to require Ahmad to know that he did not have a permit without also requiring knowledge of the permit requirement?
2. Would a properly instructed jury be likely to convict or acquit Ahmad? What evidence is probative on the issue of his claimed mistake? If you were the prosecutor, what additional evidence would you try to develop? What inferences would you ask the jury to draw?
3. At his trial, Ahmad wanted to call two witnesses who would have testified that he left the Spin-N-Market between 7:30 and 8:00 P.M. on January 25, but the district court excluded their testimony as irrelevant. The court of appeals held this evidentiary ruling was erroneous. What factual issues would the proffered testimony be relevant to?

b. Knowledge of Jurisdictional Elements

The court in *Ahmad* found that it was "eminently sensible that the phrase 'knowingly violates'" should be construed to require knowledge with respect to all elements of the violation instead of just one or two. "To hold otherwise would require an explanation as to why some elements should be treated differently from others," the court said. This interpretation of the knowledge requirement puts the Fifth Circuit at odds with several of its sister circuits.

To provide a context for considering the implications of the court's conclusion, consider the facts in Illustration F.

> **Illustration F:** Cooper, the owner of a trailer park, operates a sewage lagoon that is the sole mechanism for disposing of human waste for 20 trailers in the park. After being treated in the lagoon, the waste flows into a creek that is a tributary of a river that flows through several states. Although he has been repeatedly warned by environmental officials that the sewage discharged from the lagoon contained impermissibly high levels of E. Coli Bacteria, solid waste, and chemicals, Cooper continues to operate the lagoon without correcting the problem.
>
> Cooper is later prosecuted for knowingly discharging a pollutant into waters of the United States without a permit. After the jury finds him guilty, Cooper appeals, arguing that the conviction should be thrown out because the evidence was insufficient to show that he knew the creek was a tributary of a navigable water. Should the court vacate the conviction?

Unlike Ahmad, who claimed he thought he was discharging water instead of gasoline, Cooper undeniably knew he was discharging human waste. Cooper also undeniably knew that the waste was discharged into a creek. Should it matter whether or not he knew the creek fit within the definition of navigable waters?

The requirement that the pollutants be discharged into the waters of the United States is what is typically called a jurisdictional element of his violation. It is the factor that identifies what the federal interest is and gives Congress the power to regulate the conduct in question. Other similar jurisdictional hooks include the Commerce Clause (e.g., transmitting interstate wire communications in furtherance of a scheme to defraud)[4] and

---

[4] 18 U.S.C. § 1343 (wire fraud statute).

the power to regulate the United States mails (e.g., use of the mails in furtherance of a scheme to defraud).[5]

It has long been recognized that mens rea requirements do not ordinarily apply to jurisdictional elements contained in federal criminal statutes.[6] Yet the clear implication of the *Ahmad* court's conclusion that "knowingly" applies to each element of a Clean Water Act violation is that the defendant must know the pollutant is being discharged into waters of the United States.

What are the practical consequences of applying the statute this way? Are there legitimate policy reasons to exclude the jurisdictional element from the mens rea requirement?   Consider the following excerpt from United States v. Cooper.[7]

> The CWA offers every reason to conclude that the term "waters of the United States" as it operates in this case is "nothing more than the jurisdictional peg on which Congress based federal jurisdiction." *LeFaivre*, 507 F.2d at 1297 n.14. . . .
>
> The stated purposes of the Act provide . . . support for this view. As articulated by Congress, the principal goal of the Act is "to restore and maintain the chemical, physical, and biological integrity of the Nation's waters." 33 U.S.C. § 1251(a). This purpose would be severely undermined if polluters could only be prosecuted for knowingly polluting the nation's waters when the government could prove they were aware of the facts conferring federal jurisdiction.   Such a blanket rule would be absurd in many cases, including the present one.   Cooper's deliberate discharge of human sewage into running waters is exhaustively recorded.   He knew he was discharging sewage into them, he knew his treatment facilities were inadequate, and he knew he was acting without a permit.   It seems unlikely that Congress intended for culpability in such an instance to turn upon whether the defendant was aware of the jurisdictional nexus of these acts, any more than, for example, Congress intended conviction of a felon-in-possession offense to turn upon the defendant's knowledge of the interstate travels of a firearm.

---

[5] 18 U.S.C. § 1341 (mail fraud statute).

[6] *See, e.g.*, United States v. Yermian, 468 U.S. 63 (1984) (statute making it unlawful to knowingly make a false statement within the jurisdiction of a federal department or agency does not require knowledge of federal jurisdiction); United States v. Feola, 420 U.S. 671 (1975) (statute making it a crime to assault a federal official does not require knowledge that the intended victim is a federal official).

[7] 482 F.3d 658 (4th Cir. 2007).

This conclusion squares with the Supreme Court's analysis of congressional intent as to jurisdictional elements in *Feola*.[8] In that case, the Court considered 18 U.S.C. § 111, proscribing assault of a federal officer. The Court recognized the "federal officer" requirement as a jurisdiction conferring element and went on to consider whether it also functioned as a substantive element of the offense — that is, whether Congress intended for the statute to punish only those defendants who were aware that their victims were federal officers. The Court concluded that Congress intended for the statute both to deter conduct intended to obstruct federal law enforcement activities and to protect federal law enforcement officers to the fullest extent possible. Given the statute's clear aims, the Court said, it "cannot be construed as embodying an unexpressed requirement that an assailant be aware that his victim is a federal officer. All the statute requires is an intent to assault, not an intent to assault a federal officer." 420 U.S. at 684.

Just as Congress in 18 U.S.C. § 111 intended to "accord[] maximum protection to federal officers," *id.*, so Congress in the CWA clearly intended to provide strong protection to the nation's waterways. To attach a mens rea to the jurisdictional element would as surely undermine Congress' intent here as it would have in *Feola*. We cannot broadly exempt environmental crimes from the longstanding rule that mens rea requirements do not pertain to jurisdictional facts. Such a blanket exception would not only be astonishingly broad, but it would also suggest without objective basis that separate and less stringent rules apply to environmental harms. Finding in the CWA a broad exception to the general rule would be tantamount to assuming that Congress, in creating criminal penalties for environmental degradation, did not really mean what it said. . . .

Our conclusion today is further supported by the fact that it hardly encourages exceptionable or unfair prosecution. The Supreme Court in *Feola* justified its interpretation of § 111 by noting that it posed "no snare for the unsuspecting:"

> The situation is not one where legitimate conduct becomes unlawful solely because of the identity of the individual or agency affected. . . . The concept of criminal intent does not extend so far as to require that the actor understand not only the nature of his act but also its consequence for the choice of a judicial forum.

420 U.S. at 685. "Criminal intent serves to separate those who understand the wrongful nature of their act from those who do not, but does not require

---

[8]United States v. Feola, 420 U.S. 671 (1975). — ED.

knowledge of the precise consequences that may flow from that act once aware that the act is wrongful." United States v. X-Citement Video, Inc., 513 U.S. 64, 73 n.3 (1994). . . .

In sum, the creek's status as a "water of the United States" is simply a jurisdictional fact, the objective truth of which the government must establish but the defendant's knowledge of which it need not prove. The language of the relevant statutes — 33 U.S.C. §§ 1311(a), 1319(c)(2)(A), 1362(7) — the congressional intent that text plainly reflects, as well as relevant precedent, all require this conclusion.

DISCUSSION QUESTIONS

1. What is the rationale for the general rule that knowledge of jurisdictional elements in federal criminal statutes is not required?
2. In what sense is the requirement that pollutants must be discharged into waters of the United States purely jurisdictional?
3. *Ahmad* and *Cooper* suggest different approaches to whether "knowingly" applies only to the conduct elements of a Clean Water Act violation or whether it also extends to the jurisdictional element. Which approach is more sound?

c. Knowledge of Illegality

UNITED STATES V. SINSKEY

119 F.3d 712 (8th Cir. 1997)

ARNOLD, Circuit Judge. . . .

I

In the early 1990s, Timothy Sinskey and Wayne Kumm were, respectively, the plant manager and plant engineer at John Morrell & Co. ("Morrell"), a large meat-packing plant in Sioux Falls, South Dakota. The meat-packing process created a large amount of wastewater, some of which Morrell piped to a municipal treatment plant and the rest of which it treated at its own wastewater treatment plant ("WWTP"). After treating wastewater at the WWTP, Morrell would discharge it into the Big Sioux River.

One of the WWTP's functions was to reduce the amount of ammonia nitrogen in the wastewater discharged into the river, and the Environmental Protection Agency ("EPA") required Morrell to limit that amount to levels specified in a permit issued under the Clean Water Act ("CWA"). As well as specifying the acceptable levels of ammonia nitrogen, the permit also required Morrell to perform weekly a series of tests to monitor the amounts of ammonia nitrogen in the discharged water and to file monthly with the EPA a set of reports concerning those results.

In the spring of 1991, Morrell doubled the number of hogs that it slaughtered and processed at the Sioux Falls plant. The resulting increase in wastewater caused the level of ammonia nitrate in the discharged water to be above that allowed by the CWA permit. Ron Greenwood and Barry Milbauer, the manager and assistant manager, respectively, of the WWTP, manipulated the testing process in two ways so that Morrell would appear not to violate its permit. In the first technique, which the parties frequently refer to as "flow manipulation" or the "flow game," Morrell would discharge extremely low levels of water (and thus low levels of ammonia nitrogen) early in the week, when Greenwood and Milbauer would perform the required tests. After the tests had been performed, Morrell would discharge an exceedingly high level of water (and high levels of ammonia nitrogen) later in the week. The tests would therefore not accurately reflect the overall levels of ammonia nitrogen in the discharged water. In addition to manipulating the flow, Greenwood and Milbauer also engaged in what the parties call "selective sampling," that is, they performed more than the number of tests required by the EPA but reported only the tests showing acceptable levels of ammonia nitrogen. When manipulating the flow and selective sampling failed to yield the required number of tests showing acceptable levels of ammonia nitrogen, the two simply falsified the test results and the monthly EPA reports, which Sinskey then signed and sent to the EPA. Morrell submitted false reports for every month but one from August, 1991, to December, 1992.

As a result of their participation in these activities, Sinskey and Kumm were charged with a variety of CWA violations. After a three-week trial, a jury found Sinskey guilty of eleven of the thirty counts with which he was charged, and Kumm guilty of one of the seventeen counts with which he was charged. In particular, the jury found both Sinskey and Kumm guilty of knowingly rendering inaccurate a monitoring method required to be maintained under the CWA and Sinskey guilty of knowingly discharging a pollutant into waters of the United States in amounts exceeding CWA permit limitations. Each appeals his conviction.

II

Sinskey first challenges the jury instructions that the trial court gave with respect to 33 U.S.C. § 1319(c)(2)(A), which, among other things, punishes anyone who "knowingly violates" § 1311 or a condition or limitation contained in a permit that implements § 1311. . . .

The trial court gave an instruction, which it incorporated into several substantive charges, that in order for the jury to find Sinskey guilty of acting "knowingly," the proof had to show that he was "aware of the nature of his acts, performed them intentionally, and [did] not act or fail to act through ignorance, mistake, or accident." The instructions also told the jury that the government was not required to prove that Sinskey knew that his acts violated the CWA or permits issued under that act. Sinskey contests these instructions as applied to 33 U.S.C. § 1319(c)(2)(A), arguing that because the adverb "knowingly" immediately precedes the verb "violates," the government must prove that he knew that his conduct violated either the CWA or the NPDES [National Pollutant Discharge Elimination System] permit. We disagree.

Although our court has not yet decided whether 33 U.S.C. § 1319(c)(2)(A) requires the government to prove that a defendant knew that he or she was violating either the CWA or the relevant NPDES permit when he or she acted, we are guided in answering this question by the generally accepted construction of the word "knowingly" in criminal statutes, by the CWA's legislative history, and by the decisions of the other courts of appeals that have addressed this issue. In construing other statutes with similar language and structure, that is, statutes in which one provision punishes the "knowing violation" of another provision that defines the illegal conduct, we have repeatedly held that the word "knowingly" modifies the acts constituting the underlying conduct. *See* United States v. Farrell, 69 F.3d 891, 893 (8th Cir. 1995), and United States v. Hern, 926 F.2d 764, 766-68 (8th Cir. 1991).

In *Farrell*, for example, we discussed 18 U.S.C. § 924(a)(2), which penalizes anyone who "knowingly violates" § 922(*o*)(1), which in turn prohibits the transfer or possession of a machine gun. In construing the word "knowingly," we held that it applied only to the conduct proscribed in § 922(*o*)(1), that is, the act of transferring or possessing a machine gun, and not to the illegal nature of those actions. A conviction under § 924(a)(2) therefore did not require proof that the defendant knew that his actions violated the law.

We see no reason to depart from that commonly accepted construction in this case, and we therefore believe that in 33 U.S.C. § 1319(c)(2)(A), the word "knowingly" applies to the underlying conduct prohibited by the statute. Untangling the statutory provisions discussed above in order to define precisely the relevant underlying conduct, however, is not a little difficult. At first glance, the conduct in question might appear to be violating a permit limitation, which would imply that § 1319(c)(2)(A) requires proof that the defendant knew of the permit limitation and knew that he or she was violating it. To violate a permit limitation, however, one must engage in the conduct prohibited by that limitation. The permit is, in essence, another layer of regulation in the nature of a law, in this case, a law that applies only to Morrell. We therefore believe that the underlying conduct of which Sinskey must have had knowledge is the conduct that is prohibited by the permit, for example, that Morrell's discharges of ammonia nitrates were higher than one part per million in the summer of 1992. Given this interpretation of the statute, the government was not required to prove that Sinskey knew that his acts violated either the CWA or the NPDES permit, but merely that he was aware of the conduct that resulted in the permit's violation.

This interpretation comports not only with our legal system's general recognition that ignorance of the law is no excuse, but also with Supreme Court interpretations of statutes containing similar language and structure. In United States v. International Minerals & Chemical Corp., 402 U.S. 558 (1971), for example, the Court analyzed a statute that punished anyone who "knowingly violated" certain regulations pertaining to the interstate shipment of hazardous materials. In holding that a conviction under the statute at issue did not require knowledge of the pertinent law, the Court reasoned that the statute's language was merely a shorthand designation for punishing anyone who knowingly committed the specific acts or omissions contemplated by the regulations at issue, and that the statute therefore required knowledge of the material facts but not the relevant law. The Court also focused on the nature of the regulatory scheme at issue, noting that where "dangerous or . . . obnoxious waste materials" are involved, anyone dealing with such materials "must be presumed" to be aware of the existence of the regulations. *Id.* at 565. Requiring knowledge only of the underlying actions, and not of the law, would therefore raise no substantial due process concerns. Such reasoning applies with equal force, we believe, to the CWA, which regulates the discharge into the public's water of such "obnoxious waste materials" as the byproducts of slaughtered animals. . . .

Our confidence in this interpretation is increased by decisions of the only other appellate courts to analyze the precise issue presented here. *See* United

States v. Hopkins, 53 F.3d 533, 541 (2d Cir. 1995), and United States v. Weitzenhoff, 35 F.3d 1275, 1283-86 (9th Cir. 1993). Both cases held that 33 U.S.C. § 1319(c)(2)(A) does not require proof that the defendant knew that his or her acts violated the CWA or the NPDES permits at issue.

Contrary to the defendants' assertions, moreover, United States v. Ahmad, 101 F.3d 386 (5th Cir. 1996), is inapposite. In *Ahmad*, a convenience store owner pumped out an underground gasoline storage tank into which some water had leaked, discharging gasoline into city sewer systems and nearby creeks in violation of 33 U.S.C. § 1319(c)(2)(A). At trial, the defendant asserted that he thought that he was discharging water, and that the statute's requirement that he act knowingly required that the government prove not only that he knew that he was discharging something, but also that he knew that he was discharging gasoline. The Fifth Circuit agreed, holding that a defendant does not violate the statute unless he or she acts knowingly with regard to each element of an offense. *Ahmad*, however, involved a classic mistake-of-fact defense, and is not applicable to a mistake-of-law defense such as that asserted by Sinskey and Kumm. Indeed, the Fifth Circuit noted as much, distinguishing *Hopkins* and *Weitzenhoff* on the grounds that those decisions involved a mistake-of-law defense.

Sinskey, joined by Kumm, also challenges the trial court's instructions with respect to 33 U.S.C. § 1319(c)(4), arguing that the government should have been required to prove that they knew that their acts were illegal. This argument has even less force with respect to § 1319(c)(4) — which penalizes a person who "knowingly falsifies, tampers with, or renders inaccurate any monitoring device or method required to be maintained" by the CWA — than it does with respect to § 1319(c)(2)(A). In § 1319(c)(4), the adverb "knowingly" precedes and explicitly modifies the verbs that describe the activities that violate the act.

We have repeatedly held that, in other statutes with similar language, the word "knowingly" refers only to knowledge of the relevant activities (in this case, the defendants' knowledge that they were rendering the monitoring methods inaccurate by aiding and abetting in the flow games and selective sampling). Based on this well established constructional convention, and the equally well known principle that a term that appears in a statute more than once should ordinarily be construed the same way each time, Ratzlaf v. United States, 510 U.S. 135, 143 (1994), we see no reason to read a requirement that a defendant know of the illegal nature of his or her acts into 33 U.S.C. § 1319(c)(4). Contrary to the defendants' assertions, moreover, requiring the government to prove only that the defendant acted with awareness of his or her conduct does not render § 1319(c)(4) a strict liability offense. . . .

For the foregoing reasons, we affirm the convictions in all respects.

DISCUSSION QUESTIONS

1. Sinskey argued that the CWA requires knowledge that the conduct violates the NPDES permit. Is that tantamount to arguing that ignorance of the law is an excuse? In what sense was Morrell's NPDES permit "the law"?

2. Is the *Sinskey* court correct in asserting that *Ahmad* can be neatly distinguished as a classic mistake of fact problem?

3. Many critics of environmental criminal enforcement argue that decisions like *Sinskey* and *Weitzenhoff* (which *Sinskey* cited with approval) read the mens rea requirements out of the statute. Does *Sinskey*'s interpretation of the mens rea requirements transform CWA violations into strict liability crimes?

4. In *Weitzenhoff*, the defendants operated a municipal sewage treatment plant that had a CWA permit allowing it to discharge a limited amount of organic and solid matter in the plant's effluent. After converting to a new system, the plant experienced a buildup of excess waste that it lacked the capacity to treat. Rather than hauling the excess waste to another treatment plant as they had done before, the defendants regularly bypassed the pretreatment system and discharged the untreated sewage directly into the ocean. The majority of the en banc court in *Weitzenhoff* concluded that if the defendants knew the relevant facts — i.e., if they knew they were discharging untreated sewage from the plant — they knowingly violated the permit. Five judges dissented. Consider the following excerpt from Judge Kleinfeld's dissent.

> The harm our mistaken decision may do is not necessarily limited to Clean Water Act cases. Dilution of the traditional requirement of a criminal state of mind, and application of the criminal law to innocent conduct, reduces the moral authority of our system of criminal law. If we use prison to achieve social goals regardless of the moral innocence of those we incarcerate, then imprisonment loses its moral opprobrium and our criminal law becomes morally arbitrary.
>
> We have now made felons of a large number of innocent people doing socially valuable work. They are innocent, because

the one thing which makes their conduct felonious is something they do not know. It is we, and not Congress, who have made them felons. The statute, read in an ordinary way, does not. . . .

. . . In this case, the defendants, sewage plant operators, had a permit to discharge sewage into the ocean, but exceeded the permit limitations. The legal issue for the panel was what knowledge would turn innocently or negligently violating a permit into "knowingly" violating a permit. Were the plant operators felons if they knew they were discharging sewage, but did not know that they were violating their permit? Or did they also have to know they were violating their permit? Ordinary English grammar, common sense, and precedent, all compel the latter construction.

As the panel opinion states the facts, these two defendants were literally "midnight dumpers." They managed a sewer plant and told their employees to dump 436,000 pounds of sewage into the ocean, mostly at night, fouling a nearby beach. Their conduct, as set out in the panel opinion, suggests that they must have known they were violating their National Pollution Discharge Elimination System (NPDES) permit. But we cannot decide the case on that basis, because the jury did not. The court instructed the jury that the government did not have to prove the defendants knew their conduct was unlawful, and refused to instruct the jury that a mistaken belief that the discharge was authorized by the permit would be a defense. Because of the way the jury was instructed, its verdict is consistent with the proposition that the defendants honestly and reasonably believed that their NPDES permit authorized the discharges.

This proposition could be true. NPDES permits are often difficult to understand and obey. The EPA had licensed the defendants' plant to discharge 976 pounds of waste per day, or about 409,920 pounds over the fourteen months covered by the indictment, into the ocean. The wrongful conduct was not discharging waste into the ocean. That was socially desirable conduct by which the defendants protected the people of their city from sewage-borne disease and earned their pay. The wrongful conduct was violating the NPDES permit by discharging 26,000 more pounds of waste than the permit authorized during the fourteen months. Whether these defendants were innocent or not, in the sense of knowing that they were exceeding their permit limitation, the panel's holding will make innocence irrelevant in other permit violation cases where the defendants had no idea that they were exceeding permit limits. The only thing they have to know to be guilty is that they were dumping sewage into the ocean, yet that was a lawful activity expressly authorized by their federal permit.[9]

Are the dissenters justified in claiming that *Weitzenhoff* turns morally innocent people who do socially valuable work into felons? What are the practical implications of the dissenters' views?

5. The fact patterns in Illustrations A, B, and C at the beginning of the chapter provided a framework for considering mens rea requirements. For purposes of this chapter, we will stipulate that the spilled substances in all three fact patterns are pollutants under the Clean Water Act and that all of the waters affected by the spills are deemed navigable waters of the United States. Which of the three spills — if any — qualify as a "knowing" discharge of pollutants into navigable waters and why?

6. Environmental law scholars tend to be critical of criminal enforcement of environmental standards. One of their principal criticisms is that the culpability requirements for environmental crimes are far too low.

> They cast "knowingly" as a "minimal," "low," "slender," "relaxed," "reduced," "diminished," "diluted" or "eviscerated" level of culpability that does not require proof of "traditional criminal intent." . . . One observer actually goes so far as to suggest that when prosecutors are "unable to prove *culpable* conduct," they commonly "threaten to indict . . . on a *'knowing'* charge." . . . The implication is, of course, that knowingly is not a culpable state of mind after all.[10]

Are these criticisms justified? Is knowledge a low standard of culpability? Is it a form of traditional criminal intent?

Stated differently, does the use of "knowingly" as the principal culpable mental state in environmental criminal statutes contribute to the perception of unfairness in environmental criminal enforcement? If so, should a different level of culpability be required?

---

[9]United States v. Weitzenhoff, 35 F.3d 1275, 1293-1294 (9th Cir. 1993).

[10]Kathleen F. Brickey, *The Rhetoric of Environmental Crime: Culpability, Discretion, and Structural Reform*, 84 IOWA L. REV. 115, 120-121 (1998).

2. WILLFUL BLINDNESS

In some instances, an actor may be charged with knowledge that he does not actually possess. Under the willful blindness doctrine, deliberate ignorance of a fact or circumstance the actor suspects exists but does not want to confirm can serve as a proxy for knowledge.

UNITED STATES V. HOPKINS

53 F.3d 533 (2d Cir. 1995)

KEARSE, Circuit Judge. . . .

I. Background

The present prosecution focused on environmental problems of Spirol International Corporation ("Spirol"), a manufacturer of metal shims and fasteners in northeastern Connecticut. Spirol's manufacturing operation involved a zinc-based plating process that generated substantial amounts of wastewater containing zinc and other toxic materials; this wastewater was discharged into the nearby Five Mile River. The State of Connecticut's Department of Environmental Protection ("DEP"), pursuant to authority delegated by the United States Environmental Protection Agency, administered the CWA provisions applicable to Spirol's discharges into the river. In 1987, Spirol, then operating under the name "CEM Co.," entered into a consent order with DEP, requiring Spirol to pay a $30,000 fine for past zinc-related discharge violations and to comply in the future with discharge limitations specified in the order. In February 1989, DEP issued a modified "wastewater discharge permit" (the "DEP permit") imposing more restrictive limits on the quantity of zinc and other substances that Spirol was permitted to release into the river.

From at least 1987 through September 6, 1990, Hopkins was Spirol's vice president for manufacturing. Hopkins signed the 1987 consent order with DEP on behalf of Spirol, and he had corporate responsibility for ensuring compliance with the order and the DEP permit. The present prosecution charged that between March 1989 and September 1990 Hopkins deliberately tampered with Spirol's wastewater testing and falsified its reports to DEP. The government's proof at trial included the testimony of Dennis Mark Morrison, Aaron Anderson, and John J. Morris, who at the pertinent times were Spirol employees. Taken in the light most favorable to the government, the evidence was as follows.

A. The Evidence as to the Sampling Process Directed by Hopkins

The DEP permit required Spirol each week to collect a sample of its wastewater and send it to an independent laboratory by Friday morning of that week. Spirol was required to report the laboratory results to DEP in a discharge monitoring report once a month. Under the DEP permit, the concentrations of zinc in Spirol's wastewater were not to exceed 2.0 milligrams per liter in any weekly sample, nor to average more than one milligram per liter in any month.

During the period March 1989 to September 1990, Spirol began its weekly sampling process on Mondays. A composite sample of the plant's wastewater was aggregated over a 24-hour period by Morrison and Anderson, who were involved in the zinc-plating process. Morrison was Anderson's supervisor and reported directly to Hopkins. Before sending a sample to the independent laboratory, Morrison and Anderson measured the concentration of zinc in the sample, and Morrison reported the results to Hopkins. Morrison and Anderson testified that if the sample collected on a Tuesday contained less than one milligram of zinc per liter, it would be sent promptly to the independent laboratory with a "chain of custody" record signed by Hopkins. If the Tuesday sample was not below that level, however, it was not sent to the laboratory. Morris, Spirol's maintenance engineer, testified that Hopkins expressed concern that if the samples did "not meet the permit requirements . . . the company would be facing another fine." Accordingly, whenever the Tuesday in-house test indicated a zinc content above the one-milligram-per-liter level, Hopkins directed that that sample be discarded and that another 24-hour composite sample be taken on Wednesday. In 54 of the 78 weeks in question, Spirol's samples were sent to the laboratory later than Tuesday.

If a Wednesday sample failed the in-house test, Hopkins sometimes ordered that it too be discarded and that another sample be taken on Thursday; but he more often instructed Morrison and Anderson to dilute the Wednesday sample with tap water or to reduce the zinc concentration using an ordinary coffee filter. Similarly, if the Thursday sample failed to meet the proper standard, Hopkins usually directed that it be diluted or filtered; but, Morrison testified, "A lot of times, we would go right through Friday." Any Friday sample that failed to meet the standard was always diluted or filtered, in order that a good sample could be sent to the laboratory by the Friday deadline. Morrison testified that in some of the samples submitted to the laboratory, there was more tap water than wastewater.

From March 1989 to September 6, 1990, Hopkins filed with DEP monthly discharge monitoring reports consolidating the weekly test results from the independent laboratory. These reports showed no zinc concentrations above one milligram per liter. On each report, Hopkins signed the following certification:

> I certify under penalty of law that this document and all attachments were prepared under by [*sic*] direction or supervision in accordance with a system designed to assure that qualified personnel properly gather and evaluate the information submitted. Based on my inquiry of the person or persons who manage the system, or those persons directly responsible for gathering the information. [*sic*] The information is, to the best of my knowledge and belief, true, accurate and complete. I am aware that there are significant penalties for submitting false information, including the possibility of fine and imprisonment for knowing violations.

Contrary to Hopkins's certifications of his belief as to truth and accuracy, Morrison testified that Hopkins had caused the samples to be "tampered with" about "40 percent of the time." Morrison testified that on 25-30 occasions when he reported back to Hopkins that he had finally succeeded in getting a satisfactory sample by means of dilution or filtration, Hopkins responded, "I know nothing, I hear nothing." Anderson testified that on one occasion in the summer of 1989, he reported directly to Hopkins that an unsatisfactory sample had been collected. Hopkins's response was, " 'See what you could do with it[.]' " [W]hen Anderson returned three hours later and reported that the sample was now satisfactory, Hopkins signed the chain-of-custody record without comment, question, or sign of surprise.

Morris testified that he told Hopkins that the testing procedures being used were improper. Regardless of the test results, Spirol continued to discharge its wastewater into the river.

B. The Trial Court's Instructions as to Knowledge

In December 1993, Hopkins was charged in a three-count indictment alleging (1) that he had knowingly falsified or tampered with Spirol's discharge sampling methods, in violation of 33 U.S.C. § 1319(c)(4) (count one); (2) that he had knowingly violated the conditions of the DEP permit, in violation of 33 U.S.C. § 1319(c)(2)(A) (count two); and (3) that he had conspired to commit those offenses, in violation of 18 U.S.C. § 371.

At trial, the district court instructed the jury as follows, over Hopkins's objections, on the knowledge element of each count. As to count one, the court stated:

> Knowledge may be established by direct or circumstantial evidence. One may not willfully or intentionally remain ignorant of a fact, material or important to his conduct to escape the consequences of criminal law.
>
> If you find beyond a reasonable doubt that the defendant was aware that there was a high probability that employees of Spirol were tampering with a monitoring device or method but he deliberately and consciously avoided confirming this fact so that he could deny knowledge if apprehended, then you may treat this deliberate avoidance of [*sic*] the equivalent of knowledge, unless you find the defendant actually believed that Spirol employees were not tampering with a monitoring device or method.
>
> A showing of negligence, mistake or even foolishness on the part of the defendant is not enough to support an inference of knowledge.
>
> It is not necessary for the government to prove that the defendant intended to violate the law or that the defendant had any specific knowledge of the particular statutory, regulatory or permit requirements imposed under the Clean Water Act.
>
> The government must prove, beyond a reasonable doubt, however, that the defendant acted voluntarily or intentionally to falsify, tamper with or render inaccurate a monitoring device or method and that he did not do so by mistake, accident or other innocent reason.

The court delivered substantially the same instruction with respect to count two. . . .

B. The Conscious-Avoidance Instruction

Hopkins . . . challenges the district court's instruction that the jury could find that Hopkins had the equivalent of knowledge if it found that "there was a high probability that employees of Spirol were tampering with a monitoring device or method but [Hopkins] deliberately and consciously avoided confirming this fact so that he could deny knowledge if apprehended." Hopkins argues that such an instruction was inappropriate because it was contrary to the government's contention that he had actual knowledge. His challenge has no merit.

A conscious-avoidance charge is appropriate when (a) the element of knowledge is in dispute, and (b) the evidence would permit a rational juror to conclude beyond a reasonable doubt "that the defendant was aware of a high probability of the fact in dispute and consciously avoided confirming that fact," United States v. Rodriguez, 983 F.2d 455, 458 (2d Cir. 1993). *See generally* United States v. Civelli, 883 F.2d 191, 194-95 (2d Cir.), cert. denied, 493 U.S. 966 (1989). Such an instruction is not inappropriate merely because the government has primarily attempted to prove that the defendant had actual knowledge, while urging in the alternative that if the defendant lacked such knowledge it was only because he had studiously sought to avoid knowing what was plain. *See, e.g.*, United States v. Mang Sun Wong, 884 F.2d 1537, 1541 (2d Cir. 1989), cert. denied, 493 U.S. 1082 (1990).

Both prerequisites for a conscious-avoidance instruction were present here. Though Hopkins did not testify at trial, his knowledge plainly was in dispute, for the thrust of his cross-examination and arguments was that he did not know about the tampering. For example, in his closing argument, defense counsel argued that Hopkins could have corrected matters "if [he] had known what was going on." Further, though there was ample evidence that Hopkins himself had ordered the tampering with the samples that were to be sent to the laboratory, there was also evidence that he had studiously avoided confirming the tampering. Morrison testified, for example, that on 25-30 occasions when he presented Hopkins with satisfactory samples after having previously presented him with unsatisfactory samples, Hopkins said, "I know nothing, I hear nothing." In light of Hopkins's litigation position and the evidence at trial, the district court did not err in instructing the jury that it could find Hopkins guilty based upon his conscious attempt to avoid actual knowledge that the samples had been falsified.

Conclusion

We have considered all of Hopkins's arguments on this appeal and have found them to be without merit. The judgment of conviction is affirmed.

DISCUSSION QUESTIONS

1. What is the purpose of the willful blindness doctrine? Does it make sense to charge someone with positive knowledge of facts he does not know?

2. Is willful blindness a subjective or objective state of mind? Is Hopkins liable because of what he knew or because of what he should have known?

3. What facts would support a finding that Hopkins was willfully blind?

3. COLLECTIVE KNOWLEDGE

Although most white-collar crime prosecutions specifically target individual wrongdoers, corporations and other legal entities are sometimes criminally charged as well.[11]

The size and complexity of large corporations have, of necessity, led to greater delegation of responsibility, which in turn spreads operational responsibility among more and more subordinates. This reality of modern corporate life led the courts to develop a theory under which the aggregate knowledge of the subordinates could be imputed to the corporation without requiring proof that any individual agent had actual knowledge of all of the operative facts.

Consider, for example, the currency reporting requirements contained in the Bank Secrecy Act. The act requires banks to file a currency transaction form with the IRS for any transaction that involves more than $10,000 in currency.

Suppose a new teller is working at a branch bank window when a customer arrives with three $5,000 checks and asks for $15,000 in cash. The new teller does not know about the reporting requirements, but clearly knows the transaction involves more than $10,000 in currency. The head teller, who supervises the new teller, knows that transactions of more than $10,000 in cash must be reported, but does not know that the amounts of the customer's three checks must be aggregated. Thus, the head teller does not instruct the inexperienced teller to fill out a currency transaction report. The general counsel, who works at the bank's main office, knows all of the legal requirements but does not know about this particular transaction. Has the bank knowingly failed to file a required currency transaction report?

Under the collective knowledge doctrine, the bank's knowledge "is the sum of the knowledge of all of the employees. That is, the bank's knowledge is the totality of what all of the employees know within the scope of their

---

[11]The principles that govern when corporations and other legal entities may be held criminally liable are considered in Chapter 3.

employment."[12]   Thus, even though no one individual knew all of the relevant facts, the bank is chargeable with the aggregate knowledge of the two tellers and the general counsel and is accountable for knowingly failing to file the required currency transaction report.

C. NEGLIGENCE

Negligence is a lower degree of culpability than knowledge. Whereas knowledge ordinarily connotes awareness, and thus is a subjective state of mind, negligence is measured by an objective standard. An actor is negligent if his conduct deviates from the standard of care that a reasonable person would have observed under the circumstances. Thus, even if the actor was subjectively unaware of the risk or a relevant circumstance but should have been aware of it, he may be found to have acted negligently.

1. STANDARD OF CARE

UNITED STATES V. ORTIZ

427 F.3d 1278 (10th Cir. 2005)

LUCERO, Circuit Judge. . . .

I

[Ortiz was the operator and sole employee of a chemical distillation facility owned by Chemical Specialties. The facility produced propylene glycol, an airplane de-icing fluid, and the distillation process created significant amounts of industrial wastewater. Rather than obtaining a permit to discharge the wastewater into the local municipal waste treatment plant, Ortiz falsely told city officials that the wastewater would be shipped to another business.

Due to the city's error in connecting nearby sewer lines, the city sewer system inadvertently discharged all sanitary waste from the distillation facility into a storm sewer that discharged into the Colorado River. This prompted a complaint to the city about a pungent odor near the River. City

---

[12]United States v. Bank of New England, 821 F.2d 844, 855 (1st Cir. 1987) (quoting the trial court's instructions).

investigators subsequently discovered a foul-smelling black substance flowing into the River from a storm drain. Test samples revealed that the substance contained chemicals that were constituent ingredients of propylene glycol.]

On May 1st, a city official accompanied by an employee of the Colorado Department of Public Health and Environment met with Ortiz at Chemical Specialties. After informing Ortiz that they were investigating the source of an unusual odor downstream from Chemical Specialties, Ortiz insisted that he sent all of his wastewater to a nearby business. Six days later, after discovering more of the black discharge downstream from Chemical Specialties and none upstream, the two officials returned and told Ortiz that the substance appeared to be coming from his facility. . . . They asked Ortiz if the facility had discharged any wastewater. Again, Ortiz said no. Dubious, the officials sought and received permission to inspect the facility, whereupon they observed significant amounts of water on the bathroom floor and several hoses and pumps lying nearby. . . .

During a follow-up investigation on May 29th, a city employee collected samples from the storm drain downstream from Chemical Specialties and from a pool of water below the storm drain flapper gate. Analysis revealed propylene glycol in the samples. Because earlier investigation had ruled out surrounding businesses as the likely source of the discharges, officials turned their attention exclusively to Chemical Specialties. On June 6th, a city employee conducted a test that conclusively demonstrated a connection between the toilet in Chemical Specialties and the storm sewer. The city employee informed Ortiz that the toilet was definitely connected to the storm drain and instructed Ortiz not to discharge anything down the toilet or sink. In their words, officials "shut the water off" at Chemical Specialties and arranged for a portable toilet and handwash station to be delivered to the facility.

On June 18th, two EPA special agents were dispatched to Chemical Specialties where they discovered a tanker truck spewing a liquid with "a fermenting type of smell that comes off of [wet onions]" onto the ground at the facility. The agents then walked to the nearby storm drain outfall where yet again a black liquid with the stench of rotten onions was observed pouring into the Colorado River. Although the storm drain downstream from Chemical Specialties had the same smell, immediately upstream from the facility the storm drain was dry and odorless. Returning to Chemical Specialties, the agents interviewed Ortiz who informed them that the leaking tanker contained propylene glycol that Ortiz intended to process. Ortiz stated that he was the sole employee of Chemical Specialties, and volunteered that he was the only person with a key to the facility. When asked if he had ever discharged pollutants through the toilet, Ortiz refused to answer. City investigators again observed puddles of water on the bathroom floor and hoses lying nearby, and noted that water supply to the toilet had been turned back on and the toilet was operational.

On submission of the case to a federal grand jury, a superseding indictment was returned charging Ortiz with two violations of the Clean Water Act ("CWA"): (1) negligently discharging chemical pollutants from a point source (a storm drain) into waters of the United States (the Colorado River) without a permit on May 29, 2002 and (2) knowingly discharging chemical pollutants from a point source into waters of the United States without a permit on June 18, 2002. Having been convicted on both counts on trial to a jury, Ortiz filed a motion for judgment of acquittal. The district court denied the motion as to Count Two but granted it as to Count One, finding: "There is no evidence that the defendant had any awareness that the toilet was not connected to a sanitary sewer line before June 6, 2002. While the first count of the Superseding Indictment charges a negligent discharge, the defendant could not be guilty on that discharge in the absence of his knowledge that using the toilet would result in the discharge . . . to the river."

II . . .

A . . .

In granting Ortiz's motion for a judgment of acquittal of negligent discharge, the district court found that "the defendant could not be guilty on that discharge in the absence of his knowledge that using the toilet would result in the discharge . . . to the river." On appeal, the government argues that the court improperly imposed a mens rea requirement, and effectively conflated the elements required for a negligent discharge conviction under § 1319(c)(1)(A) and a knowing discharge conviction under § 1319(c)(2)(A). It continues with the assertion that the CWA does not saddle the government with the burden of proving that a defendant knew that waste traversed some boustrophedonic path and ended in a navigable stream. Ortiz does not dispute that ordinary negligence suffices to establish a negligent discharge violation under § 1319(c)(1)(A). Rather, Ortiz characterizes the court's judgment of acquittal as resting on the recognition "that one cannot be negligent, that is, flout a known risk, without being aware of what that risk is." Because Ortiz claims that he had no reason to suspect on May 29th that his toilet was connected to the storm drain, he argues that he cannot have been negligent in flushing dangerous chemicals down his toilet.

Even though the CWA does not define the term "negligently," we can easily determine what the government must prove to obtain a conviction under § 1319(c)(1)(A) by applying straightforward principles of statutory interpretation. . . .

Section 1319(c)(1)(A) imposes punishment upon "any person who negligently violates" certain enumerated sections of the CWA. . . . To determine what "negligently" means in this statutory context, we "start with the assumption that the legislative purpose is expressed by the ordinary meaning of the words used." Russello v. United States, 464 U.S. 16, 21 (1983). In its ordinary usage, "negligently" means a failure to exercise the degree of care that someone of ordinary prudence would have exercised in the same circumstance. Under the statute's plain language, an individual violates the CWA by failing to exercise the degree of care that someone of ordinary prudence would have exercised in the same circumstance, and, in so doing, discharges any pollutant into United States waters without an NPDES permit. Thus, contrary to the district court's reading, the CWA does not require proof that a defendant knew that a discharge would enter United States waters.

Our decision accords with the Ninth Circuit's ruling in United States v. Hanousek, 176 F.3d 1116 (9th Cir. 1999), the only case to have previously addressed this issue. . . . Hanousek argued that to establish a [negligent violation], the government had to prove that the defendant acted with criminal negligence rather than ordinary negligence. Viewing the plain language of the statute, the court disagreed, and held that one commits a negligent discharge violation by failing "to use such care as a reasonably prudent and careful person would use under similar circumstances." Id. at 1120. Further, the court determined that "if Congress intended to prescribe a heightened negligence standard, it could have done so explicitly, as it did in 33 U.S.C. § 1321(b)(7)(D)," a civil penalty provision of the CWA. Id. at 1121.

If Ortiz failed to exercise the degree of care that someone of ordinary prudence would have exercised in the same circumstance and, in so doing, discharged a pollutant into the Colorado River without a permit to do so, then he violated § 1319(c)(1)(A). Ortiz does not dispute on appeal that on May 29, 2002 he discharged some amount of propylene glycol wastewater down the toilet at Chemical Specialties. He does not deny that the wastewater flowed into the Colorado River and does not claim to have a permit to discharge untreated propylene glycol wastewater into the river. He argues, however, that when dumping the propylene glycol wastewater down the toilet, he was not acting negligently. We disagree.

In viewing the evidence in the light most favorable to the government, we have little trouble concluding that a reasonable jury could have found that Ortiz violated § 1319(c)(1)(A). Prior to May 29th, investigators told Ortiz that they had traced a black discharge with a strong onion odor from the Colorado River, up the storm drain, to the Chemical Specialties facility, and questioned him about how he was disposing of wastewater. The government presented evidence that prior to these conversations, Ortiz was dumping propylene glycol wastewater (a black substance with a strong onion odor) down the toilet. A reasonable jury could have well found that Ortiz acted negligently on May 29th when, after being alerted by investigators, he again dumped propylene glycol wastewater into the toilet.[13] Because a reasonable jury could have found beyond a reasonable doubt that Ortiz committed a violation of § 1319(c)(1)(A) on May 29, 2002, we reverse the district court's judgment of acquittal. . . .

III

We reverse the judgment of acquittal entered on Count One of the superseding indictment and reinstate the jury's verdict convicting Ortiz of negligently discharging a pollutant in violation of 33 U.S.C. §§ 1311(a) and 1319(c)(1)(A). . . .

DISCUSSION QUESTIONS

1. At what point did Ortiz's conduct become negligent? Was he negligent from the outset, when he first dumped wastewater into the company's toilet? Or was he negligent only after he had been told that his company was a likely source of the river pollution? Is his prior notice of a link between the pollution source and a navigable water relevant to the issue of negligence? If so, is it crucial?
2. The court concluded that the statute imposes criminal liability for ordinary negligence. The court observed that the Clean Water Act

---

[13]We do not imply that an individual commits a negligent discharge violation only upon prior notification from officials of a possible link between a point source and a navigable water. Here, however, the facts are more than sufficient to obtain a conviction under § 1319(c)(1)(A).

imposes civil liability for negligent violations but provides increased civil penalties where the violation is attributable to "gross negligence or willful misconduct." Is that persuasive evidence that Congress did not intend to adopt a heightened negligence standard in the criminal provision?

3. While "ordinary" negligence connotes lack of diligence — i.e., failure to perceive a risk that a reasonable person would have been aware of under the circumstances — gross negligence connotes extreme carelessness. Was Ortiz grossly negligent?

4. Is it problematic that criminal liability may be based on a level of culpability that is lower than that required for civil liability? If this seems problematic, which (if any) of the following variables are important?

   a. The civil provision the *Ortiz* court cited applies only to spills involving oil or hazardous substances, while the criminal provision applies to discharges of any pollutant, regardless of its potential harm to the environment.

   b. The criminal penalties for negligent discharges are calibrated on the basis of whether the defendant has a past history of violations.

      (1) First conviction: punishable by a fine of $2,500 to $25,000 per day of violation and/or imprisonment of up to 1 year.

      (2) Subsequent conviction: punishable by a fine of up to $50,000 per day of violation and/or imprisonment of up to 2 years.

   c. The civil penalties for discharges of oil or hazardous substances are calibrated on the basis of the defendant's level of culpability.

      (1) Discharges generally: punishable by up to $25,000 per day of violation or up to $1,000 per barrel discharged, regardless of mental state.

      (2) Grossly negligent discharges: punishable by not less than $100,000 and up to $3,000 per barrel discharged.

5. Ortiz was convicted of two crimes involving the same conduct but requiring different mental states. He was found guilty of "negligently" and "knowingly" discharging pollutants into the river. What is the difference between negligence and knowledge? At what point did Ortiz's negligence ripen into knowledge?

6. In *Ortiz*, both the negligent and knowing discharge violations were based on the same factual premise: that Ortiz dumped chemical wastewater into the toilet. From a practical standpoint, why would the prosecutor charge him with both species of violations?

7. The introduction to this chapter used Illustrations A, B, and C to provide a framework for considering mens rea requirements. Assume the spilled substances in all three fact patterns are pollutants under the Clean Water Act and that all of the waters affected by the spills are navigable. Which of the spills, if any, qualify as a "negligent" discharge of pollutants into navigable waters and why?

2. CAUSATION

The concept of causation plays a central role in both tort law and criminal law. Like the element of mens rea, the doctrine of causation helps define when an actor can be fairly held accountable for a prohibited result.

This principle can be simply illustrated by revisiting the Clean Water Act violations in *Ortiz*. The inescapable conclusion is that Mr. Ortiz, the operations manager and sole employee of the distillation facility, personally dumped chemical wastewater into the toilet and that the dumping was the source of the pollution found in the river. Ortiz thus directly caused the pollution. His causal connection with the discharge, combined with the requisite finding of negligence, provides the basis for holding him responsible for polluting the river.

a. Causation in Fact

Ordinarily, the defendant's conduct must be the actual cause of the offending result. This is often phrased as a "but for" test. In the case of Mr. Ortiz, but for his dumping industrial waste into the toilet, the pollutants would not have been discharged into the river.

b. Causation in Law

In addition, the defendant's conduct must be the legal cause — also known as the proximate cause — of the offending result. Although the concept of proximate cause is somewhat amorphous, at bottom, proximate cause is a cause that is legally sufficient to hold the actor responsible. In the run of the mill case, proximate cause and "but for" cause will coalesce. Not only was Mr. Ortiz's pouring the chemicals into the toilet the actual or "but for" cause of the water pollution. It was also the proximate cause in the sense that pollution of the river was well within the range of risks his conduct created. Stated differently, the actual result was not at variance with the result Ortiz should have anticipated.

But there may be circumstances in which the relationship between the actual result and the risk created by the actor's conduct is too attenuated to hold the actor legally responsible.

> **Illustration G:** Assume that Ortiz planned to drive a tanker truck full of wastewater to another facility for proper disposal. After starting the truck's engine, he realized that he had left his wallet — and thus his driver's license — on the desk in his office. When he went to retrieve the wallet he left the engine running and the driver's side door open.
>
> During his brief absence, a teenaged joy rider happened by, jumped in the truck, and took off in the direction of the river. Being unfamiliar with the intricacies of driving such a large vehicle, the joy rider lost control of the truck. After crashing into several concrete objects that punctured the tank of waste, the truck ran off the bank and ultimately came to rest on the river bottom. Not surprisingly, the waste spilled into the water. Was Ortiz the cause of the pollution?

While it could fairly be said that "but for" Ortiz's act of leaving the engine running and the door unlocked the truck would not have discharged chemicals into the river, a jury would be unlikely to find that he should be held criminally responsible for an essentially unforeseeable result.

c. Causation and Mens Rea

Returning to the facts in *Ortiz*, a determination that the act of pouring chemicals down the toilet was both the factual and legal cause of the discharge into the river is not the end of the matter. It is also necessary to find that when the conduct occurred, Ortiz acted with the mental state specified by the statute — in this case, knowingly or negligently — and the court found the evidence was sufficient to sustain that finding.

> **Illustration H:** But what if Ortiz had filled a glass container with waste so he could perform chemical tests to determine how it should be properly disposed of? While he carried it through the facility's lab as carefully as he could, he stumbled and dropped the container in the sink. The glass shattered and the contents spilled down the drain.

Here it is clear that he is the factual and legal cause of the discharge. But was there the necessary coalescence of act and intent? Absent additional facts, a jury would be hard put to find that he was negligent and hence criminally liable.

THE CASE OF THE RUPTURED PIPELINE

Baker was a railway company employee with supervisory responsibilities for a special construction project to realign a sharp curve in the railroad track. The project required blasting rock outcroppings near the tracks and loading the rocks onto railroad cars with a backhoe. As project supervisor, Baker's responsibilities included ensuring that the track was built safely and efficiently.

A high-pressure petroleum pipeline ran parallel to the railroad within a few feet of the tracks. Because the pipeline was at or slightly above ground level, construction workers temporarily covered it with sand and gravel so the backhoe operator could transport the rock across the pipeline and load it onto the cars without rupturing the pipe. Although the original project supervisor covered the part of the pipeline where the work was occurring with a platform made of protective railroad ties, sand, and other ballast material, when Baker assumed the job he decided it would be cheaper and more efficient just to use a few inches of sand and gravel to insulate the pipe during construction.

One day while Krause, the backhoe operator, was using the backhoe bucket to sweep rock from the tracks, the bucket struck and ruptured the pipeline, spilling 5,000 gallons of heating oil into an adjacent river.

Baker and Krause were charged with negligently discharging pollutants into the river. Is Baker the factual and/or legal cause of the spill? Is Krause? Are one or both of them negligent? What facts are critical to the resolution of these issues?[14]

D. STRICT LIABILITY

In most contexts, the requirement of a culpable state of mind is what sets criminal liability apart from its civil counterparts, and that is true in the environmental law field as well. But, of course, there are exceptions to every rule. In the universe of environmental crimes, the Refuse Act — an adjunct to other water pollution statutes — is the notable exception to the rule.

---

[14]*Cf.* United States v. Hanousek, 176 F.3d 1116 (9th Cir. 1999).

The Refuse Act makes it a crime to discharge refuse into navigable waters or to deposit any matter on the bank of navigable waters where it would be "liable" to be washed into such waters if its presence in the water could impede navigation.[15] The Act does not require proof of a culpable mental state.

In contrast with most CWA violations, Refuse Act violations are punishable as misdemeanors rather than felonies.

THE CASE OF THE LOCKED SLOP CHUTES

The Dollar Steamship Company owned, among others, a steamship called the "President Coolidge." The President Coolidge pulled into the Honolulu Harbor and tied up at a pier. Aware that the law prohibited throwing refuse from the ship into the harbor, the company had issued strict orders prohibiting the crew from doing so. As an aid to enforcement, conspicuous signs were posted throughout the ship warning crew members not to throw anything overboard, and locks had been put on the slop chutes to prevent them from being used while the ship was in harbor.

Despite these precautions, a harbor patrol boatman who was passing under the stern of the President Coolidge in his patrol boat was suddenly deluged with kitchen garbage that fell onto his boat and into the water. After clearing his eyes, he looked up in time to see a crew member walking away from the stern rail carrying what appeared to be a slop bucket.

Dollar Steamship was charged with violating the Refuse Act, which provides in pertinent part: it shall be unlawful "to throw, discharge, or deposit . . . from or out of any ship . . . any refuse matter of any kind or description whatever . . . into any navigable water of the United States." The Honolulu Harbor is classified as a navigable water under the Act.

Has Dollar Steamship violated the Act?[16] Are the company's efforts to prevent the crew from throwing debris overboard relevant? What policy (if any) would be served by applying the statute to these facts?

---

[15]33 U.S.C. § 407.
[16]*Cf.* Dollar Steamship Co. v. United States, 101 F.2d 638 (9th Cir. 1939).

3

INDIVIDUAL AND ORGANIZATIONAL LIABILITY

The requirements of foresight and vigilance imposed on responsible corporate agents are beyond question demanding, and perhaps onerous, but they are no more stringent than the public has a right to expect of those who voluntarily assume positions of authority in business enterprises whose services and products affect the health and well-being of the public that supports them.[†]

[A] fundamental law of organizational physics is that bad news does not flow upstream.[††]

Both individuals and entities are subject to criminal prosecution under most of the major environmental statutes. Although some statutes

---

[†]Chief Justice Warren E. Burger.
[††]Peter Jones, chief legal counsel for Levi Strauss.

incorporate specialized terms of more limited import,[1] the Clean Water Act, Clean Air Act, and the Resource Conservation and Recovery Act (RCRA) all define the term "person" broadly to include corporations and other entities as well as individuals.[2]

A. INDIVIDUAL LIABILITY

Since most serious violations of environmental laws occur in business settings, violations committed by or through businesses are among the most frequently prosecuted. Some criminal provisions in environmental statutes target particular business actors such as "owners," "persons in charge" of a regulated facility, and "responsible corporate officers."[3] Thus, these statutes reflect clear congressional intent to impose liability on corporate officers and employees.

But what of other statutes that impose liability on "persons" generally without specifying a particular position of responsibility within a corporation or other business entity? Are corporate officers and agents criminally liable for acts they commit while they are acting within the scope of their employment? They are, after all, acting under the cloak of authority and on behalf of the corporation.

> **Illustration A:** A plant manager instructs the facilities supervisor to clean up the plant and remove leaky drums of chemical waste from the building where they are stored. The supervisor, who has neither the means nor the budget to transport the drums to a proper disposal facility, tells a maintenance worker to throw the drums into a pond behind the plant. The maintenance worker does as he is told and dumps them in the pond. As it turns out, the chemicals are classified as hazardous waste and this method of disposal violates the Resource Conservation and Recovery Act (RCRA). Assuming the three employees all have the prescribed culpable mental state,[4] if the government prosecutes any or all of them, can they defend on the ground that they were just doing their job?

---

[1] We will encounter these specialized concepts and definitions in later chapters.

[2] *See, e.g.,* 33 U.S.C. § 1365(5) (Clean Water Act); 42 U.S.C. § 6903(15) (RCRA); 42 U.S.C. § 7602(e) (Clean Air Act).

[3] In later chapters, we will consider such specialized statutory terms of art in the context of the specific laws in which they are used. The responsible corporate officer doctrine is considered later in this chapter as well.

[4] *See supra* Chapter 2.

The Supreme Court definitively resolved this question in United States v. Wise.[5] In *Wise*, a case in which a corporate officer was charged with price fixing, the Court rejected the argument that a corporate officer or agent is not personally liable under the Sherman Act for acts committed solely in a representative capacity. The Sherman Act applies to "every person" who engages in a combination or conspiracy to restrain trade, and the term "person" includes corporations and associations.[6] Even though the defendant's acts were corporate acts in the sense that they were imputable to the corporation, the Court found no evidence of legislative intent to exempt corporate officers and agents from personal liability.

> No intent to exculpate a corporate officer who violates the law is to be imputed to Congress without clear compulsion; else the fines established by the Sherman Act to deter crime become mere license fees for illegitimate corporate business operations.... [A] corporate officer is subject to prosecution under § 1 of the Sherman Act whenever he knowingly participates in effecting the illegal contract, combination, or conspiracy ... regardless of whether he is acting in a representative capacity.[7]

Thus, it is well settled that absent clear legislative intent to exclude corporate agents from personal responsibility for crimes they commit, they "cannot use the corporate entity as a shield against liability for [their] own misdeeds."[8]

It should be noted, however, that even though environmental violations ordinarily occur in a business setting, many of the criminal provisions apply to non-business settings as well.

---

[5]370 U.S. 405 (1962).

[6]The Court found this specific inclusion of corporations and associations in the term "person" was understandable because the Sherman Act was enacted before the doctrine of corporate criminal liability had become well established. *Id.* at 408.

[7]*Id.* at 409, 416.

[8]Kathleen F. Brickey, *Corporate Criminal Liability: A Primer for Corporate Counsel*, 40 BUS. LAW. 129, 138-139 (1984).

1. DIRECT AND INDIRECT PARTICIPATION

There are several theories under which an individual may become liable for crimes. The most obvious is by directly engaging in conduct that constitutes the crime. Thus, for example, the maintenance worker in Illustration A is liable because he personally dumped the barrels into the pond. Using terminology embedded in the common law doctrine of parties to crime, he is the principal — or, in modern vernacular, the perpetrator.

But what about the facilities supervisor? He did not personally throw the barrels in the pond. He merely instructed the maintenance worker to do it. Is he liable for a violation committed by his subordinate?

Let's return to the Supreme Court's analysis in *Wise*. Wise was liable even though he was acting in his official capacity as a corporate employee. As the Court in *Wise* observed, a corporate officer or agent is personally responsible, notwithstanding that he is acting in a representative or official capacity, if he "authorizes, orders, or helps perpetrate the crime."[9]

The Court's language mirrors the rule codified in the federal complicity statute, which treats direct actors (like the maintenance worker) and those who order or assist them (like the facilities supervisor) as equally responsible for the resulting crime. All are punishable as principals — i.e., their liability for the resulting crime is precisely the same as if they had personally committed the act that resulted in the violation. The federal statute, 18 U.S.C. § 2, reads as follows:

> (a) Whoever commits an offense against the United States or aids, abets, counsels, commands, induces or procures its commission, is punishable as a principal.
>
> (b) Whoever willfully causes an act to be done which if directly performed by him or another would be an offense against the United States, is punishable as a principal.

Borrowing terminology from the statute, the maintenance worker in Illustration A is liable because he committed an offense against the United States. That is, he knowingly dumped hazardous chemicals in the pond, in

---

[9]*Wise*, 370 U.S. at 416.

violation of RCRA.[10] Under the federal complicity statute, the facilities supervisor is also guilty because he counseled or commanded the maintenance worker to dispose of the chemicals illegally.

But what about the plant manager? He instructed the supervisor to clean up the plant but did not tell him to dump the chemicals in the pond. Has he also procured the illegal disposal? The answer to this question hinges on his state of mind. What did he intend to convey when he said "clean up the plant" and "remove the leaky drums?" Was this code language for "dump the chemicals?" For "get rid of them no matter how you do it?" Did he know the supervisor had inadequate resources to dispose of them properly?

These questions are crucial because to be liable for the acts of a subordinate, the manager must act with the mental state required to commit the crime. Thus, what the manager knew and when he knew it are critical, as is what he meant when he instructed the supervisor to remove the barrels from the plant. If the message the manager intended to convey to the supervisor was "just get rid of them any way that you can," there would be a plausible case for holding him criminally responsible for the dumping. If, on the other hand, the manager had told the supervisor to "make sure we have any EPA permits we need to dispose of the drums" and the supervisor simply ignored the instruction, the manager would likely be off the hook.

Since the doctrine of parties to crime holds an accessory liable for crimes committed by another, it is necessary to consider two focal points in the prosecution's case. First, there must be evidence that someone committed a crime. In a prosecution based on the hypothetical in Illustration A, the prosecutor would introduce evidence establishing that the maintenance worker dumped hazardous chemicals in the pond. Then it would need to be shown that the accessory — here, the facilities supervisor — counseled, commanded, or otherwise encouraged the commission of the crime. On this point, the prosecutor would introduce evidence that the supervisor told the maintenance worker to throw the barrels into the pond.

This seems to be a relatively straightforward case, and if the jury is convinced beyond a reasonable doubt that the supervisor ordered the improper disposal, it can hold the supervisor personally liable for the

---

[10]The question whether he must know his conduct is illegal is considered in Chapters 2 and 4. The question whether he must know the chemicals are classified as hazardous is considered in Chapter 6.

maintenance worker's criminal act. But now for the tougher question. Is conviction of the maintenance worker a prerequisite to holding the supervisor liable for the RCRA violation? Consider the scenario in Illustration B.

> **Illustration B:** Assume the same facts as in Illustration A with the following variation. Suppose the supervisor and the maintenance worker are both prosecuted for illegally dumping the chemicals. The supervisor is convicted but the maintenance worker is acquitted. Should the supervisor's conviction be vacated because the jury found his subordinate — who allegedly committed the crime — not guilty?

Under the common law doctrine of parties to crime, technical procedural rules barred the conviction of the accessory to a crime unless the principal had been convicted first. The common-law doctrine held that a prior acquittal of the principal was a bar to prosecution of the accessory, as was reversal of the principal's conviction on appeal or his receipt of a pardon.

As the doctrine of parties to crime matured, these procedural barriers to prosecuting the accessory largely disappeared. Similarly, under the federal complicity statute quoted above, there is no formal distinction between principals and accessories. The statute provides that all participants are punishable as principals. Thus, the liability of the supervisor who counseled the illegal act is not contingent upon the conviction of his subordinate.

DISCUSSION QUESTIONS

1. Under modern law as embodied in 18 U.S.C. § 2, the supervisor's conviction in Illustration B could stand even if the maintenance worker had previously been acquitted. Is this result analytically sound?
2. What is the rationale for holding the supervisor liable in Illustration B for illegal dumping that was committed by the maintenance worker? Is the supervisor equally blameworthy? And what if liability is twice removed? Suppose the manager is found to have spoken in "code" when he told the supervisor to remove the leaky barrels. Is the manager's conduct as blameworthy as the maintenance worker's?

———————

> **Illustration C:** The facts in Illustrations A and B assume the maintenance worker knew what was in the barrels. For purposes of Illustration C, suppose the facilities supervisor tells the maintenance worker to clean out

a storage closet in the plant and discard the contents in a dumpster behind the building. The supervisor knows the closet contains a plastic bag filled with rags that have been used to wipe up spilled chemical waste. As in the previous illustrations, the chemical is hazardous.

Thinking they are ordinary cleaning rags, the maintenance worker throws the rag bag into the dumpster. The trash removal service that picks up the plant's garbage routinely disposes of the dumpster's contents at a sanitary landfill that is not authorized to receive hazardous waste. Thus, disposal of the chemical-laden rags at the landfill is illegal.

Is the driver of the garbage truck liable for illegally disposing of the rags? Is the maintenance worker? The supervisor?

The obvious problem in Illustration C is that the rags were in fact disposed of illegally, but neither the truck driver nor the maintenance worker knew or had reason to know they were handling hazardous chemical waste. Although the truck driver performed the prohibited act (disposing of the waste at the landfill) and the maintenance worker facilitated the violation (putting the rags in the trash), neither was aware that the bag contained contaminated rags. In consequence, neither could knowingly cause them to be disposed of at an unlicensed facility. Since knowing disposal of waste is an element of the crime, the driver and maintenance worker were, in effect, innocent agents. And while the facilities supervisor had the requisite knowledge, he did not personally dispose of the rags.

This is where the federal complicity statute again comes into play. Under 18 U.S.C. § 2(b), one who willfully causes an innocent agent to engage in conduct that would otherwise constitute a crime may be punished as if he had performed the act himself. Returning to Illustration C, the supervisor knew the rags were contaminated with hazardous chemicals. If he had personally thrown the bag into the landfill, he would have committed a crime, but the facts in Illustration C make it clear that the supervisor did not commit the violation himself. When he told the maintenance worker to put the rag bag in the dumpster, he consciously set in motion a chain of events that culminated in the illegal disposal of the contaminated rags. Under the complicity statute, his act of willfully causing the illegal disposal through innocent agents — the maintenance worker and the truck driver — makes him punishable as if he had put the rags there himself.

2. RESPONSIBLE CORPORATE OFFICERS

The recent fraud convictions of Enron CEOs Jeff Skilling and Ken Lay make it abundantly clear that corporate officers are personally liable for crimes they commit during the course of their employment. But what about crimes of omission? Are corporate officers personally liable for crimes they fail to prevent if they have responsibility for the business process that results in the violation?

This question gained importance with the rise of public welfare offenses. A typical public welfare offense can be found in the Food and Drug Act, which makes it a crime to introduce adulterated or misbranded drugs into the stream of commerce. As the Supreme Court observed in United States v. Dotterweich,[11] public welfare statutes like the Food and Drug Act are needed to protect the lives and health of innocent consumers who are put at risk by the marketing of adulterated or misbranded products.

In *Dotterweich*, the Court upheld the conviction of the president and general manager of a small drug jobber for violating the Food and Drug Act by shipping misbranded and adulterated drugs.[12] The Court ruled that Dotterweich was personally liable even though there was no evidence that he knew the drugs were misbranded and adulterated or that he personally participated in shipping them. The Court was of the view that the Act "puts the burden of acting at hazard upon a person otherwise innocent but standing in responsible relation to a public danger."[13] As long as Dotterweich shared "responsibility in the business process resulting in unlawful distribution," he would be personally liable.[14]

During the three decades following *Dotterweich*, most individuals prosecuted under the Food and Drug Act held relatively high office or had general authority over the business enterprise. That led to the perception that officers of small businesses were exposed to "a particularly high risk since they generally are involved in plant operations, in addition to their overall responsibilities."[15]

---

[11]320 U.S. 277 (1943).

[12]Dotterweich bought drugs from pharmaceutical manufacturers and resold them to retailers after repackaging and relabeling the products.

[13]*Id.* at 281.

[14]*Id.* at 284.

[15]Daniel F. O'Keefe, Jr. & Marc H. Shapiro, *Personal Criminal Liability Under the Federal Food, Drug, and Cosmetic Act — The* Dotterweich *Doctrine*, 30 FOOD DRUG COSM. L.J. 5, 20 (1975).

In response to a 1972 General Accounting Office report that sanitation problems in the food industry were on the increase, the Food and Drug Administration (FDA) warned industry representatives that enforcement efforts would be stepped up. Dissatisfied with the response to that warning, the FDA wrote letters to the presidents of several food chains, warning:

> We regard you as the person who ultimately has the authority to order correction of such conditions, and thus who ultimately must bear the responsibility for any failure to correct them. Should it become necessary to bring criminal action to prevent a continuation of violative conditions, therefore, we wish you to understand that you and the other high corporate officials in your organization who are specifically responsible for sanitation practices will be held accountable.[16]

The prosecution in United States v. Park was brought shortly after that.

UNITED STATES V. PARK

421 U.S. 658 (1975)

Mr. Chief Justice BURGER delivered the opinion of the Court.

We granted certiorari to consider whether the jury instructions in the prosecution of a corporate officer under § 301(k) of the Federal Food, Drug, and Cosmetic Act, 21 U.S.C. § 331(k), were appropriate under United States v. Dotterweich, 320 U.S. 277 (1943).

Acme Markets, Inc., is a national retail food chain with approximately 36,000 employees, 874 retail outlets, 12 general warehouses, and four special warehouses. Its headquarters, including the office of the president, respondent Park, who is chief executive officer of the corporation, are located in Philadelphia, Pa. In a five-count information filed in the United States District Court for the District of Maryland, the Government charged Acme and respondent with violations of the Federal Food, Drug, and Cosmetic Act. Each count of the information alleged that the defendants had received food that had been shipped in interstate commerce and that, while the food was being held for sale in Acme's Baltimore warehouse following shipment in interstate commerce, they caused it to be held in a building accessible to rodents and to be exposed to contamination by rodents. These acts were

---

[16]*Id.* at 29.

alleged to have resulted in the food's being adulterated within the meaning of 21 U.S.C. §§ 342(a)(3) and (4), in violation of 21 U.S.C. § 331(k).

Acme pleaded guilty to each count of the information. Respondent pleaded not guilty. The evidence at trial demonstrated that in April 1970 the Food and Drug Administration (FDA) advised respondent by letter of insanitary conditions in Acme's Philadelphia warehouse. In 1971 the FDA found that similar conditions existed in the firm's Baltimore warehouse. An FDA consumer safety officer testified concerning evidence of rodent infestation and other insanitary conditions discovered during a 12-day inspection of the Baltimore warehouse in November and December 1971. He also related that a second inspection of the warehouse had been conducted in March 1972. On that occasion the inspectors found that there had been improvement in the sanitary conditions, but that "there was still evidence of rodent activity in the building and in the warehouses and we found some rodent-contaminated lots of food items."

The Government also presented testimony by the Chief of Compliance of the FDA's Baltimore office, who informed respondent by letter of the conditions at the Baltimore warehouse after the first inspection.[17] There was testimony by Acme's Baltimore division vice president, who had responded to the letter on behalf of Acme and respondent and who described the steps taken to remedy the insanitary conditions discovered by both inspections. The Government's final witness, Acme's vice president for legal affairs and assistant secretary, identified respondent as the president and chief executive officer of the company and read a bylaw prescribing the duties of the chief executive officer.[18] He testified that respondent functioned by delegating

---

[17]The letter, dated January 27, 1972, included the following:

We note with much concern that the old and new warehouse areas used for food storage were actively and extensively inhabited by live rodents. Of even more concern was the observation that such reprehensible conditions obviously existed for a prolonged period of time without any detection, or were completely ignored. . . .

We trust this letter will serve to direct your attention to the seriousness of the problem and formally advise you of the urgent need to initiate whatever measures are necessary to prevent recurrence and ensure compliance with the law.

[18]The bylaw provided in pertinent part:

The Chairman of the board of directors or the president shall be the chief executive officer of the company as the board of directors may from time to time determine. He shall, subject to the board of directors, have general and active supervision of the affairs, business, offices and employees of the company. . . .

"normal operating duties," including sanitation, but that he retained "certain things, which are the big, broad, principles of the operation of the company," and had "the responsibility of seeing that they all work together."

At the close of the Government's case in chief, respondent moved for a judgment of acquittal on the ground that "the evidence in chief has shown that Mr. Park is not personally concerned in this Food and Drug violation." The trial judge denied the motion, stating that United States v. Dotterweich, 320 U.S. 277 (1943), was controlling.

Respondent was the only defense witness. He testified that, although all of Acme's employees were in a sense under his general direction, the company had an "organizational structure for responsibilities for certain functions" according to which different phases of its operation were "assigned to individuals who, in turn, have staff and departments under them." He identified those individuals responsible for sanitation, and related that upon receipt of the January 1972 FDA letter, he had conferred with the vice president for legal affairs, who informed him that the Baltimore division vice president "was investigating the situation immediately and would be taking corrective action and would be preparing a summary of the corrective action to reply to the letter." Respondent stated that he did not "believe there was anything [he] could have done more constructively than what [he] found was being done."

On cross-examination, respondent conceded that providing sanitary conditions for food offered for sale to the public was something that he was "responsible for in the entire operation of the company," and he stated that it was one of many phases of the company that he assigned to "dependable subordinates." Respondent was asked about and, over the objections of his counsel, admitted receiving, the April 1970 letter addressed to him from the FDA regarding insanitary conditions at Acme's Philadelphia warehouse. He acknowledged that, with the exception of the division vice president, the same individuals had responsibility for sanitation in both Baltimore and Philadelphia. Finally, in response to questions concerning the Philadelphia and Baltimore incidents, respondent admitted that the Baltimore problem indicated the system for handling sanitation "wasn't working perfectly" and

He shall, from time to time, in his discretion or at the order of the board, report the operations and affairs of the company. He shall also perform such other duties and have such other powers as may be assigned to him from time to time by the board of directors.

that as Acme's chief executive officer he was responsible for "any result which occurs in our company."

At the close of the evidence, respondent's renewed motion for a judgment of acquittal was denied. The relevant portion of the trial judge's instructions to the jury challenged by respondent is set out in the margin.[19] Respondent's counsel objected to the instructions on the ground that they failed fairly to reflect our decision in United States v. Dotterweich and to define "'responsible relationship.'" The trial judge overruled the objection. The jury found respondent guilty on all counts of the information, and he was subsequently sentenced to pay a fine of $50 on each count.

The Court of Appeals reversed the conviction and remanded for a new trial. That court viewed the Government as arguing "that the conviction may be predicated solely upon a showing that . . . [respondent] was the President of the offending corporation," and it stated that as "a general proposition, some act of commission or omission is an essential element of every crime." 499 F.2d 839, 841 (CA4 1974). It reasoned that, although our decision in United States v. Dotterweich, *supra*, at 281, had construed the statutory provisions under which respondent was tried to dispense with the traditional element of "'awareness of some wrongdoing,'" the Court had not construed them as dispensing with the element of "wrongful action." The Court of Appeals concluded that the trial judge's instructions "might well have left the jury with the erroneous impression that Park could be found guilty in the absence of 'wrongful action' on his part," 499 F.2d, at 841-842, and that proof of this element was required by due process. It held, with one dissent, that the instructions did not "correctly state the law of the case," *id.*, at 840, and directed that on retrial the jury be instructed as to "wrongful action," which might be "gross negligence and inattention in discharging . . . corporate

---

[19][The jury instructions provided in pertinent part:]

In order to find the Defendant guilty on any count of the Information, you must find beyond a reasonable doubt on each count. . . .

Thirdly, that John R. Park held a position of authority in the operation of the business of Acme Markets, Incorporated.

The individual is or could be liable under the statute, even if he did not consciously do wrong. However, the fact that the Defendant is pres[id]ent and is a chief executive officer of the Acme Markets does not require a finding of guilt. Though, he need not have personally participated in the situation, he must have had a responsible relationship to the issue. The issue is, in this case, whether the Defendant, John R. Park, by virtue of his position in the company, had a position of authority and responsibility in the situation out of which these charges arose.

duties and obligations or any of a host of other acts of commission or omission which would 'cause' the contamination of food." *Id.*, at 842.

The Court of Appeals also held that the admission in evidence of the April 1970 FDA warning to respondent was error warranting reversal, based on its conclusion that, "as this case was submitted to the jury and in light of the sole issue presented," there was no need for the evidence and thus that its prejudicial effect outweighed its relevancy. . . . 499 F.2d, at 843.

We granted certiorari because of an apparent conflict among the Courts of Appeals with respect to the standard of liability of corporate officers under the Federal Food, Drug, and Cosmetic Act as construed in United States v. Dotterweich, and because of the importance of the question to the Government's enforcement program. We reverse. . . .

II

The rule that corporate employees who have "a responsible share in the furtherance of the transaction which the statute outlaws" are subject to the criminal provisions of the Act was not formulated in a vacuum. Cases under the Federal Food and Drugs Act of 1906 reflected the view both that knowledge or intent were not required to be proved in prosecutions under its criminal provisions, and that responsible corporate agents could be subjected to the liability thereby imposed. *See, e.g.,* United States v. Mayfield, 177 F. 765 (N.D. Ala. 1910). Moreover, the principle had been recognized that a corporate agent, through whose act, default, or omission the corporation committed a crime, was himself guilty individually of that crime. The principle had been applied whether or not the crime required "consciousness of wrongdoing," and it had been applied not only to those corporate agents who themselves committed the criminal act, but also to those who by virtue of their managerial positions or other similar relation to the actor could be deemed responsible for its commission.

In the latter class of cases, the liability of managerial officers did not depend on their knowledge of, or personal participation in, the act made criminal by the statute. Rather, where the statute under which they were prosecuted dispensed with "consciousness of wrongdoing," an omission or failure to act was deemed a sufficient basis for a responsible corporate agent's liability. It was enough in such cases that, by virtue of the relationship he bore to the corporation, the agent had the power to prevent the act complained of. *See, e.g.,* State v. Burnam, 128 P. 218 (Wash. 1912); Overland Cotton Mill Co. v. People, 75 P. 924 (Colo. 1904).

The rationale of the interpretation given the Act in *Dotterweich*, as holding criminally accountable the persons whose failure to exercise the authority and supervisory responsibility reposed in them by the business organization resulted in the violation complained of, has been confirmed in our subsequent cases. . . .

Thus *Dotterweich* and the cases which have followed reveal that in providing sanctions which reach and touch the individuals who execute the corporate mission — and this is by no means necessarily confined to a single corporate agent or employee — the Act imposes not only a positive duty to seek out and remedy violations when they occur but also, and primarily, a duty to implement measures that will insure that violations will not occur. The requirements of foresight and vigilance imposed on responsible corporate agents are beyond question demanding, and perhaps onerous, but they are no more stringent than the public has a right to expect of those who voluntarily assume positions of authority in business enterprises whose services and products affect the health and well-being of the public that supports them.

The Act does not, as we observed in *Dotterweich*, make criminal liability turn on "awareness of some wrongdoing" or "conscious fraud." The duty imposed by Congress on responsible corporate agents is, we emphasize, one that requires the highest standard of foresight and vigilance, but the Act, in its criminal aspect, does not require that which is objectively impossible. The theory upon which responsible corporate agents are held criminally accountable for "causing" violations of the Act permits a claim that a defendant was "powerless" to prevent or correct the violation to "be raised defensively at a trial on the merits." United States v. Wiesenfeld Warehouse Co., 376 U.S. 86, 91 (1964). If such a claim is made, the defendant has the burden of coming forward with evidence, but this does not alter the Government's ultimate burden of proving beyond a reasonable doubt the defendant's guilt, including his power, in light of the duty imposed by the Act, to prevent or correct the prohibited condition. Congress has seen fit to enforce the accountability of responsible corporate agents dealing with products which may affect the health of consumers by penal sanctions cast in rigorous terms, and the obligation of the courts is to give them effect so long as they do not violate the Constitution.

III

We cannot agree with the Court of Appeals that it was incumbent upon the District Court to instruct the jury that the Government had the burden of establishing "wrongful action" in the sense in which the Court of Appeals used that phrase. The concept of a "responsible relationship" to, or a "responsible share" in, a violation of the Act indeed imports some measure of blameworthiness; but it is equally clear that the Government establishes a prima facie case when it introduces evidence sufficient to warrant a finding by the trier of the facts that the defendant had, by reason of his position in the corporation, responsibility and authority either to prevent in the first instance, or promptly to correct, the violation complained of, and that he failed to do so. The failure thus to fulfill the duty imposed by the interaction of the corporate agent's authority and the statute furnishes a sufficient causal link. The considerations which prompted the imposition of this duty, and the scope of the duty, provide the measure of culpability.

IV

Our conclusion that the Court of Appeals erred in its reading of the jury charge suggests as well our disagreement with that court concerning the admissibility of evidence demonstrating that respondent was advised by the FDA in 1970 of insanitary conditions in Acme's Philadelphia warehouse. We are satisfied that the Act imposes the highest standard of care and permits conviction of responsible corporate officials who, in light of this standard of care, have the power to prevent or correct violations of its provisions. Implicit in the Court's admonition that "the ultimate judgment of juries must be trusted," United States v. Dotterweich, 320 U.S. at 285, however, is the realization that they may demand more than corporate bylaws to find culpability.

Respondent testified in his defense that he had employed a system in which he relied upon his subordinates, and that he was ultimately responsible for this system. He testified further that he had found these subordinates to be "dependable" and had "great confidence" in them. By this and other testimony respondent evidently sought to persuade the jury that, as the president of a large corporation, he had no choice but to delegate duties to those in whom he reposed confidence, that he had no reason to suspect his subordinates were failing to insure compliance with the Act, and that, once violations were unearthed, acting through those subordinates he did everything possible to correct them.

Although we need not decide whether this testimony would have entitled respondent to an instruction as to his lack of power, had he requested it, the testimony clearly created the "need" for rebuttal evidence. That evidence was not offered to show that respondent had a propensity to commit criminal acts or that the crime charged had been committed; its purpose was to demonstrate that respondent was on notice that he could not rely on his system of delegation to subordinates to prevent or correct insanitary conditions at Acme's warehouses, and that he must have been aware of the deficiencies of this system before the Baltimore violations were discovered. The evidence was therefore relevant since it served to rebut respondent's defense that he had justifiably relied upon subordinates to handle sanitation matters.   And, particularly in light of the difficult task of juries in prosecutions under the Act, we conclude that its relevance and persuasiveness outweighed any prejudicial effect.

Reversed.

Mr. Justice STEWART, with whom Mr. Justice MARSHALL and Mr. Justice POWELL join, dissenting.

Although agreeing with much of what is said in the Court's opinion, I dissent from the opinion and judgment, because the jury instructions in this case were not consistent with the law as the Court today expounds it.

As I understand the Court's opinion, it holds that in order to sustain a conviction under § 301(k) of the Federal Food, Drug, and Cosmetic Act the prosecution must at least show that by reason of an individual's corporate position and responsibilities, he had a duty to use care to maintain the physical integrity of the corporation's food products. A jury may then draw the inference that when the food is found to be in such condition as to violate the statute's prohibitions, that condition was "caused" by a breach of the standard of care imposed upon the responsible official. This is the language of negligence, and I agree with it.

To affirm this conviction, however, the Court must approve the instructions given to the members of the jury who were entrusted with determining whether the respondent was innocent or guilty.   Those instructions did not conform to the standards that the Court itself sets out today.

The trial judge instructed the jury to find Park guilty if it found beyond a reasonable doubt that Park "had a responsible relation to the situation. . . . The issue is, in this case, whether the Defendant, John R. Park, by virtue of his position in the company, had a position of authority and responsibility in the situation out of which these charges arose." Requiring, as it did, a verdict of guilty upon a finding of "responsibility," this instruction standing alone could have been construed as a direction to convict if the jury found Park "responsible" for the condition in the sense that his position as chief executive officer gave him formal responsibility within the structure of the corporation. But the trial judge went on specifically to caution the jury not to attach such a meaning to his instruction, saying that "the fact that the Defendant is pres[id]ent and is a chief executive officer of the Acme Markets does not require a finding of guilt." "Responsibility" as used by the trial judge therefore had whatever meaning the jury in its unguided discretion chose to give it.

The instructions, therefore, expressed nothing more than a tautology. They told the jury: "You must find the defendant guilty if you find that he is to be held accountable for this adulterated food." In other words: "You must find the defendant guilty if you conclude that he is guilty." The trial judge recognized the infirmities in these instructions, but he reluctantly concluded that he was required to give such a charge under United States v. Dotterweich, which, he thought, in declining to define "responsible relation" had declined to specify the minimum standard of liability for criminal guilt.[20]

To be sure, "the day [is] long past when [courts] . . . parsed instructions and engaged in nice semantic distinctions," Cool v. United States, 409 U.S. 100, 107 (Rehnquist, J., dissenting). But this Court has never before abandoned the view that jury instructions must contain a statement of the applicable law sufficiently precise to enable the jury to be guided by something other than its rough notions of social justice. And while it might be argued that the issue before the jury in this case was a "mixed" question of both law and fact, this has never meant that a jury is to be left wholly at sea, without any guidance as to the standard of conduct the law requires. The instructions given by the trial court in this case, it must be emphasized, were a virtual nullity, a mere authorization to convict if the jury thought it

---

[20]In response to a request for further illumination of what he meant by "responsible relationship" the District Judge said:

Let me say this, simply as to the definition of the "responsible relationship." *Dotterweich* and subsequent cases have indicated this really is a jury question. It says it is not even subject to being defined by the Court. As I have indicated to counsel, I am quite candid in stating that I do not agree with the decision; therefore, I am going to stick by [my original instruction].

appropriate. Such instructions — regardless of the blameworthiness of the defendant's conduct, regardless of the social value of the Food, Drug, and Cosmetic Act, and regardless of the importance of convicting those who violate it — have no place in our jurisprudence. . . .

DISCUSSION QUESTIONS

1. The Court in *Park* stated that "[t]he concept of a 'responsible relationship' to, or a 'responsible share' in, a violation of the Act indeed imports some measure of blameworthiness. . . . The considerations which prompted the imposition of [the defendant's] duty, and the scope of the duty, provide the measure of culpability." Did the Court adopt a negligence theory of liability or a strict liability theory? Is the Court's conclusion that the Act requires a finding of minimal culpability consistent with its rejection of a requirement that the government must establish "wrongful action" in the sense that the court of appeals required it?

2. What implications do *Dotterweich* and *Park* have for the privilege of delegating authority and responsibility to subordinate agents? Is it possible that high-ranking corporate officers and managers may be held personally accountable for violations that occur in a sphere of operations in which they have little or no involvement?

3. The Court said that Park would not have been liable if he had been powerless to prevent or correct the violation. At what point during the trial does Park's responsibility for the activity that results in the violation become an issue? Is it relevant only if he raises an objective impossibility defense? Who has the burden of proving his responsibility for the offending activity?

THE CASE OF THE FDA IMPOSTER

Suppose the efforts to clean up the warehouse in *Park* had been successful. Suppose further that a competitor of Acme Markets hires a saboteur to impersonate an FDA inspector and, on the eve of the next FDA inspection, sends the saboteur to "inspect" Acme's warehouse. While in the Acme warehouse complex, the saboteur surreptitiously deposits rat and mouse pellets in strategic locations. The following day, a real FDA inspector arrives on the scene and discovers the contamination. Is Park responsible for the violation?[21]

THE CASE OF EMPLOYEE SABOTAGE

Suppose that Park was at the warehouse when the first inspection occurred and that, in the presence of the inspector, Park reprimanded the warehouse janitor and gave him specific orders to correct the problem. The janitor, who held a grudge against Park and Acme, purposely failed to follow the orders. One month later, a second FDA inspection occurred. To Park's surprise, the inspector discovered the same contamination problem. Is Park liable for the violation? Or does he have an impossibility defense based upon employee sabotage?[22]

THE CASE OF THE UNENCLOSED WAREHOUSE

Suppose that Acme had an unenclosed food storage facility in Hawaii. When the FDA inspection occurred, the inspector saw birds flying in and out of the warehouse, perching on overhead sprinklers, and eating from bags of rice stored there. When charged with the violation, Park raised the following defense: "I have been working on this contamination problem a long time, but my efforts to solve it during the past months have not been effective. I initially tried to scare the birds away with scarecrows. When I saw that scarecrows wouldn't work, I shot starter pistols every morning, thinking the noise would frighten them away. But that didn't solve the problem either. My current plan is to enclose the food storage area in a huge wire cage to keep the birds out. But right now, I can't construct the cage because the materials I need to build it haven't arrived from the mainland United States."

Does the unavailability of the materials give Park a valid impossibility defense?[23]

---

[21]*Compare* Norman Abrams, *Criminal Liability of Corporate Officers for Strict Liability Offenses — A Comment on* Dotterweich *and* Park, 28 UCLA L. Rev. 463, 468-469 (1981), *with* Kathleen F. Brickey, *Criminal Liability of Corporate Officers for Strict Liability Offenses — Another View*, 35 VAND. L. REV. 1337, 1366-1367 (1982).

[22]*Cf.* United States v. Starr, 535 F.2d 512 (9th Cir. 1976).

[23]*Cf.* United States v. Y. Hata & Co., 535 F.2d 508 (9th Cir. 1976).

Dotterweich and *Park* were the genesis of the responsible corporate officer doctrine which, in both cases, added judicial gloss to the Food and Drug Act. Although there are arguably good reasons to confine the doctrine to statutes defining public welfare offenses,[24] in some jurisdictions it has spilled over into other regulatory contexts where the statutory offenses are not — strictly speaking — public welfare crimes.[25]

Congress has also promoted expansion of the responsible corporate officer doctrine into other fields, including environmental crime. The criminal provisions in two major environmental statutes — the Clean Water Act and the Clean Air Act — expressly include "any responsible corporate officer" in the definition of the term "person."[26]

UNITED STATES V. IVERSON

162 F.3d 1015 (9th Cir. 1998)

GRABER, Circuit Judge. . . .

Background . . .

Defendant was a founder of CH2O, Inc., and served as the company's President and Chairman of the Board. CH2O blends chemicals to create numerous products, including acid cleaners and heavy-duty alkaline compounds. The company ships the blended chemicals to its customers in drums.

CH2O asked its customers to return the drums so that it could reuse them. Although customers returned the drums, they often did not clean them sufficiently. Thus, the drums still contained chemical residue. Before CH2O could reuse the drums, it had to remove that residue.

---

[24]*See* Brickey, *supra* note 21, at 1377-1381.

[25]*See, e.g.,* United States v. Jorgensen, 144 F.3d 550 (8th Cir. 1998) (applying the responsible share test to felony violations of misbranding provisions in the Federal Meat Inspection Act; defendants misrepresented that beef was 100% from producers' genetically selected cattle fed a special diet when beef had been blended with meat from outside suppliers who made no such claims).

[26]*See* 33 U.S.C. § 1319(c)(6) (Clean Water Act); 42 U.S.C. § 7413(c)(6) (Clean Air Act).

To remove the residue, CH2O instituted a drum-cleaning operation, which in turn generated wastewater. In the early to mid-1980s, defendant approached the manager of the local sewer authority to see whether the sewer authority would accept the company's wastewater. The sewer authority refused, because the wastewater "did not meet the parameters we had set for accepting industrial waste. It had too high of a metal content." Thereafter, defendant and the general manager of CH2O made two other attempts to convince the sewer authority to accept the wastewater. Both times, it refused.

Beginning in about 1985, defendant personally discharged the wastewater and ordered employees of CH2O to discharge the wastewater in three places: (1) on the plant's property, (2) through a sewer drain at an apartment complex that defendant owned, and (3) through a sewer drain at defendant's home. (The plant did not have sewer access.) Those discharges continued until about 1988, when CH2O hired Bill Brady.

Brady initially paid a waste disposal company to dispose of the wastewater. Those efforts cost the company thousands of dollars each month. Beginning in late 1991, CH2O stopped its drum-cleaning operation and, instead, shipped the drums to a professional outside contractor for cleaning.

In April 1992, CH2O fired Brady. Around that same time, defendant bought a warehouse in Olympia. Unlike the CH2O plant, the warehouse had sewer access. After the purchase, CH2O restarted its drum-cleaning operation at the warehouse and disposed of its wastewater through the sewer. CH2O obtained neither a permit nor permission to make these discharges. The drum-cleaning operation continued until the summer of 1995, when CH2O learned that it was under investigation for discharging pollutants into the sewer.

A few months before CH2O restarted its drum-cleaning operation, defendant announced his "official" retirement from CH2O. Thereafter, he continued to receive money from CH2O, to conduct business at the company's facilities, and to give orders to employees. Moreover, the company continued to list him as the president in documents that it filed with the state, and the employee who was responsible for running the day-to-day aspects of the drum-cleaning operation testified that he reported to defendant.

During the four years of the operation at the warehouse, defendant was sometimes present when drums were cleaned. During those occasions, defendant was close enough to see and smell the waste.

In some instances, defendant informed employees that he had obtained a permit for the drum-cleaning operation and that the operation was on the "up and up." At other times, however, defendant told employees that, if they got caught, the company would receive only a slap on the wrist.

[Iverson was charged in a five count indictment with violating the Clean Water Act and related water pollution laws, and was convicted on all counts.]

Responsible Corporate Officer

Defendant . . . argues that the district court erred in formulating its "responsible corporate officer" jury instruction. We are not persuaded. . . .

B. "Responsible Corporate Officer" Liability

The district court instructed the jury that it could find defendant liable under the CWA as a "responsible corporate officer" if it found, beyond a reasonable doubt:

> 1. That the defendant had knowledge of the fact that pollutants were being discharged to the sewer system by employees of CH2O, Inc.;
> 2. That the defendant had the authority and capacity to prevent the discharge of pollutants to the sewer system; and
> 3. That the defendant failed to prevent the on-going discharge of pollutants to the sewer system.

Defendant argues that the district court misinterpreted the scope of "responsible corporate officer" liability. Specifically, defendant suggests that a corporate officer is "responsible" only when the officer in fact exercises control over the activity causing the discharge or has an express corporate duty to oversee the activity. We have not previously interpreted the scope of "responsible corporate officer" liability under the CWA. We do so now and reject defendant's narrow interpretation.

. . . The CWA holds criminally liable "any person who . . . knowingly violates" its provisions. The CWA defines the term "person" to include "any responsible corporate officer." However, the CWA does not define the term "responsible corporate officer."

When a statute does not define a term, we generally interpret that term by employing the ordinary, contemporary, and common meaning of the words that Congress used. As pertinent here, the word "responsible" means "answerable" or "involving a degree of accountability." Webster's Third New Int'l Dictionary 1935 (unabridged ed. 1993). Using that meaning, "any corporate officer" who is "answerable" or "accountable" for the unlawful discharge is liable under the CWA.

The history of the "responsible corporate officer" liability supports the foregoing construction. The "responsible corporate officer" doctrine originated in a Supreme Court case interpreting the Federal Food, Drug, and Cosmetic Act (FFDCA), United States v. Dotterweich, 320 U.S. 277 (1943).

In *Dotterweich*, the president and the general manager of a corporation each argued that he was not a "person" as that term is defined in the FFDCA. The Court disagreed, holding that "the offense is committed . . . by all who do have such a responsible share in the furtherance of the transaction which the statute outlaws." *Id.* at 284. The Court refused to define the boundaries of the doctrine, however, leaving the question for district courts and juries. *See id.* at 285 ("To attempt a formula embracing the variety of conduct whereby persons may responsibly contribute in furthering a transaction forbidden by an Act of Congress . . . would be mischievous futility. . . . [T]he question of responsibility [is properly left] to the jury.").

Because Congress used a similar definition of the term "person" in the CWA, we can presume that Congress intended that the principles of *Dotterweich* apply under the CWA. Under *Dotterweich*, whether defendant had sufficient "responsibility" over the discharges to be criminally liable would be a question for the jury.

After Congress initially enacted the CWA in 1972, the Supreme Court further defined the scope of the "responsible corporate officer" doctrine under the FFDCA. In United States v. Park, 421 U.S. 658 (1975), a corporate president argued that he could not be "responsible" under *Dotterweich*, because he had delegated decision-making control over the activity in question to a subordinate. The Court rejected that argument, holding that

> the Government establishes a prima facie case when it introduces evidence sufficient to warrant a finding by the trier of the facts that the defendant had, by reasons of his position in the corporation, responsibility and authority either to prevent in the first instance or promptly to correct, the violation complained of, and that he failed to do so.

Id. at 673-74. Stated another way, the question for the jury is whether the corporate officer had "authority with respect to the conditions that formed the basis of the alleged violations." *Id.* at 674. The Court did not, however, require the corporate officer actually to exercise any authority over the activity. . . .

Moreover, this court has interpreted similar terms in other statutes consistently with the Court's decision in *Park*. . . .

Taken together, the wording of the CWA, the Supreme Court's interpretations of the "responsible corporate officer" doctrine, and this court's interpretation of similar statutory requirements establish the contours of the "responsible corporate officer" doctrine under the CWA. Under the CWA, a person is a "responsible corporate officer" if the person has authority to exercise control over the corporation's activity that is causing the discharges. There is no requirement that the officer in fact exercise such authority or that the corporation expressly vest a duty in the officer to oversee the activity. . . .

Affirmed.

DISCUSSION QUESTIONS

1. Since Iverson had "officially" retired from CH20, what is the basis for holding him liable as a responsible corporate officer? Does it matter whether he continued to have a formal affiliation with the company?[27]
2. How important is it that Iverson was occasionally present when the drums were cleaned?
3. What policy supports imposing criminal liability on an individual who is not personally involved in committing the violation?

THE CASE OF THE TOWBOAT BURN BARRELS

Marine Towing operated towboats on the Mississippi, Ohio, and Tennessee Rivers. Giles, who served as the company's marine superintendent and vice president of operations, had operational control over all of the company's boats. During the period in question, the towboats were not equipped with dumpsters. Instead, they used 55-gallon burn barrels to incinerate solid waste and debris while the boats were out of port, often for long stretches of time and under crowded conditions. Every two or three days the barrels would fill up and deck hands, in accordance with informal company policy, dumped ash and unburned debris into the river. When the

---

[27]*Cf.* United States v. Hong, 242 F.3d 528 (4th Cir. 2001).

barrels were no longer usable, deck hands dumped them overboard as well. The dumping occurred only at night and while the boat was on a remote stretch of the river.

A more environmentally friendly (and costlier) alternative for disposing of the debris would have been to hire a barge to offload waste from the towboats while they were out of port.   Since Giles exercised ultimate supervision over the towboats, only he had the authority to implement an alternative disposal routine. Quigley, a towboat captain for Marine Towing, knew Marine's policy was to incinerate trash and debris. Although Quigley was unhappy about the incineration policy, he had no control over it. And while he could have asked Giles to provide a barge, he didn't ask because he knew Giles was satisfied with the current policy and didn't want to "make waves with the top brass."

A federal grand jury indicted Giles and Captain Quigley, charging them with knowingly discharging pollutants into navigable waterways in violation of the Clean Water Act. At trial, the defense produced witnesses who testified that the use of burn barrels on river vessels was a common practice, even on United States Coast Guard boats. Some deck hands also testified that there was no other practicable way to dispose of the waste on Marine's boats.

Which, if either, of the defendants should be held criminally responsible for the dumping?[28]

A finding that Giles and/or Quigley are responsible would not preclude holding other crew members liable as well. Should any other members of the crew be prosecuted? If so, should it matter that they were just following orders?

B. ORGANIZATIONAL LIABILITY

1. PRINCIPLES OF LIABILITY

In the federal system, corporations and other legal entities may be held criminally liable for the acts of their officers and agents under a modified respondeat superior theory. It goes without saying that a corporation can be said to "act" only in the sense that it acts through its agents — that is, the acts of corporate officers and employees can be imputed to the corporate entity

---

[28]*Cf.* United States v. M/G Transp. Servs., Inc., 173 F.3d 584 (6th Cir. 1999).

itself. There are, of course, discrete limits on this principle, and to explore them we'll turn separately to each.

First, whose acts are imputable to the corporation? Although there is some disagreement about whether it is the most desirable approach to defining the appropriate bounds of corporate liability,[29] the federal rule allows imposition of criminal liability based on the acts of corporate agents regardless of their status in the corporate hierarchy. Thus, while this rule would hold the organization liable for criminal acts of those at the highest policy-making levels of the corporate hierarchy (e.g., policy makers like the CEO and members of the board of directors), it also holds the entity liable for acts of mid-level managers (e.g., plant managers) and those in the lowest echelons of the organizational ladder (e.g., truck drivers, pesticide applicators, and maintenance workers).

Consider the following instructions to the jury in a leading state case, Commonwealth v. Beneficial Finance Co.:[30]

> [T]he Commonwealth must prove beyond a reasonable doubt that there existed between the guilty individual or individuals and the corporation which is being charged with the conduct of the individuals, such *a relationship that the acts and the intent of the individuals were the acts and intent of the corporation.* . . .
>
> *It does not mean that the Commonwealth must prove that the individual who acted criminally was a member of the corporation's board of directors, or that he was a high officer in the corporation, or that he held any office at all.* . . . The Commonwealth must prove that the individual for whose conduct it seeks to charge *the corporation criminally was placed in a position by the corporation where he had enough power, duty, responsibility and authority to act for and in behalf of the corporation to handle the particular business or operation or project of the corporation in which he was engaged at the time that he committed the criminal act, with power of decision as to what he would or would not do while acting for the corporation, and that he was acting for and in behalf of the corporation in*

---

[29]The Model Penal Code corporate liability provision, for example, reflects the view that corporations and other legal entities should be held responsible for conventional crimes only if the board of directors or a high managerial agent engaged in the prohibited conduct or authorized, condoned, or ratified it. *See* MODEL PENAL CODE AND COMMENTARIES § 2.07 (Official Draft and Revised Comments 1985). This approach is critiqued in Kathleen F. Brickey, *Rethinking Corporate Liability Under the Model Penal Code*, 19 RUTGERS L.J. 593 (1987-1988).

[30]275 N.E.2d 33 (Mass. 1971).

the accomplishment of that particular business or operation or project, and that he committed a criminal act while so acting. . . .

You will note from what I said that it is not necessary that the Commonwealth prove that an individual had any particular office or any office at all or that he had any particular title or any title at all. It isn't the title that counts. *It isn't the name of the office that counts, but it's the position in which the corporation placed that person with relation to its business, with regard to the powers and duties and responsibilities and authority which it gave to him which counts.* If it placed him in a position with such power, duty, authority, and responsibility that it can be found by you that, when he acted in the corporation's business, the corporation was acting, then you may find the corporation equally guilty of the criminal acts which he commits and of the intent which he holds, if you first find that the individual was guilty of the crime.

Now, this test doesn't depend upon the power, duty, the responsibility, or the authority which the individual has with reference to the entire corporation business. The test should be applied to his position with relation to the particular operation or project in which he is serving the corporation. [Emphasis supplied by the court.]

Upholding the instructions as consistent with established case law, the Supreme Judicial Court of Massachusetts explained:

It is obvious that criminal conspiratorial acts are not performed within the glare of publicity, nor would we expect a board of directors to meet officially and record on the corporate records a delegation of authority to initiate, conduct or conclude proceedings for the purpose of bribing a public official. Of necessity, the proof [of] authority to so act must rest on all the circumstances and conduct in a given situation and the reasonable inferences to be drawn therefrom.

Additional factors of importance are the size and complexity of many large modern corporations which necessitate the delegation of more authority to lesser corporate agents and employees. As the judge pointed out: "There are not enough seats on the Board of Directors, nor enough offices in a corporation, to permit the corporation engaged in widespread operations to give such a title or office to every person in whom it places the power, authority, and responsibility for decision and action." This latter consideration lends credence to the view that the title or position of an individual in a corporation should not be conclusively determinative in ascribing criminal responsibility. In a large corporation, with many numerous and distinct departments, a high ranking corporate officer or agent may have no authority or involvement in a particular sphere of corporate activity, whereas a lower ranking corporate executive might have much broader power in dealing with a matter peculiarly within the scope of his authority. Employees who are in the lower echelon of the corporate hierarchy often exercise more responsibility in the *everyday operations* of the corporation than the directors or officers. Assuredly, the title or office that the person holds may be considered, but it should not be the decisive criterion upon which to predicate corporate responsibility. . . .

———————

This broad respondeat superior rule is not without limits, of course.

(1) The agent must be acting on behalf of the corporation and within the scope of employment. As the instructions in *Beneficial Finance* make clear, this does not mean that the agent must be specifically authorized to commit a crime. It means, instead, that the agent must commit the offense while performing a job-related responsibility.

(2) Even if the conduct is contrary to general corporate policy or contrary to specific instructions not to engage in it, if the agent commits the crime pursuant to his authority to handle that part of the corporation's business, that is enough to make his acts and intent those of the corporation.

Thus, for example, the maintenance worker in Illustration A had general responsibility for keeping the plant clean and orderly. When the facilities supervisor told him to remove the leaking drums of waste from the building, he was directed to perform a function that was well within his assigned range of duties. Even though he committed a crime when he dumped the chemical drums into the pond, he was acting on behalf of the corporation as part of the cleanup operation. And even if he knew that dumping the chemicals in the pond was against company policy or if he had been specifically told to have the drums transported to a proper disposal facility, he was still performing a job-related function when he disposed of the drums. Removing them from the plant as part of the cleanup was clearly within his job description, and that is enough to make his acts imputable to the corporation.

(3) If the crime requires proof of mens rea, the agent must possess the prescribed culpable mental state[31] and act with the intent to benefit the corporation. In reality, however, the intent to benefit rule boils down to an intent to forward corporate business. Although the corporation must have

———————

[31]The exception to this principle is that a corporation may be found to have the requisite mens rea by imputing the collective knowledge of a group of employees to the entity if it cannot be shown that any individual agent possessed the prescribed mental state. *See* United States v. Bank of New England, 821 F.2d 844 (1st Cir. 1987), and *supra* Chapter 2.

some expectation of benefit from the agent's performance of his function, no actual benefit is required.

DISCUSSION QUESTIONS

1. Assume the same facts as in the Case of the Towboat Burn Barrels, but with the following variation. Suppose the indictment charged Marine Towing with the unlawful dumping. Is the company liable for the violation?
2. Is it relevant that Marine's practice of burning and dumping was relatively common on towboats and that the Coast Guard had used similar disposal methods on its vessels as well? Should industry-wide observance of illegal practices be a defense?
3. Why would the government want to charge the corporation if there are identifiable individual wrongdoers who can be prosecuted?

2. POLICY CONSIDERATIONS

As a practical matter, corporate prosecutions are relatively few and far between.[32] But the practice of prosecuting corporate entities appears to be more prevalent in environmental crime cases. A study of hazardous waste prosecutions found that prosecutors charged corporate defendants in nearly 60 percent of the cases.[33] When contrasted with the prosecutions arising out of the recent corporate fraud scandals — which have produced criminal charges against only a handful of entities (Arthur Andersen being the most notable among them) — the prevalence of corporate defendants in environmental crime prosecutions is striking.

---

[32]Corporate prosecutions have become even less common with the recent increase in deferred prosecution and nonprosecution agreements in cases of corporate wrongdoing. *See* REPORT, CRIME WITHOUT CONVICTION: THE RISE OF DEFERRED AND NON PROSECUTION AGREEMENTS (Dec. 28, 2005), *available at* www.corporatecrimereporter.com; Vanessa Blum, *Justice Deferred: The Fed's New Weapon of Choice Makes Companies Turn Snitch to Save Themselves*, LEGAL TIMES, Mar. 21, 2005, at 1.

[33]Kathleen F. Brickey, *Charging Practices in Hazardous Waste Crime Prosecutions*, 62 OHIO ST. L.J. 1077, 1121 (2001).

The liability rules underlying corporate criminal liability are well settled, if infrequently invoked. Yet the proposition that corporations can be held criminally responsible still provokes controversy.

Francis T. Cullen, Gray Cavender, William J. Maakestad & Michael L. Benson, Corporate Crime Under Attack: The Fight to Criminalize Business Violence

362-364 (2006)

Despite . . . the relatively small number of corporate prosecutions, the concept of organizational crime remains controversial, and some critics continue to argue against the application of criminal sanctions to corporate and other business enterprises, primarily on three grounds. First, they challenge the deterrent effect of the sanction, essentially because "corporations don't commit crimes, people do." Second, they question the retributive function because corporate criminal sanctions may actually end up punishing innocent shareholders (by reducing the value of their shares) and consumers (by increasing the costs of goods and services). Third, they contest the efficiency of organizational liability, arguing that economic analysis shows that, on the whole, civil liability may deter unlawful corporate conduct at less cost than criminal liability. Although a detailed analysis of each objection is beyond the scope of this chapter, a few comments are in order, particularly because the [Ford] Pinto prosecution — along with other important cases like the Arthur Andersen prosecution — involved organizational rather than individual defendants. We suggest that, in many instances, sanctioning the organization is the most prudent and equitable policy, and thus prosecutors' options should not be confined to imposing individual criminal liability.

The critics' first objection — that people, not corporations, commit crimes — ignores the reality that the labyrinthian structure of many modern corporations often makes it extremely difficult to pinpoint individual responsibility for specific decisions. Even in cases in which employees who carried out criminal activities can be identified, controversial questions remain. John S. Martin, a former U.S. Attorney who actively prosecuted corporate and white-collar crime cases, comments that when individual offenders can be identified they "often turn out to be lower-level corporate employees who never made a lot of money, who never benefited personally from the transaction, and who acted with either the real or mistaken belief that if they did not commit the acts in question their jobs might be in jeopardy." Further, says Martin, "they may have believed that their superior was aware and approved of the crime, but could not honestly testify to a specific conversation or other act of the superior that would support an indictment of the superior." Thus, a thorough investigation may well lead a prosecutor to conclude that indictments against individuals simply cannot be justified, even though the corporation benefited from a clear violation of a criminal statute. Such a result would disserve the deterrent function.

The existence of corporate criminal liability also provides a powerful incentive for top officers to supervise middle- and lower-level management more closely. Individual liability, in the absence of corporate liability, encourages just the opposite: top executives may take the attitude of "don't tell me, I don't want to know." In the words of Peter Jones, former chief legal counsel at Levi Strauss, "a fundamental law of organizational physics is that bad news does not flow upstream." Only when directives come from the upper echelon of the corporation "will busy executives feel enough pressure to prevent activities that seriously threaten public health and safety." For a similar reason, proponents of the conservative "Chicago School" of law and economic thought advocate corporate rather than individual sanctioning: a firm's control mechanisms will be more efficient than the state's in deterring misconduct by its agents and will bring about adequate compliance with legal standards as long as the costs of punishment outweigh the potential benefits.

The second objection — that the cost of corporate criminal fines is actually borne by innocent shareholders and consumers — also seems unfounded. With regard to shareholders, whether individual or institutional, incidents of corporate criminal behavior may give the owners the right to redress the diminution of their interest by filing a derivative suit against individual officers and/or members of the board of directors. Although the cost and the uncertainty of winning such a suit may be high, shareholders must regard this cost as one of the risks incurred when they invest in securities. Just as shareholders may occasionally be enriched unjustly through undetected misbehavior by their company, it is only fair to expect them to bear a part of the burden on those occasions when illegality is discovered and duly sanctioned.

Next, it is simplistic, if not untenable, to argue that corporate criminal fines will simply be passed on to the consuming public through higher prices. Stephen Yoder, among others, notes that in such instances our economic system allows consumers to exert a type of indirect, collective control. If we assume that competition exists in the offending corporation's industry, the firm cannot simply decide to raise its prices to absorb the fine or the costs related to the litigation. If it does so, it risks becoming less competitive and suffering such concomitant problems as decreased profits, difficulty in securing debt and equity financing, curtailed expansion, and the loss of investors to more law-abiding corporations.

The final objection — that civil remedies may be a cheaper and hence more efficient deterrent of unlawful conduct than criminal sanctions — also misses the mark. First, as we have seen throughout the book, it is common for corporate wrongdoing to be met by both criminal and civil responses, each seeking different moral and instrumental ends. Second, as Lawrence Friedman reminds us, deterrence and efficiency are not the only interests in play. Deterrence has never been regarded as the sole justification for criminal liability, and efficiency is but one basis for social policy. The pursuit of justice and the imposition of just deserts are also traditional and worthwhile considerations. Civil and criminal liabilities have distinct social meanings, and in the real world findings of civil and criminal liability are not transmutable for purposes of moral condemnation. Recalling a theme we explored earlier in discussing why criminal rather than civil sanctions were sought against Ford in the Pinto case, Dan Kahan concludes his broad investigation of social meaning in the context of corporate wrongdoing with a passage that emphasizes the civil-criminal distinction:

> Just as crimes by natural persons denigrate social values, so do corporate crimes. Members of the public show that they feel this way, for example, when they complain that corporations put profits ahead of the interests of workers, consumers, or the environment. Punishing corporations, just like punishing natural persons, is also understood to be the right way for society to repudiate the false valuations that their crimes express. Criminal liability "sends the message" that people matter more than profits and reaffirms the value of those who were sacrificed to "corporate greed."

DISCUSSION QUESTIONS

1. It is true that in large corporations it may be difficult to pinpoint the particular individual who is directly responsible for committing the crime. But if mid- to low-level employees can be identified as the responsible individuals, what is to be gained by prosecuting both the individuals and the corporation?[34]

2. Are there circumstances under which it would arguably be preferable to prosecute the corporation rather than mid- to low-level employees who are identifiable as individual wrongdoers? Should the perception that prosecuting the individuals might smack of "scapegoating" be a factor in the decision whether to prosecute the individuals? And, if so, does that leave the corporation as the designated scapegoat?

3. Some of the arguments for holding corporations criminally responsible — e.g., the labyrinthian structure of modern corporations and the concomitant diffusion of responsibility in them — presuppose large corporations with complex structures. Do the arguments that favor corporate criminal liability apply with equal force to small "mom and pop" operations as well?[35]

4. Is there a ready explanation for why corporations would be prosecuted in a higher percentage of environmental crime cases than in cases charging other crimes like financial accounting fraud?

---

[34]In the hazardous waste crime study mentioned in the text, the typical corporate prosecution charged both the corporation and at least one individual. *Id.* at 1122.

[35]*Cf.* Kathleen F. Brickey, *Close Corporations and the Criminal Law: On "Mom and Pop" and a Curious Rule*, 71 WASH. U. L.Q. 189 (1993).

4

WATER POLLUTION

*In a reversal of terms that is worthy of Alice in Wonderland, . . . a landowner who places clean fill dirt on a plot of subdivided dry **land** may be imprisoned for the statutory felony offense of "discharging pollutants into the navigable **waters** of the United States."*[†]

The defendants' conduct here was utterly reprehensible and may have violated any number of other criminal laws; but it did not violate . . . the Clean Water Act.[††]

A. THE CLEAN WATER ACT

The Clean Water Act (CWA) was among the first modern environmental statutes to impose criminal penalties. Enacted in 1972, the CWA adopted lofty and ambitious goals. The Act's primary objective is "to restore and maintain the chemical, physical, and biological integrity of the Nation's waters"[1] and eliminate the discharge of pollutants into navigable waterways

---

[†]Judge Susan M. Novotny, U.S. District Court, Northern District of Florida.
[††]Judge D. Brock Hornby, U.S. District Court, District of Maine.
[1]33 U.S.C. § 1251(a).

by 1985. Needless to say, while some progress has been made, the latter goal has yet to be achieved.

The CWA's first priority is to set water quality standards and regulate the discharge of pollutants into public waterways. Although the Act flatly prohibits polluting navigable waters,[2] it establishes a permit system that allows controlled discharges of pollutants provided that they are consistent with the protection of public water supplies, marine and wildlife, and agricultural, industrial, and recreational uses of the waters.[3]

B. KEY CONCEPTS

The CWA prohibits the "discharge" of "pollutants" from a "point source" into "navigable waters of the United States." Thus, we will begin our consideration of the Act's regulatory scheme by looking individually at each of these four discrete but interrelated concepts.

1. DISCHARGE

The CWA regulates discharges of pollutants. Under the Act, a "discharge" is the release of a pollutant into navigable waters from a point source.[4]

> **Illustration A:** Corey Construction Company buys a large tract of land next to a river to build luxury waterfront condominiums. To prepare the land for the project, Corey bulldozes all of the trees on the property and dumps them into the river. Does the dumping constitute a discharge?

Here, the answer is undoubtedly yes. Corey has clearly introduced the trees into the water. Thus, assuming for the moment that uprooted trees constitute a pollutant, dumping them in the river is an addition of pollutants to the water, and hence constitutes a discharge.

---

[2] "[T]he discharge of any pollutant by any person shall be unlawful." 33 U.S.C. § 1311(a).

[3] 33 U.S.C. § 1312(a). A permit to discharge pollutants may be obtained from the Environmental Protection Agency (EPA) or a state through the National Pollutant Discharge Elimination System (NPDES). 33 U.S.C. § 1342.

[4] 33 U.S.C. § 1362(12).

Illustration B: Acme Canning operates a seafood processing plant in New England next to the Atlantic Ocean. In the spring, Acme buys herring directly from the local fishermen who catch them in the ocean. Then, after sorting and processing the herring for pickling, Acme disposes of unsuitable fish and fish parts in wastewater it releases into the ocean. Is this a discharge under the CWA?

Yes, this also constitutes a discharge even though the herring are being returned to the same water from which they were caught. When the fishermen caught the herring, they removed the fish from the water. When Acme released wastewater containing fish and fish parts, it reintroduced them back into the ocean and this is an addition of the fish to the water.[5]

Illustration C: Back to Corey Construction. Suppose the entire tract of land Corey bulldozes is classified as wetlands. After uprooting the trees, the bulldozer operator gathers them into several piles to burn. When some of the uprooted trees won't burn, the crew uses a backhoe to dig several pits and buries the unburned trees in the pits. They also use tractors to plow the ashes from the burned vegetation into the soil. Do these facts support a claim that Corey has discharged pollutants into the wetlands?

This is a somewhat closer case. Corey would clearly want to argue that all it had done was *remove* the vegetation from the wetlands, and removing is the opposite of adding to. But at least one court confronted with this issue disagreed. In Avoyelles Sportsmen's League, Inc. v. Marsh,[6] the court found that this type of conduct amounts to more than mere removal. The vegetation was removed from the wetlands and then redeposited back onto the land. And, according to the court, the term "discharge" can reasonably be construed to include "redeposit." Thus, when Corey's employees plowed the ashes into the soil and buried the unburned logs, they reintroduced the bulldozed vegetation into the wetlands, and this constituted a discharge.

2. POINT SOURCE

To violate the Clean Water Act, the discharge of pollutants must be from a point source. "Point source" is a term of broad import that includes:

---

[5]We will consider whether the fish are pollutants later in this chapter.
[6]715 F.2d 897 (1983).

any discernable, confined and discrete conveyance, including but not limited to any pipe, ditch, channel, tunnel, conduit, well, discrete fissure, container, rolling stock, concentrated animal feeding operation, or vessel or other floating craft, from which pollutants are or may be discharged.[7]

Illustration D: Dale's Painting and Decorating is a fashionably upscale decorating service. Unfortunately, Dale doesn't have room to store used cans of customized paint after finishing a job. Since leaving them with the client would not be fashionably upscale, Dale routinely pours the rest of the paint into a stream behind her office before discarding the cans in the trash. Does this constitute a discharge from a point source?

The paint cans are containers, which the definition of point source specifically includes. Thus, since the paint is poured into the water from the cans, this is a discharge from a point source.

Illustration E: Assume the facts in Illustration D with the following variation. As she pulls into the parking lot behind the office after finishing a job, the door to Dale's van flies open and a bucket of paint falls out, spilling all of its contents onto the pavement. Dale attaches a power nozzle to a garden hose and hoses the paint off of the parking lot and into the stream. Does hosing the paint into the stream constitute a discharge from a point source?

The problem in Illustration E is that the point source is the bucket from which the paint spilled. Although the spill constituted a discharge from a point source,[8] it wasn't a discharge into the stream. Once the paint is spilled on the ground, we need to find another point source for the discharge. Contrast the facts in Illustration F.

Illustration F: Suppose that rather than applying paint with a brush, Dale uses a spray applicator with a nozzle. When she is ready to discard the leftover paint, she sprays it into the stream.

How does Illustration F differ from Illustration E? Even though the spray applicator operates like a hose, it is the source of the discharge. It is

---

[7]33 U.S.C. § 1362(14).

[8]Query whether this accident would be a "knowing" discharge — a point we will consider later in the chapter.

undoubtedly a "discrete conveyance" and, in addition, is connected to a "container" that holds the paint. Thus, this is a discharge of a pollutant from a point source. In Illustration E, the hose is a point source, but it is not the source of the *pollutant* (i.e., the paint). But can we make the garden hose a point source of pollution? Suppose that the water pipe the hose is connected to is old and rusty. If the hose sprays rusty water into the stream, that would be a discharge of a pollutant from a point source.

UNITED STATES V. PLAZA HEALTH LABORATORIES, INC.

3 F.3d 643 (2d Cir. 1993)

PRATT, Circuit Judge. . . .

Facts and Background

Villegas was co-owner and vice president of Plaza Health Laboratories, Inc., a blood-testing laboratory in Brooklyn, New York. On at least two occasions between April and September 1988, Villegas loaded containers of numerous vials of human blood generated from his business into his personal car, and drove to his residence at the Admirals Walk Condominium in Edgewater, New Jersey. Once at his condominium complex, Villegas removed the containers from his car and carried them to the edge of the Hudson River. On one occasion he carried two containers of the vials to the bulkhead that separates his condominium complex from the river, and placed them at low tide within a crevice in the bulkhead that was below the high-water line.

On May 26, 1988, a group of eighth graders on a field trip at the Alice Austin House in Staten Island, New York, discovered numerous glass vials containing human blood along the shore. Some of the vials had washed up on the shore; many were still in the water. Some were cracked, although most remained sealed with stoppers in solid-plastic containers or ziplock bags. Fortunately, no one was injured. That afternoon, New York City workers recovered approximately 70 vials from the area.

On September 25, 1988, a maintenance worker employed by the Admirals Walk Condominium discovered a plastic container holding blood vials wedged between rocks in the bulkhead. New Jersey authorities retrieved numerous blood vials from the bulkhead later that day.

Ten of the retrieved vials contained blood infected with the hepatitis-B virus. All of the vials recovered were eventually traced to Plaza Health Laboratories.

Based upon the May 1988 discovery of vials, Plaza Health Laboratories and Villegas were indicted on May 16, 1989, on two counts each of violating § 1319(c)(2) and (3) of the Clean Water Act. A superseding indictment charged both defendants with two additional CWA counts based upon the vials found in September 1988.

[Two of the counts in the indictment charged the defendants with knowingly discharging pollutants from a point source without a permit. They were convicted on both counts. On appeal, Villegas argued that his conviction could not stand because the definition of point source did not contemplate individual human beings.]

Discussion . . .

A. Navigating the Clean Water Act . . .

As applied to the facts of this case, . . . the defendant "added" a "pollutant" (human blood in glass vials) to "navigable waters" (the Hudson River), and he did so without a permit. The issue, therefore, is whether his conduct constituted a "discharge," and that in turn depends on whether the addition of the blood to the Hudson River waters was "from any point source." . . .

> (14) The term "point source" means any discernible, confined and discrete conveyance, including but not limited to any pipe, ditch, channel, tunnel, conduit, well, discrete fissure, container, rolling stock, concentrated animal feeding operation, or vessel or other floating craft, from which pollutants are or may be discharged. This term does not include agricultural stormwater discharges and return flows from irrigated agriculture.

33 U.S.C. § 1362(14).

During and after Villegas's trial, Judge Korman labored over how to define "point source" in this case. At one point he observed that the image of a human being is not "conjured up" by [C]ongress's definition of "point source." Ultimately, he never defined the "point source" element but he did charge the jury:

Removing pollutants from a container, and a vehicle is a container, parked next to a navigable body of water and physically throwing the pollutant into the water constitutes a discharge from a point source.

. . . Judge Korman held that the element "point source" may reasonably be read

> to include any discrete and identifiable conduit — *including a human being* — designated to collect or discharge pollutants produced in the course of a waste-generating activity (emphasis added).

As the parties have presented the issue to us in their briefs and at oral argument, the question is "whether a human being can be a point source." Both sides focus on the district court's conclusion . . . that, among other things, the requisite "point source" here could be Villegas himself. . . .

I. Language and Structure of Act

Human beings are not among the enumerated items that may be a "point source." Although by its terms the definition of "point source" is nonexclusive, the words used to define the term and the examples given ("pipe, ditch, channel, tunnel, conduit, well, discrete fissure," etc.) evoke images of physical structures and instrumentalities that systematically act as a means of conveying pollutants from an industrial source to navigable waterways.

In addition, if every discharge involving humans were to be considered a "discharge from a point source," the statute's lengthy definition of "point source" would have been unnecessary. It is elemental that Congress does not add unnecessary words to statutes. Had Congress intended to punish any human being who polluted navigational waters, it could readily have said: "any person who places pollutants in navigable waters without a permit is guilty of a crime."

The Clean Water Act generally targets industrial and municipal sources of pollutants, as is evident from a perusal of its many sections. Consistent with this focus, the term "point source" is used throughout the statute, but invariably in sentences referencing industrial or municipal discharges. *See, e.g.,* 33 U.S.C. § 1311 (referring to "owner or operator" of point source); § 1311(e) (requiring that effluent limitations established under the Act "be applied to all point sources of discharge"); § 1311(g)(2) (allows an "owner or operator of a point source" to apply to EPA for modification of its limitations requirements); § 1342(f) (referring to classes, categories, types, and sizes of point sources); § 1314(b)(4)(B) (denoting "best conventional pollutant control technology measures and practices" applicable to any point source within particular category or class); § 1316 ("any point source . . . which is constructed as to meet all applicable standards of performance"); § 1318(a) (administrator shall require owner or operator of any point source to install, use and maintain monitoring equipment or methods); and § 1318(c) (states may develop procedures for inspection, monitoring, and entry with respect to point sources located in state).

This emphasis was sensible, as "[i]ndustrial and municipal point sources were the worst and most obvious offenders of surface water quality. They were also the easiest to address because their loadings emerge from a discrete point such as the end of a pipe." David Letson, *Point/Nonpoint Source Pollution Reduction Trading: An Interpretive Survey*, 32 NAT. RESOURCES J. 219, 221 (1992).

Finally on this point, we assume that Congress did not intend the awkward meaning that would result if we were to read "human being" into the definition of "point source." Section 1362(12)(A) defines "discharge of a pollutant" as "any addition of any pollutant to navigable waters from any point source." Enhanced by this definition, § 1311(a) reads in effect "the addition of any pollutant to navigable waters *from any point source by any person* shall be unlawful" (emphasis added). But were a human being to be included within the definition of "point source," the prohibition would then read: "the addition of any pollutant to navigable waters *from any person by any person* shall be unlawful," and this simply makes no sense. As the statute stands today, the term "point source" is comprehensible only if it is held to the context of industrial and municipal discharges. . . .

Convictions reversed; cross-appeal affirmed.

OAKES, Circuit Judge, dissenting:

I agree that this is not the typical Clean Water Act prosecution — though, as criminal prosecutions under the Act are infrequent, or at least result in few published judicial opinions, what is "typical" is as yet ill-defined. I also agree that the prosecutors in this case may not have defined the theory of their case before proceeding to trial as well as they might have, thereby complicating the task of determining whether the jury was asked to resolve the proper factual questions. However, because I do not agree that a person can never be a point source, and because I believe that Mr. Villegas' actions, as the jury found them, fell well within the bounds of activity proscribed by the Clean Water Act's bar on discharge of pollutants into navigable waters, I am required to dissent.

Point Source . . .

I begin with the obvious, in hopes that it will illuminate the less obvious: the classic point source is something like a pipe. This is, at least in part, because pipes and similar conduits are needed to carry large quantities of waste water, which represents a large proportion of the point source pollution problem. Thus, devices designed to convey large quantities of waste water from a factory or municipal sewage treatment facility are readily classified as point sources. Because not all pollutants are liquids, however, the statute and the cases make clear that means of conveying solid wastes to be dumped in navigable waters are also point sources. *See, e.g.*, 33 U.S.C. § 1362(14) ("rolling stock," or railroad cars, listed as an example of a point source); Avoyelles Sportsmen's League, Inc. v. Marsh, 715 F.2d 897, 922 (5th Cir. 1983) (backhoes and bulldozers used to gather fill and deposit it on wetlands are point sources).

What I take from this look at classic point sources is that, at the least, an organized means of channeling and conveying industrial waste in quantity to navigable waters is a "discernible, confined and discrete conveyance." . . .

In short, the term "point source" has been broadly construed to apply to a wide range of polluting techniques, so long as the pollutants involved are not just humanmade, but reach the navigable waters by human effort or by leaking from a clear point at which waste water was collected by human effort. . . .

. . . [T]o further refine the definition of "point source," I consider what it is that the Act does not cover: nonpoint source discharges.

Nonpoint source pollution is, generally, runoff: salt from roads, agricultural chemicals from farmlands, oil from parking lots, and other substances washed by rain, in diffuse patterns, over the land and into navigable waters.[9] The sources are many, difficult to identify and difficult to

---

[9]   According to the EPA, nonpoint source pollution is caused by diffuse sources that are not regulated as point sources and normally is associated with agricultural, silvicultural and urban runoff, runoff from construction activities, etc. Such pollution results in the human-made or human-induced alteration of the chemical, physical, biological, and radiological integrity of water. In practical terms, nonpoint source pollution does not result from a discharge at a specific, single location (such as a single pipe) but

control. Indeed, an effort to greatly reduce nonpoint source pollution could require radical changes in land use patterns which Congress evidently was unwilling to mandate without further study.[10] The structure of the statute which regulates point source pollution closely, while leaving nonpoint source regulation to the states under the Section 208 program — indicates that the term "point source" was included in the definition of discharge so as to ensure that nonpoint source pollution would not be covered. Instead, Congress chose to regulate first that which could easily be regulated: direct discharges by identifiable parties, or point sources.

This rationale for regulating point and nonpoint sources differently — that point sources may readily be controlled and are easily attributable to a particular source, while nonpoint sources are more difficult to control without radical change, and less easily attributable, once they reach water, to any particular responsible party — helps define what fits within each category. Thus, Professor Rodgers has suggested, "the statutory 'discernible, confined and discrete conveyance' . . . can be understood as singling out those candidates suitable for control-at-the-source." 2 William H. Rodgers, Jr., Environmental Law: Air and Water § 4.10 at 150 (1986). . . .

While Villegas' activities were not prototypical point source discharges . . . they much more closely resembled a point source discharge than a nonpoint source discharge. First, Villegas and his lab were perfectly

---

generally results from land runoff, precipitation, atmospheric deposition, or percolation.

EPA Office of Water Regulations and Standards, Nonpoint Source Guidance 3 (1987).
[10]As Professors Anderson, Mandelker, and Tarlock have observed,

Congress expressed great faith in the ability of engineers to limit what came out of pipes but less faith in the ability of engineers to fix non[]point source pollution:

There is no effective way as yet, other than land use control, by which you can intercept that runoff and control it in the way that you do a point source. We have not yet developed technology to deal with that kind of a problem. . . . [Senate Debate on S. 2770, Nov. 2, 1971, reported in 1972 Legislative History, at 1315.]

FREDERICK R. ANDERSON, DANIEL R. MANDELKER, & A. DAN TARLOCK, ENVIRONMENTAL PROTECTION: LAW AND POLICY 377 (2d ed. 1990).

capable of avoiding discharging their waste into water: they were, in Professor Rodgers' terms, a "controllable" source.

Furthermore, the discharge was directly into water, and came from an identifiable point, Villegas. Villegas did not dispose of the materials on land, where they could be washed into water as nonpoint source pollution. Rather, he carried them, from his firm's laboratory, in his car, to his apartment complex, where he placed them in a bulkhead below the high tide line. I do not think it is necessary to determine whether it was Mr. Villegas himself who was the point source, or whether it was his car, the vials, or the bulkhead: in a sense, the entire stream of Mr. Villegas' activity functioned as a "discrete conveyance" or point source. The point is that the source of the pollution was clear, and would have been easy to control. Indeed, Villegas was well aware that there were methods of controlling the discharge (and that the materials were too dangerous for casual disposal): his laboratory had hired a professional medical waste handler. He simply chose not to use an appropriate waste disposal mechanism.

Villegas' method may have been an unusual one for a corporate officer, but it would undermine the statute — which, after all, sets as its goal the elimination of discharges — to regard as "ambiguous" a Congressional failure to list an unusual method of disposing of waste. I doubt that Congress would have regarded an army of men and women throwing industrial waste from trucks into a stream as exempt from the statute. . . . A different reading would encourage corporations perfectly capable of abiding by the Clean Water Act's requirements to ask their employees to stand between the company's trucks and the sea, thereby transforming point source pollution (dumping from trucks) into nonpoint source pollution (dumping by hand). . . .

Conclusion

Accordingly, I would affirm the rulings of the district court.

DISCUSSION QUESTIONS

1. Which of the following would constitute a discharge from a point source under the majority's view?
   a. A dump truck parks beside a river and dumps a load of manure directly into the water.

b. The dump truck dumps the manure onto the river bank. The next day a heavy rain washes the manure from the bank into the water.

c. The dump truck dumps the manure onto the river bank. Three laborers then shovel it into the water.

d. The dump truck parks on the river bank. The three laborers climb onto the truck bed and shovel the manure over the side into the water.

2. Judge Oakes could not believe that Congress would exempt an army of men and women throwing industrial waste into the river from the requirements of the CWA. In his view, this would encourage corporations that are perfectly capable of complying with the Act "to ask their employees to stand between the company trucks and the sea." What did he mean by that?

3. Could Judge Oakes' reading of the statute lead to imposition of felony penalties for throwing a candy wrapper into navigable waters? If so, would it be possible to avoid this result while at the same time recognizing that an individual could be a point source?

3. POLLUTANTS

The CWA regulates the discharge of "pollutants" into navigable waters. Like other key concepts in the Act, the term "pollutant" is broadly defined. It includes:

dredged spoil, solid waste, incinerator residue, sewage, garbage, sewage sludge, munitions, chemical wastes, biological materials, radioactive materials, heat, wrecked or discarded equipment, rock, sand, cellar dirt and industrial, municipal and agricultural waste discharged into water.

One of the primary goals of the CWA is to reduce the flow of industrial wastewater and sewage sludge into the nation's waterways. Examples are legion. Consider, for example, an electroplating company that drains untreated industrial wastewater containing high levels of cyanide and zinc into a local sewer system,[11] or a chemical hauler that rinses out its tankers and discharges the wastewater into municipal sewer lines. No one would quibble about the need to curb practices like these. Nor would it be

---

[11]*See, e.g.*, United States v. Wells Metal Finishing, 922 F.2d 54 (1st Cir. 1991). *See also* United States v. Distler, 671 F.2d 954 (6th Cir. 1981) (chemical storage facility discharged toxic chemicals into a local sewer system).

surprising that the leftover paint in Illustrations D - F is a pollutant. Even though it may still be suitable for its intended use, the leftover paint is clearly a chemical waste that does not belong in rivers and streams.

But what about the unusable herring and discarded herring parts in Illustration B and the uprooted trees in Illustration A? Do they qualify as pollutants? If you read the definition again carefully, you will see that biological materials are identified as pollutants. Thus, fish, trees, and other vegetation that are native to water or wetlands where they are deposited may nonetheless be deemed pollutants under the Act.

> **Illustration G:** In Illustrations A and C, Corey Construction Company is preparing a tract of land for a riverfront condominium development. Suppose the company wants to deepen the riverbed next to the development so that large yachts can dock at a pier near the complex. Corey brings in a barge equipped with a crane to deepen the channel. The crane lowers a large, hinged bucket to scoop up rock, sand, and silt from the river bottom. The crane operator drops the scooped-up material into shallow water about a hundred yards downstream and forms a small dike. Has the crane operator discharged a pollutant into the river?

4. NAVIGABLE WATERS

The CWA regulates pollution discharges into the nation's navigable waterways, including territorial seas. There are two discrete questions to address in this regard.

First, what is the source of power to exercise federal jurisdiction under the CWA? Congress has power under the Commerce Clause to regulate things and activities that are in or affect commerce, and it is clear that navigation occurs in interstate commerce or, when it is wholly intrastate, can be found to affect commercial activity.

Second, what does "navigable" mean in this context? The term "navigable waters" is defined to mean "the waters of the United States, including the territorial seas."[12] This leaves much to the imagination and has led courts to conclude that Congress intended to exercise its power expansively "to regulate at least some waters that would not be deemed 'navigable' under the classical understanding of that term."[13]

---

[12]33 U.S.C. § 1362(7).
[13]United States v. Riverside Bayview Homes, Inc., 474 U.S. 121, 133 (1985).

Congress can regulate waterways used to transport people and goods in interstate or foreign commerce. Those are the waterways that the term "navigable waters" conventionally denotes (though a river could be navigable even though it was entirely within one state). The Wisconsin River, not to mention the Mississippi River into which it flows, is a navigable waterway in the conventional sense. The most elementary type of federal regulation of such waterways that the commerce clause authorizes is regulation aimed at making sure they remain navigable, in the sense of usable in interstate or foreign commerce, rather than allowing them to become obstructed by low-lying bridges, or to become too shallow for navigation by large vessels because the sources of their water are being diminished by dams, silting, or real estate development. There are believed to be more than 100 million acres of wetlands in the lower 48 states, and they supply some of the water in navigable waterways. Also, by temporarily storing storm water, wetlands reduce flooding, which can interfere with navigation. . . .

. . . Congress may forbid the pollution of navigable waters even if the pollution has no effect on navigability, which is the usual case. In fact navigability is a red herring from the standpoint of constitutionality. The power of Congress to regulate pollution is not limited to polluted navigable waters; the pollution of groundwater, for example, is regulated by federal law because of its effects on agriculture and other industries whose output is shipped across state lines, and such regulation has been held to be authorized by the commerce clause. . . .

[Thus, nothing] in the Constitution forbids interpreting the Clean Water Act to cover any wetlands that are connected to navigable waters. . . .[14]

DISCUSSION QUESTIONS

1. It seems clear that a body of water may be considered navigable under the CWA even though it is not navigable in fact. What prompts courts to embrace such an expansive reading of this jurisdictional term?
2. As noted in Chapter 2, knowledge of jurisdictional facts is generally not required in federal criminal law.[15] Thus, even though the primary mental state for CWA violations is "knowingly" (e.g., knowingly discharging

---

[14]United States v. Gerke Excavating, Inc., 412 F.3d 804, 806-807 (7th Cir. 2005).

[15]*See, e.g.,* United States v. Feola, 420 U.S. 671 (1975) (defendants may be guilty of assaulting or conspiring to assault a federal official without proof that they knew the intended victim was a federal agent).

chemical waste into a stream), the defendant need not be shown to know the facts that bring the discharge within the jurisdiction of the federal government (i.e., that the stream is classified as "navigable"). Is this a sound rule?

5. APPLYING THE CONCEPTS

As the preceding discussion of key concepts suggests, successful prosecution of a polluter under the Clean Water Act requires proof that the polluter discharged pollutants from a point source into navigable waters. The Case of the Recycled Fish is designed to test your understanding of these concepts and how they work together.

THE CASE OF THE RECYCLED FISH

Hydro Power Company operates a hydroelectric facility on Lake Wobegon. The facility diverts water from the lake into a manmade reservoir that holds nearly 30 billion gallons of water. The diversion is accomplished by pumping lake water uphill into the reservoir through a series of large pipes connected to reversible pump/turbines. Power is generated when the water is allowed to flow downhill back through the pipes and the force of gravity turns the pump/turbines. Hydro Power can move more than 20 billion gallons of water between the reservoir and the lake in a single day.

Fish and other aquatic organisms from the lake are "entrained" during the course of this process. That is, they are carried through the power-generating system by the force of the moving water. Although some of the fish and other organisms survive, a substantial number are destroyed during the pumping process. Thus, both live and dead fish re-enter the lake when the water is released back downhill.

Is Hydro Power's release of live fish and dead fish remains into Lake Wobegon a discharge under the CWA? Are the fish and fish remains pollutants? Is Hydro Power a point source?[16] Is Lake Wobegon a water of the United States?

---

[16]*Cf.* Nat'l Wildlife Fed'n v. Consumers Power Company, 862 F.2d 580 (6th Cir. 1988).

C. PERMIT VIOLATIONS

1. THE PERMIT SYSTEM

Notwithstanding that one of the primary goals of the CWA is to rid the nation's waterways of pollution, the Act establishes the National Pollutant Discharge Elimination System [NPDES], a permit system that allows controlled discharges of specified pollutants into navigable waters in specified amounts. Without a permit, all discharges of pollutants into public waterways are presumptively illegal. With a permit, discharges are legal provided that the permit holder complies with the permit's terms and conditions.[17]

Judge Boggs succinctly explained the permit system in National Wildlife Federation v. Consumers Power Company.[18]

> Generally, the objective of the Clean Water Act is to "restore and maintain the chemical, physical, and biological integrity of the Nation's waters." The CWA establishes a comprehensive statutory system for controlling water pollution. To that end, it establishes the § 402 NPDES permit system for regulating discharges of pollutants into waters of the United States. The District of Columbia Circuit Court of Appeals recently indicated that "the cornerstone of the Clean Water Act's pollution control scheme is the National Pollut[ant] Discharge Elimination System (NPDES) permit program. . . ." Natural Resources Defense Council, Inc. v. EPA, 822 F.2d 104, 108 (D.C. Cir. 1987). The United States Environmental Protection Agency (EPA) is principally responsible for administering the NPDES permit system, and it may lawfully delegate permit issuing authority to state government.
>
> The CWA has been held to divide the sources of water pollution into categories: "point source" and "nonpoint source." As the *Gorsuch* court explained, "the latter category is defined by exclusion and includes all water quality problems not subject to § 402." 693 F.2d at 166. The NPDES permit program was designed to control "point sources" of pollution, and the legislative history behind CWA indicates that Congress's focus was on the discharge of traditional industrial and municipal wastes.

---

[17]33 U.S.C. § 1342(a)(1). The permit holder must also comply with applicable effluent limitations and performance standards.

[18]862 F.2d 580 (6th Cir. 1988).

Under § 402, an NPDES permit is required for the "discharge of a pollutant" from a "point source." Unless the EPA issues an NPDES permit, "the discharge of any pollutant by any person [is] unlawful." 33 U.S.C. § 1311(a). Where the source of a pollutant is a point source, and the pollutant is discharged into navigable waters, the source *must* obtain a § 402 permit limiting and controlling both the amount and type of pollutants which can be lawfully discharged. The general prohibition of CWA § 301(a) regarding point source pollution is self-executing. In order to avoid liability under § 301(a), a polluter must apply for and obtain an NPDES permit from the EPA, or from an authorized state water pollution control agency. EPA, or an authorized state agency, may in its discretion exempt a specific pollutant discharge from § 301(a)'s general prohibition by issuing an NPDES permit. Alternatively, the agency may choose not to issue such a permit, leaving the discharge unlawful under § 301(a). We have indicated that "under § 402(a)(2) of the Act, the Administrator of EPA is required to prescribe the conditions of such permits and to assure compliance with those conditions and other requirements of the Act." United States ex rel. Tennessee Valley Authority v. Tennessee Water Quality Control Board, 717 F.2d 992, 998 (6th Cir. 1983).

Section 502(12) of the CWA, a key portion of the statute, defines the term "discharge of pollutants" as "any addition of any pollutant to navigable waters from any point source." 33 U.S.C. § 1362(12)(A). The District of Columbia Circuit has held that for NPDES requirements to apply to any given set of circumstances, "five elements must be present: (1) a *pollutant* must be (2) *added* (3) *to navigable waters* (4) *from* (5) *a point source*." National Wildlife Federation v. Gorsuch, 693 F.2d 156, 165 (D.C. Cir. 1982). . . .

As the excerpt from Judge Boggs' opinion suggests, the NPDES permit system is the capstone of the CWA's pollution control regime. Under this regulatory scheme, there are essentially two types of violations, as illustrated below.

Illustration H: Acme Electroplating discharges untreated chemical waste directly into the ocean through a concealed pipe. Acme has never sought a permit to discharge the waste.

Here, it is clear that this is a discharge of pollutants from a point source into navigable waters. Because this activity is prohibited unless the actor first obtains a permit, a violation has occurred. That would be true whether Acme had failed to apply for a permit or had applied and a permit was refused.

Illustration I: Acme applies for and receives a permit to discharge the waste into the ocean. The permit allows Acme to discharge wastewater containing lead, but only if the amount of lead does not exceed 1 part per billion gallons. Acme routinely discharges wastewater containing 50 parts per billion gallons.

Acme has violated the CWA even though it has a permit to discharge chemical wastewater from its plant. Whether Acme has failed to treat the wastewater to reduce the lead content or has treated it but failed to maintain the allowable ratio of lead to water, Acme's discharge violates the terms and conditions of the permit.

UNITED STATES V. FREZZO BROTHERS, INC.

602 F.2d 1123 (3d Cir. 1979)

ROSENN, Circuit Judge.

Since the enactment in 1948 of the Federal Water Pollution Control Act ("the Act"), the Government has, until recent years, generally enforced its provisions to control water pollution through the application of civil restraints. In this case, however, the Government in the first instance has sought enforcement of the Act as amended in 1972, against an alleged corporate offender and its officers by criminal sanctions. . . .

I

Frezzo Brothers, Inc., is a Pennsylvania corporation engaged in the mushroom farming business near Avondale, Pennsylvania. The business is family operated with Guido and James Frezzo serving as the principal corporate officers. As a part of the mushroom farming business, Frezzo Brothers, Inc., produces compost to provide a growing base for the mushrooms. The compost is comprised mainly of hay and horse manure mixed with water and allowed to ferment outside on wharves.

The Frezzo's farm had a 114,000 gallon concrete holding tank designed to contain water run-off from the compost wharves and to recycle water back to them. The farm had a separate storm water run-off system that carried rain water through a pipe to a channel box located on an adjoining property owned by another mushroom farm. The channel box was connected by a pipe with an unnamed tributary of the East Branch of the White Clay Creek. The waters of the tributary flowed directly into the Creek.

Counts One through Four of the indictment charged the defendants with discharging pollutants into the East Branch of the White Clay Creek on July 7, July 20, September 20, and September 26, 1977. On these dates Richard Casson, a Chester County Health Department investigator, observed pollution in the tributary flowing into the Creek and collected samples of wastes flowing into the channel box. The wastes had the distinctive characteristics of manure and quantitative analysis of the samples revealed a concentration of pollutants in the water. The Government introduced meteorological evidence at trial showing that no rain had been recorded in the area on these four dates. Based on this evidence, the Government contended that the Frezzos had willfully discharged manure into the storm water run-off system that flowed into the channel box and into the stream.[19]

Investigator Casson returned to the Frezzo farm on January 12, 1978, to inspect their existing water pollution abatement facilities. Guido and James Frezzo showed Casson both the holding tank designed to contain the waste water from the compost wharves, and the separate storm water run-off system. Casson returned to the farm on May 9, 1978 with a search warrant and several witnesses. This visit occurred after a morning rain had ended. The witnesses observed the holding tank overflowing into the storm water run-off system. The path of the wastes from the Frezzo holding tank to the channel box and into the stream was photographed. James Frezzo was present at the time and admitted to Casson that the holding tank could control the water only 95% of the time. Samples were again collected, subjected to quantitative analysis and a high concentration of pollutants was found to be present. This incident gave rise to Count Five of the indictment.

Additional samples were collected from the channel box on May 14, 1978, after a heavy rain. Again, a concentration of pollutants was found to be present. This evidence served as the basis for Count Six of the indictment. At trial, the Government introduced evidence of the rainfall on May 9 and May 14 along with expert hydrologic testimony regarding the holding capabilities of the Frezzos' tank. The Government theorized that the holding tank was too small to contain the compost wastes after a rainstorm and that

---

[19]At the time when the violations occurred, the statute punished "willful" violations as well as negligent ones. A subsequent amendment deleted willfulness as a culpable mental state and replaced it with knowledge. — ED.

the Frezzos had negligently discharged pollutants into the stream on the two dates in May.

The jury returned guilty verdicts on all six counts against the corporate defendant, Frezzo Brothers, Inc., and individual defendants, Guido and James Frezzo. . . .

III

The Frezzos . . . contend that the indictment should have been dismissed because the EPA had not promulgated any effluent standards applicable to the compost manufacturing business.   The Frezzos argue that before a violation of § 1311(a) can occur, the defendants must be shown to have not complied with existing effluent limitations under the Act.   The district court disagreed, finding no such requirement.   We agree with the district court.

The core provision of the Act is found in § 1311(a) which reads:

> Except as in compliance with this section and sections 1312, 1316, 1317, 1328, 1342, and 1344 of this title, the discharge of any pollutants by any person shall be unlawful.

Section 1311(b) then sets out a timetable for the promulgation of effluent limitations for point sources and section 1312 provides for the establishment of water quality related effluent limitations.   The Frezzos contend that they cannot have violated the Act because the EPA has not yet promulgated effluent limitations which they can be held to have violated. . . .

. . . The basic policy of the Act is to halt uncontrolled discharges of pollutants into the waters of the United States.   In fact, the Act sets forth "the national goal that the discharge of [all] pollutants into the navigable waters be eliminated by 1985." 33 U.S.C. § 1251(a)(1).   We see nothing impermissible with allowing the Government to enforce the Act by invoking § 1311(a), even if no effluent limitations have been promulgated for the particular business charged with polluting.   Without this flexibility, numerous industries not yet considered as serious threats to the environment may escape administrative, civil, or criminal sanctions merely because the EPA has not established effluent limitations.   Thus, dangerous pollutants could be continually injected into the water solely because the administrative process has not yet had the opportunity to fix specific effluent limitations. Such a result would be inconsistent with the policy of the Act.

We do not believe . . . that the permit procedure urged by the Government is unduly burdensome on business. If no effluent limitations have yet been applied to an industry, a potential transgressor should apply for a permit to discharge pollutants under section 1342(a). The Administrator may then set up operating conditions until permanent effluent limitations are promulgated by EPA. The pendency of a permit application, in appropriate cases, should shield the applicant from liability for discharge in the absence of a permit. EPA cannot be expected to have anticipated every form of water pollution through the establishment of effluent limitations. The permit procedure, coupled with broad enforcement under § 1311(a) may, in fact, allow EPA to discover new sources of pollution for which permanent effluent standards are appropriate.

In the present case, it is undisputed that there was no pending permit to discharge pollutants; nor had Frezzo Brothers, Inc., ever applied for one. This case, therefore, appears to be particularly compelling for broad enforcement. . . . The Frezzos, under their interpretation of the statute, could conceivably have continued polluting until EPA promulgated effluent limitations for the compost operation. The Government's intervention by way of criminal indictments brought to a halt potentially serious damage to the stream in question, and has no doubt alerted EPA to pollution problems posed by compost production. We therefore hold that the promulgation of effluent limitation standards is not a prerequisite to the maintenance of a criminal proceeding based on violation of section 1311(a) of the Act . . . .

Accordingly, the judgment of the district court will be affirmed.

DISCUSSION QUESTIONS

1. The national goal of the CWA is to eliminate the discharge of pollutants into navigable waters. Is the permit system consistent with that goal? Is the government's issuance of a CWA permit equivalent to granting the applicant a license to pollute? Why would Congress make the permit system the heart of the regulatory scheme?
2. The Frezzos argued, unsuccessfully, that the EPA must provide written notice of the violation as a prerequisite to filing criminal charges. If they were operating without the guidance of either an effluent standard for mushroom compost or a warning from the EPA, why would they be on notice that their conduct violated the law? How does "no effluent standard" + "no prior notification" = a willful or knowing violation?

3. What special problems of proof does the government face in a case like this?

———————

To constitute a criminal violation of the permit requirements, the violator must act "knowingly" or "negligently." These mental states were considered at greater length in Chapter 2, but we will briefly recap here. Recall that *Sinskey* and *Ahmad* construed the knowledge component of CWA violations, while *Ortiz* construed the standard for negligence under the CWA.

In *Sinskey* and *Ahmad,* the courts ruled that while the knowledge requirement applies to each factual element of the offense, the defendant need not know of the permit requirement or, if the operator had a permit, that the discharge violated the terms of the permit. Thus, Ahmad's claim that he thought that he was only pumping water from the underground storage tank must be countered by evidence that he knew each factual element of the crime — here, that the substance in the tank was something other than water. Similarly, Sinskey's claim that the statute requires proof that he knew the discharge of wastewater from the meat-packing plant was in violation of the plant's permit was off the mark. The term "knowingly" modifies the conduct elements of the offense. Thus, he must be shown to have known that the plant discharged wastewater containing ammonia nitrates at levels that exceeded one part per million.

In *Ortiz,* the court ruled that negligent violations of CWA permit requirements can be established by proof of ordinary negligence. Thus, the government was required to prove only that Ortiz failed to exercise ordinary care when he decided to dispose of dangerous chemicals by dumping them into the toilet. It was not necessary to show that he knew that flushing them down the drain would result in a discharge into the river or that his conduct was criminally negligent or grossly negligent. He need not have been aware of the actual risk his conduct created as long as a reasonable person should have been aware of the risk.

2. AN ALTERNATIVE REGULATORY REGIME

Although the CWA is now the principal federal water pollution statute, the Refuse Act serves as an ancillary enforcement tool. Also known as the Rivers and Harbors Act, the Refuse Act is a turn of the century statute that prohibits discharging "any refuse matter of any kind or description" (excluding certain kinds of sewage) into navigable waters.[20] While the Act does not define the term "refuse," the Supreme Court has construed it to mean all foreign substances and pollutants that threaten navigation or pollute the water.[21] No actual impediment to navigation is required, however.

The Refuse Act contains two distinct prohibitions: (1) the act of discharging refuse into navigable waters; and (2) depositing refuse on the bank of navigable waters where the refuse is "liable" to be washed into the water. Do these prohibitions provide a useful backup to the liability scheme in the CWA? How would they apply to the four hypotheticals posed in Discussion Question #1 after *Plaza Health Laboratories*?

Unlike the CWA, the Refuse Act does not require proof of a culpable mental state to establish a criminal violation. Instead, it imposes strict liability. And unlike criminal violations of the CWA, which are felonies, Refuse Act violations are misdemeanors. How would these differences influence a prosecutor's decision about which statute to invoke?

D. KNOWING ENDANGERMENT

The CWA makes it a separate crime to knowingly violate a permit requirement or a term or condition imposed by a permit if, by doing so, the actor knowingly puts another person in imminent danger of death or serious bodily injury.[22] Under this provision, "serious bodily injury" is an injury that poses a "substantial risk of death, unconsciousness, extreme physical pain, protracted and obvious disfigurement, or protracted loss or impairment of the function of a bodily member, organ, or mental faculty."[23] Under the endangerment statute, the risk of harm must be "imminent," which means the government must prove that it is "highly probable" that the illegal discharge would cause death or serious injury.

The knowing endangerment statute recognizes a limited defense of consent. The actor has an affirmative defense if he can prove, by a preponderance of the evidence, that the person who was endangered by the violation consented to the charged conduct and that the danger and the

---

[20]33 U.S.C. § 407.

[21]United States v. Standard Oil Co., 384 U.S. 224, 230 (1966).

[22]The knowing endangerment provision also applies to violations of other provisions of the CWA, including violations of effluent limitations or performance standards.

[23]33 U.S.C. § 1319(c)(3)(B)(iv).

conduct were "reasonably foreseeable hazards" of: (1) an occupation, business, or profession; or (2) medical treatment or medical or scientific experimentation that conforms to professionally approved protocols and was conducted with the endangered person's informed consent.[24]

1. PROTECTED PARTIES

UNITED STATES V. BOROWSKI

977 F.2d 27 (1st Cir. 1992)

HORNBY, District Judge. . . .

Facts

The defendant John Borowski was the President and owner of Borjohn Optical Technology, Inc. and Galaxie Laboratory, Inc. ("Borjohn"). Borjohn operated a manufacturing facility in Burlington, Massachusetts, producing optical mirrors for use in aerospace guidance and sighting systems.

Borjohn used various rinses, dips and nickel plating baths to plate nickel onto its mirrors. When a mirror was improperly plated, Borjohn used a nitric acid bath to strip the nickel off. From time to time the nickel plating solutions and nitric acid stripping baths had to be replaced.

Borjohn disposed of its spent nickel plating baths and nitric acid baths by crudely dumping them directly into plating room sinks, without any form of pretreatment. Those sinks drained immediately into Borjohn's underground pipes which, at the property border line, fed into the Burlington municipal sewer system and from there into the Massachusetts Water Resource Authority's treatment works. Because the pollutants were ultimately discharged into a publicly-owned treatment works, Borjohn was subject to the EPA's pretreatment regulations. The EPA regulations prohibited nickel discharges into the publicly-owned treatment works in amounts exceeding 3.98 milligrams per liter and also prohibited concentrations of nitric acid discharges into the publicly-owned treatment works if they had a pH balance of less than 5. The nickel and nitric acid baths Borjohn discharged greatly exceeded these pretreatment standards.

---

[24]33 U.S.C. § 1319(c)(3)(B)(ii).

According to medical experts, enormous health concerns are associated with exposure to nitric acid and nickel in the amounts involved here. Contact with the chemicals causes severe allergic reactions, chemical burns, serious skin disorders such as rashes and dermatitis, and cancer. Inhalation of nickel vapors and nitric acid fumes can cause breathing problems, nasal bleeding and serious damage to a person's respiratory tract. Various Borjohn employees testified to symptoms consistent with these health problems. Employees testified to having had "daily nose bleeds," headaches, chest pains, breathing difficulties, dizziness, rashes and blisters.

Repeated employee exposure to the chemicals was unavoidable. In discharging the spent nickel plating baths and nitric acid baths, for instance, Borjohn employees were told to bail out the harmful solutions by hand using a plastic bucket or a portable pump. Once a tank was nearly empty it was tipped over the edge of the sink and a scoop or small cup was used to scoop out any remaining solution. The employees were required to scrape the sides and bottom of nickel baths to extricate a layer of nickel byproduct called "extraneous plate out." Sometimes employees were told to dump "hot" nitric acid solutions into the sinks. This created an "alka seltzer" like appearance on the surface of the sink. Employees testified that the nickel and nitric acid solutions sometimes splashed and spilled directly onto their skins. Indeed, one employee complained that he was always "wet" with the solution and at times was scalded by the chemicals.

[The protective gear made available to the employees was grossly inadequate, and it was clear that Borjohn and Borowski knew the employees were exposed to serious health risks. Borjohn and Borowski were indicted under the CWA's knowing endangerment provision for knowingly discharging the nickel and nitric acid baths into the city sewer system and the publicly owned treatment plant, thereby placing the employees in imminent danger of death or serious bodily injury. Both Borjohn and Borowski were convicted.]

Discussion

Section 1317(b) of the Clean Water Act directs the EPA to promulgate pretreatment standards for pollutants going into publicly-owned treatment works.[25] Subsection (d) prohibits the owner or operator of any source (a term that includes Borjohn and Borowski) from violating these standards. Section 1319(c)(3)(A) provides that anyone who "knowingly violates section . . . 1317 . . ., and who knows at that time that he thereby places another person in imminent danger of death or serious bodily injury" is guilty of a felony.[26]

We assume for purposes of this appeal that both defendants knowingly violated § 1317 and knew of the dangers to the Borjohn employees. It is undisputed that Borjohn employees were placed in imminent danger of serious bodily injury during their employment and that some of this danger occurred at the time of dumping chemical solutions into sinks that ultimately led to a publicly-owned treatment works. The question is whether the defendants, in knowingly violating § 1317, knew that they "thereby" placed the employees in imminent danger.

There is no single correct answer to this semantic puzzle. In one sense, it can be said that the knowing violation "thereby" placed the employees in danger. After all, the defendants knew that the sinks were connected to the publicly-owned sewer and treatment works and that the wastes would therefore illegally proceed without interruption to the publicly-owned treatment works. They also knew that the employees' actions in performing

---

[25]Specifically, the EPA is to promulgate:

> regulations establishing pretreatment standards for introduction of pollutants into treatment works . . . which are publicly owned for those pollutants which are determined not to be susceptible to treatment by such treatment works or which would interfere with the operation of such treatment works. . . . Pretreatment standards under this subsection . . . shall be established to prevent the discharge of any pollutant through treatment works . . . which are publicly owned, which pollutant interferes with, passes through, or otherwise is incompatible with such works.

33 U.S.C. § 1317(b).

[26] Knowing endangerment. (A) General rule. Any person who knowingly violates section . . . 1317 . . ., and who knows at that time that he thereby places another person in imminent danger of death or serious bodily injury, shall, upon conviction, be subject to a fine of not more than $250,000 or imprisonment of not more than 15 years, or both. A person which is an organization shall, upon conviction of violating this subparagraph, be subject to a fine of not more than $1,000,000.

33 U.S.C. § 1319(c)(3).

the dumping as instructed placed them in imminent danger. Arguably, therefore, through the knowing violation the defendants "thereby" endangered the employees. On the other hand, there could be no violation unless the wastes ultimately ended up in a publicly-owned sewer and treatment works. But the risks and dangers to these employees would have been the same if the plugs had always remained in the sinks so that no discharge to the publicly-owned treatment works (and therefore no § 1317 violation) ever occurred. The danger to the employees was inherent in their handling of the various chemical solutions, solutions that were part of the defendant's manufacturing process. They would have been subject to the identical hazards had they been dumping the chemicals into drums or other containers for appropriate treatment under the Act. In that respect, therefore, although the defendants knew that their employees were placed in imminent danger, that danger was not caused by the knowing violation of § 1317.

Since semantic analysis alone is insufficient, how is this puzzle to be resolved? Several factors assist us. First, the purpose of the statute is clear. The Clean Water Act is not a statute designed to provide protection to industrial employees who work with hazardous substances. Instead, section 1251(a) states: "The objective of this Act is to restore and maintain the chemical, physical, and biological integrity of the Nation's waters." The EPA is directed to promulgate pretreatment standards only so as to "prevent the discharge of any pollutant" that will pass through publicly-owned treatment works, interfere with the works, be incompatible with the works, or otherwise violate effluent standards for the works. The EPA regulations reflect this same focus of concern on publicly-owned treatment works. The regulations' goals are:

> To prevent the introduction of pollutants into POTWs which will interfere with the operation of a POTW, including interference with its use or disposal of municipal sludge;
> To prevent the introduction of pollutants into POTWs which will pass through the treatment works or otherwise be incompatible with such works; and
> To improve opportunities to recycle and reclaim municipal and industrial wastewaters and sludges.

40 C.F.R. § 403.2. One can read the entire statute and regulations in vain for any protection mechanism for industrial employees who work with wastes

at the point of discharge.[27] Instead, other laws deal with industrial employee health and safety. The Occupational Safety and Health Act (OSHA) is the best known. 29 U.S.C. §§ 651 et seq. . . .

Second, Congress has passed a separate law dealing with the general handling, treatment and storage of hazardous substances. Specifically, the Resource Conservation and Recovery Act (RCRA) is a cradle-to-grave statute providing a full range of remedies designed to protect both health and the environment. The Clean Water Act, on the other hand, is not directed at the *handling* of pollutants. Indeed, under the Clean Water Act, if the publicly-owned treatment works were itself capable of removing the nickel and acid from Borjohn's discharges (thereby satisfying Clean Water Act goals), the works could seek to avoid the prohibition placed on Borjohn's discharge — yet the health hazard to the employees would obviously remain

---

[27]Any concern for employees reflected in the regulations deals with "downstream" employees, i.e., employees of the publicly-owned works. *See* 40 C.F.R. § 403.5(b)(7) (prohibiting "pollutants which result in the presence of toxic gases, vapors, or fumes *within the POTW* in a quantity that may cause acute worker health and safety problems") (emphasis supplied).

At only three other points do the regulations reflect concern with health. First, 40 C.F.R. § 403.8(f)(1)(vi)(B) provides:

> *The POTW* shall have authority and procedures (after informal notice to the discharger) immediately and effectively to halt or prevent any discharge of pollutants *to the POTW* which reasonably appears to present an imminent endangerment to the health or welfare of persons (emphasis supplied).

This provision apparently permits a municipal works to take steps to prevent a discharge from reaching it. The danger contemplated, therefore, is to persons who would be endangered once the discharge reaches the municipal sewers or works. Second, 40 C.F.R. § 403.8(f)(2)(vii)(C) lists as a "significant noncompliance" any discharge that causes "interference or pass through (including endangering the health of POTW personnel or the general public)." Conspicuously missing is any reference to source employees. Third, the very next sentence lists as a significant noncompliance "any discharge of a pollutant that has caused imminent endangerment to human health, welfare or to the environment. . . ." 40 C.F.R. § 403.8(f)(2)(vii)(D). "Discharge" is defined as "the introduction of pollutants into a POTW. . . ." 40 C.F.R. § 403.3(g). The concern again, therefore, is for "downstream" effects.

None of these regulations was referred to by either the United States Attorney's Office or the defendants.

the same.[28] Moreover, unlike the Clean Water Act, RCRA exhibits explicit concern for industrial health. It has a provision specifically requiring the EPA to provide information about employee hazards to the Secretary of Labor and OSHA for OSHA enforcement purposes. The Clean Water Act exhibits no equivalent concern for workplace dangers.

Finally, the well-known rule of lenity in applying criminal statutes applies here. Where there is ambiguity in a criminal statute, the ambiguity is to be construed in favor of the defendant. Our initial semantic exercise reveals the ambiguity in this statute.

These three factors lead us to conclude that a knowing endangerment prosecution cannot be premised upon danger that occurs before the pollutant reaches a publicly-owned sewer or treatment works. Section 1319(c)(3)(A) therefore does not apply to the defendants' conduct as set forth in this indictment.

[The CWA provides a defense to a knowing endangerment charge if the endangerment "was consented to by the person endangered," and the danger and charged conduct were reasonably foreseeable hazards of a particular occupation. The government argued that the court's interpretation of the knowing endangerment provision made this language meaningless because only employees of the source of the discharge could be endangered and consent to the endangerment.]

. . . We find the premise to be faulty. In the course of ordinary industrial activity, illegal discharges will undoubtedly occur from time to time (human or mechanical failure) that the industrial manufacturer or other entity physically cannot correct or halt immediately. Such an entity, if it is also a good citizen, will inform the publicly-owned treatment works of the discharge so that any corrective steps possible can be taken downstream. These publicly-owned treatment works may then hire professional consultants to advise the publicly-owned treatment works how to handle these fully disclosed but illegal discharges until they are corrected or halted. These "downstream" actors — consciously and freely dealing with illegal substances after they have reached the publicly-owned sewers or treatment works — are legitimate subjects for the affirmative defense and give it appropriate content. The section does not, therefore, require us to give

---

[28]Conversely, there may be remedial measures (proper respirators and ventilation, protective clothing and procedures) that could alleviate the health risks to the workers, yet have no value in addressing Clean Water Act concerns of cleaning up the discharges.

section 1319 the reading the United States Attorney urges, a reading that is inconsistent with the overall thrust of the Clean Water Act.

Conclusion

The endangered persons on whom this prosecution is based had no connection to the publicly-owned treatment works or municipal sewers, but were endangered solely as a result of their employment activities at their private place of employment prior to any illegal discharge reaching the public sewer or works. The defendants' conduct here was utterly reprehensible and may have violated any number of other criminal laws; but it did not violate the knowing endangerment provision of the Clean Water Act.

Accordingly, the judgments of conviction are vacated, judgments of acquittal shall be entered for both defendants on both counts.

DISCUSSION QUESTIONS

1. What is the point of having a knowing endangerment provision if its protections do not extend to Borjohn's employees? Whom does the statute protect and why?
2. If the court had concluded that the endangerment provision protected Borjohn employees, would the defendants have been able to prevail on the defense of consent? What is the reason for recognizing consent as a defense?
3. Unlike violations of the CWA permit requirement, violations of the knowing endangerment provision require proof that the actor either had actual knowledge or actually believed that he was placing another person in imminent danger. Proof of actual knowledge or belief does not require direct evidence of the violator's state of mind, however. Circumstantial evidence, including evidence that the defendant "took affirmative steps to shield himself from relevant information" — i.e., was willfully blind to the truth — may be used to prove his state of mind.[29]

    The court in *Borowski* assumed, without deciding, that Borjohn and Borowski knew that dumping the chemicals directly into the sink endangered Borjohn's employees. What evidence is relevant to the issue

---

[29]33 U.S.C. § 1319(c)(3)(B)(i).

of knowledge in *Borowski*? Is the evidence sufficient to support a finding of actual knowledge or belief?

2. WILLFUL BLINDNESS

We encountered the willful blindness doctrine in Chapter 2 in *Hopkins*, where the court ruled that deliberate ignorance can serve as a proxy for knowledge. Thus, Hopkins could be charged with knowledge that his employees were tampering with the monitoring process if he was aware of a high probability that tampering had occurred and he deliberately closed his eyes to the truth.

The following excerpt from United States v. Carrillo[30] provides a metaphorical glimpse at the willful blindness doctrine and the problem of drawing an inference of knowledge from evidence of ignorance.

> . . . Evidence of deliberate ignorance can be placed into two general categories: evidence of "overt physical acts," and evidence of "purely psychological avoidance, a cutting off of one's normal curiosity by an effort of will." *Craig*, 178 F.3d at 896. The first category, as we have explained, is generally the easy case, because there is evidence the defendant physically acted to avoid knowledge. United States v. Giovannetti, 919 F.2d 1223, 1228 (7th Cir. 1990). As an example of such a case we gave United States v. Diaz, 864 F.2d 544, 550 (7th Cir. 1988), where the defendant attempted to distance himself from a drug transaction by "absenting himself from the scene of the actual delivery and sometimes by pretending to be fussing under the hood of his car." *Giovannetti*, 919 F.2d at 1228.
>
> The second category, psychological avoidance, is more troublesome. The act in this category is a mental act — "a cutting off of one's normal curiosity by an effort of will." *Id.* at 1229. . . . The difficulty in a psychological avoidance case — one without any outward physical manifestation of an attempt to avoid facts — lies in distinguishing between a defendant's mental effort of cutting off curiosity, which would support an ostrich instruction, and a defendant's simple lack of mental effort, or lack of curiosity, which would not support an ostrich instruction. There is generally no way to peer directly into the defendant's thought process to determine whether he or she has become suspicious and then dismissed the

---

[30]435 F.3d 767 (7th Cir. 2006).

uncomfortable thought for fear of its consequences. A person may admit to such thoughts, but these instances are rare, and not necessary to the giving of an ostrich instruction.

Our precedent establishes that the circumstances surrounding the defendant alone can be sufficient to allow the jury to infer that the defendant was suspicious but deliberately cut off his or her curiosity in an effort to remain ignorant of guilty knowledge. The logic behind these cases is that given what the defendant knew, it would be permissible for a jury to conclude that the defendant strongly suspected involvement in illegal activity, but purposely avoided finding out for sure. There is no need to search in vain for an "act" that occurred in the veiled isolation of a defendant's psyche. The focus is on what the defendant knew and whether the defendant knew enough to support an inference that he or she remained deliberately ignorant of facts constituting criminal knowledge.

Great caution must be exercised, however, in determining which circumstances support the inference of deliberate ignorance. The most important principle for the district court to keep in mind is that the ostrich "instruction is not meant to allow a jury to convict a person for negligence." *Giovannetti*, 919 F.2d at 1228. . . .

. . . The focus of the ostrich instruction is on the particular defendant, and not a reasonable person. It asks whether the defendant deliberately avoided knowledge by "shutting his or her eyes." . . . [T]he instruction should only be given where "there are facts and evidence that support an inference of deliberate ignorance," and evidence merely supporting a finding of negligence — that a reasonable person would have been strongly suspicious, or that a defendant should have been aware of criminal knowledge — does not support an inference that a particular defendant was deliberately ignorant. . . .[31]

DISCUSSION QUESTION

1. The CWA knowing endangerment provision allows proof of actual knowledge or belief to be based on evidence that the defendant took "affirmative steps to shield himself from relevant information." Should this statutory language be read literally to mean that willful blindness can support an inference of knowledge only if there is evidence that the defendant physically distanced himself from the wrongdoing to avoid

---

[31]*Id.* at 780-782.

learning the truth?   Or should evidence of "purely psychological avoidance" be enough?

3. IMMINENT DANGER

THE CASE OF THE BEACHED BLOOD VIALS

Recall the facts in *Plaza Health Laboratories*, where the defendant hid vials of blood in a bulkhead in the Hudson River. Suppose the following additional evidence will be presented at trial.

Witness number 1, a former employee at Plaza, will testify that Villegas had worked at two other blood testing laboratories before becoming co-owner and vice president of marketing at Plaza. She will also testify that Villegas regularly handled blood samples and took precautions when he did so.

Witness number 2, a medical technologist at Plaza, will testify that nearly half of the blood samples sent to the lab were tested for hepatitis. Plaza had set aside a separate area with a separate machine to conduct the tests.

Witness number 3, the director of pathology at Plaza, will testify that Villegas had written the lab's safety manual on handling blood samples and that Plaza employees regularly followed the safety guidelines.

Witness number 4, an expert in virology, will testify that the primary risk of contracting hepatitis would be that a vial of contaminated blood could break and a piece of the broken glass could pierce someone's skin. While the risk of contracting hepatitis under these circumstances would be "very high," he will testify that the risk that this would actually occur is "low." If the vials were to be washed onto the beach and someone stepped on one that contained infected blood, the risk of infection would be great. But, of course, not all of the vials contained infected blood, and it was unlikely that many of them would be washed ashore.

Assuming the court will entertain the possibility that placing the vials in the bulkhead constituted a discharge from a point source, is the evidence sufficient to prove that Villegas "[knew] at that time that he thereby place[d] another person in imminent danger of death or serious bodily injury?"[32]

---

[32]*Cf.* United States v. Villegas, 784 F. Supp. 6 (E.D.N.Y. 1991).

E. WETLANDS

Wetlands serve as nature's sponge. Marshes, bogs, swamps, mangroves, mud flats, and other saturated areas that are classified as wetlands filter out pollutants like fertilizers and industrial chemicals that would otherwise pollute nearby streams, rivers, and lakes. Because they are porous and absorb billions of gallons of rain, wetlands are also natural protection against flooding.[33] And, of course, wetlands provide essential habitats for countless species of plants, birds, mammals, and aquatic life. In short, wetlands are vitally important — if under-appreciated — ecosystems.

Just as the Frezzo Brothers needed a permit to discharge their mushroom composting waste into the creek, landowners whose property is classified as wetlands must get a permit to develop it.[34] Because the wetlands permit system often interferes with landowners' use of their own land, wetlands regulation is far more controversial than application of CWA permit requirements to conventional examples of water pollution like those found in Illustrations H and I.

The civil and criminal enforcement programs have provoked landowners to use intimidation and other coercive means to induce their own environmental consultants to keep unfavorable reports from regulators, to threaten — in the presence of a government inspector — to "shoot the next person" who enters the property, and to accuse government enforcers of being "Bureaucratic Enviro-Nazis."

Given the important ecological roles that wetlands play, what makes this regulatory regime such a volatile social and political lightning rod?

KATHLEEN F. BRICKEY, WETLANDS REFORM AND THE CRIMINAL ENFORCEMENT RECORD: A CAUTIONARY TALE

76 WASH. U. L.Q. 71, 71-76 (1998)

Marinus Van Leuzen was a pretty lucky man. Van Leuzen owned a waterfront lot. Because the lot contained wetlands, local officials informed

---

[33]The destruction of wetlands made New Orleans far more vulnerable to flooding from Hurricane Katrina. *See* Daniel A. Farber & Jim Chen, DISASTERS AND THE LAW: KATRINA AND BEYOND 210-211 (2006).

[34]The wetlands protection program is administered under the auspices of the EPA and the Army Corps of Engineers.

him that it could not be developed without a permit from the Corps of Engineers. Notwithstanding this advice, Van Leuzen raised the elevation of the site by about three feet and built a pole house. Unfazed by repeated warnings that his construction activity was illegal, Van Leuzen added a shell driveway, a concrete deck and sidewalks. He installed a septic system, sodded the lawn and added more fill.[35] Van Leuzen's development of the site in clear violation of the Clean Water Act[36] triggered a lengthy criminal investigation that culminated in high level discussions at the Justice Department about whether he should be prosecuted for filling wetlands without a permit. To Van Leuzen's good fortune, the criminal case was closed without further action and the matter was referred for civil enforcement.

John Pozsgai had far worse luck. Pozsgai owned and operated a truck repair business. In order to expand his business, Pozsgai bought an adjacent lot that his lawyer described as a neighborhood dumpsite. Because the entire tract was legally classified as wetlands, local authorities notified Pozsgai that he could not develop the land without a permit from the Corps. Equally unfazed by repeated warnings that his construction activities were illegal, Pozsgai filled and graded the site in preparation for building a garage. To Pozsgai's misfortune, a lengthy criminal investigation of his case culminated in his indictment, conviction and three year prison term for violating the Clean Water Act.[37] . . .

In the meantime, a successful media campaign orchestrated by several conservative groups had made Pozsgai a cause célèbre of the property rights movement. At House oversight hearings on the status of wetlands and wetlands regulation, Pozsgai's prosecution was described as an example of "enforcement overkill" that bordered on the "incomprehensible." Critics charged that the government pursued Pozsgai "as if he were Public Enemy No. 1," even though his crime was minor. Pozsgai was portrayed as the victim of an absurd wetlands enforcement policy that irrationally imprisoned "senior citizens whose only crime was to realize the American dream of

---

[35]See United States v. Van Leuzen, 816 F. Supp. 1171 (S.D. Tex. 1993).

[36]See 33 U.S.C. §§ 1311(a), 1319(c)(2) (1994). Although Van Leuzen could have legally constructed the pole house if he had obtained a permit from the Corps, he would have had to comply with whatever terms and conditions the permit imposed.

[37]See United States v. Pozsgai, 757 F. Supp. 21 (E.D. Pa. 1991). His sentence was reported to be the longest ever imposed for an environmental crime as of that point in time. Pozsgai was also sentenced to pay a $200,000 fine.

owning and developing their own property." Needless to say, conservative journalists eagerly joined in the cause.

Pozsgai was only one of several wetlands violators who achieved notoriety through criminal prosecution. A media blitz orchestrated by the Fairness to Landowners Committee, for example, generated more than four thousand petitions and letters to President Bush on behalf of William Ellen, a marine construction project manager. Ellen was convicted of illegally filling more than eighty acres of wetlands on a large tract of land that was being developed as a commercial hunting preserve. Notwithstanding that Ellen was not his constituent and that the sentence was a modest six months, Senator David Pryor sought a presidential pardon for Ellen, calling his case "a prime example of the strange and twisted consequences that can result from a bureaucracy out of touch with reality." The Ellen prosecution prompted conservative writers to label wetlands regulators and enforcement officials as "Bureaucratic Enviro-Nazis" and led property rights advocates to complain that something is terribly wrong when the government wants to jail a mere "dirt mover" while murderers and rapists are being released due to prison overcrowding.

In view of the extensive publicity that these and similar prosecutions received, it should come as no surprise that when Congress considered a Clean Water Act reauthorization bill in 1995, wetlands regulation reform was high on the agenda. Responding to calls to inject "balance and common sense" into water pollution laws, supporters of regulatory reform vowed to replace "oppressive wetlands regulations" conceived by environmental "extremists" with a simplified law that would preserve the "best" wetlands while at the same time protecting the rights of property owners. The Clean Water Act Amendments of 1995 would have accomplished all that and more. Dubbed by detractors as the "dirty water bill," the amendments would have resulted in the loss of protection for at least half of the nation's existing wetlands, eliminated the Environmental Protection Agency's ("EPA") authority to enforce wetlands regulations, abolished all administrative enforcement of wetlands regulations,[38] and made criminal enforcement of

---

[38]The bill's civil enforcement procedures would have required the following steps: (1) issuance of a compliance order to the violator by the Corps of Engineers; (2) notifying the violator of the compliance order; (3) waiting for the outcome of an appeal if the violator disputed the determination that he was not in compliance; (4) filing civil suit within 60 days of a decision denying the appeal or, if there was no appeal, filing suit within 150 days from the date of notification.

wetlands regulations to prevent environmental harm literally impossible. The bill would have forbidden initiating a criminal prosecution until after the violator had disobeyed a compliance order and the government could show that the violation had caused "actual" (and perhaps irreversible) environmental "degradation." Notably, proof of actual degradation of the environment is not a prerequisite for criminal enforcement of any other environmental law. . . .

The furor over the wetlands enforcement program can be best understood when placed in its statutory context. Apart from concerns about unreasonable government interference with private property rights,[39] and about ambiguity and complexity found in water pollution laws, the fundamental bone of contention is the breathtaking reach of wetlands regulations. The Clean Water Act defines the term "navigable waters" to be "waters of the United States, including the territorial seas."[40] While regulations promulgated by the Corps of Engineers and EPA define waters of the United States[41] to include bodies of water that would be recognized as such in common parlance,[42] they also include wetlands that are adjacent to traditional waters, thus taking "a quantum leap onto land."[43] In consequence, a property owner could run afoul of wetlands regulations not only by filling in marshes, swamps and bogs, but by dumping dirt into a dry arroyo or ditch as well.[44] As one court put it:

> In a reversal of terms that is worthy of *Alice in Wonderland*, the regulatory hydra which emerged from the Clean Water Act mandates . . . that a

---

[39]Property rights activists claim that government regulation of privately owned property constitutes an uncompensated "taking" of the property. . . .

[40]33 U.S.C. § 1362(7) (1994).

[41]*See* 33 C.F.R. § 328.3(a) (1986) (Army Corps definition); 40 C.F.R. § 230.3(s) (1980) (EPA definition).

[42]"Waters of the United States" include lakes, rivers and streams, for example. 33 C.F.R. § 328.3(a)(3) (1986).

[43]United States v. Mills, 817 F. Supp. 1546, 1551 (N.D. Fla. 1993). The definition includes "those areas that are inundated or saturated by surface or ground water at a frequency and duration sufficient to support, and that under normal circumstances do support, a prevalence of vegetation typically adapted for life in saturated soil conditions. Wetlands generally include swamps, marshes, bogs and similar areas." 33 C.F.R. § 328.3(b); 40 C.F.R. § 230.3(t).

[44]*Cf.* United States v. Wilson, 133 F.3d 251, 258 (4th Cir. 1997) (holding erroneous a jury instruction that defined waters of the United States to include adjacent wetlands having no direct or indirect surface connection to other waters of the United States).

landowner who places clean fill dirt on a plot of subdivided dry *land* may be imprisoned for the statutory felony offense of "discharging pollutants into the navigable *waters* of the United States."[45]

———————

It is against this backdrop that the Supreme Court has endeavored to define the outer bounds of federal wetlands enforcement authority. And, as we shall see, a definitive rule is yet to come.

Although the CWA applies only to discharges into navigable waters, "navigable" is a term of limited import. In 1985, the Supreme Court ruled in United States v. Riverside Bayview Homes, Inc. that navigable waters may include some waters that are not navigable in fact — e.g., wetlands adjacent to a navigable waterway.[46] Thus, for example, in *Riverside Bayview Homes*, a commercial developer that owned 80 acres of low-lying marshy land abutting a navigable lake was required to obtain a permit before putting fill materials on the property to prepare it for construction of a housing development.

But the Supreme Court has recently been chipping away at the Corps of Engineers' expansive reading of its power to regulate wetlands that have only tenuous relationships to navigable waters. In Solid Waste Agency of Northern Cook County v. Army Corps of Engineers[47] (*SWANCC*), the Court struck down the "migratory bird rule." The Corps had asserted that it had jurisdiction over isolated, nonnavigable, intrastate waters such as ponds if they were used by migratory birds as habitat. The high Court ruled that the Corps had exceeded its statutory authority by promulgating regulations giving the agency jurisdiction over ponds that are not adjacent to open water.

Although the precise impact of the Court's decision in *SWANCC* on wetlands regulation was not immediately apparent, it was inevitable that commercial developers, property rights advocates, and conservative journalists would use the decision as a springboard for renewed criticism of the government's use of CWA regulations to curb private and commercial development of areas designated as wetlands.[48]

———————————————————

[45]*Mills*, 817 F. Supp. at 1548 (emphasis in original).

[46]474 U.S. 121, 133 (1985).

[47]531 U.S. 159 (2001).

[48]*See generally* Kathleen F. Brickey, *Wetlands Reform and the Criminal Enforcement Record: A Cautionary Tale*, 76 WASH. U. L.Q. 71 (1998). *Cf.* United States v. Rapanos, 376 F.3d 629 (6th Cir.) (although a minority of courts read *SWANCC* expansively to require that nonnavigable waters must directly abut navigable waters to be covered under the CWA,

As it turned out, *SWANCC* was indeed a harbinger of change. At the end of its 2005 Term, the Supreme Court handed down Rapanos v. United States,[49] a plurality decision that revealed deeply divided views about the appropriate scope of wetlands jurisdiction.

Justice Scalia, joined by Chief Justice Roberts and Justices Thomas and Alito, decried the Corps' expansive reading of its jurisdiction under the CWA and called its regulatory approach the improbable equivalent of "Land is Waters."[50]

Justice Scalia's plurality opinion advocated a highly restrictive two-part test for determining whether wetlands are "adjacent" to navigable waters for purposes of CWA jurisdiction. In the plurality's view, wetlands should be deemed "waters of the United States" within CWA jurisdiction only if two conditions are fulfilled:

> First, that the adjacent channel contains a wate[r] of the United States (*i.e.*, a relatively permanent body of water connected to traditional interstate navigable waters); and second, that the wetland has a continuous surface connection with that water, making it difficult to determine where the "water" ends and the "wetland" begins.[51]

The plurality's goal, in short, was to limit CWA jurisdiction to "relatively *permanent* bodies of water"[52] and to exclude places where the presence of water is intermittent or ephemeral.

Justice Kennedy, concurring only in the judgment, wrote a separate opinion rejecting the plurality's narrow adjacency requirement, arguing instead for a broader "significant nexus" test as a threshold for establishing Clean Water Act jurisdiction.[53]

Writing in dissent for the remaining members of the Court, Justice Stevens argued that the Corps had reasonably interpreted its jurisdiction to

---

a majority of courts have read *SWANCC* more narrowly to allow CWA jurisdiction to extend to nonnavigable waters having only a hydrological connection to navigable waters), cert. denied, 541 U.S. 972 (2004).

[49] 547 U.S. 715 (2006).

[50] *Id.* at 734.

[51] *Id.* at 742.

[52] *Id.* at 733.

[53] *Id.* at 779.

cover non-isolated wetlands under the Act, and he pointedly rejected the two "novel conditions" the plurality would impose.[54]

In a brief separate opinion, Chief Justice Roberts fretted that the *Rapanos* Court's inability to agree on a rationale that commanded a majority left the lower courts and regulators to grapple with this problem on a case-by-case basis.[55]

And that's where things stood when the first post-*Rapanos* court of appeals decision was handed down.

NORTHERN CALIFORNIA RIVER WATCH V. CITY OF HEALDSBURG

457 F.3d 1023 (9th Cir. 2006)

SCHROEDER, Chief Judge.

Defendant/Appellant City of Healdsburg ("Healdsburg") appeals the district court's judgment in favor of Plaintiff/Appellee Northern California River Watch ("River Watch"), an environmental group, in this litigation under the Clean Water Act ("CWA"). Plaintiff alleges that Healdsburg, without first obtaining a National Pollutant Discharge Elimination System ("NPDES") permit, violated the CWA by discharging sewage from its waste treatment plant into waters covered by the Act. Healdsburg discharged the sewage into a body of water known as "Basalt Pond," a rock quarry pit that had filled with water from the surrounding aquifer, located next to the Russian River. . . .

. . . The district court held that discharges into the Pond are discharges into the Russian River, a navigable water of the United States protected by the CWA. . . .

. . . We affirm the district court's holding that Basalt Pond is subject to the CWA. . . .

Background . . .

Basalt Pond was created in approximately 1967 when the Basalt Rock Company began excavating gravel and sand from land near the Russian River. After the top soil was ripped away, large machines tore out rock and

---

[54]*Id.* at 788, 797-798, 800-807.
[55]*Id.* at 757, 758.

sand. The result was a pit. The pit filled with water up to the line of the water table of the surrounding aquifer. Today, Basalt Pond, measuring one half mile in length and a quarter mile in breadth, contains 58 acres of surface water. The Pond lies along the west side of the Russian River, separated from the River by a levee.

It is undisputed that the Russian River is a navigable water of the United States. Its headwaters originate in Mendocino County, California. Its main course runs about 110 miles, flowing into the Pacific Ocean west of Santa Rosa.

The horizontal distance between the edge of the River and the edge of the Pond varies between fifty and several hundred feet, depending on the exact location and the height of the river water. Usually, there is no surface connection, because the levee blocks it and prevents the Pond from being inundated by high river waters in the rainy season.

In 1971, Healdsburg built a secondary waste-treatment plant on a 35-acre site located on the north side of Basalt Pond about 800 feet from and west of the Russian River. Prior to 1978, Healdsburg discharged the plant's wastewater into another water-filled pit located to the north. In 1978, Healdsburg began discharging into Basalt Pond. Although Healdsburg did not obtain an NPDES permit, it received a state water emission permit as well as permission from Syar Industries, Inc., the current owner and manager of land and operations at Basalt Pond.

The wastewater discharged into Basalt Pond from the plant was about 420 to 455 million gallons per year between 1998 and 2000. The volume of the Pond itself is somewhat larger — 450 to 740 million gallons. The annual outflow from the sewage plant, therefore, is sufficient to fill the entire Pond every one to two years. Basalt Pond would, of course, soon overflow in these circumstances were it not for the fact that the Pond drains into the surrounding aquifer.

Pond water in the aquifer finds its way to the River over a period of a few months and seeps directly into the River along as much as 2200 feet of its banks. . . .

The district court found that the concentrations of chloride in the groundwater between the Pond and the Russian River are substantially higher than in the surrounding area. Chloride, which already exists in the Pond due to naturally occurring salts, reaches the River in higher concentrations as a direct result of Healdsburg's discharge of sewage into the Pond. . . .

Discussion

A. Wetlands Constituting Waters of the United States

Congress passed the Clean Water Act in 1972. The Act's stated objective is "to restore and maintain the chemical, physical, and biological integrity of the Nation's waters." 33 U.S.C. § 1251(a). To that end, the statute, among other things, prohibits "the discharge of any pollutant by any person" except as provided in the Act. § 1311(a).

After the CWA was passed, an issue arose concerning the extent to which wetlands adjacent to navigable waters constitute "waters of the United States." In 1978, the Army Corps of Engineers ("ACOE") issued a regulation defining "waters of the United States" to include "adjacent wetlands." The regulations specifically provide that "[t]he term 'waters of the United States' means," among other things, "[w]etlands adjacent to waters." The regulations further specify that "[w]etlands separated from other waters of the United States by man-made dikes or barriers, natural river berms, beach dunes and the like are 'adjacent wetlands.'" 33 C.F.R. § 328.3(c).

The first issue is therefore whether Basalt Pond and its surrounding are "wetlands adjacent to waters" within the meaning of the regulations. If so, we must decide whether such adjacent wetlands constitute "waters of the United States" protected under the Act.

[T]he Pond itself and its surrounding area are wetlands under the regulatory definition. The applicable regulations define wetlands as "those areas that are inundated or saturated by surface or groundwater." The record here reflects that the Russian River and surrounding area rest on top of a vast gravel bed extending as much as sixty feet into the earth. The gravel bed is a porous medium, saturated with water. Through it flows an equally vast underground aquifer. This aquifer supplies the principal pathway for a continuous passage of water between Basalt Pond and the Russian River. Beneath the surface, water soaks in and out of the Pond via the underground aquifer. This action is continuous, 24 hours a day, seven days a week, 365 days a year. Indeed, the parties have stipulated that the Pond and the River overlie the same unconfined aquifer and that the land separating the two is saturated below the water table.

Because Basalt Pond and surrounding wetlands were created by quarrying, they are man-made. This fact is not determinative of whether they qualify as navigable waters. Since Basalt Pond contains wetlands, the only remaining question is whether the adjacent wetlands constitute waters of the United States subject to the CWA.

The Supreme Court has consistently held, when interpreting the meaning of "adjacent wetlands" in the regulations, that in order for the Act to apply there must be some relationship between wetlands and an identifiable navigable water. The leading case is *Riverside Bayview Homes*, 474 U.S. 121 decided in 1985. The Supreme Court there upheld CWA jurisdiction over wetlands that directly abutted a navigable creek. The Court held that "the relationship between waters and their adjacent wetlands provides an adequate basis for a legal judgment that adjacent wetlands may be defined as waters under the Act." *Id.* at 134. The Court left open the question of whether the CWA also protected wetlands other than those adjacent to open waters. *Id.* at 131-32.

In Solid Waste Agency of Northern Cook County v. United States Army Corps of Engineers, 531 U.S. 159 (2001) (SWANCC), the Supreme Court again interpreted the CWA term "navigable waters" and held that isolated ponds and mudflats, unconnected to other waters covered by the Act, were not "waters of the United States." The case involved ponds that had been formed as a result of an abandoned sand and gravel pit mining operation and were not "adjacent wetlands." The ACOE regulations defined the ponds nevertheless to be "waters of the United States," because they were "used as habitat by other migratory birds which cross state lines." Under this "Migratory Bird Rule," ponds that are isolated from navigable waters may constitute "waters of the United States" if they are used as habitat by migratory birds. The Supreme Court rejected that theory and held that the CWA does not protect isolated ponds without a significant nexus. The Court explained that, "[i]t was the significant nexus between wetlands and 'navigable waters' that informed our reading of the [Act] in *Riverside Bayview Homes*." *Id.* at 167.

The Supreme Court in *SWANCC*, therefore, invalidated the Migratory Bird Rule but did not purport to reconsider its prior holding regarding adjacent wetlands in *Riverside Bayview Homes....*

In the last term, however, the Supreme Court discussed the intersection between *Riverside Bayview Homes* and *SWANCC*. United States v. Rapanos, 126 S. Ct. 2208 (2006). The *Rapanos* decision involved two consolidated cases.

The first consolidated case, *Rapanos I*, involved three land parcels near Midland, Michigan. [All three parcels contained at least several dozen acres of wetlands.] The wetlands at issue in all three parcels were neither directly adjacent to or entirely isolated from a navigable water of the United States. . . .

In *Rapanos*, a 4-4-1 plurality opinion, the Supreme Court addressed how the term "navigable waters" should be construed under the Act. The plurality, written by Justice Scalia for four Justices, would have reversed on the grounds that only those wetlands with a continuous surface connection to bodies that are "waters of the United States" are protected under the CWA. Justice Stevens, writing the dissent for four Justices, would have affirmed on the grounds that wetlands not directly adjacent to navigable waters, but adjacent to tributaries of navigable waters, are protected under the CWA. Justice Stevens argued that *Riverside Bayview Homes* is still the controlling precedent and does not require a "significant nexus" test.

Justice Kennedy, constituting the fifth vote for reversal, concurred only in the judgment and, therefore, provides the controlling rule of law. See Marks v. United States, 430 U.S. 188, 193 (1977) (explaining that "[w]hen a fragmented Court decides a case and no single rationale explaining the result enjoys the assent of five Justices, the holding of the Court may be viewed as that position taken by those Members who concurred in the judgments on the narrowest grounds"). Justice Kennedy took the view that wetlands come within the statutory phrase "navigable waters," if the wetlands have a "significant nexus" to navigable-in-fact waterways. He explained that a significant nexus exists "if the wetlands, either alone or in combination with similarly situated lands in the region, significantly affect the chemical, physical, and biological integrity of other covered waters more readily understood as 'navigable.' " *Rapanos*, 126 S. Ct. at 2248. "When, in contrast, wetlands' effects on water quality are speculative or insubstantial, they fall outside the zone fairly encompassed by the statutory term 'navigable waters.' " *Id.*

In addressing whether a hydrological connection satisfies the "significant nexus" test, Justice Kennedy explained that a "mere hydrologic connection should not suffice in all cases; the connection may be too insubstantial for the hydrologic linkage to establish the required nexus with navigable waters as traditionally understood." *Id.* at 2251. Rather, the "required nexus must be assessed in terms of the statute's goals and purposes," which are to "restore and maintain the chemical, physical, and biological integrity of the Nation's waters."

Justice Kennedy made clear that *SWANCC*'s holding "is not an explicit or implicit overruling of *Riverside Bayview Homes*. Rather, *SWANCC* provides further clarification of *Riverside Bayview Homes'* construction of the term "navigable waters." As Justice Kennedy explained in *Rapanos*:

> ... Taken together these cases establish that in some instances, as exemplified by *Riverside Bayview*, the connection between a nonnavigable water or wetland and a navigable water may be so close, or potentially so close, that the Corps may deem the water or wetland a "navigable water" under the Act. In other instances, as exemplified by *SWANCC*, there may be little or no connection. Absent a significant nexus, jurisdiction under the Act is lacking.

Id. at 2241.

Applying these principles in this case, it is apparent that the mere adjacency of Basalt Pond and its wetlands to the Russian River is not sufficient for CWA protection. The critical fact is that the Pond and navigable Russian River are separated only by a man-made levee so that water from the Pond seeps directly into the adjacent River. This is a significant nexus between the wetlands and the Russian River and justifies CWA protection.... The district court's findings of fact support the conclusion that Basalt Pond and its wetlands "significantly affect the chemical, physical, and biological integrity of other covered waters understood as navigable in the traditional sense."

Moreover, there is an actual surface connection between Basalt Pond and the Russian River when the River overflows the levee and the two bodies of water commingle. Thus, there are several hydrological connections between Basalt Pond's wetlands and the Russian River that affect the physical integrity of the River. Basalt Pond drains into the aquifer and at least 26 percent of the Pond's volume annually reaches the River itself. There is also an underground hydraulic connection between the two bodies, so a change in the water level in one immediately affects the water level in the other.

In addition to these physical connections between Basalt Pond and the Russian River, the district court found that there is also a significant ecological connection. The wetlands support substantial bird, mammal and fish populations, all as an integral part of and indistinguishable from the rest of the Russian River ecosystem. Many of the bird populations at the Pond are familiar along the River, including cormorants, great egrets, mallards, sparrows, and fish-eaters. Fish indigenous to the River also live in the Pond due to the recurring breaches of the levee. As the district court observed, these facts make Basalt Pond indistinguishable from any of the natural wetlands alongside the Russian River that have extensive biological effects on the River itself.

The district court also found that Basalt Pond significantly affects the chemical integrity of the Russian River by increasing its chloride levels. The chloride from Basalt Pond reaches the River in higher concentrations as a direct result of Healdsburg's discharge of sewage into the pond. Mr. John Lambie testified at trial that the average concentration of chloride appearing upstream in the river is only 5.9 parts per million. In contrast, the average concentration of chloride seeping from Basalt Pond into the River is 36 parts per million, and the chloride concentration on the west side of the River adjacent to the Pond is 18 parts per million.

In sum, the district court made substantial findings of fact to support the conclusion that the adjacent wetland of Basalt Pond has a significant nexus to the Russian River. The Pond's effects on the Russian River are not speculative or insubstantial. Rather, the Pond significantly affects the physical, biological and chemical integrity of the Russian River, and ultimately warrants protection as a "navigable water" under the CWA. Appellant's discharge of wastewater into Basalt Pond without a permit, therefore, violates the CWA. . . .

DISCUSSION QUESTIONS

1. Is it important that the Pond is adjacent to the River? Why isn't adjacency, standing alone, sufficient to confer CWA jurisdiction? Would the dissenters in *Rapanos* have found that adjacency alone is enough?
2. Is the hydrological link between the Pond and the River enough to satisfy Justice Kennedy's significant nexus test?
3. How would the Justices who formed the plurality in *Rapanos* likely have decided *River Watch*?
4. Why was Justice Kennedy's concurrence the "controlling" opinion in *Rapanos*?

F. MISCELLANEOUS CWA CRIMES

While it is clear that the organizing principle for the CWA regulatory regime is the permit system, other components of the regulatory scheme have somewhat different emphases. To flesh out the picture, this section briefly surveys several other provisions that can also lead to criminal prosecution.

1. PRETREATMENT STANDARDS

In *Borowski*, the knowing endangerment charge did not stem from a permit violation. Instead, the underlying CWA violation was a discharge that violated pretreatment standards applicable to businesses like Borjohn, which discharge pollutants into publicly owned treatment works (POTWs). POTWs are facilities that "store, treat, recycle and reclaim municipal and industrial liquid wastes"[56] and are generally owned and operated by municipalities or similar governmental units.

Instead of regulating these types of discharges through the permit system, the CWA requires the EPA to promulgate national pretreatment standards applicable to specified industrial users who discharge pollutants into POTWs.[57] The pretreatment standards are designed to prevent discharges that might interfere with the effectiveness of a POTW's treatment system and thereby indirectly cause pollutants to be discharged into navigable waters through the POTW.

Mechanisms to ensure that industrial users are in compliance with pretreatment requirements include use of specified monitoring procedures (e.g., periodic or continual testing of industrial wastewater for the amount of lead it contains) and submission of periodic reports that reflect the discharger's compliance record.

Negligently or knowingly violating these requirements can lead to criminal penalties.[58]

2. DISCHARGE OF DANGEROUS POLLUTANTS OR HAZARDOUS SUBSTANCES

The CWA imposes criminal penalties for negligently or knowingly introducing a pollutant or hazardous substance into a sewer system or POTW

---

[56]33 U.S.C. § 1292(2).
[57]33 U.S.C. § 1317(d).
[58]33 U.S.C. § 1319(c).

if the polluter knew or reasonably should have known that the discharged substance could cause personal injury or property damage.[59]

3. NOTIFICATION REQUIREMENTS

The CWA requires any "person in charge" of a vessel or facility from which a discharge of oil or a hazardous substance has occurred to immediately notify the appropriate federal agency that the discharge has occurred.[60] The duty to notify arises as soon as the person in charge knows about the discharge.[61]

This provision is potentially problematic, as is shown by Illustration J.

Illustration J: B & B Shipping operates a fleet of oil tankers. Captain Bligh, the captain of the flagship, drinks five martinis before getting behind the wheel. Thus inebriated, he runs the ship aground on a reef. The impact ruptures one of the ship's oil storage compartments, and thousands of gallons of oil immediately begin to gush from the hull. Thinking he can handle the problem himself, Captain Bligh does not notify the Coast Guard (an appropriate federal agency) that the spill has occurred. Twelve hours later, he tells the Coast Guard about the spill.

Did Captain Bligh have a duty to notify the Coast Guard when the ship ran aground? As is so often the case, the answer is "it depends." The duty to notify arises as soon as the person in charge (here, the captain) knows the discharge has occurred. If the accident occurred at night and it was too dark to see the oil gushing out, perhaps he could argue that he did not know until much later that the spill had occurred. On the other hand, if the strong stench of crude oil suddenly filled the air when the ship ran aground, or the sound of thousands of gallons of oil rushing through the hull was an unmistakable sign of a rupture, or the spill occurred during the day when the escaping oil could readily be seen, Bligh was required to immediately notify the Coast Guard.

---

[59]33 U.S.C. § 1319(c)(2)(B). The term "hazardous substance" includes any substance classified as hazardous or toxic under the CWA or select other environmental statutes.

[60]In addition to natural persons, a corporate owner/operator of a facility may be a person in charge of a facility.

[61]33 U.S.C. § 1321(b)(5).

So assuming he knew the spill had occurred, why might Captain Bligh be reluctant to report it?

Let's begin by harkening back to the basic CWA regulatory scheme. How should we characterize what has happened here? The oil is a pollutant, the ocean is a navigable water, the ship is a point source, and J & J does not have a permit to discharge oil into the water.

But what does this have to do with Captain Bligh? He assumed control of the ship while he was drunk and ran the ship aground. One can only conclude that at minimum, he acted negligently. And if he negligently caused the unpermitted discharge of oil into the water, he committed a crime.

The obvious dilemma is that if Captain Bligh complies with the reporting requirement, in effect he admits responsibility for a criminal violation of the CWA. If he does not notify the Coast Guard, he has committed an independent crime because he violated the notification requirements.

Under these circumstances, his lawyer could reasonably be expected to argue that requiring him to notify federal authorities amounts to compelling him to implicate himself in criminal misconduct in violation of his Fifth Amendment privilege against self-incrimination. And this is where the statute steps in to save Captain Bligh from himself.

The notification provision grants limited immunity to the Captain Blighs of the world if they jump through all the necessary hoops. Modeled on the federal use immunity statute,[62] the CWA immunity provision provides that the notification may not be used against Captain Bligh in any criminal proceeding, except a prosecution for perjury or giving a false statement.[63]

Thus, as long as Captain Bligh complies with the immediate notification requirement *and* if the notification truthfully discloses what has happened, the contents of the notification cannot be used in a criminal prosecution to prove that he negligently discharged the oil.

Although an earlier version of the CWA immunity provision applied to both natural persons and corporations, in its current iteration it applies only to natural persons like Captain Bligh. Thus, because corporations have no Fifth Amendment privilege against self-incrimination,[64] the fact and contents of the notification may be used in a criminal prosecution against the corporation that provides it.

---

[62]18 U.S.C. § 6002.

[63]*Cf.* United States v. Apfelbaum, 445 U.S. 115 (1980) (construing the use immunity statute in the context of a perjury prosecution against an immunized witness).

[64]*See, e.g.*, George Campbell Painting Corp. v. Reid, 392 U.S. 286 (1968).

4. FALSE STATEMENTS

The CWA places a premium on truthfulness in connection with recordkeeping, reporting, and monitoring requirements. It is a crime under the Act to knowingly make a false material statement in any application, record, or other document required to be filed or maintained under the Act, or to knowingly falsify, tamper with, or render inaccurate any monitoring device or method the Act requires to be maintained.[65]

The CWA false statements provision overlaps with the general federal false statements statute,[66] but it neither preempts nor is preempted by the Title 18 provision. We will take a closer look at the intersection of these false statements statutes when we consider liability for environmental wrongdoing under conventional criminal statutes in Chapter 8.

[65]33 U.S.C. § 1319(c)(4).
[66]18 U.S.C. § 1001.

5

AIR POLLUTION

Modern science has not established a safe level for asbestos exposure for which there is no increased risk of disease.[†]

They said, "Our asbestos isn't bad asbestos." And "These fibers are too short or the wrong shape to be harmful" and "Our mining process doesn't result in the kind of asbestos exposure that would cause the disease."[††]

Companies will tell you that asbestos isn't a problem. "Go back to work, George. There's nothing to worry about." Senators, they lied. We need to worry about asbestos.[†††]

A. THE CLEAN AIR ACT

The Clean Air Act (CAA) was enacted in part "to protect and enhance the quality of the Nation's air resources" and thus promote public health and welfare.[1] Toward that end, the Act establishes a multifaceted regulatory

---

[†]Indictment, United States v. W.R. Grace.

[††]David McAteer, Assistant Secretary for Mine Safety and Health, Department of Labor.

[†††]George Biekola, Michigan taconite miner debilitated by asbestos-related disease.

[1]42 U.S.C. § 7401(b)(1).

scheme that, *inter alia*, regulates stationary and mobile sources of air pollution, limits the release of "criteria pollutants" (e.g., ozone, lead, and sulfur dioxide) that endanger public health or welfare, and establishes a national ambient air quality standard for each criteria pollutant. The Act also directs the EPA to set and enforce national emissions standards for hazardous air pollutants (NESHAPs) where feasible or, when control of such emissions is not feasible, to adopt work practice guidelines to reduce them.

But the Act does not rely exclusively on federal enforcement mechanisms. Indeed, the congressional statement of findings explicitly states that prevention and control of air pollution at the source is "the primary responsibility of States and local governments."[2] The Act thus requires states to adopt state implementation plans (SIPs) that set emission limits, establish systems for monitoring compliance, and provide enforcement mechanisms.

The Clean Air Act Amendments of 1990 made sweeping changes, including revamping the basic civil and criminal enforcement provision. The changes included increasing some criminal penalties and expanding the scope of the criminal provisions to include five different categories of crimes: (1) violating an implementation plan, permit, compliance order, or other regulation; (2) making false statements, failing to give required notification, or tampering with a required monitoring device;[3] (3) failing to pay any required federal fee; (4) negligent endangerment; and (5) knowing endangerment.

B. KEY CONCEPTS

Although the preceding overview of the CAA describes a variety of approaches to preventing and reducing air pollution, asbestos provides the unifying theme in CAA criminal enforcement actions. The vast majority of CAA prosecutions are cases in which building demolition or renovation is performed in violation of the asbestos work practice guidelines.

The following sections provide a glimpse at some of the key concepts that we will encounter when we begin considering asbestos-related crimes.

---

[2]42 U.S.C. § 7401(a)(3).

[3]We will consider the false statements and tampering crimes in Chapter 8.

1. PERSON

The CAA's criminal enforcement scheme is generally directed at any "person" who commits a violation. The term "person" is defined broadly to include individuals, organizations, and governmental entities.[4] The criminal provisions also expressly apply to "any responsible corporate officer,"[5] but the Act does not specify who might fit that description.[6]

Although "person" is a term of broad import under the CAA, low-level employees are insulated from criminal liability for most criminal violations. Unless a violation is both knowing and willful, the term "person" excludes employees who are carrying out their normal responsibilities and are acting under the employer's orders.[7] This provision makes the CAA the only environmental statute whose criminal enforcement provisions generally immunize mid- to low-level employees from criminal prosecution for job-related violations.

2. STATIONARY SOURCE

The CAA regulates both mobile and stationary sources of air pollution. A stationary source is "any building, structure, facility, or installation" that emits or might emit air pollutants.[8]

Illustration A: A coal-burning power plant emits high levels of sulphur dioxide through its smokestack.

The plant (or its smokestack) is a stationary source of pollution.

Illustration B: An old and poorly maintained pick-up truck that runs on leaded gasoline emits unacceptably high amounts of lead and carbon monoxide through its tail pipe.

---

[4]Specifically, the definition includes "an individual, corporation, partnership, association, State, municipality, political subdivision of a State, and any agency, department, or instrumentality of the United States and any officer, agent or employee thereof." 42 U.S.C. § 7602(e). Governmental entities may not, however, be prosecuted for knowing endangerment under the CAA. 42 U.S.C. § 7413(c)(5)(E).

[5]42 U.S.C. § 7413(c)(6).

[6]The responsible corporate officer doctrine is considered in greater detail in Chapter 3.

[7]42 U.S.C. § 7413(h).

[8]42 U.S.C. § 7411(a)(3).

Although the tail pipe is roughly equivalent to a smokestack as a conduit for emitting pollutants into the air, the truck is a mobile rather than stationary source of pollution and hence is subject to a different regulatory regime than the power plant.

Because the bulk of CAA prosecutions arise out of improper asbestos removal from aging buildings, most of these prosecutions involve modification of stationary sources of pollution. "Modification" in this context means making a physical change in the structure or a change in its method of operation that increases emissions of air pollutants from the facility or causes it to emit air pollutants that it did not previously emit.[9]

3. HAZARDOUS POLLUTANT

The CAA is concerned primarily with pollutants that pose a risk to human health or welfare. Hazardous Air Pollutants (sometimes called Air Toxics) are substances and compounds that EPA must regulate. Before the CAA Amendments of 1990 were enacted, EPA had listed about 30 pollutants as hazardous, but had adopted national emission standards for only 8.[10]   The 1990 Amendments classified nearly 200 compounds and substances — including asbestos — as hazardous air pollutants and authorized EPA to add other substances that may pose a risk of adverse environmental or human health effects.[11]

4. NATIONAL EMISSIONS STANDARDS FOR HAZARDOUS POLLUTANTS (NESHAPS)

The CAA directs the EPA Administrator to establish National Emissions Standards for Hazardous Air Pollutants to reduce or eliminate emissions of hazardous air pollutants. Rather than focusing on a quantitative threshold for emissions, the asbestos NESHAP focuses on preventing emissions by regulating asbestos-related activities such as demolition and renovation of structures that contain friable asbestos. Asbestos is friable if it can be easily crumbled and reduced to powder and thus is capable of becoming airborne. The asbestos NESHAP requires those who engage in demolition and

---

[9]42 U.S.C. § 7411(a)(4).
[10]They included asbestos, benzene, beryllium coke oven emissions, inorganic arsenic, mercury, radio nuclides, and vinyl chloride. 40 C.F.R. § 61.01(a).
[11]42 U.S.C. § 7412(b)(1)-(3).

renovation activities to notify EPA in advance, to adequately wet exposed friable asbestos, and to follow work practice standards to prevent the emission of asbestos particulates into the outside air.

> **Illustration C:** A commercial building owner decides to replace old and crumbling insulation on steam pipes in the building's basement. The owner instructs the maintenance supervisor to strip all of the insulation off of the pipes. The supervisor loosens the insulation with a saw and then scrapes the crumbling insulation from the pipe with a chisel. The insulation contains a large amount of asbestos, and the removal process creates clouds of dust. Assuming there are no undisclosed facts, does the removal of the insulation violate the asbestos NESHAP?

C. ASBESTOS DEMOLITION AND RENOVATION

As noted above, the asbestos NESHAP requires those involved in asbestos demolition and renovation activities to provide the EPA advance written notice of proposed asbestos removal and to follow EPA work practice rules and standards designed to prevent the release of asbestos into the environment. Because the rules and standards focus on steps those who engage in asbestos-related demolition and renovation activities must follow, it is the violation of the work practice rules — dry removal of asbestos-containing material without an EPA waiver and failure to keep asbestos material adequately wet — that triggers liability. For purposes of these rules, the question whether asbestos particulates were actually emitted into the ambient air is ordinarily not relevant.[12]

1. OWNERS AND OPERATORS

The asbestos demolition and renovation rules are directed primarily at owners and operators of a removal or renovation operation. The term "operator" is defined to include senior management personnel and corporate officers. Unless the violation is both knowing and willful, stationary engineers or technicians who are responsible for operating, maintaining, repairing, or monitoring equipment and facilities are not deemed operators unless they are senior management personnel or corporate officers. That is

---

[12]Under EPA rules, ambient air is outside air that is accessible to the public.

true even if the engineers or technicians often perform supervisory or training functions.

UNITED STATES V. DIPENTINO

242 F.3d 1090 (9th Cir. 2001)

THOMPSON, Circuit Judge. . . .

Background

The Las Vegas Convention and Visitors Authority ("Visitors Authority") hired Ab-Haz Environmental, Inc. ("Ab-Haz"), an asbestos abatement consulting firm, to oversee the removal of asbestos-containing materials from the Landmark Hotel and Casino in Las Vegas, Nevada, prior to its demolition. Rafiq Ali was the president and sole proprietor of Ab-Haz; Rocco Dipentino was an industrial hygienist employed by Ab-Haz as the on-site inspector at the Landmark. Under the terms of its contract with the Visitors Authority, Ab-Haz was required to: (1) survey the Landmark and identify the asbestos-containing materials that needed to be removed prior to demolition; (2) prepare specifications for how the asbestos removal job was to be performed; (3) assist the Visitors Authority in selecting an asbestos-removal contractor to remove the asbestos-containing materials; (4) serve as the Visitors Authority's on-site representative, providing day-to-day monitoring and oversight of the work to ensure that it was being performed in accordance with the law; and (5) inspect and certify that the site was free from asbestos following the completion of the asbestos-removal work.

The Clean Air Act classifies asbestos as a hazardous air pollutant. Emissions of hazardous air pollutants in violation of work practice standards promulgated by the Environment Protection Agency are prohibited. Under the work practice standard relevant to this case, an owner or operator of a demolition activity is required to remove all asbestos prior to demolition and must "adequately wet the [asbestos-containing] material and ensure that it remains wet until collected and contained" in leak-tight containers for proper disposal. An owner or operator of a demolition activity who knowingly violates a work practice standard is subject to criminal penalties. An employee who is carrying out his or her normal activities and acting under orders from the employer is liable only for knowing and willful violations.

The grand jury for the District of Nevada returned a two-count indictment against Ab-Haz, Rafiq Ali, Rocco Dipentino, and a defendant who was later acquitted, Richard Lovelace, who was the on-site inspector of the asbestos-removal contractor hired by the Visitors Authority. Count 1 of the indictment charged the defendants with knowingly conspiring to violate the Clean Air Act by removing regulated asbestos-containing materials from surfaces in the Landmark without complying with the applicable work practice standards. Count 2 charged each defendant with knowingly violating the Clean Air Act by leaving scraped asbestos-containing debris on floors and other surfaces, where it was allowed to dry out, instead of placing the debris, while wet, into leak-proof containers for removal from the site. Count 2 [also] charged each defendant with knowingly violating the Clean Air Act by causing asbestos-covered facility components to fall from the ceiling to the floor, rather than carefully lowering such components so as not to dislodge asbestos. One government inspector described the removal project as "the worst [asbestos] abatement job I've seen."

[The jury convicted Ali and Dipentino of knowingly allowing asbestos-containing debris to dry out before placing it into leak-proof containers.]

B. Sufficiency of the Evidence

Dipentino asserts that the evidence was insufficient to support his conviction for violating the Clean Air Act. . . .

The Clean Air Act imposes criminal liability on an owner or operator if he or she knowingly violates the Act. The term "owner or operator" is defined under the asbestos regulations as "any person who owns, leases, operates, controls, or supervises the facility being demolished or renovated or any person who owns, leases, operates, controls or supervises the demolition or renovation operation, or both." 40 C.F.R. § 61.141. In determining whether a person is an owner or operator within the meaning of the Clean Air Act, the question is whether the person "had significant or substantial or real control and supervision over [the] project." United States v. Walsh, 8 F.3d 659, 662 (9th Cir. 1993).

The evidence established that Dipentino "had significant or substantial or real control and supervision" over the asbestos-abatement project at the Landmark and that he knowingly violated the relevant work practice standards charged in the indictment. The government presented evidence that Dipentino was employed by Ab-Haz as the Landmark's "on-site representative during the term of work"; that he was present at the site on a daily basis; that he performed inspections of areas that the asbestos-removal contractor had allegedly abated; that he prepared and signed final inspection reports certifying that rooms in the Landmark were clear of asbestos-containing material; and that he had the power to stop the asbestos-removal contractor's work for improper performance.

The government also presented evidence that Dipentino was licensed by the State of Nevada as an asbestos-abatement supervisor and consultant; that in support of his applications for those licenses, Dipentino certified that he had completed courses and training in environmental law requirements; that Dipentino co-authored with Rafiq Ali the asbestos survey of the Landmark, which revealed that the Landmark contained 328,000 square feet of asbestos-containing acoustical ceiling spray, 1250 linear feet of asbestos-containing fireproofing material on structural components such as beams, as well as asbestos-containing pipe insulation and other materials found throughout the facility; and that piles of asbestos-containing debris were discovered by inspectors after the Landmark abatement job was certified as completed. Although Dipentino argues that the jury could not reasonably have concluded that he knew, simply by looking, that the debris left to dry on the floors of the Landmark contained asbestos, the district court properly rejected this argument in a post-judgment order stating: "Knowledge that a debris pile contains asbestos, however, can also result from knowing the source and nature of the material in the debris pile. Plainly it can be concluded that a person knows a debris pile contains asbestos if that person knew that the debris pile was created from material that the person knew to contain asbestos." In sum, there was sufficient evidence to convict Dipentino. . . .

DISCUSSION QUESTIONS

1. Ali was the president and sole proprietor of Ab-Haz. Dipentino was an industrial hygienist employed by Ab-Haz as the on-site inspector at the Landmark. As a "hired gun," in what sense was Dipentino an owner or operator? What did he own or operate? Was Ali also an owner or operator? Was Ab-Haz? Was Landmark?
2. Is it immediately apparent why liability would be limited to owners and operators?
3. Dipentino was convicted of knowingly violating the Clean Air Act. What must he know to be guilty? What evidence supports a finding that he had the requisite knowledge?

4. Although prosecutions under the Clean Air Act are few in number, they may not provide an accurate barometer of the level of criminal enforcement relating to air pollution. When reportable quantities of hazardous pollutants are released into the environment — including the air — the Comprehensive Environmental Response, Compensation, and Liability Act (CERCLA) imposes a duty to notify regulators. Failure to comply with the notification requirements provides an independent basis for criminal prosecution.

UNITED STATES V. PEARSON

274 F.3d 1225 (9th Cir. 2001)

RAWLINSON, Circuit Judge. . . .

Factual Background

In 1995, the Navy embarked on a project to remove asbestos-containing material, as part of an upgrade and renovation of the Central Heating Plant at the Whidbey Island Naval Air Station. The Navy contracted with Metcalf Grimm to carry out the renovations. Metcalf Grimm, in turn, subcontracted with Environmental Maintenance Service, Inc. ("EMS") to conduct both the asbestos abatement and the demolition work.

Work on the project took place in three phases, only the third of which is relevant to this appeal. The third phase of the project involved the removal of asbestos from the main part of the boiler house, including the removal of asbestos from the boilers and associated equipment. While the project was being performed, a containment structure constructed from plastic sheeting was placed around the area designated for asbestos removal. The purpose of the containment structure is to prevent the release of asbestos fibers to the outside air. This goal is further accomplished by using negative air machines to create lower pressure within the containment area, thereby preventing the release of air from the containment area. Inside the containment area, asbestos removal was performed by workers with respiratory protection.

Asbestos work practice regulations promulgated pursuant to the CAA require that asbestos be adequately wet before removal. The regulations also govern the proper handling of asbestos during its removal.

Around June 17, 1996, Pearson was hired by EMS, in part because he was a certified asbestos supervisor. Witnesses testified at trial that Pearson was their supervisor for the entire period he worked on the project. According to witnesses, Pearson performed functions such as correcting time cards, instructing others on how much water to use, and conducting daily meetings to give instructions to the crew.

Pearson was charged with two counts of knowingly causing the removal of asbestos-containing materials without complying with the applicable work practice standards, in violation of the CAA.

Each count carries a statutory maximum penalty of five years imprisonment.

During trial, testimony was presented that the work practice standards were not followed, at Pearson's direction. Less than the appropriate amount of water was used to wet the asbestos. Additionally, dry asbestos was "all over the place." Containment walls were pulled away from the ceiling, with work continuing. Some of the negative air machines were clogged, and one Navy inspector testified that she saw bags of asbestos outside the containment area, with asbestos material on the exterior surface of the bags.

Pearson's defense was that he was not involved at any time with the removal of asbestos, either as a supervisor or as a worker. He asserted that he was only involved with the demolition phase of the project. Pearson was acquitted of Count 1 and convicted of Count 2, with the jury specifically finding that Pearson acted in a supervisory capacity. . . .

Discussion

The CAA was passed to protect and enhance the quality of the Nation's air resources. To accomplish this goal, the CAA directs the Environmental Protection Agency ("EPA") to prescribe and enforce emission standards for the control of hazardous air pollutants. Where control is not feasible, the EPA is to promulgate work practice standards designed to achieve a reduction in emissions. Under the CAA, asbestos is a hazardous air pollutant. The EPA has determined that asbestos contamination cannot be feasibly addressed by promulgating emission standards. Thus, work practice standards were devised for the removal of asbestos-containing material during the demolition and renovation of affected buildings.

42 U.S.C. § 7413(c) provides criminal penalties for a limited class of individuals who fail to follow the CAA's regulations. Individuals who may be criminally liable include the "owner or operator of a demolition or renovation activity" that involves "regulated asbestos-containing material." The owner or operator of a demolition or renovation activity is defined in the

federal regulation as any person who "owns, leases, operates, controls or supervises" the facility being demolished or renovated, or supervises the demolition or renovation activity, or both. This definition parallels that found in 42 U.S.C. § 7412, where "owner or operator" for purposes of that section is defined as "any person who owns, leases, operates, controls, or supervises a stationary source." Persons excluded from the definition of "a person" are employees carrying out their normal activities, acting under orders from their employer, except in the case of knowing and willful violations.

I. The Jury Instructions . . .

A. Supervisor Liability

Pearson contends the district court failed to properly define the term "supervisor" as it is used in the CAA.[13] He alleges control and authority are hallmarks of the definition of the term "supervisor." Additionally, he posits that the definition of "supervisor" should include some degree of dominion. According to Pearson, the acts that would make someone a "supervisor" are responsibilities for reporting; applying for permits; designing the work plan; interfacing with multiple contractors and regulatory agencies; signing off on waste disposal manifests[;] designing and building the containment area; determining the number of negative air machines and the type of respiratory protective equipment; ordering and receiving supplies; and firing people for cause. In sum, Pearson contends he did not have enough authority to be liable as a "supervisor" under the CAA.

The district court defined the term "supervisor" as follows:

> In order to be a supervisor, it is not enough that the defendant was present at the job site or participated in asbestos abatement/removal activities, or even that he had the job title "supervisor." The defendant must have had significant and substantial control over the actual asbestos abatement work practices.

In determining the scope of authority necessary to meet the definition of "supervisor" under the CAA, we have held that "substantial control" is the

---

[13]The degree of authority necessary to be a "supervisor" is not defined in either 42 U.S.C. § 7412 or § 7413.

governing criterion. Under the CAA, a defendant need not possess ultimate, maximal, or preeminent control over the actual asbestos abatement work practices. Significant and substantial control means having the ability to direct the manner in which work is performed and the authority to correct problems. On any given asbestos abatement project there could be one or more supervisors. The term "supervisor" is not limited to the individual with the highest authority. Accordingly, we find the district court did not abuse its discretion in instructing the jury that Pearson had to have significant and substantial control to be liable as a supervisor.

Under this definition, Pearson was clearly a supervisor.

B. The Exclusion of Certain "[P]ersons" under § 7413(h)

An employee "who is carrying out his normal activities and who is acting under orders from the employer," cannot be liable under the CAA's criminal provisions as an operator, except in the case of knowing and willful violations. 42 U.S.C. § 7413 (h). Whether an individual found to be a supervisor under § 7412 can also be an employee under § 7413(h) is an issue of first impression. We find that an individual can be both. . . .

The CAA itself does not define the term employee. The government argues "the term [employee] cannot apply to those in supervisory positions that are responsible for giving orders to others." Pearson contends the jury could have plausibly found he was a supervisor, but still carried out his normal activities and acted under orders from his employer. . . .

[Since the statute does not explicitly exclude senior management personnel or corporate officers from the definition of "employees," a supervisor "who is carrying out his normal activities and is acting under orders from the employer" may be an employee who is exempt from criminal liability unless the violation is knowing and willful.]

While we agree that a supervisor under § 7412 may also be an employee, failure to give such an instruction in this case was not error because Pearson failed to meet his initial burden of establishing the provision was applicable in this case. Pearson contends his "status as a supervisor or non-supervisory employee who was just following orders is not an affirmative defense." He asserts that the Act defines affirmative defenses to criminal prosecution at 42

U.S.C. § 7413(c)(5)(C);[14] thus, the government had the burden of establishing he was not an excluded "person" for purposes of § 7413(h).

Pearson's contention is erroneous. When a statutory prohibition is broad and a defendant seeks to apply a narrow exception to the prohibition, it is more likely than not that the exception is an affirmative defense. Such a construction was clearly intended by Congress. The Conference Committee stated in unambiguous terms:

> These provisions create a new affirmative defense to criminal actions under certain parts of section [7413]. As such, once the government has satisfied its burden to prove a "knowing" violation in the traditional sense, the burden will shift to the person seeking to claim the defense and the defendant must prove that he was acting under his employer's orders or carrying out normal activities. Only after a defendant has satisfied that burden will the government be required to prove that the defendant's actions were willful.

Conference Report, 136 Cong. Rec. at § 16952.

Pearson did not raise or establish that he was an employee carrying out his normal activities and acting under orders from his employer. In fact, Pearson consistently maintained that he had nothing to do with asbestos clean-up. Accordingly, the district court properly excluded such an instruction. . . .

Affirmed.

DISCUSSION QUESTIONS

1. Pearson argued that the trial court incorrectly defined the term "supervisor." How did the court define it? How would Pearson's proposed definition differ? What facts would be important in determining whether Pearson was a supervisor?
2. Who, if anyone, in the following hypotheticals would qualify under the statute as an owner or operator of a demolition or renovation activity?
   a. Pearson holds the title of "estimator" at an asbestos removal contracting business. On Project A, he wrote the asbestos removal proposal for the general contractor on the renovation work. He also

---

[14]Like its counterpart in the Clean Water Act, section (c)(5)(C) provides that consent is an affirmative defense to a knowing endangerment charge. — ED.

signed the EPA Notice of Intent to Remove Asbestos, and met twice with the local Air Pollution Control Board to discuss asbestos removal issues.

   b.   Pearson is vice president of the company during Project B, and he signs the contract for the asbestos removal. At this time, Smith holds the title of estimator and prepares the asbestos removal proposal. Jones is the foreman on this project. Pearson is never on the job site while asbestos-removal work is being performed. Smith and Jones are usually present at the job site.

   c.   Pearson owns 80 percent of the company's stock. He is president of the company during Project C but is not involved in the day-to-day operational decisions about asbestos removal projects. He has never been present at a job site while asbestos removal work was being performed.

3.   What is the significance of the court's finding that someone like Pearson could serve in dual roles as a "supervisor" and an "employee" at the same time?

4.   Under ordinary principles of criminal law, the explanation that "I was just following orders from my superior" is not a defense. Why would Congress make an express exception to that rule in the CAA?

The CAA charges in *Dipentino* and *Pearson* focused primarily on failure to adequately wet down asbestos-containing materials before removing them, in violation of the asbestos work practice standard. While neither case involved allegations that the improper removal activities had actually released asbestos fibers into the air, one obvious reason for requiring the owner or operator to keep asbestos wet during demolition and renovation is to prevent its release.

But the asbestos NESHAP also provides that the owner or operator of a demolition site shall not discharge "visible emissions to the outside air" while collecting, processing, packaging, or transporting any asbestos-containing waste material coming from the source.[15] Visible emissions are emissions that are "visually detectable without the aid of instruments" and

---

[15] 40 C.F.R. § 61.150(a).

that come from the asbestos-containing material.[16] Outside air means air that is "outside buildings and structures."[17]

> **Illustration D:** A demolition contractor is hired to remove asbestos insulation from steam pipes located in an apartment building. The contractor decides to use a "dry removal" technique (i.e., scraping the insulation from the pipes without wetting them down) that emits a substantial quantity of asbestos dust inside the building. After all of the pipes are scraped clean, the contractor directs the workers to throw the insulation out the windows into a large dump truck. Large clouds of dust rise when the insulation hits the bed of the truck.

There are several obvious problems with this demolition operation. First, the contractor has not wet the insulation down before or after removing it, and the failure to take these required steps is manifested by emission of asbestos dust into the air. But even though the dust can be readily seen, emissions that are contained *inside* the building are not "visible emissions" within the meaning of this regulation. They must be emitted into the outside air. On the other hand, the dust that is created by throwing the insulation into the truck and hauling it away uncovered is a visible emission. The dust is visible without the aid of instruments and is emitted into the air outside the building.

THE CASE OF THE INVISIBLE "VISIBLE EMISSIONS"

Johnson bought an old hospital building for the purpose of renovating and developing it as commercial property. Before the sale, the owner told Johnson that a recent inspection revealed extensive amounts of asbestos in the building's fireproofing and that asbestos abatement could be very expensive. Johnson later discovered that no licensed asbestos-removal contractor would do the job for less than $400,000 — far more than he was willing or able to pay — so he skipped a few steps and hired his handyman to supervise the removal of the fireproofing material.

---

[16]40 C.F.R. § 61.141. This definition also applies to visually detectable emissions that come from asbestos milling, manufacturing, or fabricating operations.
    [17]*Id.*

The handyman then hired a dozen illegal aliens to perform the work, but he did not tell them the fireproofing contained asbestos. None of the workers had experience or training in asbestos removal work.

The workers scraped the fireproofing from the walls with putty knives and placed it in plastic bags that were left open inside the building. This dry removal operation released large amounts of asbestos dust inside the building.

Once the operation was under way, a local building inspector visited the site in response to a complaint that the renovation was being done without a city building permit. When the inspector arrived, he noticed the building was not sealed (windows and doors were left open and there was a gaping hole in one wall), saw airborne fireproofing dust inside, and observed the workers scraping the asbestos fireproofing from the walls. The inspector immediately issued a stop-work order and posted a large notice that work could not continue without a permit.

To overcome this unexpected hurdle, Johnson told the handyman to have the remainder of the work done at night. Thus, the remaining asbestos removal was completed over the next few weeks under cover of darkness. After all the fireproofing had been scraped off, Johnson told the handyman to have the workers hose down the inside of the building using an outside water line.

The handyman removed the cap from what he mistakenly believed was the water line (it was actually a pressurized gas line), and then got in his nearby van. When he started the engine, a spark from the ignition caused an explosion that blew a second large hole in the exterior wall of the building.

Local department of health officials who inspected the site after the explosion found fine, loose fireproofing dust all over the floors and shelves and nearly a hundred open and unsealed bags of fireproofing residue in the building.

In addition to charging Johnson with failure to notify the EPA of intent to remove asbestos and failure to adequately wet and contain asbestos dust, the prosecutor decided to charge him with violating the visible emission rule. If there are no eyewitnesses who can testify that they saw asbestos emissions outside the building, is that an insurmountable hurdle to proving a violation of the rule? Is there other evidence that could lead a jury to conclude — beyond a reasonable doubt — that a visible emission occurred?[18]

---

[18]*Cf.* United States v. Technic Servs., Inc., 314 F.3d 1031 (9th Cir. 2002); United States v. Ho, 311 F.3d 589 (5th Cir. 2002).

2. JURISDICTION

The Constitution grants Congress the power "to regulate Commerce . . . among the several States."[19] Although the Constitution does not directly confer the power to exercise general criminal jurisdiction, during the twentieth century the Commerce Clause became "the chief engine for federal regulatory and criminal statutes"[20] and the source of extraordinary expansion of federal criminal jurisdiction.[21]

Under modern Commerce Clause jurisprudence, the commerce power may be used to regulate: (1) use of the channels of interstate commerce; (2) instrumentalities of commerce, or people or things in commerce; and (3) intrastate activities that substantially affect interstate commerce.

We encountered the first category of regulation in Chapter 4, where the jurisdictional hook under the Clean Water Act was the discharge of pollutants into "navigable waters," which are clearly channels of interstate commerce. The second category of regulation — regulation or protection of instrumentalities of interstate commerce — might be exemplified by federal statutes forbidding destruction of an aircraft, carjacking, or carrying a gun on a commercial aircraft.

The third category — regulation of activities that substantially affect interstate commerce — enables Congress to reach activities that are purely intrastate. This kind of regulation can apply to an activity that, by itself, has a substantial effect on commerce or to activities that, in the *aggregate*, affect commerce.

Classic examples of this type of regulation come from NLRB v. Jones & Laughlin Steel Corp.[22] and Wickard v. Filburn.[23] In *Jones & Laughlin Steel*, the NLRB had accused the firm of engaging in unfair labor practices at one of its mills and ordered the company to cease and desist. Jones & Laughlin challenged the order, arguing that it was an impermissible attempt to regulate purely intrastate economic activity. The Supreme Court disagreed, finding that if labor problems at the mill caused its manufacturing operations to

---

[19]U.S. Const. Art. I, § 8, cl. 3.
[20]United States v. Ho, 311 F.3d 589, 596 (5th Cir. 2002).
[21]*See generally* Kathleen F. Brickey, *Criminal Mischief: The Federalization of American Criminal Law*, 46 HASTINGS L.J. 1135 (1995).
[22]301 U.S. 1 (1937).
[23]317 U.S. 111 (1942).

cease, that would have an "immediate" and potentially "catastrophic" effect on interstate commerce.[24]

In *Wickard*, the Court upheld a provision in the Agricultural Adjustment Act that limited the amount of wheat farmers could grow, even if the wheat was produced for home consumption. Production of excess wheat fulfilled the individual farmer's need for wheat that he would have otherwise purchased in the open market. Although the link between one farmer's intrastate production of excess wheat for home consumption would have only a negligible effect on commerce, if many farmers fulfilled their individual needs by producing excess wheat, their conduct — in the aggregate — would affect price and market conditions. Thus, this intrastate activity could be regulated under the commerce power.

The Supreme Court's most recent pronouncements on Commerce Clause jurisdiction are instructive. In United States v. Lopez,[25] the Court struck down a congressional exercise of Commerce Clause jurisdiction for the first time in more than 50 years, when it declared the Gun-Free School Zones Act unconstitutional. Since the Gun-Free School Zones Act did not purport to regulate the use of the channels of interstate commerce or to protect persons or things in commerce, the Court found that the Act could be upheld only if the statute regulated activities that "substantially affect" interstate commerce. The Court ruled that the Act did not pass muster under this test because gun possession in school zones is unrelated to commerce, because the Act contained no express jurisdictional element (e.g., that the gun or its possessor must have traveled in interstate commerce), and because there were no congressional findings supporting a nexus between the regulated conduct and commercial intercourse.

In a second Commerce Clause case decided just a week later, the Court put to rest speculation about whether the "substantial effects" test applies to all statutes that rely on commerce-based jurisdiction. United States v. Robertson[26] made clear that it does not. In *Robertson*, a unanimous Court held that to pass constitutional muster, a substantial effect on commerce need be shown only when the regulated activity is wholly intrastate. Thus, if the person or entity in question is *engaged in* commerce — e.g., Robertson operated a gold mine that purchased equipment from out-of-state suppliers

---

[24]*Jones & Laughlin Steel*, 301 U.S. at 41.
[25]514 U.S. 549 (1995).
[26]514 U.S. 669 (1995).

and hired out-of-state workers — no showing that the mining activity *affected* commerce is required.

Five years later, the Court reconsidered the constitutional boundaries of commerce-based jurisdiction in United States v. Morrison.[27] The Court in *Morrison* struck down a provision of the Violence Against Women Act that authorized victims of gender-motivated violence to bring private civil suits in federal court. Although the challenged provision contained no express jurisdictional element, Congress had relied on its Commerce Clause power as a basis for enacting the statute. In addition, Congress had accumulated a "mountain of data" detailing harmful effects that domestic violence has on interstate commerce, and — in contrast with the Gun-Free School Zones Act — included specific findings to that effect. The Court in *Morrison* nonetheless invalidated the statute, holding that Congress lacks power under the Commerce Clause to regulate "noneconomic, violent criminal conduct based solely on that conduct's aggregate effect on interstate commerce."[28] Although the Court stopped short of ruling that Commerce Clause jurisdiction can never be based on the aggregate effects of noneconomic activity on commerce, it emphasized that in all of the prior cases that had upheld aggregate effects jurisdiction, the statutes in question regulated economic activity.

Morrison's "economic/noneconomic" distinction is amorphous at best. Is a gang of street muggers who regularly prey on elderly victims and steal their valuables engaged in economic activity for purposes of Commerce Clause jurisdiction? Would the answer be clearer if the gang only targeted victims who were withdrawing money at automated teller machines? Would it be clearer still if the gang's principal activity was robbing commercial banks? It is likely that *Morrison*'s "economic/noneconomic" distinction will be difficult to apply and will require courts to indulge in ad hoc line-drawing exercises with little concrete guidance.[29]

---

[27]529 U.S. 598 (2000).

[28]*Id.* at 617.

[29]*Cf.* Solid Waste Agency v. Army Corps of Eng'rs, 531 U.S. 159 (2001) (holding, as a matter of statutory construction, that the Army Corps of Engineers exceeded its authority under the Clean Water Act by promulgating regulations that broadly asserted jurisdiction over all intrastate waters that provide habitat for migratory birds, and noting that the government's constitutional argument that the Corps has the power to regulate such waters would stretch Commerce Clause jurisdiction to its outer bounds). *Solid Waste Agency* and its progeny are considered in the discussion of wetlands regulation in Chapter 4.

In the meantime, despite the *Lopez* Court's insistence that intrastate conduct must have a "substantial" effect on interstate commerce before federal jurisdiction kicks in, the lower courts have continued to construe the substantial effects test to require only a minimal effect on commerce. Thus, for example, one who causes a party to cancel an $8,800 contract with an out-of-state company[30] or who makes seasonal use of a truck to transport, intrastate, a pecan harvest a short distance to an out-of-state broker[31] have been found to substantially affect interstate commerce.

DISCUSSION QUESTIONS

1. Suppose a coal-burning power plant on the campus of a private university spews high levels of sulphur dioxide into the air. The sulphur dioxide levels greatly exceed emission limits imposed under the CAA. Does the EPA have jurisdiction under the Commerce Clause to enforce the emission limits against the university? If so, under what theory or theories?

2. A local asbestos demolition contractor is hired to remove asbestos ceiling tiles from a podiatrist's office in a rural part of the state. Although there is no evidence that any asbestos particulates entered the ambient air, the contractor did not give the EPA prior written notice of the demolition, did not wet the asbestos tiles down before removing them, and did not keep the tiles adequately wet until they were placed in sealed containers for disposal. The contractor does not have any other employees.
   a. Does the Commerce Clause confer jurisdiction to enforce the CAA asbestos work practice standard against the contractor? If so, under what theory or theories? Are there additional factual questions you would like to explore before reaching your conclusion?
   b. Does it make any difference whether the contractor is licensed by the state?

3. Suppose the podiatrist leases her office from the building owner. The owner is not interested in renovating the office but gives the podiatrist permission to have the ceiling tiles removed at her own expense. After soliciting and receiving two bids, the podiatrist decides to remove the tiles herself. As in Question 2, the work is done in violation of the CAA

---

[30]Defalco v. Bernas, 244 F.3d 286 (2d Cir. 2001).
[31]United States v. Grassie, 237 F.3d 1199 (10th Cir. 2001).

asbestos work practice standard. Does the Commerce Clause confer jurisdiction to enforce the standard against her?

4. Suppose the asbestos demolition described in Question 2 had occurred with the following variations on the theme. The contractor's business was located in an urban area, the contractor had 20 permanent employees, and the building under renovation was a large hospital. Although the same CAA violations occurred, there was still no evidence that asbestos dust was released from the hospital into the ambient air. Would this affect your analysis of Commerce Clause jurisdiction?

3. PARALLEL STATE AND FEDERAL ENFORCEMENT

Although the federal government has taken the lead in environmental regulation, state and local governments often have their own parallel pollution control tools. While it is not uncommon for state and local authorities to target problems that may not be on the federal enforcers' radar screens, federal and state enforcement efforts occasionally overlap one another.

UNITED STATES V. LOUISVILLE EDIBLE OIL PRODUCTS, INC.

926 F.2d 584 (6th Cir.), cert. denied, 502 U.S. 859 (1991)

MARTIN, Jr., Circuit Judge.

We have before us the denial of a motion to dismiss a nine count indictment charging asbestos related violations of the Clean Air Act and the Comprehensive Environmental Response Compensation and Liability Act. Defendants claim this federal prosecution is barred by the double jeopardy clause of the fifth amendment because previous fines levied by a local environmental enforcement agency were, in effect, federal punitive measures carried out through a state agency to regulate the same conduct. Defendants also argue that prosecution under both the Clean Air Act and the Comprehensive Environmental Act violates the double jeopardy clause by subjecting them to multiple prosecution for the same conduct. Because the actions taken by the federal and state government are those of independent sovereigns, and because the Clean Air Act and the Comprehensive Environmental Act encompass separate offenses requiring differing elements of proof, we affirm the judgment of the district court that double jeopardy has not attached.

Louisville Edible Oils Products is a Kentucky corporation engaged in the business of producing edible oils such as salad oil. A federal indictment charges that Louisville Edible owned two facilities in Louisville, one at 2500 South Seventh Street and the other at 1303 South Shelby Street, from which it knowingly emitted friable asbestos, an air pollutant, and demolished or renovated a stationary asbestos source in violation of the Clean Air Act and the Comprehensive Environmental Act. These actions were allegedly carried out in whole or in part by Louisville Edible and its co-defendants: Presidential, Inc., an Indiana corporation affiliated with Louisville Edible operating as its construction and demolition unit, [and three executives who worked for one or both of the corporations].

The local environmental enforcement agency, the Jefferson County Air Pollution Control District, had repeatedly fined Louisville Edible for its disregard of state environmental legislation. Beginning in April of 1977, the Air Pollution Board fined Louisville Edible $25,000 for the release of asbestos from its Seventh Street facility. Louisville Edible was cited on several other occasions and was fined an additional $24,000 in July of 1988 for an illegal renovation of the asbestos containing facility at Shelby Street. Another $125,000 was assessed against Louisville Edible in July of 1989 for asbestos violations at both facilities. These fines were levied only against Louisville Edible.

[The defendants argued that since the Jefferson County Air Pollution Control District had already punished them for the asbestos violations at the Seventh Street and Shelby Street facilities, the double jeopardy clause barred the federal government from prosecuting them again for the same offenses.]

The dual sovereignty doctrine holds that the double jeopardy clause "does not apply to suits by separate sovereigns, even if both are criminal suits for the same offense." United States v. A Parcel of Land, Etc., 884 F.2d 41, 43 (1st Cir. 1989). The doctrine is based on the premise that

> [w]e have here two sovereignties, deriving power from different sources, capable of dealing with the same subject matter within the same territory. . . . Each government in determining what shall be an offense against its peace and dignity is exercising its own sovereignty, not that of the other.
>
> It follows that an act denounced as a crime by both national and state sovereignties is an offense against the peace and dignity of both and may be punished by each.

United States v. Lanza, 260 U.S. 377, 382 (1922). Here the state prosecution was directed by the Air Pollution Board, which derives its jurisdiction from state law; as a state actor the Air Pollution Board is a "separate sovereign[ ] with respect to the Federal Government because each state's power to prosecute is derived from its own 'inherent sovereignty,' not from the federal government." Heath v. Alabama, 474 U.S. 82, 88 (1985). Accordingly, the Jefferson County Air Pollution Board and the United States, through the Environmental Protection Agency, may each pursue claims against Louisville Edible for the same conduct without subjecting the defendant to double jeopardy.

Louisville Edible argues that the dual sovereignty doctrine does not apply in this case because the Air Pollution Board and the United States Environmental Protection Agency were not acting as separate entities; but rather, that the Jefferson County Board was acting as a "tool" for federal enforcement. *See, e.g.*, Bartkus v. Illinois, 359 U.S. 121 (1959) (discussing exception to dual sovereignty doctrine where state prosecution is merely a "cover and tool of federal authorities"). Louisville Edible claims that correspondence between the Chief of Air Compliance of Region IV of the Environmental Protection Agency, and the Secretary-Treasurer of the Air Pollution Control District for Jefferson County, establishes that the local agency was acting at the direction of the Environmental Protection Agency in imposing civil fines.

We agree with the district court that a review of these documents does not suggest that the Jefferson County Air Pollution Board was acting as a conduit for federal government enforcement. Indeed, these documents establish that the Board rejected a number of the Environmental Protection Agency's recommendations, including a request to defer prosecution pending Agency action. Rather than acting as a "tool," the Board engaged in inter-sovereign dialogue before pursuing its own prosecution. *See Bartkus*, 359 U.S. at 123 (discussing benefits of federal-state cooperation in law enforcement).

The Environmental Protection Agency has no statutory authority to control the actions of the local board. Indeed, the record demonstrates that the Jefferson County Board often conflicted with the Environmental Protection Agency over the way to properly address Louisville Edible's actions, before the Environmental Protection Agency determined to initiate its own claim. . . .

For the foregoing reasons, the judgment of the district court is affirmed.

DISCUSSION QUESTIONS

1. The dual sovereignty doctrine allows a defendant to be punished twice for the same conduct. What rationale supports this rule? Does the dual sovereignty doctrine unfairly give the government two bites at the apple?
2. What is the significance of the court's finding that the Jefferson County Air Pollution Control Board and the EPA sometimes disagreed on how to address Louisville Edible Oil's asbestos removal violations? Would it have made a difference if the Jefferson County Board had acquiesced in the EPA's request that it defer pursuing its own prosecution pending EPA action?

4. KNOWING VIOLATIONS

As is true under the Clean Water Act, CAA violations typically require proof that the accused acted knowingly. Consistent with general principles of criminal law, a knowing violation requires proof that the actor had knowledge of the conduct elements of the crime, but knowledge of illegality is not required. Thus, for example, to be liable for violating the asbestos work practice standard, a contractor would need to know the material being removed contained asbestos, but would not need to be aware of the specific requirements imposed by the work practice rule (e.g., the requirement that asbestos-containing materials be adequately wet down before removal).

But let's consider one component of the asbestos rules that we haven't encountered before. The regulations impose criminal penalties on any person who knowingly fails to give the EPA advance notice of intent to remove asbestos-containing materials.

> **Illustration E:** An art gallery hires a general contractor to extensively renovate the second floor. The renovation plans include removing and replacing old ceiling tiles and wallboard. The gallery owner does not know the ceiling and wall materials contain asbestos. Although the general contractor discovers the asbestos during his initial inspection, he is not a licensed asbestos remover and is unaware of the CAA regulatory requirements for asbestos demolition and renovation. The contractor nonetheless removes the asbestos-containing material without giving the EPA written notice of his intent to do so. Have either the gallery owner or the contractor violated the CAA work practice standard requiring advance written notice?

The gallery owner seems to be off the hook. Assuming the contractor did not tell the owner that his inspection had revealed the presence of asbestos, the owner does not have knowledge of the underlying facts that trigger the notice requirement. And absent factual knowledge, the owner cannot knowingly violate the requirement.

But the contractor is differently situated. Although he has no expertise in the intricacies of the CAA's asbestos regulatory scheme, he learned that the material he was hired to remove contained asbestos. Did he knowingly violate the notification requirement?

This raises an interesting question. Is it possible to knowingly fail to notify the EPA if one is unaware of the notice requirement? What level of knowledge is required in this circumstance?

Although case law on this point under the CAA is scarce,[32] it is consistent with the maxim that ignorance of the law is no excuse. Factual knowledge — i.e., knowledge of the facts that constitute the offense — rather than knowledge of the law is required. That point carries special weight where, as here, the law regulates hazardous materials. As the Supreme Court reasoned in United States v. International Minerals & Chemical Corp.,[33] where "dangerous or deleterious devices or products or obnoxious waste materials are involved, the probability of regulation is so great that anyone who is aware that he is in possession of them or dealing with them must be presumed to be aware of the regulation."[34] Asbestos clearly fits in this category of dangerous substances that are highly regulated, so the presumption of awareness applies.

THE CASE OF THE AMISH WEATHERVANE SHOP

Robert owns and manages a small shop that produces handcrafted weathervanes. When demand for these high-quality products began to rise, Robert decided to enlarge the workshop space so he could bring in additional craftsmen. The renovation required tearing down the rear wall of the shop to expand the work space beyond the existing building. As Robert was well aware, the wall contained asbestos insulation.

---

[32]United States v. Ho, 311 F.3d 589 (5th Cir. 2002), appears to be a case of first impression interpreting the knowledge requirement in the context of CAA failure to notify offenses.

[33]402 U.S. 558 (1971).

[34]Id. at 565.

When he was ready to begin the renovation, Robert hired some day workers to tear down the wall and haul the debris away. Neither Robert nor the workers notified the EPA of their intent to remove asbestos-containing material. Not long after the project was complete, Robert was charged with knowingly failing to give the required notice.

Robert told his lawyer that he didn't think he could be convicted because he did not know about the notification requirement and was acting in good faith. The lawyer then gave Robert the bad news, explaining the *International Minerals* case and its presumption of awareness of regulation where the regulated material is dangerous. The lawyer also told him about another case, United States v. Weintraub,[35] which stated that a knowing violation of the asbestos work practice standards does not require proof of knowledge of illegality because "no one can reasonably claim surprise that asbestos is regulated and that some form of liability is possible for violating those regulations."[36]

Robert replied that the presumption of awareness should not apply to him because he lives in an insular Amish religious community in which the dangers of asbestos are not a matter of common knowledge or interest and where members of the community are not influenced by outside media. Thus, he argued, members of his community are not the "reasonable" people the *Weintraub* court had in mind and, unlike their more worldly counterparts, they do not appreciate the hazards of asbestos.

Should Robert's good faith defense prevail?[37] Is the presumption of awareness that the *International Minerals* Court recognized rebuttable?

D. KNOWING ENDANGERMENT

Like the Clean Water Act, the CAA makes knowing endangerment a crime. The CAA provision proscribes knowingly releasing a hazardous pollutant or extremely hazardous substance into the ambient air if the actor knows his conduct places another person in imminent danger of death or serious bodily injury. The CWA and CAA provide identical definitions of the term "serious bodily injury" — an injury that involves a "substantial risk of death, unconsciousness, extreme physical pain, protracted and obvious

---

[35]273 F.3d 139 (2d Cir. 2001).
[36]*Id.* at 151.
[37]*Cf.* United States v. Rubenstein, 403 F.3d 93 (2d Cir. 2005).

disfigurement, or protracted loss or impairment of the function of a bodily member, organ, or mental faculty."[38]

Under both endangerment statutes, the standard for determining whether the defendant committed a knowing violation is whether he had "actual awareness" or "actual belief" that the conduct posed an imminent risk of death or serious bodily injury to another. Although the actual awareness or belief standard might seem to preclude the use of willful blindness as a proxy for knowledge, the statute explicitly provides that circumstantial evidence — "including evidence that the defendant took affirmative steps to be shielded from relevant information"[39] — may be used to prove the defendant possessed actual knowledge.

Both endangerment statutes also recognize identical affirmative defenses. They both require proof that: (1) the person who was endangered by the violation freely consented to the conduct; (2) the danger and the conduct were "reasonably foreseeable hazards" of an occupation, business, or profession, or of medical treatment or medical or scientific experimentation that conforms to professionally approved methods; and (3) the person endangered was informed of the risks before giving consent.[40] The defendant has the burden of proving consent by a preponderance of the evidence.

1. THE W.R. GRACE PROSECUTION

W.R. Grace & Co. is a global supplier of a broad array of industrial products and services, including chemicals and materials for commercial and residential construction such as attic insulation (marketed as "Zonolite Attic Insulation") and fireproofing products (marketed as "Monokote").[41] Both of these products contain vermiculite, a mineral that greatly expands when processed at high temperatures. Vermiculite is also an ingredient used in masonry fill and is used as an additive in potting soils and lawn care products.

In February 2005, Grace and seven of its officers and executives were indicted for conspiracy, fraud, obstruction of justice, and knowing

---

[38]42 U.S.C. § 7413(c)(5)(A).
[39]42 U.S.C. § 7413(c)(5)(B).
[40]42 U.S.C. § 7413(c)(5)(C).
[41]Grace has more than 6,000 employees in nearly 40 countries and annual sales of about $2 billion.

endangerment under the CAA in connection with its mining and production of vermiculite.[42]

a. Background

The saga begins in 1963, when W.R. Grace acquired the Zonolite Company, which mined and processed vermiculite in Libby, Montana. For nearly 30 years, Grace operated 3 facilities in Libby: the Libby Mine, which was the source of vermiculite ore; a Screening Plant, where Grace processed the ore; and a facility known as the Export Plant, where processed vermiculite was stockpiled and held for shipment to other Grace facilities and to industrial customers throughout the country. Grace disposed of mining waste and milling tailings (a byproduct of the milling process) at the Libby Mine.

The vermiculite deposits at the Libby Mine were contaminated with a highly toxic form of asbestos called "tremolite," and during the early years after Grace took it over, the Libby Mine spewed as many as 5,000 pounds of asbestos fibers a day into the air. Obeying the law of gravity, the detritis drifted back to earth, of course, blanketing Libby and its neighboring communities in a shroud of asbestos-contaminated dust. Exposure to airborne asbestos can cause serious, often fatal diseases, including asbestosis (a debilitating lung disease), and cancer.

Those who worked at the mine would be literally coated with dust containing asbestos fibers by the end of the day. And because Grace did not require the miners and other workers to wear respirators and coveralls or to shower and change clothes before they left, when the miners went home, the asbestos went home with them.

Pulitzer Prize winning journalists Andrew Schneider and David McCumber provide a compelling chronicle of Les Skramstad, who worked for the mine for two years and was dying from asbestosis.[43] Although Skramstad was initially hired at the mine for a temporary construction job, his first day on the job was beyond his wildest expectations.

---

[42]The trial is tentatively scheduled to begin sometime between September 2007 and February 2008, pending resolution of the government's appeal of several pre-trial rulings.
We will consider the conspiracy, fraud, and obstruction of justice charges in Chapter 8.
[43]ANDREW SCHNEIDER & DAVID MCCUMBER, AN AIR THAT KILLS (2004).

ANDREW SCHNEIDER & DAVID MCCUMBER, AN AIR THAT KILLS

66-68 (2004)

Les would never forget that first ride up to the mine. He had no idea what to expect, and when he arrived, he couldn't believe his eyes. Everything — ground, trucks, buildings, people — was brownish-gray in color, covered with fine dust. It was like stepping into a sepia-tone photograph. Everything he could see but himself was the same color, and it wouldn't be long before he matched exactly.

When he reported to the construction office, the boss said, "Have you ever been up here at the mine, or in the mill?"

"No."

"Well, you're going to have some fun today. We're going to start you over at the dry mill, as a sweeper."

"I thought I was supposed to be on construction."

"Don't worry, we don't pay any attention to that. You start as a sweeper. You need to go over to the warehouse and get yourself a respirator, then head over to the dry mill."

So, just as [his friend] Perley Vatland had done five years earlier, Les started his Zonolite career sweeping out the mill. That first day, he walked over to the warehouse and got his respirator. "Wear it if you can," he was told. He didn't exactly know what that meant, but he just fitted it together and put it on. Somebody directed him to the manlift — a foot-wide conveyor belt with steps on it — and told him to ride it to the top of the mill, seven floors up. "Start up there at the top and just sweep it all down," he was told.

When he got off at the top level, it was obvious what he had to do. The dust was more than a foot deep in places. Each floor had shovels and brooms, so Les set to with determination. But after about 15 minutes, his respirator was clogged with dust and he couldn't breathe.

He rode the lift down to the bottom, saw a couple of workers, and asked, "How do you clean these things out?"

"Oh, just use an air hose and blow them out, or you can wash them out with water," he was told. So he blew the fine, feathery dust out of his respirator, went back up and kept working.

By the time he'd finished one floor he'd cleaned his mask out four times. And of course the second-highest floor was twice as deep, because it held all the dust he'd swept down from above. By the time he got the second level done it was time for lunch. Les tried to clean as much of the dust from his head and face as he could. He found that it wasn't easy — the dust would cling to his skin. He looked around, and noticed respirators hanging on hooks all around the mill, and nobody else seemed to be wearing one.

When he went into the lunchroom, a couple of the supervisors were there, Tom DeShazer and Pete Watts, and a couple of the other miners.

"How do you like that dust?" one of them asked.

"That's the damnedest stuff I've ever seen in my life," Les responded with feeling, and the miners all laughed as though he'd told the funniest joke you could imagine.

"You don't worry about that dust," one of the supervisors said. "It's a nuisance, but there's nothing in it that will hurt you. You'll get used to it."

Les ate his lunch and went back to work.

He tried washing his respirator out, and that proved to be a big mistake. He'd tried to blow the moisture out of it, but what remained made it clog up faster than ever. So eventually his found its way to a hook like all the rest.

Each floor was worse than the last. Les's battle with the never-ending blizzard of dust was truly mythical in proportion, like Hercules cleaning the Augean stables. People would normally think of dust being light, but in such quantity it is surprisingly heavy. Finally he got the place swept down to the basement, where there was a waste conveyor that took the accumulation to the tailing pile. Of course, every time he moved the stuff, he sent more dust into the air.

When he got on the bus to ride back to town that night, he was covered in dust, just like everybody else. His hair was coated, his ears and nose were plugged up. His throat felt like sandpaper. The dust clogged his mouth and nose with what felt like thick brown syrup.

He cleaned up the best he could when he got home, and he didn't say much to Norita about his battle with the dust. He knew she wasn't very happy about his taking the job in the first place, and he didn't want her to be concerned.

He looked at his lovely pregnant wife, and hugged [his kids], and smiled. Its okay, he thought to himself. *I'll bet there's always something that needs doing up there. Sooner or later they'll move me to something else. And if I do a really good job at this, maybe they'll keep me.*

After working in various capacities at the mine, Skramstad applied for a job at the expansion plant, where raw vermiculite ore was heated to 2,000 degrees and transformed into a featherweight substance that was up to twenty times larger than the original ore. There was also an experimental lab at the expansion plant where Grace developed new commercial uses for Zonolite and the mine's major byproduct — tremolite asbestos. Employees performed occasionally bizarre experiments in the quest for marketable uses for Zonolite and tremolite, including baking loaves of bread whose ingredients included animal-feed mixtures that contained Zonolite. Les Skramstad's experience is once again telling.

ANDREW SCHNEIDER & DAVID McCUMBER, AN AIR THAT KILLS

73-75 (2004)

The first time Les Skramstad ever heard the word "asbestos" was in 1960.

"I want you to go up to the mine and bring back a pickup load of asbestos," Dave Robinson said that day.

"What's that?" Les asked.

"Oh, you know, it's that grayish-white stuff that's around in the rock. That's called asbestos."

So Les and Bob Cohenour got picks and shovels and drove up to the mine in a short-box Dodge pickup. They ran into Thorny, who asked, "What are you fellows after?"

"We're supposed to get a load of asbestos."

"Oh, we got lots of that," he said. "Follow me."

So they drove up to one of the levels where the miners were working, and Thorny showed them how the asbestos lay across the other rock, in seams. He pointed to one. "That's probably the easiest to get right there, but if you need more of it, just let me know. It's everywhere up here."

So Les backed the pickup up to that seam. It wasn't hard shoveling — it was soft, almost soapy in consistency. It didn't take them long to get a load and head back to town with it. They didn't bother to cover the load with a tarp — why would they?

When they got back to the plant, they put down a sheet of Kraft paper, maybe 12 feet square, and dumped the load on it. They spread it out shallow so it would dry.

"Now, this has got to be plumb dry and pure," Robinson said. "You've got to get everything else out of it. No rocks, no vermiculite, no nothing."

It took them about two weeks of work. They found they couldn't put fans on it, because when it dried it would turn to dust and blow away. They put electric heaters around it, and got down on their hands and knees, right over it, picking rocks out of it.

The asbestos got very fluffy as it dried, and they were gradually getting it "clean." But they realized that in order to do so more efficiently, they had to come up with some method other than picking through it by hand. So they built a jig that would vibrate the stuff and shake out the heavier impurities. They had to run each batch through time and time again, but finally they got down to pure asbestos. They put it in 30-gallon garbage cans and closed them tight, so a draft wouldn't blow through and take it away.

Les remembers workers from the mine coming in and razzing him and Bob about their little project — particularly a friend, Don Riley, who would say, "You still playing with that stuff?" They'd take the tops off the cans and stick their arms in, and they'd go right through the stuff, clear to the bottom, and when they drew their arms out they'd look like they had feathers.

Les and Bob would brush them off and say, "Damn it, don't do that, we're trying to save that stuff." Finally, they took small sacks, like cement sacks, filled them and sewed them shut. That first time, they produced maybe 20 sacks.

Bob and Les were relieved when they got done with that load, because it was a nasty job. Of course, nobody had said anything to them about any danger, so they didn't wear respirators while they were cleaning the stuff, trying to get 100-percent obscenely pure tremolite asbestos.

But pretty soon, Robinson came back and said, "Go up and get another load of that asbestos. We've got so much of it up there, we've got to find a use for it. There's enough of it to last a hundred years."

Of course, Bob and Les were excited by that idea, because if they found a use for the asbestos, it could mean jobs for them and other men for a long time. So back they went, and Thorny said, "You boys after another load of asbestos? Well, you know where it is." They spent a full month shoveling and cleaning and packing the asbestos.

Robinson was an engineer of some sort, and he was full of ideas. He had one that Les actually thought made a lot of sense. Robinson wanted to develop a fire retardant that firefighters could take to a fire and spray on it, along with the water, and the asbestos and vermiculite would slow the fire down much more than just straight water. So they took No. 4 ore, very fine stuff, and mixed it into a slurry and experimented with pumping it through a two-inch fire hose with a nozzle on it.

Here is Les Skramstad's worst nightmare, even worse than the month of inhaling the pure asbestos that probably sealed his own fate:

"We demonstrated this on several different occasions to people who came in from somewhere. I thought it could be the ideal product. This stuff didn't weigh anything, and it could be taken to a fire easily. So we were gung ho on it, and again we thought anything that was good for the company was good for our jobs. So we worked really hard on this."

He pauses for a moment. He can't tell the rest of it without choking up. It's easy to say he shouldn't have any guilt, this kind, smiling man who loves music, this principled man who would never hurt anyone if he could help it, who was just doing the best he could for his family. It's easy to say that he was following orders, that he had no idea what the stuff could do.

But the guilt is in his eyes, the way they glisten, and in his voice as it cracks:

"And oh, Jesus, what I did was I sprayed that stuff all over near that building, over by the ball fields, on the trees and the brush to see how it would stick. Those ball fields, where everybody's kids played.

"Where my kids played."

Thus, it is clear that Libby residents who did not have relatives working at the mine were exposed to asbestos in countless harmful ways. But we've only begun to scratch the surface.

ANDREW SCHNEIDER & DAVID MCCUMBER, AN AIR THAT KILLS

85-87 (2004)

Before they sent Les to dig a truckload of asbestos, before they made him "clean" it on his hands and knees, they knew. Before they hired him in 1959 to sweep the dust that gathered in the windows on each floor of the dry mill, they knew. Probably, even before they took Perley Vatland on in 1954 to sweep the same mill, they knew.

* * *

On August 8, 1956, Benjamin Wake, a young industrial-hygiene engineer for the state Health Department's Division of Disease Control, arrived at the mine for its first inspection since 1944. . . .

For two days . . . Wake gathered samples of dust from everywhere. . . . He used vacuum pumps to pull air into filters so the level of dust the workers were breathing could be measured, but the dust was so thick it often clogged the filters.

"The asbestos in the air is of considerable toxicity," Wake wrote in his report, adding that he found "enormous quantities of dust and inoperable exhaust systems." The company told him that the asbestos content in the dust ranged from 8 to 21 percent. There is no evidence, however, that the state determined for itself how much asbestos was in the dust.

Wake cited "poor policy in matters of maintenance and operation of this plant," and submitted a four-page list of repairs to ventilating systems, conveyors and other work areas that he considered mandatory to protect workers. He warned that "inhalation of asbestos dust must be expected sooner or later to produce pulmonary fibrosis . . . pulmonary asbestosis, once established, is a progressive disease with a bad prognosis."

Wake returned two and a half years later, in late 1958, and again in 1960. Both times, he found that little had been done to protect workers. In 1962, the workforce had been increased to about 150 when he returned for his fourth inspection in six years. After spending three more days at the plant, he found that the dry mill was again "extremely dusty and in the need of repair and modification to reduce dust to safe levels." He found the concentration of dust, "especially asbestos," substantially higher than in earlier inspections, and for the fourth time he submitted a long list of changes needed to protect workers. Again, it warned of the dangers of asbestos.

Wake's reports were largely ignored. They were stamped "confidential" and produced no discernable safety improvements. And none of this information was shared with the miners.

But what Grace knew went far beyond hypothetical "what if" scenarios. A 1959 chest x-ray program for the mine workers revealed that 48 of the 130 workers screened had lung abnormalities. Eight already had asbestosis.[44] Ten years later, a confidential study of the Libby miners concluded that:

> although 17 percent of our 1 to 5 years' service group have or are suspect of lung disease, there is a marked rise (45 percent) beginning with the 11th year of service, climbing to 92 percent in the 21 to 25 years' service group. This suggests that chances of getting lung disease increase as years of exposure increase.[45]

A 1962 internal memo from the company's safety chief even suggested that 32 workers whose x-rays showed serious signs of disease should be reassigned to work at less dirty jobs. "If we minimize their exposure to dust . . . chances are we may be able to keep them on the job until they retire, thus precluding the high cost of total disability."[46]

Yet despite management's documented knowledge of serious health risks and existing diseases, Grace withheld critical information from its workers — often with the connivance of local doctors who were pressured to "stop making waves."[47] Simply put, Grace and its predecessor, Zonolite, did everything they could to conceal the awful truth.

Further compounding the Libby tragedy, Grace donated asbestos-contaminated materials for a variety of uses throughout the community,

---

[44]*Id.* at 89.
[45]*Id.* at 93.
[46]*Id.* at 92.
[47]*Id.* at 123.

including the foundation for an outdoor ice skating rink at a local elementary school and the surface for running tracks at the junior and senior high schools. Grace also leased some of its contaminated properties for use as baseball fields and commercial buildings, all the while concealing its knowledge of the enormous risk of harm to the community.

As time went by, Grace decided to sell off its contaminated properties to minimize its liability. In 1990, the 3M Company expressed interest in buying the Libby Mine, but later wrote a letter to Grace indicating that it had decided against buying it because of "potential environmental problems."[48] Phelps Dodge Mining Company similarly declined to buy the property, attributing the decision primarily to "the presence of so much asbestos."[49]

This newfound lack of marketability prompted yet another change in strategy.

> For the same reasons that 3M would not buy the mine, I doubt that any other large corporation will come forward with an offer to buy the entire property. If Grace is going to be able to transfer all of the future responsibilities and liabilities to someone else, they are going to have to be willing to sell to some small organization.[50]

Thus, with no large buyers in sight, Grace simply gave much of the contaminated real estate to the City of Libby and sold what property it could, including land on which the buyers established their personal residence and started a commercial nursery. And so it went on down the line.

b. Indictment

The indictment charged Grace and others with conspiring to expose Libby residents to imminent danger of death or serious bodily harm by releasing asbestos into the ambient air, and to obstruct government agencies' enforcement of laws protecting public health and the environment. The indictment charged that the defendants pursued these objectives to enrich themselves, to increase corporate profits, and to avoid liability. It also identified the acts of giving contaminated vermiculite to the Libby

---

[48]Indictment, United States v. W.R. Grace, CR 05-07-M-DWM (indictment filed in United States District Court for the District of Montana) ¶ 152 (Feb. 7, 2005) (on file with the author).

[49]*Id.* at ¶ 153.

[50]*Id.* at ¶ 155.

community, placing mill tailings at Libby Schools, and the property transactions described above as overt acts in furtherance of the conspiracy.

Liability had to be a major concern for Grace because it was widely known at the time that breathing asbestos can cause debilitating diseases and death, and the harm to the Libby community from long term and widespread exposure to tremolite is incalculable.

UNITED STATES V. W.R. GRACE

INDICTMENT

CR 05-07-M-DWM (D. Mont. 2005)

* * *

B. Asbestos Related Diseases

47. Modern science has not established a safe level for asbestos exposure for which there is no increased risk of disease.

48. Airborne exposure to tremolite asbestos by breathing into human lungs causes scarring of the lung tissues and can cause the disease known as "asbestosis."

49. Asbestosis is a progressive disease that destroys the human lung's ability to absorb oxygen, and in severe cases, results in severe disability or death.

50. The rate of asbestosis mortality of the Libby population is 40 to 80 times higher than expected when compared to rates for Montana and the United States.

51. Airborne exposure to tremolite asbestos causes lung cancer in humans.

52. The rate of lung cancer mortality of the Libby population is approximately 30 percent higher than expected when compared to rates for Montana and the United States.

53. Airborne exposure to tremolite asbestos can cause an aggressive and fatal form of cancer in humans known as "mesothelioma." This form of cancer is extremely rare, resulting in no more than 9 cases per 1 million individuals in the United States general population, and is uniquely associated with exposure to asbestos. This form of cancer is not related to cigarette smoking.

54. Over twenty cases of mesothelioma have been identified to date among persons who lived or worked in Libby. This is a significant finding for this small population of approximately 8,000 people.

55. Airborne exposure to tremolite asbestos can cause the disease of pleural fibrosis, which is scarring of the pleural tissues surrounding the lungs. Pleural fibrosis can result in impaired functioning of the lungs, and in more severe cases, disability and death. The development and progression of pleural fibrosis is not related to cigarette smoking.

56. Pleural fibrosis is associated with a greater risk of developing mesothelioma and lung cancer.

57. To date, approximately 1,200 residents of the Libby, Montana area have been identified as having asbestos related pleural abnormalities as a result of being exposed to tremolite asbestos produced by W.R. GRACE at the Libby Mine. Of this group, 70 percent are not former employees at the Libby Mine. Individuals have been identified with asbestos related disease whose only exposure to asbestos has been through asbestos containing vermiculite from the Libby Mine located throughout the community.

58. Asbestos related diseases have a latency period ranging from 3 to 40 years or more. That is, a person exposed to asbestos by breathing will not manifest symptoms of disease until 3 to 40 or more years after exposure.

59. Airborne exposure to tremolite asbestos can cause bloody pleural effusions. A bloody pleural effusion is a pathological collection of bloody fluid between the pleural lining and the lung. They are considered to be a possible manifestation of early stages of mesothelioma.

The indictment alleges the defendants knew the vermiculite was contaminated with tremolite asbestos, knew the contaminated vermiculite released tremolite fibers into the air, knew how hazardous tremolite was to human health, concealed the dangers of being exposed to tremolite, and misled the government by withholding information about the contamination to forestall the EPA from recognizing and declaring a public health emergency.

UNITED STATES V. **W.R. GRACE**
INDICTMENT

CR 05-07-M-DWM (D. Mont. 2005)

* * *

Manner and Means of the Conspiracy

The following manner and means, among others, were used by the defendants to effectuate and perpetuate the conspiracy set forth above:

74. It was part of the conspiracy that the defendants obtained knowledge of the hazardous nature of the tremolite asbestos contaminated vermiculite through various means, including, but not limited to: scientific testing and analysis, including animal studies; epidemiological studies of employees; employee medical screening and examinations; employee medical record reviews; collection and evaluation of a deceased employee's lung tissue; review of employee death certificates; conducting employee morbidity and mortality studies; employee autopsy reviews; review of medical and scientific literature; reviewing reports from insurance carriers; and reviewing employee worker[s'] compensation claims.

75. It was part of the conspiracy that the defendants obtained knowledge of the propensity of tremolite asbestos contaminated vermiculite, when disturbed, to release fibers into the ambient air (also known as "friability") through various means, including, but not limited to: product testing, including attic simulation and vermiculite materials handling tests ("drop tests"); and air and bulk sampling at the Libby Mine and other defendant W.R. GRACE facilities in and around Libby, Montana, at defendant W.R. GRACE owned and licensed expansion plants, at the facilities of customers using vermiculite materials, and at the Libby High School track.

76. It was part of the conspiracy that the defendants concealed the full extent of their knowledge of the hazardous nature and friability of the tremolite asbestos contaminated vermiculite from employees of defendant W.R. GRACE Libby vermiculite mining and processing operations; families of employees of defendant W.R. GRACE Libby vermiculite mining and processing operations; industrial customers of defendant W.R. GRACE Libby vermiculite products; employees of industrial customers of defendant W.R. GRACE Libby vermiculite products; residents of Libby, Montana and surrounding communities in Lincoln County, Montana; and government authorities.

77.   It was part of the conspiracy that the defendants obstructed, impeded, and frustrated the governmental authorities by withholding information regarding the hazardous nature and friability of the tremolite asbestos contaminated vermiculite and asserting that the Libby Mine operations and Libby vermiculite posed no risk to public health and safety and the environment.

Counts II - IV of the indictment charged Grace and three of the individual defendants — Alan Stringer, who was the Libby Mine Supervisor and later the General Manager of Operations; Jack Wolter, who served as Vice President of Mining and Engineering for the Construction Products Division (CPD) and later as Vice President and General Manager of CPD; and Robert Bettacchi, who first served as General Manager of CPD, then as CPD Vice President, and finally as CPD President and Senior Vice President of W.R. Grace — with knowing endangerment.

UNITED STATES V. **W.R. GRACE**
INDICTMENT

CR 05-07-M-DWM (D. Mont. 2005)

* * *

Count II
(Clean Air Act - Knowing Endangerment)

* * *

186.   [B]eginning on or about November 15, 1990, and continuing until the present, at Libby, within the State and District of Montana, defendant W.R. GRACE did knowingly release and caused to be released into the ambient air a hazardous air pollutant, namely, asbestos, and at the time, knowingly placed another person, namely the residents of the town of Libby and Lincoln County in imminent danger of death or serious bodily injury by providing and distributing asbestos contaminated vermiculite material to the community; and by causing defendant W.R. GRACE employees and their personal effects to be contaminated with asbestos, in violation of 42 U.S.C. § 7413(c)(5)(A), 18 U.S.C. § 2.

Count III
(Clean Air Act - Knowing Endangerment)

* * *

188. [B]eginning on or about December, 1993, and continuing until on or about June 15, 2000, at Libby within the State and District of Montana, the defendants, W.R. GRACE, ALAN R. STRINGER, JACK W. WOLTER, and ROBERT J. BETTACCHI did knowingly release and caused to be released into the ambient air a hazardous air pollutant, namely, asbestos, and at the time knowingly placed another person in imminent danger of death or serious bodily injury by selling real property known as the "Screening Plant" to the Parker family, in violation of 42 U.S.C. § 7413(c)(5)(A), 18 U.S.C. § 2.

Count IV
(Clean Air Act - Knowing Endangerment)

* * *

190. [B]eginning on or about November 15, 1990, and continuing until on or about the summer of 2000, at Libby within the State and District of Montana, the defendants, W.R. GRACE, ALAN R. STRINGER, JACK W. WOLTER, and ROBERT J. BETTACCHI did knowingly release and caused to be released into the ambient air a hazardous air pollutant, namely, asbestos, and at the time knowingly placed another person in imminent danger of death or serious bodily injury by leasing a property known as the "Export Plant" to the Burnetts and selling the property known as the "Export Plant" to the City of Libby, in violation of 42 U.S.C. § 7413(c)(5)(A), 18 U.S.C. § 2.

DISCUSSION QUESTIONS

1. What evidence supports three separate knowing endangerment counts? Why would prosecutors charge multiple violations of the same statute?

2. The knowing endangerment counts in the indictment identify the persons who were endangered as the residents of the town of Libby (Count II) and the Parker family (Count III). Who was endangered by the conduct alleged in Count IV? Are there others who were endangered by the asbestos but who were not specified as "another person" in any of the

three counts? If so, could the prosecutors have added more knowing endangerment counts to the indictment?

3. Asbestos-related diseases usually have a long latency period and may not manifest themselves for years. If the government did not have evidence that termolite had actually caused any deaths or illnesses in Libby, would that undermine the prosecution's ability to prove violations of the knowing endangerment statute? Apart from evidence of actual harm, what other kinds of evidence could the prosecution rely on?

4. The knowing endangerment statute requires proof of actual knowledge or belief. Precisely what does that mean in this context?

5. The government decided to prosecute W.R. Grace in addition to seven of its officers and agents. Why would the government want to hold the corporation criminally responsible?

6. It is widely known that asbestos is hazardous. When he began working at the expanding plant, Les Skramstad knew he was working with asbestos. Is that enough to give the defendants an affirmative defense of consent under the knowing endangerment statute?

2. NEGLIGENT ENDANGERMENT

The Clean Air Act's negligent endangerment provision parallels the knowing endangerment statute in many respects, but there are several significant differences. First, the negligent endangerment provision ordinarily does not apply to employees who are performing their regular job-related responsibilities. This exception does not apply to senior management personnel and corporate officers, however.

Second, prosecutors enjoy a relaxed burden of proof under the negligent endangerment provision. A violation occurs when the actor *negligently* releases a hazardous air pollutant or extremely hazardous substance and thereby *negligently* places another in imminent danger of death or serious injury. And third, consent is not a defense under the negligent endangerment provision.[51]

---

[51]One other notable difference is that, while knowing endangerment is a felony, negligent endangerment is a misdemeanor.

DISCUSSION QUESTION

1. Suppose that in the W.R. Grace prosecution, the asbestos contamination was restricted to the Libby Mine. The prosecutor is contemplating charging Grace and some of its officers with endangering the mine workers, including Les Skramstad. The prosecutor believes there is a better than even chance that the defendants can prove that Skramstad and his co-workers consented to their asbestos exposure, but feels confident that the government can prove the defendants knew they were exposing the workers to an extreme health hazard. Could the prosecutor charge them with negligent endangerment and deprive them of the defense of consent? What are (or should be) the limits of prosecutorial discretion in deciding what offense to charge?

E. ALTERNATIVE REGULATORY SCHEMES

As is often the case, federal regulatory schemes may address the same or similar concerns under different but overlapping statutes. In the context of the conditions at the Libby Mine, the Occupational Safety and Health Act (OSHA) is a case in point.

Congress enacted OSHA in 1970 to reverse a "worsening trend" in workplace safety in American industry. OSHA's goal is to provide all American workers "safe and healthful working conditions" through mandatory safety and health standards for businesses that affect interstate commerce.

> OSHA's scheme of liability derives from the imposition of two duties upon employers. The first is a general duty to furnish employees "employment and a place of employment which are free from recognized hazards that are causing or are likely to cause death or serious physical harm." The second is a duty to comply with specific occupational safety and health rules promulgated by the Secretary of Labor. Violation of either of these duties is punishable by a civil fine that may be imposed administratively, and willful violation of a specific rule or regulation is punishable as a crime when the violation results in an employee's death.
>
> OSHA's regulatory scheme seems well tailored to [the Grace prosecution]. The regulations, for example, require employers to instruct employees in the safe and proper handling of poisonous or toxic materials used in the workplace; to advise them of potential hazards and of personal protective measures needed to avoid injury; to provide appropriate first aid

services and medical attention; to provide personal protective equipment for employees exposed to hazardous conditions. . . .[52]

Two years after Congress enacted the enabling legislation, the Occupational, Safety and Health Administration promulgated regulations limiting workplace exposure to asbestos — including tremolite found in vermiculite.[53] But from the outset, it was reasonably clear that the OSHA regulatory regime was seriously flawed.

> First, the civil enforcement scheme is relatively weak. The Act is directed primarily toward prevention of work-related injuries and illnesses. Although an employer may be cited and fined for violations that have yet to produce a single injury, a principal purpose of these citations is abatement of the unsafe condition or practice. Imposition of a monetary penalty is purely discretionary unless the violation is designated as "serious" [i.e., there is a substantial probability of death or serious physical harm], and the maximum civil penalty for serious violations is $1,000.[54] Thus the civil penalty structure has no *in terrorem* deterrent value, especially where correction of the violation would be more costly than the penalty.[55]

Historically, these limited compliance incentives have been exacerbated by budgetary and staffing constraints and the lack of an aggressive enforcement policy. Civil penalties are shockingly low,[56] and more often than not they are the product of a negotiated compromise between regulators and the employer who committed the violation. Thus, OSHA's civil penalty scheme has been largely ineffective.

> OSHA's criminal enforcement mechanism has proven no more effective. For a number of possible reasons, only seven criminal OSHA prosecutions were instituted during the first twelve years the statute was in

---

[52]Kathleen F. Brickey, *Death in the Workplace: Corporate Liability for Criminal Homicide*, 2 NOTRE DAME J.L. ETHICS & PUB. POL'Y 753, 776-777 (1987) [hereinafter Brickey, *Death in the Workplace*].

[53]SCHNEIDER & MCCUMBER, *supra* note 43, at 249.

[54]The maximum fine for serious violations has since been increased to $7,000 per violation. — ED.

[55]Brickey, *Death in the Workplace*, *supra* note 52, at 777-778.

[56]In 1983, when the maximum fine was $1,000, the average penalty assessed for violations that created a probability of death or serious physical harm was less than $200.

effect. One obvious disincentive to proceeding under OSHA's criminal provision is that for first time offenders, the maximum fine for willful criminal violations is the same as the maximum fine for willful civil violations.[57] Thus, when the employer is a corporation or other entity that cannot suffer imprisonment, the Commission may perceive little or no immediate value in referring the matter to the Justice Department for criminal prosecution. Unless the conduct of an employer who is an individual — as opposed to an entity — is so egregious that imprisonment seems an appropriate sanction to pursue, OSHA provides little incentive to follow the criminal enforcement route.[58]

OSHA's criminal enforcement scheme is notable for the laxity of its penalties. Willful violations of an OSHA standard, rule, or regulation that cause the death of an employee are only misdemeanors. For a first offense, the maximum penalty is a fine[59] and/or a maximum term of six months' imprisonment. If the violator is convicted of a subsequent violation, the offense is punishable by a fine and/or a maximum one-year prison term.[60] In contrast, CAA knowing endangerment offenses are felonies punishable by a maximum term of 15 years in prison and/or a fine. For a subsequent knowing endangerment conviction, the maximum fine and term of imprisonment are doubled.[61]

And then there is the question of who can be held criminally responsible under the two regulatory regimes. In the Grace prosecution, the government charged both the corporation and seven of its officers and agents. Under OSHA, the government's options might have been more limited.

---

[57]Originally, the maximum fine for both willful civil and criminal violations was $10,000. The maximum civil fine for willful or repeated violations has since been increased to $70,000, and there is a minimum fine of $5,000 per violation. Criminal fines were substantially increased by the Criminal Fine Enforcement Act of 1984. *See infra* note 59. — ED.

[58]Brickey, *Death in the Workplace, supra* note 52, at 780-781.

[59]The maximum fine for criminal OSHA violations was originally $10,000 for a first violation, or $20,000 for a subsequent conviction. In 1984, Congress enacted the Criminal Fine Enforcement Act, which raised fines across the board for virtually all federal crimes. Because the Fine Enforcement Act increased fines for misdemeanors resulting in death, the maximum fine for criminal OSHA violations is the same as the maximum fine for most felonies — $250,000 for individuals and $500,000 for organizations. 18 U.S.C. § 3571.

[60]29 U.S.C. § 666(e).

[61]42 U.S.C. § 7413(c)(5)(A).

Whether Congress meant to extend liability beyond the corporate employer to the corporation's responsible officers and agents is not entirely clear. . . . The term "employer" is defined to mean "a person engaged in a business affecting commerce who has employees." Although a number of individual agents have been cited for civil and criminal OSHA violations courts have, on occasion, cast doubt on the question whether individual corporate agents are employers within the contemplation of this definition. Thus, it remains uncertain whether OSHA's scheme of liability ascribes personal fault to individual business managers, except in the case of a sole proprietor who [lacked] the foresight to do business in corporate form.[62]

And, of course, in the context of the Libby Mine, OSHA's regulatory scheme would be concerned only with the *miners'* exposure to asbestos. OSHA's jurisdiction does not extend to the exposure of miners' families and other Libby residents. Thus, the CAA regulatory scheme seems better suited to address problems of the magnitude that existed at the Libby Mine.

The Mine Safety and Health Administration (MSHA) also has jurisdiction to regulate, and inspect for hazardous conditions in, American mines. Although MSHA limits the amount of airborne asbestos that miners may be exposed to, the permissible MSHA limit is 20 times higher than the allowable limit under OSHA. Thus, a vermiculite mine with levels of asbestos that would be unsafe under OSHA regulations would often be legal under MSHA's weaker regulatory standard.[63]

And this is where politics come into play. The safety standard under which MSHA regulates asbestos is nearly 30 years old and does not reflect more recent advances in knowledge about the dangers asbestos poses to human health. Although MSHA tried to bring its asbestos standard in line with OSHA's in 1989, industry resistance and a pro-industry administration forestalled any modernizing change.[64] Industry-funded studies contradicted

---

[62]Brickey, *Death in the Workplace, supra* note 52, at 781-782.

[63]SCHNEIDER & MCCUMBER, *supra* note 43, at 262.

[64]This is not, of course, a phenomenon that is unique to MSHA. The EPA recently announced that it will enhance the role of its political appointees and diminish the role of scientists in setting standards for controlling dangerous air pollutants. Felicity Barringer, *Greater Role for Nonscientists in E.P.A. Pollution Decisions*, N.Y. TIMES, Dec. 8, 2006, at A22.

Perhaps reflecting the Agency's capture by the mining industry, a recent assessment of the Mine Safety and Health Administration's enforcement record found the Agency had failed to assess penalties for violations it had cited in thousands of cases since at least 1995. *Mining Agency Finds Penalties Lapse*, N.Y. TIMES, Feb. 28, 2008, at A13.

union charges that miners were dying because of asbestos and claimed that the risk of asbestos exposure was minimal.[65] As one MSHA administrator put it:

> The efforts to prevent the new standard were pretty much made by the same people making the same statements they made in defending Libby. . . . They said, "Our asbestos isn't bad asbestos." And "Those fibers are too short or the wrong shape to be harmful" and "Our mining process doesn't result in the kind of asbestos exposure that would cause the disease."[66]

Simply put, industry told the regulators the same thing mining company officials routinely told the miners: "Go back to work, George. There's nothing to worry about."[67]

---

[65]SCHNEIDER & MCCUMBER, *supra* note 43, at 262-263.
[66]*Id.* at 264.
[67]*Id.*

6

HAZARDOUS WASTE

RCRA is *"a regulatory cuckoo land of definition. . . . I believe we have five people in the agency who understand what 'hazardous waste' is."*[†]

The Resource Conservation and Recovery Act (RCRA) is a far-reaching regulatory statute that establishes cradle to grave regulation of hazardous waste. RCRA is designed to regulate the more than half million individuals and firms that generate hazardous waste as well as those who treat, store, dispose of, or transport it. The regulatory scheme is called "cradle to grave" because it monitors hazardous waste from the moment it is created up through the time it is finally disposed of. The primary objective of the statute is to ensure proper disposal of hazardous waste and to eliminate waste management practices that endanger human health or the environment. And, as its title suggests, RCRA also secondarily endeavors to promote recycling and resource recovery.

[†]Don. R. Clay, EPA Assistant Administrator for the Office of Solid Waste and Emergency Response.

The critical link in the chain is the manifest system. Those who produce hazardous waste (i.e. "generators") must prepare a manifest that enables EPA to identify and trace the transportation, treatment, and disposal of the waste. RCRA also imposes stringent standards for handling hazardous waste as well as numerous recordkeeping and labeling requirements. As is true under many environmental statutes, a permit system is the capstone of the regulatory scheme.

A. THE RESOURCE CONSERVATION AND RECOVERY ACT

RCRA was a long overdue legislative response to a national environmental emergency brought about by environmentally irresponsible disposal of hazardous and toxic contaminants. Enacted in 1976, RCRA was intended to close "the last remaining loophole in environmental law, that of unregulated land disposal of discarded material and hazardous wastes."[1]

Although technological innovations during the Industrial Revolution produced new types and amounts of hazardous waste, the end of World War II marked the beginning of the hazardous waste crisis. With the shift from military to predominantly domestic industrial output, the quantity of industrial hazardous waste byproducts soared from an annual output of 500 *thousand* metric tons of hazardous waste in the 1940s to 275 *million* metric tons by the 1980s. Not surprisingly, the dramatic increase in hazardous waste production occurred without a corresponding improvement in safe waste management practices or parallel growth of a waste management industry that could effectively address the impending crisis. The problem was compounded by too little information about hazardous waste disposal practices: no one knew how many hazardous waste dumpsites there were, where they were located, or what they contained.

The exponential increase in the quantity of hazardous waste was only the tip of the iceberg, however. Industry's reliance on petroleum as a principal component of synthetic organic chemicals, the growth of the organic chemistry industry, and the production of new and lucrative products like plastics and electronic components only made matters worse. These

---

[1]HOUSE COMM. ON INTERSTATE AND FOREIGN COMMERCE SUBCOMM. ON OVERSIGHT AND INVESTIGATIONS OF THE 96TH CONG., REPORT ON HAZARDOUS WASTE DISPOSAL 2 (COMM. PRINT 1979).

industrial advances spawned new environmental challenges on the safe handling and disposal of unfamiliar hazardous byproducts. Although the environmental effects of these byproducts might not become immediately apparent, some could be toxic for hundreds or even thousands of years.

Ironically, the government's first ambitious programs to reduce environmental pollution contributed to the hazardous waste crisis in their own right. The Clean Water Act required industries to remove toxic and hazardous materials from effluents discharged into navigable waters. The Clean Air Act similarly required industries and municipalities to install scrubbers in smokestacks to remove hazardous particulates from emissions released into the air. Yet neither Act addressed how and where to properly dispose of the hazardous waste these steps inevitably produced. In accordance with conventional wisdom that industrial waste could be commingled with household garbage in municipal and nontoxic landfills, the regulated community routinely disposed of the hazardous byproducts of environmental compliance by depositing them in solid form onto the ground. Thus, industry and government alike treated the ground in and onto which hazardous wastes came to rest as a "bottomless sponge" capable of absorbing hazardous waste and toxic residues with little or no effect.[2]

It has since become clear that the "bottomless sponge" theory of hazardous waste disposal cannot be sustained, either from an environmental or public health perspective. The effects of improper disposal practices like those in Love Canal,[3] Times Beach,[4] and the Valley of the Drums,[5] can be

---

[2]Sydney M. Wolf, *Hazardous Waste Trials and Tribulations*, 13 ENVTL. L. REV. 367, 413 (1983) (quoting House Ground Water Contamination Hearings).

[3]   Love Canal provided the nation's first serious warning that hazardous waste contamination could decimate an entire community. After years of disposing of hazardous chemicals contaminated with dioxin and pesticides in Love Canal in New York, Hooker Chemical Company deeded the dumpsite to the Niagara Falls Board of Education in 1953. The city built a public school on the banks of the canal and allowed residential development in adjacent areas. In 1978, the New York State Health Department declared a public health emergency after women in the homes closest to the canal experienced unusually high rates of miscarriages. Officials evacuated more than two hundred families living closest to the canal.

Although the Health Department concluded that the families in the 850 remaining homes were not at increased risk, a privately administered health questionnaire revealed a geographical clustering of serious health problems, including birth defects, asthma, and diseases of the central

irreversible and severe, ranging in their most extreme forms from public health emergencies to potentially catastrophic environmental harm.

The potentially far reaching effects of improper hazardous waste disposal set the stage for considering RCRA's cradle to grave regulatory scheme, to which we now will turn.

---

nervous system and the urinary system. The government spent millions of dollars to relocate the families from the first two rows of homes. In the end, more than a thousand households were evacuated, and the state of New York installed a clay cap over the most severely contaminated sixteen acres. Over time, the state extended the clay cover to more than forty surrounding acres.

Kathleen F. Brickey, *Charging Practices in Hazardous Waste Crime Prosecutions*, 62 OHIO ST. L.J.1077, 1088 n.37 (2001).

   [4] In the early 1970s, Times Beach, Missouri, hired a firm to spray oil on its unpaved streets to control dust. The firm, which also hauled toxic chemical waste from a downstate pharmaceutical company, sprayed the city's streets with dioxin-contaminated waste oil. In 1982, flooding from the nearby Meramec River washed high levels of dixoin into the northern part of the town. Fearful that the floodwaters would contaminate the residents' homes, the government evacuated all 2,200 Times Beach residents. The following year, the EPA took the unprecedented step of buying out the entire town, which was later razed.

Id. at 1080 n.3.

   [5] In Shepardsville, Kentucky, a hauler dumped more than 17 thousand drums of chemical waste on a seven-acre site in his own back yard, which came to be known as the Valley of the Drums. In addition to environmental contamination caused by hazardous materials leaking from the deteriorating drums, an undetermined amount of waste had also been buried or dumped on the ground at the site. When the EPA tested soil and surface waters leading to the Ohio River from the dump site in 1979, it identified two hundred organic chemicals and thirty heavy metals, including alkyl aromatics, ketones, alcohols, and organic acids.

Id. at 1088 n.38.

B. KEY CONCEPTS

1. HAZARDOUS WASTE

As is true under other environmental laws, statutory definitions are pivotal. In RCRA, the threshold inquiry is whether "waste" qualifies as "hazardous" waste. The statute provides the following guidance on what substances are deemed hazardous waste:

> A solid waste, or combination of solid wastes, which because of its quantity, concentration, or physical, chemical or infectious characteristics may —
> (1) cause, or significantly contribute to an increase in mortality or an increase in serious irreversible, or incapacitating reversible, illness; or
> (2) pose a substantial present or potential hazard to human health or the environment when improperly treated, stored, transported, or disposed of, or otherwise managed.[6]

Although this definition provides a somewhat helpful starting point, it leaves a number of questions unresolved. One obvious point is that you can't determine whether a substance is hazardous waste without first determining that it is a "solid waste."[7] RCRA gets us to the next step by providing another definition that informs us that solid waste is discarded material that is not excluded from the definition by other regulations. In addition to including ordinary garbage and sludge from waste treatment plants and air pollution control facilities, solid waste includes "solid, liquid, semisolid, or contained gaseous material" that is a product of "industrial, commercial, mining, and agricultural operations."[8] Thus, in this context, "solid" can mean "liquid" or "gas."

Some discarded material is excluded from regulation under RCRA. Specifically, solid or dissolved materials found in household sewage or irrigation return flows are excluded, as are industrial discharges from a point source that are subject to the Clean Water Act permit requirements.

---

[6]42 U.S.C. § 6903(5).
[7]*Cf.* FREDERICK R. ANDERSON, ROBERT L. GLICKSMAN, DANIEL R. MANDELKER & A. DAN TARLOCK, ENVIRONMENTAL PROTECTION: LAW AND POLICY 896 (3d ed. 1999) ("[t]he issue of whether a material is or is not a waste is probably the single most perplexing question raised by RCRA").
[8]42 U.S.C. § 6903(27).

So far, so good. But is it clear what "discarded" means in this context? EPA regulations provide that discarded means "abandoned" or (in some instances) "recycled," "inherently waste-like," or a "military munition."[9] And so it goes on down the line.

THE CASE OF THE PESTICIDE RINSEATES

DeMott is a licensed pesticide applicator. Although he has a diverse clientele, the bulk of his business comes from farmers who hire him to spray agricultural crops with various types of pesticides. He and his employees spray the crops from trucks mounted with large tanks and sprayers. When a job is complete, the employees rinse the tanks and other equipment to eliminate any remaining pesticide residue.

DeMott is, of necessity, cost conscious. While the profit margin for pesticide applicators is relatively low, disposing of pesticides and pesticide rinseates is difficult and expensive because of strict laws regulating hazardous waste disposal. To reduce the volume of rinseates and produce a corresponding savings in the cost of disposing of them, DeMott decided to buy an evaporator tank and have his employees pump the pesticide rinseates into the tank until it was full. DeMott did not keep records of what pesticides went into the tank.

When the evaporator tank was nearly full, DeMott hired B & O, Inc., a hazardous waste disposal company, to advise him on what he should do about the rinseates. The B & O representative told him that if the rinseates were waste, they would be classified as hazardous waste under RCRA and he would need a permit to store or dispose of them. But if DeMott could find a use for the rinseates that was consistent with their intended use and with applicable Department of Agriculture rules, they would not be classified as waste and thus would not be subject to RCRA's regulatory requirements.

When the evaporation tank later became full, DeMott and his employees pumped its contents into a truck and sprayed the rinseates on a field. After receiving complaints of nausea and severe headaches experienced by homeowners who lived next to the field, local public health officials suspected the illnesses were related to the spraying and asked EPA to investigate. EPA investigators concluded that the rinseates had constituted hazardous waste and that spraying them on the field was illegal.

---

[9]40 C.F.R. § 261.2.

The investigators referred the matter to the U.S. Attorney, who convened a grand jury and obtained an indictment charging DeMott with illegally storing and disposing of the waste without a RCRA permit. DeMott moved to dismiss the indictment on the ground that because the contents of the evaporator tank were not a solid waste, they could not be deemed hazardous waste under RCRA.

What is DeMott's basis for making this claim? Does his argument have a plausible ring?[10]

Once it is determined that a substance is a solid waste, the next step is determining what the waste is and whether it is hazardous. The EPA again fleshes out the picture with a detailed set of regulations that lists hundreds of specific compounds and substances (called "listed" wastes) that are deemed hazardous under RCRA. But of course the list can't be all encompassing. Does that necessarily mean that a substance that is not listed is not hazardous?

By now you have probably guessed that the answer couldn't be that simple. And you would be right. If a solid waste is not listed, then it must be determined whether it should be deemed a "characteristic" waste — that is, whether it is solid waste that has physical characteristics such as toxicity, ignitability, volatility, or reactivity that warrant treating it as hazardous.[11] And that, in turn, once again sends us back to the regulations to consult detailed specific standards for determining whether the substance in question is characteristic waste.[12]

In view of the complex process for determining whether a compound constitutes hazardous waste, it is no small wonder that an EPA administrator is reported to have called RCRA "a regulatory cuckoo land of definition."[13] RCRA, he went on to say, "is *very* complex. I believe we have five people in the agency who understand what 'hazardous waste' is. What's hazardous

---

[10]*Cf.* United States v. White, 766 F. Supp. 873 (E.D. Wash. 1991).

[11]*See* 42 U.S.C. § 6921(a); 40 C.F.R. §§ 261.3, 261.20-.24.

[12]*See, e.g.,* 40 C.F.R. § 261.21 (defining the characteristic of ignitability to mean "a liquid, other than an aqueous solution containing less than 23 percent alcohol by volume" that has a flash point below 140° F, as determined by specified test methods).

[13]United States v. White, 766 F. Supp. 873, 882 (E.D. Wash. 1991) (quoting Don R. Clay, EPA Assistant Administrator for the Office of Solid Waste and Emergency Response).

one year isn't [the next] — [what] wasn't hazardous yesterday, is hazardous tomorrow, because we've changed the rules."[14]

DISCUSSION QUESTIONS

1. Are the terms "hazardous" and "dangerous" synonymous under RCRA? Would RCRA be clearer (and, perhaps, simpler) if Congress had used the term "dangerous" instead of "hazardous" in the statute?
2. Defendants charged under laws that are complex or whose contours are otherwise indeterminate often challenge them as impermissibly vague. In essence, this type of argument is intended to persuade the court to rule that, as written, the statute or regulation in question does not give fair notice of what conduct is criminal. The Supreme Court has addressed this issue in many contexts and has given the following general guidance for evaluating vagueness arguments.

> Vague laws offend several important values. First, because we assume that man is free to steer between lawful and unlawful conduct, we insist that laws give the person of ordinary intelligence a reasonable opportunity to know what is prohibited, so that he may act accordingly. Vague laws may trap the innocent by not providing fair warning. Second, if arbitrary and discriminatory enforcement is to be prevented, laws must provide explicit standards for those who apply them. A vague law impermissibly delegates basic policy matters to policemen, judges, and juries for resolution on an *ad hoc* and subjective basis, with the attendant dangers of arbitrary and discriminatory applications.[15]

Needless to say, the need for clarity is even greater when the arguably vague law imposes criminal penalties.

Are the terms "hazardous waste" and "solid waste" impermissibly vague? Do the definitions give a person of ordinary intelligence fair notice of what conduct is criminal? Who is the person of ordinary intelligence in the context of RCRA prosecutions? Is it important that the typical RCRA prosecution occurs in a business setting, as in The Case of the Pesticide Rinseates?

---

[14]*Id.*
[15]Grayned v. City of Rockford, 408 U.S. 104, 108-109 (1972).

3. If the owner of an electroplating facility stores waste from the manufacturing process in the plant, it is hazardous waste subject to RCRA regulation. But what if the owner pours the waste down a pipe that empties into a stream? Must he still comply with RCRA? Or is there an argument that the second scenario is exempt from RCRA's regulatory scheme?

2. GENERATORS

The initial regulatory burden under RCRA is imposed on generators of hazardous waste. To be a generator, one must first be deemed a "person," which includes individuals and entities, including state and local governments. RCRA does not define the term "generator," but under EPA regulations a generator is a person whose activity produces hazardous waste or "first causes a hazardous waste to become subject to regulation."[16] Although generators are typically engaged in industrial manufacturing or service industries, the definition also encompasses those who produce hazardous waste "infrequently or accidentally."[17]

Hazardous waste generators are heavily regulated. Once they determine that wastes they produce are hazardous, generators must obtain an EPA identification number; observe restrictions on temporarily storing the waste on site; comply with detailed regulations on labeling, packaging, and transporting the waste; track the waste through the RCRA manifest system; and maintain records and file reports in accordance with EPA requirements.[18]

C. TREATMENT, STORAGE, OR DISPOSAL

RCRA's regulatory regime requires anyone who treats, stores, or disposes of hazardous waste to obtain a permit and manage the waste in accordance with the terms of the permit. The permit application and review process serves a number of important functions. The filing of an application puts the EPA on notice that the applicant intends to engage in activity that is

---

[16]40 C.F.R. § 260.10.

[17]CHRISTOPHER HARRIS, RAYMOND C. MARSHALL & PATRICK O. CAVANAUGH, ENVIRONMENTAL CRIMES 2-222 n.1185 (1992).

[18]Regulatory requirements vary depending on whether the generator is deemed a large quantity, intermediate, or small quantity hazardous waste generator.

regulated by RCRA. The application must provide a detailed description of the applicant's business operations and its facility, as well as relevant technical information such as the chemical composition of the waste the facility will handle.

EPA's in-depth review of the application enables the Agency to determine whether the facility will be in compliance with RCRA requirements and to prescribe the precise conditions (if any) under which the business will be allowed to manage hazardous waste. Once a permit is issued, RCRA's recordkeeping and reporting requirements enable EPA to closely monitor the facility's compliance with the terms of its permit.

RCRA's criminal provisions come into play when the actor "knowingly" treats, stores, or disposes of hazardous waste "without a permit" or "in knowing violation of" a permit. As is so often the case, the difficult question is what the term "knowingly" modifies.

UNITED STATES V. JOHNSON & TOWERS, INC.

741 F.2d 662 (3d Cir. 1984)

SLOVITER, Circuit Judge. . . .

I

The criminal prosecution in this case arose from the disposal of chemicals at a plant owned by Johnson & Towers in Mount Laurel, New Jersey. In its operations the company, which repairs and overhauls large motor vehicles, uses degreasers and other industrial chemicals that contain chemicals such as methylene chloride and trichloroethylene, classified as "hazardous wastes" under the Resource Conservation and Recovery Act (RCRA) and "pollutants" under the Clean Water Act. During the period relevant here, the waste chemicals from cleaning operations were drained into a holding tank and, when the tank was full, pumped into a trench. The trench flowed from the plant property into Parker's Creek, a tributary of the Delaware River. Under RCRA, generators of such wastes must obtain a permit for disposal from the Environmental Protection Agency (E.P.A.). The E.P.A. had neither issued nor received an application for a permit for Johnson & Towers' operations.

The indictment names as defendants Johnson & Towers and two of its employees, Jack Hopkins, a foreman, and Peter Angel, the service manager in the trucking department. According to the indictment, over a three-day period federal agents saw workers pump waste from the tank into the trench, and on the third day observed toxic chemicals flowing into the creek. [The indictment charged all three defendants with RCRA and CWA violations and conspiracy.]

The counts under RCRA charged that the defendants "did knowingly treat, store, and dispose of, and did cause to be treated, stored and disposed of hazardous wastes without having obtained a permit . . . in that the defendants discharged, deposited, injected, dumped, spilled, leaked and placed degreasers . . . into the trench. . . ." The indictment alleged that both Angel and Hopkins "managed, supervised and directed a substantial portion of Johnson & Towers' operations . . . including those related to the treatment, storage and disposal of the hazardous wastes and pollutants" and that the chemicals were discharged by "the defendants and others at their direction." The indictment did not otherwise detail Hopkins' and Angel's activities or responsibilities.

Johnson & Towers pled guilty to the RCRA counts. Hopkins and Angel pled not guilty, and then moved to dismiss [the RCRA counts]. The court concluded that the RCRA criminal provision applies only to "owners and operators," i.e., those obligated under the statute to obtain a permit. Since neither Hopkins nor Angel was an "owner" or "operator," the district court granted the motion as to the RCRA charges but held that the individuals could be liable on these . . . counts under 18 U.S.C. § 2 for aiding and abetting. The court denied the government's motion for reconsideration and the government appealed to this court.

We hold that section 6928(d)(2)(A) covers employees as well as owners and operators of the facility who knowingly treat, store, or dispose of any hazardous waste, but that the employees can be subject to criminal prosecution only if they knew or should have known that there had been no compliance with the permit requirement of section 6925. . . .

III

A

Since we must remand this case to the district court because the individual defendants are indeed covered by section 6928(d)(2)(A), it is incumbent on us to reach the question of the requisite proof as to individual defendants under that section. . . .

We focus again on the statutory language:

[a]ny person who — [. . .]

(2) *knowingly* treats, stores, or disposes of any hazardous waste identified or listed under this subchapter either —

(A) without having obtained a permit under section 6925 of this title . . . or

(B) in *knowing violation* of any material condition or requirement of such permit. [. . .]

42 U.S.C. § 6928(d) (1982) (emphasis added).

If the word "knowingly" in section 6928(d)(2) referred exclusively to the acts of treating, storing or disposing, as the government contends, it would be an almost meaningless addition since it is not likely that one would treat, store or dispose of waste without knowledge of that action. At a minimum, the word "knowingly," which introduces subsection (A), must also encompass knowledge that the waste material is hazardous. Certainly, "[a] person thinking in good faith that he was [disposing of] distilled water when in fact he was [disposing of] some dangerous acid would not be covered." United States v. International Minerals & Chemical Corp., 402 U.S. 558, 563-64 (1971).

Whether "knowingly" also modifies subsection (A) presents a somewhat different question. The district court concluded that it is not necessary to show that individual defendants prosecuted under section 6928(d)(2)(A) knew that they were acting without a permit or in violation of the law. Since we have already concluded that this is a regulatory statute which can be classified as a "public welfare statute," there would be a reasonable basis for reading the statute without any mens rea requirement. However, whatever policy justification might warrant applying such a construction as a matter of general principle, such a reading would be arbitrary and nonsensical when applied to this statute.

Treatment, storage or disposal of hazardous waste in violation of any material condition or requirement of a permit must be "knowing," since the statute explicitly so states in subsection (B). It is unlikely that Congress could have intended to subject to criminal prosecution those persons who acted when no permit had been obtained irrespective of their knowledge (under subsection (A)), but not those persons who acted in violation of the terms of a permit unless that action was knowing (subsection (B)). Thus we are led to conclude either that the omission of the word "knowing" in (A) was inadvertent or that "knowingly" which introduces subsection (2) applies to subsection (A).

As a matter of syntax we find it no more awkward to read "knowingly" as applying to the entire sentence than to read it as modifying only "treats, stores or disposes." . . .

B

However, our conclusion that "knowingly" applies to all elements of the offense in section 6298(d)(2)(A) does not impose on the government as difficult a burden as it fears. On this issue, we are guided by the Court's holding in United States v. International Minerals & Chemical Corp., 402 U.S. at 563, that under certain regulatory statutes requiring "knowing" conduct the government need prove only knowledge of the actions taken and not of the statute forbidding them. . . .

The Court recognized that under certain statutes, such as the income tax law, the government must show a purpose by defendant to bring about the forbidden result. However, the Court in *International Minerals*, construing a statute and regulations which proscribed knowing failure to record shipment of chemicals, stated,

> [W]here, as here . . . *dangerous or deleterious devices or products or obnoxious waste materials are involved*, the probability of regulation is so great that anyone who is aware that he is in possession of them or dealing with them must be presumed to be aware of the regulation.

402 U.S. at 565 (emphasis added).

Even the dissenting Justices, viewing the highly regulated shipping industry, agreed that the officers, agents, and employees

> are under a species of absolute liability for violation of the regulations despite the "knowingly" requirement. This, no doubt, is as Congress intended it to be. *Cf.* United States v. Dotterweich, 320 U.S. 277; United States v. Balint, 258 U.S. 250. Likewise, prosecution of regular shippers for violations of the regulations could hardly be impeded by the "knowingly" requirement for triers of fact would have no difficulty whatever *in inferring knowledge on the part of those whose business it is to know, despite their protestations to the contrary.*

402 U.S. at 569.

The indictment in this case specified the crime in the language of the statute. Thus it did not include language spelling out the knowledge requirements of the statute. . . . Nevertheless, in light of our interpretation of section 6928(d)(2)(A), it is evident that the district court will be required to instruct the jury, inter alia, that in order to convict each defendant the jury must find that each knew that Johnson & Towers was required to have a permit, and knew that Johnson & Towers did not have a permit. Depending on the evidence, the district court may also instruct the jury that such knowledge may be inferred. . . .

IV

In summary, we conclude that the individual defendants are "persons" within section 6928(d)(2)(A), that all the elements of that offense must be shown to have been knowing, but that such knowledge, including that of the permit requirement, may be inferred by the jury as to those individuals who hold the requisite responsible positions with the corporate defendant.

For the foregoing reasons, we will reverse the district court's order dismissing portions of . . . the indictment, and we will remand for further proceedings consistent with this opinion.

UNITED STATES V. HOFLIN

880 F.2d 1033 (9th Cir. 1989)

THOMPSON, Circuit Judge.

Douglas Hoflin appeals his felony conviction for aiding and abetting the disposal of hazardous waste during his tenure as Director of Public Works for the City of Ocean Shores, Washington, in violation of 42 U.S.C. § 6928(d)(2)(A). Hoflin also appeals his misdemeanor conviction for aiding and abetting the burial of sludge at the Ocean Shores sewage treatment plant, contrary to the conditions of the plant's operating permit in violation of 33 U.S.C. § 1319(c)(1).

Hoflin contends his conviction under 42 U.S.C. § 6928(d)(2)(A) requires proof that he knew there was no permit for disposal of the waste, and that the jury instructions omitted this element of the offense. He also contends that the jury instructions were inadequate to define the misdemeanor offense created by 33 U.S.C. § 1319(c)(1). We affirm.

Background

Hoflin was the Director of the Public Works Department for Ocean Shores, Washington ("City"), from 1975 to 1980, when he left for personal reasons. In 1982, he returned as Assistant Director until he again became Director in 1983. As Director, Hoflin's responsibilities included supervising maintenance of roads and operation of a sewage treatment plant. The criminal prosecution in this case arose from the disposal of two types of waste generated by the City: paint left over from road maintenance and sludge removed from the kitchen of the City's golf course. These wastes were buried at the City's sewage treatment plant.

A. Leftover Road Paint

Hoflin and his successor, John Hastig, bought 3,500 gallons of paint for road maintenance from 1975 through 1982. As painting jobs were finished, 55-gallon drums which had contained paint were returned to the Public Works Department's yard. Drums which were empty were used elsewhere or given away. Fourteen drums which still contained paint remained. In the fall of 1982, Hastig moved these drums inside a building located on the Public Works Department yard to keep the paint from freezing. The fire marshal, however, ordered Hastig to return the drums to the outdoors because of the risk of explosion. Hoflin was aware that the drums had to be moved because of the flammable nature of their contents.

When Hoflin again became Director in 1983, he told Fred Carey, director of the sewage treatment plant, that he planned to dispose of the drums by burying them at the plant. Carey replied that burying the drums might jeopardize the plant's NPDES certificate,[19] but Hoflin said he was going to do it anyway.

Hoflin instructed an employee to haul the paint drums to the sewage treatment plant and bury them. Hoflin claimed he told the employee to bury only drums in which the contents had solidified, but the employee testified that Hoflin gave no such instruction. Around August, 1983, employees of Hoflin's department took the drums to the treatment plant, dug a hole on the

---

[19]The National Pollutant Discharge Elimination System ("NPDES") certificate is an operating permit issued to the City pursuant to the Clean Water Act, 33 U.S.C. § 1342. Any person seeking to discharge a pollutant directly into the navigable waters of the United States must obtain an NPDES certificate either from the Administrator of the Environmental Protection Agency ("EPA") or from a state agency authorized by the EPA.

grounds of the plant, and dumped the drums in. Some of the drums were rusted and leaking, and at least one burst open in the process. The hole was not deep enough, so the employees crushed the drums with a front end loader to make them fit. The refuse was then covered with sand.

Almost two years later, in March 1985, Carey reported the incident to state authorities. After inspecting the plant, the state authorities referred the matter to the Environmental Protection Agency ("EPA"). EPA employees recovered the drums, but because several of the drums had no lids or had been crushed, paint had already leaked into the soil. Ten of the fourteen drums recovered contained liquid material. [EPA tests confirmed that the contents of the drums were hazardous and could not be legally disposed of without a permit.] No such permit had been obtained.

B. Kitchen Sludge from the Golf Course Restaurant

The City owns a golf course which houses a restaurant. Periodically, the grease trap in the kitchen septic system is pumped out and the sludge is taken to the sewage treatment plant. Because this sludge contains so much grease, it kills the bacteria necessary for the treatment process and has to be specially burned. In September 1984, three truck loads of this sludge were transported to the City's sewage treatment plant, but Carey refused to accept delivery. Carey told Hoflin that accepting the sludge could jeopardize the plant's NPDES certificate. Hoflin told him to take it anyway and to bury it rather than treat it.[20] The sludge was then dumped into a depression on the grounds of the plant and covered with a backhoe. This burial violated the plant's NPDES permit.

C. The Indictment

[The indictment charged Hoflin with conspiracy, disposing of the paint without a permit in violation of RCRA (42 U.S.C. § 6928(d)(2)), and disposing of the kitchen sludge in violation of the CWA. The jury acquitted him of conspiracy but convicted him on the RCRA and CWA charges.]

---

[20]The City's sewage treatment plant, run by Carey, has an NPDES permit for treating and discharging sewage. The plant operators treat waste water with bacteria in clay-lined lagoons to break down organic materials, and then discharge the waste into ground waters. Section 54 of the NPDES permit requires the permit holder to provide all known, available and reasonable methods of treatment to prevent leachate from its solid waste material from entering surface waters or adversely affecting state ground waters.

Discussion

A. Section 6928(d)(2)(A)

On appeal from his conviction on Count II, Hoflin contends he did not know the City did not have a permit to dispose of the paint. . . .

. . . Section 6928(d) provides in pertinent part:

(d) Criminal Penalties
Any person who — [. . .]
    (2) *knowingly* treats, stores or disposes of any hazardous waste identified or listed under this subchapter either —
        (A) without having obtained a permit under section 6925 of this title . . . ; or
        (B) in *knowing* violation of any material condition or requirement of such permit; [. . .]
shall, upon conviction, be subject to [fines, imprisonment, or both] (emphasis added).

It is Hoflin's position that "knowingly" in subsection (2) modifies both subsections (A) and (B). Under this interpretation, knowledge becomes an essential element of the crime defined by section 6928(d)(2)(A), and Hoflin could not be convicted on Count II without proof that he knew no permit had been obtained. . . .

. . . The absence of the word "knowing" in subsection (A) is in stark contrast to its presence in the immediately following subsection (B). The statute makes a clear distinction between non-permit holders and permit holders, requiring in subsection (B) that the latter knowingly violate a material condition or requirement of the permit. To read the word "knowingly" at the beginning of section (2) into subsection (A) would be to eviscerate this distinction. Thus, it is plain that knowledge of the absence of a permit is not an element of the offense defined by subsection (A). The statute is not ambiguous. On the contrary, "the language is plain and the meaning is clear. Our statutory construction inquiry, therefore, is at an end." United States v. Patterson, 820 F.2d 1524, 1526 (9th Cir. 1987).

Hoflin relies on United States v. Johnson & Towers, Inc., 741 F.2d 662 (3d Cir. 1984), to argue that this interpretation of the statute is unreasonable and could not have been intended by Congress. . . .

We respectfully decline to follow the Third Circuit's analysis in *Johnson & Towers*. Had Congress intended knowledge of the lack of a permit to be an element under subsection (A) it easily could have said so. It specifically inserted a knowledge element in subsection (B), and it did so notwithstanding the "knowingly" modifier which introduces subsection (2). In the face of such obvious congressional action we will not write something into the statute which Congress so plainly left out. . . . To adopt the Third Circuit's interpretation of subsection (A) would render the word "knowing" in subsection (B) mere surplusage.

The result we reach is also consistent with the purpose of RCRA. The overriding concern of RCRA is the grave danger to people and the environment from hazardous wastes. Such wastes typically have no value, yet can only be safely disposed of at considerable cost. Millions of tons of hazardous substances are literally dumped on the ground each year; a good deal of these can blind, cripple or kill. Many of such substances are generated and buried without notice until the damage becomes evident. . . .

Finally, our conclusion is consistent with RCRA's goals and the treatment Congress gave "knowledge" in 42 U.S.C. § 6928(d)(2)(A) and (B) to achieve these goals. The statute requires knowledge of violation of the terms of a permit under subsection (B) but omits knowledge that a permit is lacking as an element of disposing of hazardous waste without a permit under subsection (A). There is nothing illogical about this. Knowledge of the location of hazardous waste, from its generation through its disposal, is a major concern of RCRA. Those who handle such waste are, therefore, affirmatively required to provide information to the EPA in order to secure permits. Placing this burden on those handling hazardous waste materials makes it possible for the EPA to know who is handling hazardous waste, monitor their activities and enforce compliance with the statute. On the other hand, persons who handle hazardous waste materials without telling the EPA what they are doing shield their activity from the eyes of the regulatory agency, and thus inhibit the agency from performing its assigned tasks. We hold that knowledge of the absence of a permit is not an element of the offense defined by 42 U.S.C. § 6928(d)(2)(A).

Hoflin next argues that even if knowledge of the absence of a permit is unnecessary to a prosecution under section 6928(d)(2)(A), the government nonetheless must prove, and the jury must be instructed, that the defendant knew the material being disposed of was hazardous. We agree.

Subsection (2) applies to anyone who "knowingly treats, stores or disposes of any hazardous waste. . . ." The term "knowingly" modifies "hazardous waste" as well as "treats, stores or disposes of," and thus, one who does not know the waste he is disposing of is hazardous cannot violate section 6928(d)(2)(A). But this does not help Hoflin. The district court's instructions to the jury embodied this interpretation of the statute. The district court instructed the jury that in order to find Hoflin guilty on Count II, the jury had to find:

> First: That [Hoflin] knowingly disposed of or commanded and caused others to dispose of chemical wastes on or about August 1, 1983;
> Second: Defendant knew that the chemical wastes had the potential to be harmful to others or to the environment, or in other words, it was not an innocuous substance like water;
> Third: The wastes were listed or identified by the United States Environmental Protection Agency ("EPA") as a hazardous waste pursuant to RCRA;
> Fourth: The defendant had not obtained a permit from either EPA or the State of Washington authorizing the disposal under RCRA.

While these instructions did not use the word "hazardous" in paragraph Second, they did require the jury to find that Hoflin disposed of chemical waste which he knew "had the potential to be harmful to others or to the environment." This instruction was sufficient. . . .

Affirmed.

DISCUSSION QUESTIONS

1. The holdings in *Hoflin* and *Johnson & Towers* conflict with one another. Which decision is more analytically sound? Is § 6928(d)(2) free from ambiguity, as the *Hoflin* court maintained? Should Congress rewrite § 6928(d)(2)? If so, how should it be redrafted?

2. The indictment in *Johnson & Towers* alleged that both Angel and Hopkins managed and directed a substantial part of the company's operations — including hazardous waste management operations — and that the chemicals in question were discharged at their direction. How important is their status as managers? Would subordinate employees acting under their direction and supervision also be liable?

3. Courts considering this issue routinely analogize RCRA to public welfare statutes, often citing *Dotterweich*, *Park*, and *International Minerals*. In what respects are the regulatory schemes considered in those cases analogous to RCRA?

4. The RCRA provision at issue in *Hoflin* and *Johnson & Towers* imposes felony penalties. The violations at issue in *Dotterweich*, *Park*, and

International Minerals were misdemeanors. How important is this difference?[21]

5. Hoflin argued that the statute requires knowledge that the waste is hazardous, and the court of appeals agreed. But precisely what does that mean? Courts consistently conclude that knowledge that the waste is regulated — i.e., that EPA regulations identify it as hazardous — is not required. Nor is it required that the defendant know exactly what the substance is. All that is required is "knowledge of the general hazardous character" of the waste — i.e., that it has "the potential to be harmful to others or the environment."[22] The court in *Hoflin* held that an instruction to that effect is sufficient. Is this a meaningful standard?

The indictments in *Hoflin* and *Johnson & Towers* alleged violations of § 6928(d)(2)(A), which prohibits treatment, storage, or disposal of hazardous waste without a permit. These are typical charges. During the first ten years of the Justice Department's environmental criminal enforcement program, more than half of the indictments in RCRA prosecutions charged that the defendants managed hazardous waste without a permit. In contrast, only a handful of prosecutions alleged violations of § 6928(d)(2)(B), which prohibits treating, storing, or disposing of hazardous waste in violation of the terms and conditions of a permit. It thus appears that the government gives priority to prosecuting cases in which the defendants are "rogue" operators who engage in highly regulated business activities without subjecting themselves to the rules of the game.[23]

THE CASE OF THE MISLABELED PAINT WASTE

Franklin, an independent waste hauler, owns and operates Franklin Trucking. Chem-Co, a manufacturer of paint and paint solvents, pays Franklin $45 per drum to haul away sixteen 55-gallon drums of hazardous paint waste. Before he transfers the drums to Franklin's possession, Chem-Co's manager instructs a subordinate to remove or paint over labels on the side of the drums that identify the contents as paint waste and solvents. The manager neither tells Franklin the waste is hazardous nor provides a manifest

---

[21]*Cf.* Staples v. United States, 511 U.S. 600 (1994).

[22]United States v. Goldsmith, 978 F.2d 643, 646 (11th Cir. 1992).

[23]*See generally* Brickey, *supra* note 3.

that identifies the contents of the drums. Franklin suspects, but does not know, that the drums may contain paint waste or solvents.

After loading the drums onto his truck, Franklin takes them to the outskirts of town and dumps them in a junkyard. After being charged with illegal disposal of hazardous waste, he argues that he wasn't sure what kind of waste he was hauling and that even if he had known what it was, he didn't know that paint waste was harmful. Will either of these arguments fly?[24]

D. TRANSPORTATION

Like generators, hazardous waste transporters are subject to significant regulation under RCRA. Every hazardous waste transporter must obtain an EPA identification number, which must be used on all transportation documents, including the manifest. The transporter must ensure that the waste is properly labeled and contained, comply with the manifest requirements, keep detailed records of all hazardous waste shipments — including their source and destination — and ensure that the waste is delivered only to a treatment, storage, or disposal facility (TSD) that has a permit to treat, store, or dispose of the particular type of waste.

RCRA's criminal provision makes it an offense to knowingly transport or cause hazardous waste to be transported to a facility that does not have a permit.

UNITED STATES V. HAYES INTERNATIONAL CORP.

786 F.2d 1499 (11th Cir. 1986)

KRAVITCH, Circuit Judge. . . .

I. Background

Hayes International Corp. (Hayes) operates an airplane refurbishing plant in Birmingham, Alabama. In the course of its business, Hayes generates certain waste products, two of which are relevant to this case. First, Hayes must drain fuel tanks of the planes on which it works. Second, Hayes paints

---

[24]*Cf.* United States v. Sellers, 926 F.2d 410 (5th Cir. 1991).

the aircraft with spray guns and uses solvents to clean the paint guns and lines, thereby generating a mix of paint and solvents.

L. H. Beasley was the employee of Hayes responsible for disposal of hazardous wastes. In early 1981, Beasley orally agreed with Jack Hurt, an employee of Performance Advantage, Inc., to dispose of certain wastes. Under the agreement, Performance Advantage would obtain from Hayes the valuable jet fuel drained from the planes; Performance Advantage would pay twenty cents per gallon for the jet fuel, and, at no charge, would remove other wastes from the Hayes plant including the mixture of paint and solvents. Performance Advantage was a recycler, and used the jet fuel to make marketable fuel. Wastes were transported from Hayes to Performance Advantage on eight occasions between January 1981 and March 1982.

Beginning in August 1982, government officials discovered drums of waste generated by Hayes and illegally disposed of by Performance Advantage. Approximately six hundred drums of waste were found, deposited among seven illegal disposal sites in Georgia and Alabama. The waste was the paint and solvent which Performance Advantage had removed from Hayes. Some of the drums were simply dumped in yards, while others were buried.

The prosecutions in this case were brought under the Resource Conservation and Recovery Act. The Act creates a cradle to grave regulatory scheme to ensure that hazardous wastes are properly disposed of. Generators of waste are required to identify hazardous wastes and use a manifest system to ensure that wastes are disposed of only in facilities possessing a permit.

[Both Beasley and Hayes were convicted of eight counts of transporting hazardous waste to a facility that had no permit to treat, store, or dispose of hazardous waste. The allegation that Performance Advantage did not have a permit was undisputed.]

II. The Elements of a Section 6928(d) Offense . . .

Whether Knowledge of the Permit Status Is Required

The government argues that the statute does not require knowledge of the permit status of the facility to which the wastes are transported. The Supreme Court has noted that statutes similarly drafted in the manner of section 6928(d) are linguistically ambiguous: it is impossible to tell how far down the sentence "knowingly" travels. . . .

In this case, the congressional purpose indicates knowledge of the permit status is required. The precise wrong Congress intended to combat through section 6928(d) was transportation to an unlicensed facility. Removing the knowing requirement from this element would criminalize innocent conduct; for example, if the defendant reasonably believed that the site had a permit, but in fact had been misled by the people at the site. If Congress intended such a strict statute, it could have dropped the "knowingly" requirement. . . .

The government does not face an unacceptable burden of proof in proving that the defendant acted with knowledge of the permit status. Knowledge does not require certainty; a defendant acts knowingly if he is aware " 'that that result is practically certain to follow from his conduct, whatever his desire may be as to the result.' " United States v. United States Gypsum Co., 438 U.S. 422 (1978). Moreover, in this regulatory context a defendant acts knowingly if he willfully fails to determine the permit status of the facility.

Moreover, the government may prove guilty knowledge with circumstantial evidence. In the context of the hazardous waste statutes, proving knowledge should not be difficult. The statute at issue here sets forth certain procedures transporters must follow to ensure that wastes are sent only to permit facilities. Transporters of waste presumedly are aware of these procedures, and if a transporter does not follow the procedures, a juror may draw certain inferences. Where there is no evidence that those who took the waste asserted that they were properly licensed, the jurors may draw additional inferences. Jurors may also consider the circumstances and terms of the transaction. It is common knowledge that properly disposing of wastes is an expensive task, and if someone is willing to take away wastes at an unusual price or under unusual circumstances, then a juror can infer that the transporter knows the wastes are not being taken to a permit facility.

In sum, to convict under section 6928(d)(1), the jurors must find that the defendant knew what the waste was (here, a mixture of paint and solvent), and that the defendant knew the disposal site had no permit. Knowledge does not require certainty, and the jurors may draw inferences from all of the circumstances, including the existence of the regulatory scheme.

III. Analysis

A

We now turn to the three defenses appellees rely upon. The first is simply a mistake of law defense. They contend that they held a good faith belief that any waste sent to a recycler was exempt from the regulations, regardless of whether the waste was actually recycled. The discussion set forth above indicates that ignorance of the regulatory status is no excuse. There is no dispute that the appellees knew that the waste was a combination of paint and solvents; nor is there any dispute that the mixture was a hazardous waste. Accordingly, the evidence was sufficient for the jury to find the appellees knowingly transported hazardous waste.

B

The appellees' second defense is that the evidence was insufficient to show they knew that Performance Advantage did not have a permit. . . . The evidence shows that Hayes was not following the regulatory procedure for manifesting waste sent to a permit site, from which the jury could have inferred that the appellees did not believe Performance Advantage had a permit. This inference is strengthened by Hayes' own documents, which set forth this requirement. Performance Advantage also was not charging to haul away the waste (although obviously they found the overall deal advantageous), and Beasley thought he had made a good deal; accordingly the terms were such as to raise suspicion.

The appellees rely on Hurt's testimony that he had had an EPA "number," and that he could not recall whether he had given it to Beasley. Drawing all reasonable inferences in favor of the government, the jury could have found that Hurt did not give the EPA "number" to Beasley. In addition, the "number" was not a permit, and the jury could have inferred that Beasley did not believe the number evidenced an actual permit.[25] Accordingly, the jury could have found that there was no evidence that Performance Advantage professed to be a permit facility. Based on all the above, the jury could have found beyond a reasonable doubt that appellees knew Performance Advantage did not have a permit.

C

Appellees' third defense is that they believed that Performance Advantage was recycling the waste. At the outset, we accept the theory of this mistake of fact defense. As the Supreme Court stated in United States v. International Minerals, 402 U.S. 558, 563-64 (1971), a case involving "knowing" shipment of dangerous chemicals, a person who believed "in good faith that he was shipping distilled water when in fact he was shipping

---

[25]Indeed no permit actually existed.

some dangerous acid would not be covered." In this case, had the wastes been recycled, then no violation of the statute would have occurred. Accordingly, a good faith belief that the materials were being recycled is analogous to the good faith belief in *International Minerals* that the acid was actually water.

We believe, however, that there is sufficient evidence for the jury to have rejected the defense of mistake of fact. . . . In this case, three areas of the evidence could have led the jury to reject the mistake of fact defense.

First, are the negotiations that led to the arrangement. Jack Hurt, who negotiated the deal for Performance Advantage, testified at trial. He contacted Beasley in late 1980 or early 1981 about purchasing jet fuel from Hayes. After Hurt asked "what it would take" to obtain the right to purchase the jet fuel, the parties agreed that Performance Advantage would take away a load of the paint wastes, at no charge, and attempt to run them through their system to make fuel. The proposed deal was that Performance Advantage would obtain the jet fuel for twenty cents per gallon if it would also haul away the paint waste. Thirty drums of the paint waste were then shipped to the Performance Advantage plant. Hurt was not responsible for the test run at the plant, but his supervisor, Lyn Bolton, instructed him to find out if Performance Advantage could obtain the jet fuel without the paint waste. Hurt then told Beasley that Bolton did not want the paint waste, but Beasley replied that "he liked the deal the way it was; to take it all." Bolton then decided to take the paint waste as well as the jet fuel.

The inferences that the jury could have drawn from the above testimony are clear. Beasley knew that Performance Advantage had tested the paint sludge in its recycling system, and that after this test Performance Advantage did not want the paint sludge, even for free. If Performance Advantage found it desirable to run the waste through its system, it would not have objected to a deal in which it obtained the waste at no cost. Accordingly, the jury could infer from this exchange that Beasley knew that Performance Advantage did not intend to recycle the paint waste.

The second type of evidence showing appellees' knowledge consisted of internal documents from Hayes. For example, one document, a compliance memorandum from Hayes official Charles Reymann to Beasley, stated:

> Hazardous waste with no resale value, which must be disposed of, shall be hauled to an EPA-approved disposal site. The hauler and the disposal site must both have an EPA interim permit number. A manifest must be used to identify the materials hauled, the hauler, and the disposal site. A copy of the manifest must be returned to Hayes by the disposal site operator.

The evidence showed that Performance Advantage did not want the paint waste, even at no charge, and Beasley therefore knew it had no resale value. The memorandum directed that wastes with no resale value be sent to EPA approved sites, and that manifests must be used to confirm disposition of the wastes. The jury could infer from Beasley's violation of company procedures that he knew the disposition of the waste was improper. The documentary evidence also showed that proper disposition of the waste was Beasley's responsibility; the jury could infer from the fact that it was Beasley's business to know what happened to the waste, that indeed he did know.

Third, subsequent conversations between Hurt and Beasley removed any doubt whether Beasley thought the wastes were being recycled. . . .

. . . Beasley was directly told that the waste was being disposed of rather than recycled, and he nevertheless continued to ship waste to Performance Advantage; this indicates that the agreement was never premised on recycling of the waste. Accordingly, we conclude that the inferences would support conviction for shipments both before and after the conversation. . . .

DISCUSSION QUESTIONS

1. Suppose a transporter of hazardous waste does not know that a permit is required but knows that the facility does not have one. Would that knowledge be sufficient under *Hayes*? What if the transporter is ignorant of the permit requirement but knows that he has not asked whether the facility has a permit?
2. What if the transporter knows that the disposal facility has a permit but that the permit does not cover the substance being delivered to the facility?[26]
3. Does proof of shipment of hazardous waste to a facility without a permit always (or almost always) justify an inference of knowledge of the facility's permit status? If not, what more is needed?

THE CASE OF THE CAUSTIC CARBURETOR CLEANER

Ready Reclamation Services hired Franklin Trucking to haul away 30,000 gallons of wastewater that Ready had used to rinse out storage tanks

---

[26]*Cf.* United States v. MacDonald & Watson Waste Oil Co., 933 F.2d 35 (1st Cir. 1991).

in which carburetor cleaner had been stored. The rinse water was highly caustic and was classified as hazardous waste under RCRA. When Ready's manager called Franklin, he falsely told Franklin he had 30,000 gallons of diesel fuel he needed to have hauled away.

A few days later when Franklin's driver came to do the job, the driver asked the manager whether the holding tanks contained some kind of solvent. The manager said they did not and insisted that they contained diesel fuel. The manager also signed a manifest stating the material to be hauled away was not hazardous. The manager did not ask the driver whether Franklin had a permit to transport hazardous waste or whether its disposal facility had a permit to store or dispose of hazardous waste. In point of fact, neither Franklin Trucking nor its disposal facility had a RCRA permit.

Ready and its manager were indicted for knowingly transporting hazardous waste to a disposal facility that lacked a RCRA permit. After the government rested its case at trial, the defense lawyers moved for a directed verdict of acquittal. Citing *Hayes*, they argued that the government had failed to prove a crucial element of its case — namely, that the defendants knew the facility to which the wastewater had been shipped did not have a hazardous waste permit.

Should the court grant the motion?[27] What factors are relevant to the issue of knowledge in this context? Is the price per drum that Ready paid Franklin to haul the waste away among them?

UNITED STATES V. FIORILLO

186 F.3d 1136 (9th Cir. 1999)

PER CURIAM . . .

Facts and Procedural History

Diversey Corp. ("Diversey") is a company engaged in the manufacture and sale of industrial cleaning products. In 1992, Diversey discovered that two of its products, Slurry and Eclipse, would leak out of their containers in warm or humid weather. The two products are industrial-strength cleansers used in institutional settings and both are highly caustic. After determining that the products were unsaleable, Diversey authorized its corporate

---

[27]*Cf.* United States v. Overholt, 307 F.3d 1231 (10th Cir. 2002).

distribution manager, Adrian Farris, to dispose of 30,000 gallons of the products.

Frank Fiorillo was the president and CEO of West Coast Industries, Inc. ("West Coast"). The company's primary business was the storage of a number of products at a warehouse located in Sacramento, California. Fiorillo, who had provided warehouse services to Diversey in the past, submitted a proposal for the disposal of the products to Farris on behalf of West Coast and SafeWaste Corp. ("SafeWaste"), Art Krueger's company. Farris agreed to the proposal and the parties entered into a contract on February 24, 1993, for the disposal of 10,000 gallons of Slurry and Eclipse. Under the contract, Diversey agreed to pay 50% of the contract costs when the products were transported to Fiorillo's warehouse and the remaining 50% upon submission of compliance documentation.

Diversey periodically received compliance documentation from Fiorillo and Krueger in the form of certificates of disposal, which were signed by Krueger. Ultimately, Diversey paid Krueger and Fiorillo $254,000 for the disposal of 30,000 gallons of the hazardous products. In reality, Fiorillo and Krueger only properly disposed of two of the eleven truckloads of Slurry and Eclipse by sending it to a facility in Nevada, which met the requirements set out in RCRA. The rest of the Slurry and Eclipse was stored at Fiorillo's warehouse in Sacramento in a cold room that Krueger leased from Fiorillo.

In August 1993, Rick Knighton, a former West Coast employee, informed David DeMello, a Sacramento County Fire Department official, that West Coast was storing Class A explosives at its warehouse,[28] and another fire inspector, Robert Billett, went to the warehouse where they informed the receptionist that they were there to conduct an inspection. . . .

. . . Fiorillo agreed to accompany the inspectors during the inspection. DeMello and Billett then discovered the Class A explosives, consisting of approximately 17,000 artillery shells, taking up about one-third of the warehouse. DeMello also discovered hazardous material, which covered an additional one-third of the warehouse, leaking from its containers about six feet from the explosives.

Over the course of the next few days, members of the fire department returned to the warehouse to ensure that proper cleanup was occurring and that no further violations were happening. About eight days after DeMello's

---

[28]When Knighton was a West Coast employee, he had contacted DeMello to inquire whether West Coast met the requirements to store Class A explosives in the Sacramento warehouse. DeMello informed Knighton that West Coast would not be approved to store Class A explosives at its warehouse.

discovery, the fire captain, Ed Vasques, received an anonymous tip that additional hazardous materials were being stored in a room that the fire inspectors had not discovered. DeMello, Vasques, and other officials conducted a re-inspection of the warehouse and discovered an unmarked door that was hidden behind several pallets of food and beverages.

Peter Bishop, an independent contractor hired by West Coast to assist in the cleanup, entered Fiorillo's office to get keys to the room. An investigator from the Sacramento County environmental office overheard Fiorillo say that there was nothing in the room, that he had done everything they wanted and that he had had enough. Nevertheless, Bishop came back out with the keys. A door outside the warehouse led into the cold room as did a door inside the warehouse. The keys did not work on the outside door, and when Bishop went to unlock the inside door, it was apparently unlocked. At this point, the county officials discovered the Slurry and Eclipse, which Krueger and Fiorillo had told Diversey was destroyed. . . .

C. Title 42 U.S.C. § 6928(d)(1)

The indictment charged Fiorillo and Krueger with "knowingly storing corrosive hazardous waste" in violation of 42 U.S.C. § 6928(d)(2) and with "knowingly transporting and causing to be transported a corrosive hazardous waste" in violation of 42 U.S.C. § 6928(d)(1).[29] The jury found both defendants guilty on both counts. Fiorillo and Krueger challenge their convictions for violating subsection 6928(d)(1), asserting that its "causes to be transported" provision applies only to those who generate hazardous waste for transport by others. The Government argues that the "causes to be transported" prohibition is not limited to hazardous waste generators and that the defendants properly were convicted of both storing and causing transportation of hazardous waste. We agree with the defendants that a person who merely receives hazardous waste does not "cause[]" that waste

---

[29]This subsection of the statute provides:

Any person who —
    (1) knowingly transports or causes to be transported any hazardous waste identified or listed under this subchapter to a facility which does not have a permit under this subchapter . . .
shall, upon conviction, be subject to [a fine or imprisonment, or both].

42 U.S.C. § 6928(d)(1).

"to be transported" under section 6928(d)(1). We nevertheless affirm the defendants' convictions because the record shows that Fiorillo and Krueger took responsibility for and carried out the transportation of the Eclipse and Slurry from Diversey's storage location to the West Coast warehouse. . . .

Fiorillo and Krueger assert that their actions of unlawfully receiving and storing hazardous waste did not "cause[]" the transportation of that waste under section 6928(d)(1); the Government refutes this contention. The word "cause" has a plethora of meanings. Among its common definitions are "to bring about," "to compel," *see* Black's Law Dictionary 200 (5th ed. 1979), and "to effect by command, authority, or force," *see* Webster's New Collegiate Dictionary 175 (1979). Various legal standards draw fine lines between types of "causation" — ranging from an indirect, peripheral contribution to an immediate and necessary precedent of an event. Looking at the word "cause" itself, therefore, does not allow us to discern the specific actions to which Congress intended to attach criminal liability under section 6928(d)(1). The statute's overall structure reveals, however, that as Congress used the phrase here, "causes to be transported" does not include a warehouse's receipt of hazardous waste pursuant to a contract. . . .

. . . Subsection (d)(1) addresses transporting and causing to be transported hazardous waste to a facility lacking a permit, whereas subsection (d)(2) addresses treating, storing, and disposing of hazardous waste without or in violation of a permit. By dividing these activities into two categories, Congress demonstrated that, despite the similarities between the prohibitions in subsections (d)(1) and (d)(2), it intended to distinguish between these two groups of conduct in some way. The principal distinction is that subsection (d)(1) describes activities connected to the creation and shipping of hazardous waste, while subsection (d)(2) covers only the receipt and processing of the waste. Stated another way, subsection (d)(1) pertains to the direction of hazardous waste to a facility that lacks a permit, whereas subsection (d)(2) addresses activities occurring at the unpermitted facility.

We acknowledged this distinction between subsections (d)(1) and (d)(2) when discussing a different aspect of those provisions in United States v. Speach, 968 F.2d 795 (9th Cir. 1992). *Speach* presented the issue of whether the Government must prove that a section 6928(d)(1) defendant knew that the recipient facility of the hazardous waste lacked a permit. We answered this question in the affirmative, relying in part upon the following reasoning:

> The two provisions [(d)(1) and (d)(2)] target different groups of defendants. Section 6928(d)(2)(A) imposes criminal liability on the person who

knowingly treats, stores, or disposes of waste, when he or his facility lacks a permit, whether or not he knew that the permit was lacking. . . .

In contrast, section 6928(d)(1) deals not with the violator's lack of a permit, but with the lack of a permit on the part of the person to whom the violator delivers hazardous waste.

Id. at 797. In this passage, *Speach* implicitly recognized that the violator of subsection (d)(1) is the person responsible for making the delivery of hazardous waste, not the person who merely accepts the shipment.[30]

The duplicate coverage of the same conduct that would result if we adopted the Government's interpretation of section 6928(d)(1) supplies additional structural evidence supporting our understanding of this provision. The Government contends that any person who, without a permit, "receives hazardous waste after it has been shipped from the generating facility" "causes to be transported" that hazardous waste in violation of subsection (d)(1). If this interpretation of the statute were correct, the same act — receiving hazardous waste — would subject the actor to liability under subsection (d)(2)(A) as well as subsection (d)(1). This construction would contradict logic and ignore the basic assumption that Congress does not use different language in different provisions to accomplish the same result. Following this presumption, therefore, we construe section 6928(d)(1) as applying to conduct other than that covered under section 6928(d)(2).

. . . Subsection (d)(5) imposes criminal penalties on any person who "knowingly transports without a manifest, or causes to be transported without a manifest, any hazardous waste [required] to be accompanied by a manifest." A "manifest" is "the form used for identifying the quantity, composition, and the origin, routing, and destination of hazardous waste," 42 U.S.C. § 6903(12); various provisions of the federal hazardous waste management laws hold *generators* of hazardous waste responsible for providing this form to the transporter. Subsection (d)(5), therefore,

---

[30] . . . Subsection (d)(1) logically holds liable transporters and those causing transportation only for sending or delivering hazardous waste to a facility lacking a permit, because what the recipient does with the waste after accepting it is beyond the transporter's control. In contrast, subsection (d)(2)'s proscription of treating, storing, or disposing of hazardous waste without a permit, as well as in violation of any material condition or requirement of a permit, demonstrates Congress's concern in this provision with regulating the activities of processors, who, unlike transporters, "are in a position to control" those activities. United States v. MacDonald & Watson Waste Oil Co., 933 F.2d 35, 49 (1st Cir. 1991); *see generally Speach*, 968 F.2d at 797 (discussing each provision's limitation of liability to person in best position to know law's requirements). . . .

proscribes the same two activities that subsection (d)(1) addresses — transporting and causing to be transported — and imposes conditions with which only a generator of hazardous waste reasonably can comply. This provision reinforces our understanding that subsection (d)(1) pertains to persons responsible for the delivery of hazardous waste, not merely the receipt of it, because only a generator (who supplies the manifest) or a transporter (who must obtain it before undertaking the transportation) reasonably could be expected to comply with these requirements.

In light of our conclusion, based upon our examination of the face of the statute, that Congress did not intend section 6928(d)(1) to apply to persons who do no more than receive hazardous waste, we examine the provision's legislative history only to determine whether Congress failed to express its actual intent in the language of the statute. When Congress enacted section 6928 in 1976, subsection (d)(1) prohibited only "knowingly" "transporting . . . hazardous waste . . . to a facility which does not have a permit." In 1984, Congress amended the statute, adding the "causes to be transported" language. The House Report accompanying the 1984 amendments explains the reasoning behind this addition:

> This provision clarifies the criminal liability of generators of hazardous waste who knowingly cause the waste to be transported to an unpermitted facility. Because the generator is in the best position to know the nature of his waste material, the regulatory scheme established by RCRA places a duty on the generator in the first instance to make arrangements to transport and dispose of his waste properly. EPA's ability to obtain criminal penalties against generators who knowingly cause the transportation of hazardous waste to an unpermitted facility is essential to the regulatory scheme.

H.R. Rep. No. 98-198, pt. I (1984), reprinted in 1984 U.S.C.C.A.N. 5576, 5613. Far from indicating that Congress meant subsection (d)(1) to apply to anyone who merely accepts delivery of a shipment of hazardous waste, the House Report strengthens our understanding, based upon the statute's language and structure, that this provision applies only to those persons responsible for initiating, arranging for, or actually performing the transportation of the waste. . . .

. . . In comparing subsection (d)(1) to subsection (d)(2), the First Circuit stated:

> Since *generators and transporters* have little control over either the operation of the facility or the manner of disposal after the wastes are

delivered to the facility, it is not surprising that *subsection (d)(1)* omits a provision relating to manner of disposal, and limits *generator and transporter* responsibility to ensuring that the facility has an appropriate permit for the type of waste being delivered.

[United States v. MacDonald & Watson Waste Oil Co., 933 F.2d 35, 49 (1st Cir. 1991)] (emphasis added).

We must clarify that our interpretation of this provision does not mean that a person must be in the business of generating or transporting hazardous waste in order to run afoul of section 6928(d)(1). In some circumstances, the intended recipient of hazardous waste may also violate subsection (d)(1) by personally undertaking the transportation of the hazardous waste or by making arrangements for a third party to perform that task. Recognizing this possibility, we decline to adopt the interpretation of the statute, advocated by the defendants, that subsection (d)(1) applies only to generators and transporters of hazardous waste. Instead, we hold that the language of section 6928(d), its structure, and its legislative history dictate that subsection (d)(1) does not apply to a person who does not participate in or direct the transportation of hazardous waste, but merely receives that waste.

Turning our attention to these defendants' conduct, we first note that, because the jury found both defendants guilty of violating subsection (d)(1), we must construe the record in the light most favorable to the Government. According to Farris, he solicited bids from three companies, including SafeWaste, when he learned Diversey needed to dispose of the Eclipse and Slurry. In response to this inquiry, Fiorillo submitted to Farris a written proposal, dated January 26, 1993. Farris accepted Fiorillo's bid because it was the lowest and because they previously had had a good working relationship. On February 24, 1993, Farris, Fiorillo, and Krueger signed another document printed on West Coast letterhead that was substantially identical to the January 26 letter and that also was styled as a proposal letter from Fiorillo to Farris. As Farris testified, however, and as the writing itself indicates, the February 24 document actually was a memorialization of a meeting among the three men, and it constituted the contract to which all three were parties. The contract states:

> Per our meeting today with yourself [Farris], Art Krueger (Safewaste Corp.) and myself [Fiorillo], regarding your warehoused hazardous material. The following is our proposal for handling, *transportation*, disposal and EPA compliance documentation for Diversey products Eclipse, Slurry, and PEP in one and six gallon containers.

Service	*Cost*
. . . Freight (from current warehouse location or any 'in-line' multiple stop locations to disposal site).	$1,760.00 per load . . .

Terms

A.   On a load by load basis, 50% of the billing amount is to be paid upon confirmed pick-up of the product from your warehouse site or the last stop on a multiple site pick-up. . . .

Assumptions . . .

2.   You will deliver to us an accurate location, address, contact name and phone number of all inventory as described on your product disposal form.
3.   You will give us the authority to request an accurate inventory and product condition description for each location.

Below Fiorillo's signature is the heading "Sign Off An [sic] Approval." Signature lines for Fiorillo, Krueger, and Farris as representatives of their respective corporations appear under this heading; all three signed this document on February 24, 1993.

Other evidence exists that Krueger and Fiorillo actually arranged for and conducted the transportation of the Eclipse and Slurry from Diversey's storage facilities. Throughout his extensive testimony, Farris frequently asserted that Fiorillo undertook the transportation and that Krueger participated in this activity, as well. Farris also offered examples of contacts he had had with both defendants that supported his account of Fiorillo's and Krueger's responsibilities. Significantly, there is no evidence in the record contradicting Farris's account that defendants undertook and incurred the costs of transporting the Eclipse and Slurry. Based upon this evidence, the jury reasonably could have determined that Fiorillo and Krueger did much more than simply receive the hazardous waste and store it: they proposed (and Farris agreed) that Diversey would pay them to make arrangements for transporting the waste to the West Coast warehouse. . . .

Conclusion . . .

The judgment is affirmed in part and reversed and remanded in part. . . .

DISCUSSION QUESTIONS

1. Why does § 6928(d)(1) require generators and transporters to assume responsibility for ensuring that the facility receiving the shipment has a permit for the type of waste being delivered? Doesn't the ultimate responsibility rest with the facility itself?
2. The court in *Fiorillo* ruled that mere receipt of hazardous waste is not equivalent to causing its transportation. What criteria determine whether the intended recipient violates § 6928(d)(1)? In what sense did Fiorillo cause transportation of the waste? Was his participation in facilitating the transportation more than minimal? Would something less suffice? What if he simply had said to Diversey, "You bring me the hazardous waste and I'll get rid of it for you"?
3. Which, if any, of the defendants in *Fiorillo* could have been charged with violating § 6928(d)(2)?
4. Which, if any, of the participants in the waste disposal operations in *Hoflin* could have been charged with violating § 6928(d)(1)?

E. KNOWING ENDANGERMENT

Like the Clean Water and Clean Air Acts, RCRA contains a felony provision that punishes knowing endangerment. The RCRA endangerment section criminalizes transporting, treating, storing, or disposing of a waste that is deemed hazardous under RCRA when the actor "knows at that time that he thereby places another person in imminent danger of death or serious bodily injury."[31] As is true under the other two endangerment statutes, "serious bodily injury" means bodily injury that involves a substantial risk of death, unconsciousness, extreme physical pain, protracted and obvious disfigurement, or protracted loss or impairment of the function of a bodily member, organ, or mental faculty.[32]

1. KNOWLEDGE

For purposes of RCRA's endangerment provision, a person acts knowingly with respect to his *conduct* if he is *aware* of its nature. He acts

---

[31]42 U.S.C. § 6928(e).
[32]42 U.S.C. § 6928(f)(6).

knowingly with respect to an attendant *circumstance* if he is *aware* or *believes* the circumstance exists. And he acts knowingly with respect to a *result* if he is *aware* or *believes* that his conduct is *substantially certain* to cause the result.

An individual knows his conduct places another person in imminent danger of death or serious bodily injury if he is actually aware or actually believes that it does. Knowledge that another person possesses may not be imputed to the actor. But even though the statutory standard is actual knowledge or belief, circumstantial evidence — including evidence of willful blindness — may be used to establish actual knowledge.

> **Illustration A:** A plant manager instructs the maintenance supervisor to get a crew to remove 50 pounds of cleaning rags from the plant and dispose of them. The rags, which have been used to clean machinery, have accumulated on the floor in the back of the plant over a period of several months. The manager, knows — but does not tell the supervisor — that solvent was poured onto the machinery before the rags were used to wipe the machines clean. Because the rags are now laden with solvent, they are deemed hazardous waste.
>
> Thinking they are ordinary cleaning rags, the supervisor tells three employees to put them in large plastic bags and take them to a local landfill. He does not tell them to wear protective gloves and masks while handling the rags. Direct contact with the solvent in the rags can cause a severe and disfiguring skin rash.

DISCUSSION QUESTIONS

1. Under RCRA's endangerment provision, in what sense — if at all — has the supervisor acted knowingly?
2. Suppose that the manager did not tell the supervisor about the solvent on the rags, but the supervisor smelled an odor that "reminded me of turpentine." Would that affect the outcome?
3. Suppose the manager had specifically told the supervisor there was solvent on the rags. Would the supervisor have knowingly endangered the three workers by telling them to bag them up if he failed to advise them to wear protective gear?
4. Suppose the supervisor knew that inhaling fumes from the solvent-laden rags could cause serious breathing complications for asthmatics. Thinking that none of the three workers had asthma, the supervisor advised them to wear gloves — but not masks — while handling the

rags. One of the workers in fact had chronic asthma. Did the supervisor knowingly expose the asthmatic worker to the risk of breathing complications?

THE CASE OF THE CYANIDE SLUDGE

Bowers owned a fertilizer company called Bowers' Botanicals. Bowers told four of his employees to enter an 11-foot high tank containing several tons of cyanide-laced sludge and begin removing the sludge. The only way to enter or leave the tank was through a 22-inch manhole at the top.

Although Bowers told the workers to wash the sludge out through a valve opening in the end of the tank, it soon became apparent that the valve opening was too small. When the workers left the tank to tell Bowers that the plan wouldn't work, they complained of sore throats and irritated nasal passages and asked for protective gear. Bowers insisted that they continue working in the tank, but provided none of the safety equipment they had requested.

After cutting a bigger hole around the valve opening, the workers re-entered the tank and resumed the sludge removal operation. About 45 minutes later, a worker named Randall collapsed in severe respiratory distress and in danger of dying. After firefighters removed him from the tank and rushed him to a hospital, the fire chief asked Bowers whether there was any cyanide in the tank. Bowers said "no," there was "only sludge," which the fire chief understood to mean mud.

The attending physician in the emergency room concluded that the most likely cause of Randall's condition was cyanide poisoning. But when the doctor called Bowers to ask whether there had been any cyanide in the tank, Bowers once again lied and said "no." The doctor nonetheless had a medical helicopter bring a cyanide antidote kit to the hospital and administered the antidote to Randall. The results from Randall's blood tests later revealed highly toxic levels of cyanide in his system, which caused severe and permanent brain damage that left him barely able to speak, walk, or care for himself.

Within weeks after Randall was hospitalized, Bowers told a new employee to bury the sludge that other workers had removed from the tank, again providing neither safety training nor protective gear.[33]

Has Bowers knowingly endangered Randall and his co-workers? What are the relevant inquiries on the issue of knowledge?

DISCUSSION QUESTIONS

1. As is true of other endangerment statutes we have considered, RCRA's knowing endangerment provision recognizes a limited defense of consent. One of the circumstances that will trigger the defense is that "the danger and conduct charged were reasonably foreseeable hazards of . . . an occupation, a business, or a profession."[34] In The Case of the Cyanide Sludge, Randall and his co-workers knew the fumes from the sludge were making them ill, yet they voluntarily re-entered the tank. Does this constitute consent under the knowing endangerment statute?

2. If the supervisor in Illustration A had advised the three workers to wear masks so they wouldn't inhale fumes from the solvent but the workers decided not to wear them, would the supervisor have a defense of consent?

2. IMMINENT DANGER

THE CASE OF THE PSYCHO-ORGANIC SYNDROME

Morris & Co. is in the drum recycling business. It buys used 55-gallon drums, cleans and repaints them, and then sells them back to chemical companies. Many of the drums it buys have previously been used to store toxic chemicals. In accordance with longstanding instructions, Morris employees clean toxic residue from the drums and dump the residue into nearby sewers. Ever conscious of the need to contain costs, Morris takes virtually no safety precautions to protect the workers who clean out the drums.

---

[33]*Cf.* United States v. Elias, 269 F.3d 1003 (9th Cir. 2001); *Ninth Circuit Upholds Prison Sentence, Federal RCRA Enforcement in Idaho Case*, Daily Env't Rep. (BNA) No. 204, at AA-1 (Oct. 24, 2001).

[34]42 U.S.C. § 6928(f)(3)(A).

One of the dangers of working with these chemicals without proper protective gear is solvent poisoning, which can cause one of three types of psycho-organic syndrome.

Type 1: Type 1 can cause sleeping disorders and disorders that affect thinking, behavior, and personality. These symptoms disappear quickly once exposure to the chemicals ends.

Type 2-A: Type 2-A can cause personality changes, affect the ability to control impulses, and result in loss of motivation and severe mood swings. As with Type 1, once exposure to the chemicals ends, the symptoms of Type 2-A will clear up and the affected person will recover.

Type 2-B: Type 2-B produces additional symptoms, including irreversible concentration and memory problems, impaired learning ability, and cognitive impairment.

Type 3: Type 3, the most severe form of psycho-organic syndrome, can cause acute learning impairment, severe memory loss, serious psychiatric problems, and gross tremor.

Prolonged exposure to toxic chemicals also increases the long-term risk of developing cancer.

After the practices at Morris & Co. come to light, a grand jury indicts Morris for violating RCRA. The indictment charges Morris with one count of disposing of hazardous waste without a permit and three counts of knowing endangerment. The indictment alleges that the company unlawfully endangered three of its employees: (1) Adams, who has symptoms of Type 1 syndrome; (2) Baker, who has symptoms of Type 2-A and possibly Type 2-B; and (3) Carter, who complained of sleep disorders and mood swings but was found not to be affected by psycho-organic syndrome at the time he was examined by a doctor.

Morris moves to dismiss the indictment on the following grounds:

1. If Adams, Baker, and Carter were endangered, the danger they were exposed to was the possibility of developing Type 2-A psycho-organic syndrome, which does not qualify as "serious bodily injury" under the knowing endangerment statute.
2. The speculative risk of developing some unspecified type of cancer at an unspecified point in the future is not "serious bodily injury."
3. The indictment alleges that Adams, Baker, and Carter were placed in "imminent danger" of death or serious bodily injury because it "could reasonably be expected" that their exposure to the toxic chemicals would cause death or serious bodily injury. The risk of developing psycho-organic syndrome or some type of cancer at a distant point in

time does not constitute "imminent" danger. Congress contemplated that the conduct must be "substantially certain" to cause death or serious injury.[35]

Do any of the points that Morris makes in its motion to dismiss have persuasive force?[36]

DISCUSSION QUESTIONS

1. Would it make any difference if medical experts had not yet defined psycho-organic syndrome at the point in time when Adams, Baker, and Carter were exposed to the chemicals without proper protective gear?
2. Suppose that, unlike the original scenario, Morris had a RCRA permit to dispose of chemical residue by placing it in EPA approved sealed containers. Suppose further that the workers who cleaned out the drums always followed the approved containment procedures. But while Morris scrupulously obeyed EPA rules and regulations, the company failed to provide proper protective gear to the workers who cleaned out the drums, in violation of workplace safety rules promulgated by the Occupational Health and Safety Administration. In consequence, the workers who cleaned out the drums were exposed to a serious risk of developing psycho-organic syndrome. Assuming arguendo that this would qualify as imminent danger of serious bodily injury, has Morris violated RCRA's knowing endangerment provision?

RCRA targets industrial production and disposal of hazardous waste. Although there is evidence that — in at least a few parts of the country — there has been some organized crime involvement in the hazardous waste industry,[37] the bulk of RCRA enforcement is directed toward legitimate businesses that circumvent environmental regulations

---

[35]To support this argument, Morris cites § 6928(f)(1)(C), which provides that a person acts knowingly with respect to a result (here, death or serious injury) "if he is aware or believes that his conduct is *substantially certain* to cause danger of death or serious bodily injury." (Emphasis added.)

[36]*Cf.* United States v. Protex Indus., Inc., 874 F.2d 740 (10th Cir. 1989).

[37]*See* DONALD J. REBOVICH, DANGEROUS GROUND: THE WORLD OF HAZARDOUS WASTE CRIME 59-76 (1992).

applicable to their business processes. And as we have seen in Chapter 1,[38] the expense and inconvenience of complying with RCRA provide legitimate businesses powerful economic incentives to operate outside the regulatory system.

But what about wholly illegitimate businesses? Did Congress intend to bring them into the regulatory loop?

THE CASE OF THE CLANDESTINE COCAINE LAB

Douglas manufactures cocaine at a large, if clandestine, laboratory he operates on the outskirts of a mid-size city. Production of cocaine requires the use of a number of highly volatile chemicals, including ether and other substances whose explosive power is equivalent to dynamite. Douglas stores hundreds of barrels of the chemicals in a windowless concrete warehouse about 100 yards behind the lab.

The manufacturing process produces an equally volatile mix of spent chemicals, which he temporarily keeps in barrels behind the warehouse. At least once a week he loads the barrels onto a truck, drives to a relatively rural area, and dumps the barrels onto a vacant lot by a stream.

After receiving an anonymous tip, law enforcement authorities raided the laboratory and, to their great surprise, discovered that it housed one of the largest illegal drug processing operations in the country. Once the full extent of the chemical storage and disposal problem became apparent, the authorities called in a team of hazardous materials experts to supervise removal of the chemicals from the warehouse and to clean up the vacant lot where Douglas had dumped the spent chemicals.

The U.S. Attorney obtained an indictment charging Douglas with knowing endangerment. Which facts, if any, support such a charge? Who, if anyone, was in imminent danger of death or serious bodily injury? Assuming arguendo that the facts would support a knowing endangerment charge, would multiple counts be warranted? Would the defense of consent apply?

---

[38]*See supra* Chapter 1, at text accompanying notes 36-37.

F. DOUBLE JEOPARDY

In *Fiorillo*, Krueger and Fiorillo were each charged with and convicted of two crimes: (1) transportation of hazardous waste to an unpermitted facility; and (2) disposal of hazardous waste without a permit. Both charges were based on the same course of conduct — illegal transportation and disposal of the Slurry and Eclipse products. Although the primary issue on appeal was a question of statutory construction raised by the illegal transportation charge, another issue that was not raised on appeal lurks in the background. To what extent is it constitutionally permissible to convict and punish defendants for committing multiple crimes arising out of a common course of conduct?

The Fifth Amendment protects criminal defendants from being "twice put in jeopardy of life or limb" for "the same offense." Over time, the Supreme Court construed the double jeopardy clause to include prohibitions against prosecuting the defendant for the same offense following conviction or acquittal and against imposing multiple punishments for the same offense.

In their simplest form, these prohibitions can be illustrated by considering the captain of a ship who dumps toxic sludge into the ocean by opening a valve that releases the sludge from a holding tank. If the captain is tried and acquitted on a single count indictment, he cannot be retried simply because the prosecutor does not like the outcome. Similarly, if the trial results in a conviction, the prosecutor cannot retry the captain merely because the sentence the judge imposed seems too low. Nor can the judge impose two separate prison terms for the single count of conviction just because the captain is unrepentant.

That much is clear. But when are offenses the "same" in this context? What if two different statutes prohibit dumping sewage into the ocean? Could the captain be charged and convicted of violating both laws based on his single act of turning the valve?

Although the Supreme Court has struggled for years to construct a coherent theory of when two offenses are the "same" for double jeopardy purposes, its most enduring test is articulated in Blockburger v. United States.[39] Under *Blockburger*, when "the same act or transaction constitutes a violation of two distinct statutory provisions," the act or transaction may be punished twice if "each provision requires proof of a fact which the other

---

[39]284 U.S. 299 (1932).

does not."[40]   Thus, if each statute requires proof of an element that is not required by the other, *Blockburger* permits imposition of multiple punishments, even though the evidence used to establish each of the crimes may be substantially the same.

DISCUSSION QUESTIONS

1. Suppose that in The Case of the Clandestine Cocaine Lab, the U.S. Attorney obtains an indictment against Douglas charging him with violating RCRA by: (1) illegally storing the chemicals without a permit, in violation of 42 U.S.C. § 6928(d)(2)(a);[41] illegally transporting the chemicals to a facility that does not have a permit, in violation of 42 U.S.C. § 6928(d)(1);[42] and illegally disposing of the chemicals without a permit, in violation of 42 U.S.C. § 6928(d)(2)(a).[43]

   Suppose Douglas is convicted on all three counts. On appeal, he argues that convicting him of more than one of these offenses amounts to punishing him twice for the same crime in violation of the Double Jeopardy Clause. Does he have a strong argument under *Blockburger*?[44]

   To provide an analytical framework for your answer, it may be helpful to address several ancillary questions. What brought Douglas' conduct under § 6928(d)(1) in the first instance? What brought his conduct under § 6928(d)(2)(a)? In what sense are the three crimes the same? In what sense are they different?

2. What if Douglas had not driven the truckloads of chemicals to the vacant lot, but instead had hired Franklin Trucking to transport the barrels and dump them on the lot. Would there still be a basis for holding him liable for illegally transporting and disposing of the chemical waste?

3. Suppose that, as in The Case of the Clandestine Cocaine Lab, the indictment also charges Douglas with knowing endangerment, in

---

[40]*Id.* at 304.

[41]The operative statutory language is "[a]ny person who . . . treats, stores, or disposes of any hazardous waste . . . without a permit."

[42]The operative statutory language is "[a]ny person who . . . knowingly transports or causes to be transported any hazardous waste . . . to a facility which does not have a permit."

[43]*See supra* note 41.

[44]*Cf.* United States v. Wasserson, 418 F.3d 225 (3d Cir. 2005).

violation of 42 U.S.C. § 6928(e).[45]   If he is convicted of knowing endangerment in addition to the three charges described in Question 1, does he have a stronger double jeopardy argument under *Blockburger*? Does each crime require proof of an element that the other does not?

---

[45]The operative statutory language is "[a]ny person who knowingly transports, treats, stores, or disposes of . . . any hazardous waste" without a permit knowing that "he thereby places another person in imminent danger of death or serious bodily injury."

7

HAZARDOUS AND TOXIC SUBSTANCES

Con Ed had, and was aware of, records that the manhole where the explosion occurred contained over 200 pounds of asbestos [and was aware of] broad areas of contamination.[†]

Given the extraordinary amount of media coverage of the incident and the [company's] knowledge that government officials were carrying out their own independent asbestos tests, allegations of a cover-up are not credible.[††]

[T]here were people at Con Edison . . . who clearly knew and who should have been jumping up and down saying, "there is asbestos there, we know it." It was obvious that they didn't say it because they were intimidated. . . .[†††]

[†]Mary Jo White, United States Attorney for the Southern District of New York.
[††]Spokesman for Consolidated Edison of New York, Inc.
[†††]Judge John S. Martin, United States District Court, Southern District of New York.

A. THE COMPREHENSIVE ENVIRONMENTAL RESPONSE, COMPENSATION, AND LIABILITY ACT

The Comprehensive Environmental Response, Compensation, and Liability Act (CERCLA) was enacted to deal with the increasingly serious problem of hazardous waste sites. Also known as the Superfund Act, the basic purpose of the statute is to get hazardous waste sites cleaned up. Thus, unlike the Clean Water Act, the Clean Air Act, and the Resource Conservation and Recovery Act, CERCLA's principal focus is remedial rather than regulatory.

CERCLA allows private parties who clean up hazardous waste sites to sue the polluters and hold them financially responsible for the costs of the cleanup, which can be — and usually are — considerable. CERCLA also authorizes the government to clean up hazardous waste sites using funds from a multi-million dollar trust fund known as the Superfund[1] and recover the costs from the polluters. The primary emphasis, then, is on cleaning up sites that create the danger of causing significant harm to human health and the environment and allocating civil liability among the responsible parties.

CERCLA's regulatory side focuses on notification and recordkeeping requirements. The notification requirements, which require the reporting of a release of hazardous substances into the environment, are designed to facilitate timely government responses to dangers posed by such releases in order to minimize the harm to human health and the environment. The notification and recordkeeping provisions are backed by criminal penalties.

B. KEY CONCEPTS

The touchstone of CERCLA's criminal enforcement scheme is its notification requirements. CERCLA requires a "person in charge" of a "vessel or facility" to report the "release" of a "reportable quantity" of a "hazardous substance" into the "environment."

---

[1]The Superfund's official title is the Hazardous Substance Response Trust Fund.

1. RELEASE INTO THE ENVIRONMENT

a. Release

CERCLA's notification requirements are triggered by the "release" of a hazardous substance into the environment. A release is:

> any spilling, leaking, pumping, pouring, emitting, emptying, discharging, injecting, escaping, leaching, dumping, or disposing into the environment (including the abandonment or discarding of barrels, containers, and other closed receptacles containing any hazardous substance or pollutant or contaminant). . . .[2]

The term "release" thus extends to virtually any means by which a substance can be introduced into the environment.

Illustration A: A ship's captain orders the crew to open a valve to get rid of raw sewage at sea.

Illustration B: Barrels of hazardous waste that are stored outdoors begin to corrode on the bottom and their contents drain onto the ground.

Illustration C: A storage tank containing hazardous chemicals collapses and ruptures after being struck by lightning.

Illustration D: Smoke that comes out of a factory smokestack contains high levels of sulfur dioxide.

Illustration E: A demolition contractor's use of a wrecking ball to knock down a building containing large amounts of asbestos spews clouds of asbestos dust into the air.

---

[2] 42 U.S.C. § 9601(22). Some releases are exempt from the notification requirements. They include releases that occur pursuant to permits issued under the Clean Water Act and RCRA; application of registered pesticides; engine exhaust from automobiles, airplanes, other motorized vehicles or pipeline pumping stations; and releases that expose persons to hazardous substances only within the workplace. Releases of radionuclides that are the product of mining and excavation activities and releases of nuclear material that is regulated under the Atomic Energy Act are also exempt.

Illustration F: A business owner buries ten barrels of hazardous chemicals in the woods. The barrels are brand new, sealed tightly, and do not leak.

DISCUSSION QUESTION

1. Which of the events in Illustrations A-F qualify as a release under CERCLA? Among the events that do qualify, what is the relevant definitional term that best describes why the event should be deemed a release?

b. Environment

To be reportable, a release must introduce a hazardous substance into the environment. But "environment" is also a term of broad import. It includes navigable waters and contiguous zones, ocean waters under the exclusive management of the United States, and any "surface water, ground water, drinking water supply, land surface or subsurface strata, or ambient air within the United States" or under its jurisdiction.[3]

DISCUSSION QUESTIONS

1. Is abandoning sealed containers that are in good condition equivalent to releasing their contents into the environment? Why would Congress include abandonment of the sealed barrels in the definition of "release?"
2. Does CERCLA make the conduct in any of the examples illegal? If not, is the conduct in any of them independently punishable under other environmental statutes we have previously considered? How do the regulatory schemes in the Clean Water Act, the Clean Air Act, and RCRA mesh with CERCLA's regulatory requirements?
3. Why would Congress exempt releases that expose others to hazardous substances only in the workplace?
4. Given the inclusiveness of the definitions of the terms "release" and "environment," are there activities that would qualify as a release but would not constitute a release into the environment?

---

[3]40 C.F.R. § 302.3.

2. HAZARDOUS SUBSTANCE

To be reportable under CERCLA, the material that is released into the environment must be classified as a hazardous substance. This is another point at which CERCLA is intertwined with other key environmental statutes. Substances are hazardous under CERCLA if they are classified as hazardous or toxic pollutants under the Clean Water Act, as RCRA hazardous wastes, as hazardous pollutants under the Clean Air Act, and a host of other substances classified as hazardous by EPA pursuant to CERCLA or the Toxic Substances Control Act.

Specific substances and compounds that are designated by EPA as hazardous are known as "listed" hazardous substances and are explicitly classified as hazardous in the Code of Federal Regulations.[4] Unlisted solid wastes are also subject to regulation under CERCLA if they are "characteristic" hazardous wastes — i.e., if they possess ignitable, corrosive, or reactive characteristics as determined in accordance with EPA standards.[5]

3. REPORTABLE QUANTITY

Not all hazardous substance releases are subject to CERCLA's notification requirements. Only those that meet or exceed a reportable quantity (RQ) within a 24 hour period will trigger the notification requirement. What constitutes a reportable quantity is determined in some instances by statute[6] and in others by EPA regulations.[7]

EPA sets the RQ for individual hazardous substances based on the potential harm they can cause to human health and the environment, which in turn is based on the toxicity and quantity of the particular substance. Absent a specific RQ set by EPA, the default amount for most substances is one pound. The RQ for hazardous wastes that are deemed "characteristic" hazardous waste — i.e., those that are ignitable, corrosive, or reactive — is ordinarily 100 pounds.[8]

---

[4]*See, e.g.*, 40 C.F.R. § 302.4.

[5]40 C.F.R. § 302.4(b), §§ 261.20-.23. The petroleum exception excludes petroleum, including crude oil, that is not specifically listed as hazardous under CERCLA. Natural gas and synthetic gas are also excluded. 42 U.S.C. § 9601(14).

[6]*See* 42 U.S.C. § 9602(a).

[7]*See, e.g.*, 40 C.F.R. § 302.4(a)-(b) tbl. 302.4.

[8]Less stringent reporting rules apply to routine, continuous releases that are stable in quantity and rate. *See* 40 C.F.R. § 302.8(a).

Determining whether a release should be reported can be difficult because of the complexity of calculating how much of the substance has evaporated into the air or has leached into the soil. The problem is compounded when the substance is mixed with other hazardous or nonhazardous material. If the quantity of one of the hazardous substances in the mixture is known, then the release must be reported if the known quantity equals or exceeds the RQ for that substance. If the mixture contains an unknown quantity of one or more hazardous substances, then the release must be reported if the total quantity of the mixed substance exceeds the RQ for the hazardous substance or substances.

Illustration G: Midwest Chemical Company hires Oscar, the owner of a waste recycling plant, to dispose of two truckloads of soil contaminated with ammonia. Midwest, an environmentally friendly company, tells Oscar that approximately 150 pounds of ammonia are present in the soil. Although Oscar's recycling plant has a RCRA permit to dispose of ammonia-contaminated soil, Oscar decides to cut costs and dumps the contaminated soil into a landfill, in violation of Midwest's permit. The RQ for ammonia is 100 pounds. The total weight of the contaminated soil is 3,000 pounds. Is Oscar's dumping of the soil a reportable release?

The release in Illustration G is reportable. Oscar knows that the quantity of ammonia exceeds the RQ.

Illustration H: Assume the facts in Illustration G with the following variation. Midwest tells Oscar that the soil is contaminated with an unknown quantity of ammonia. Oscar dumps the two truckloads of soil into the landfill. As in Illustration G, the total weight of the two truckloads of soil is 3,000 pounds, and the RQ for ammonia is 100 pounds. But in this variation of the facts, the contaminated soil contains only 5 pounds of ammonia. Is the dumping a reportable release?

There are two critical differences in this variation: (1) the quantity of contaminants is unknown to Oscar; and (2) the actual quantity of ammonia in the soil is well below the applicable RQ. How, if at all, do these differences affect the outcome?

If Oscar had known there were only five pounds of ammonia in the soil, this would not be a reportable release because the quantity is insignificant compared with the RQ. But here, the total amount of waste is 30 times higher than the RQ for ammonia. The default rule in this case is that the release must be reported because the total amount of the mixture exceeds the

RQ for ammonia.[9] Is there a persuasive rationale for this default rule? Does it make sense to make the release of five pounds of a highly diluted form of ammonia reportable when releasing five pounds of pure ammonia would not be?

There are infinite variations on this theme. Consider, for example, a situation in which Oscar knows the soil is contaminated with a mixture of ammonia and toluene, a toxic industrial solvent, but does not know how much of either substance is present. Under the applicable EPA rules, this does not change the outcome in Illustration H because the default rule is virtually the same. The release must be reported if the *total amount of waste* that Oscar dumped exceeds the RQ for *either* of the substances. Because the 3,000 pounds of waste exceeded the 100 pound RQ for ammonia, the release was reportable.[10] The result would be the same even if only minuscule amounts of ammonia and toluene were actually in the soil.

DISCUSSION QUESTION

1. While determining how much of a particular substance has been released can be dauntingly complex, the determination is critically important to the decision whether a release must be reported. In view of the importance of that decision — the actor's potential criminal liability hangs in the balance — wouldn't it make sense to err on the side of caution and report most spills and accidental releases as a matter of course? Are there countervailing incentives not to notify the authorities even when the question whether a spill must be reported appears to be a close judgment call?

4. VESSEL OR FACILITY

To be subject to the CERCLA notification requirements, the release of the hazardous substance must originate from a vessel or facility. The term "facility" means:

(A) any building, structure, installation, equipment, pipe or pipeline . . . , well, pit, pond, lagoon, impoundment, ditch, landfill, storage container, motor vehicle, rolling stock, or aircraft, or (B) any site or area where a

---

[9]40 C.F.R. § 302.6(b)(1)(ii).
[10]40 C.F.R. § 302.6(b)(1)(ii).

hazardous substance has been deposited, stored, disposed of, or placed, or otherwise come to be located; but does not include any consumer product in consumer use or any vessel.[11]

DISCUSSION QUESTION

1. Which of the following would be releases from a facility?
    a. The driver of a tanker truck carrying industrial sludge opens the valve to allow the sludge to spill onto the highway on a rainy day.
    b. A farmer shovels pesticide-contaminated soil into a shallow depression on his farm.
    c. The pesticide in the contaminated soil in 1b leaches into the ground.
    d. The farmer pours leftover pesticides from a bottle into the shallow depression on the farm.

5. PERSON IN CHARGE

CERCLA does not require everyone who has knowledge of a reportable release to notify the authorities. Instead, the duty to notify applies only to a "person in charge" of the vessel or facility. Although CERCLA does not define what persons should be deemed "in charge" of a facility, it does define the term "person" to include individuals, organizations, and federal, state, and local governmental entities.[12]

While owners and operators of a facility would ordinarily be considered "in charge," a duty to notify can be imposed on operatives farther down the organizational chain of command. Most courts that have considered the issue have concluded that Congress intended to impose reporting duties on those who are in a position to detect, prevent, and abate the release of hazardous substances, and that is inevitably a fact-specific inquiry.

---

[11]42 U.S.C. § 9601(9).
[12]42 U.S.C. § 9601(21).

UNITED STATES V. CARR

880 F.2d 1550 (2d Cir. 1989)

PIERCE, Circuit Judge . . .

Appellant David James Carr appeals from a judgment . . . convicting him under section 103 of the Comprehensive Environmental Response, Compensation and Liability Act of 1980 (CERCLA), 42 U.S.C. § 9603. Under section 103, it is a crime for any person "in charge of a facility" from which a prohibited amount of hazardous substance is released to fail to report such a release to the appropriate federal agency. Appellant, a supervisor of maintenance at Fort Drum, New York, directed a work crew to dispose of waste cans of paint in an improper manner, and failed to report the release of the hazardous substances — the paint — to the appropriate federal agency. At appellant's trial, the district court instructed the jury that appellant could be found to have been "in charge" of the facility so long as he had any supervisory control over the facility.

Appellant contends on appeal that this instruction was erroneous because (1) it extended the statutory reporting requirement to a relatively low-level employee, and (2) it allowed the jury to find that appellant was "in charge" so long as he exercised *any* control over the dumping. . . .

Background

Appellant was a civilian employee at Fort Drum, an Army camp located in Watertown, New York. As a civilian employee at a military installation, he was supervised by Army officers. His position was that of maintenance foreman on the Fort's firing range, and as part of his duties he assigned other civilian workers to various chores on the range. In May 1986, he directed several workers to dispose of old cans of waste paint in a small, man-made pit on the range; at that time, the pit had filled with water, creating a pond. On Carr's instructions, the workers filled a truck with a load of cans and drove to the pit. They backed the truck up to the water, and then began tossing cans of paint into the pond. After the workers had thrown in fifty or so cans, however, they saw that paint was leaking from the cans into the water, so they decided instead to stack the remaining cans of paint against a nearby target shed. At the end of the day, the workers told Carr of the cans leaking into the pond, and warned him that they thought that dumping the cans into the pond was illegal. Two truckloads of paint cans remained to be moved the next day, so Carr told the workers to place those cans alongside the target shed.

Approximately two weeks later, Carr directed one of the workers to cover up the paint cans in the pond by using a tractor to dump earth into the pit. Another worker, however, subsequently triggered an investigation by reporting the disposal of the cans to his brother-in-law, a special agent with the Department of Defense. A 43-count indictment was returned against appellant, charging him with various violations of federal environmental laws. The indictment included charges under the Resource Conservation and Recovery Act (Counts 1-4), the CERCLA charges here at issue (Counts 5-6), and multiple charges under the Clean Water Act (Counts 7-43). Appellant pleaded not guilty, and a 6-day trial before a jury began on October 3, 1988.

After the government had presented its evidence, it filed with the court various proposed jury instructions, including one regarding the definition of the term "in charge." Over appellant's objection, the district court gave the government's proposed instruction to the jury, essentially unchanged, as follows:

> There has been testimony that the waste paint was released from a truck assigned to the workers by the Defendant David Carr. The truck, individually, and the area of the disposal constitute facilities within the meaning of [CERCLA]. So long as the Defendant had supervisory control or was otherwise in charge of the truck or the area in question, he is responsible under this law. The Defendant is not, however, required to be the sole person in charge of the area or the vehicle. If you find that he had any authority over either the vehicle or the area, this is sufficient, regardless of whether others also exercised control.

The jury acquitted appellant of all charges except Counts 5 and 6, the CERCLA charges. The district court imposed a suspended sentence of one year's imprisonment, and sentenced appellant to one year of probation. This appeal followed.

Discussion

I. The Meaning of "In Charge" Under Section 103

Appellant raises two claims on this appeal, both of which arise out of the district court's instruction quoted above. The first claim turns on the meaning of the statutory term "in charge." Under section 103, only those who are "in charge" of a facility must report a hazardous release. There is, however, no definition of the term "in charge" within CERCLA. Appellant argues that the district court's instruction was erroneous because Congress never intended to extend the statute's reporting requirement to those, like Carr, who are relatively low in an organization's chain of command.

Our analysis of appellant's claim requires a review of the statute and its legislative history. The language of the statute itself sheds little light on the meaning of the term "in charge." Section 103 of CERCLA states only that:

> Any person in charge of a vessel or an offshore or an onshore facility shall, as soon as he has knowledge of any release (other than a federally permitted release) of a hazardous substance from such vessel or facility in quantities equal to or greater than those determined pursuant to [42 U.S.C. 9602], immediately notify the National Response Center established under the Clean Water Act of such release. The National Response Center shall convey the notification expeditiously to all appropriate Government agencies, including the Governor of any affected State.

42 U.S.C. § 9603(a) (1982). The regulations implementing the statute fail to define the term "in charge." See 40 C.F.R. § 302 (1988) (EPA regulations). Since its meaning is unclear, we turn to the legislative history in an effort to determine the scope Congress intended the term "in charge" to have.

When CERCLA was enacted in late 1980, Congress sought to address the problem of hazardous pollution by creating a comprehensive and uniform system of notification, emergency governmental response, enforcement, and liability. The reporting requirements established by section 103 were an important part of that effort, for they ensure that the government, once timely notified, will be able to move quickly to check the spread of a hazardous release. [CERCLA's reporting requirements were modeled on § 311 of the Clean Water Act.]

The legislative history of section 311 bears out appellant's argument that CERCLA's reporting requirements should not be extended to *all* employees involved in a release. "The term 'person in charge' [was] deliberately designed to cover only supervisory personnel who have the responsibility for the particular vessel or facility and not to include other employees," H.R. Conf. Rep. No. 940, 91st Cong., 2d Sess. 34 (1970), reprinted in 1970 U.S. Code Cong. & Admin. News 2712, 2719. Indeed, as the Fifth Circuit has stated, "to the extent that legislative history does shed light on the meaning of 'persons in charge,' it suggests at the very most that Congress intended the provisions of [section 311] to extend, not to every person who might have knowledge of [a release] (mere employees, for example), but only to persons who occupy positions of responsibility and power." United States v. Mobil Oil Corp., 464 F.2d 1124, 1128 (5th Cir. 1972).

That is not to say, however, that section 311 of the Clean Water Act — and section 103 of CERCLA — do not reach lower-level supervisory employees. The reporting requirements of the two statutes do not apply only to owners and operators, but instead extend to any person who is "responsible for the operation" of a facility from which there is a release, Apex Oil Co. v. United States, 530 F.2d 1291, 1294 (8th Cir. 1976). As the Fifth Circuit noted in *Mobil Oil*, imposing liability on those "responsible" for a facility is fully consistent with Congress' purpose in enacting the reporting requirements. Those in charge of an offending facility can make timely discovery of a release, direct the activities that result in the pollution, and have the capacity to prevent and abate the environmental damage.

Appellant's claim that he does not come within the reporting requirements of section 103 fails because we believe Congress intended the reporting requirements of CERCLA's section 103 to reach a person — even if of relatively low rank — who, because he was in charge of a facility, was in a position to detect, prevent, and abate a release of hazardous substances. Appellant's more restrictive interpretation of the statute would only "frustrate congressional purpose by exempting from the operation of the [statute] a large class of persons who are uniquely qualified to assume the burden imposed by it." *Mobil Oil*, 464 F.2d at 1127.

II. The Breadth of the Instruction Given

Appellant's second claim focuses more closely on the specific instruction given by the district court. The district court instructed the jury that "[i]f you find that [Carr] had any authority over either the vehicle or the area, this is sufficient [to convict], regardless of whether others also exercised control." Appellant contends that the district court, by instructing the jury that it had only to find that appellant exercised "any authority" over the facility at issue, effectively broadened the statute to reach any employee working at the facility. . . .

A careful review of the challenged instruction indicates that the district court sought, through the charge, to explain two important principles to the jury: (1) that the appellant must have exercised supervisory control over the facility in order to be held criminally liable for his failure to report the release, but (2) that the appellant need not have exercised *sole* control over the facility. By taking the language of the instruction out of context — by focusing too narrowly on the district court's use of the word "any" — appellant ignores the broader point that the district court was attempting to make to the jury. The court had already explained that the appellant must have had "supervisory control" over the facility in order to be found guilty. The subsequent, challenged portion of the instruction was therefore not directed at the breadth of authority that appellant must have had, but instead was intended to make clear that the appellant need not have been the sole person in charge of the facility. . . . [W]e hold that the instruction, though not ideal, was not erroneous. . . .

The judgment of the district court is, therefore, affirmed.

DISCUSSION QUESTIONS

1. The jury was instructed that the defendant did not have to be the sole person in charge to be liable. Can more than one person be in charge of a facility at the same time? If so, do they all share responsibility for a failure to notify?
2. Who else might be deemed to be a person in charge in *Carr*?
3. Why would CERCLA exempt employees who know about a hazardous substance release from the notification requirements if they were not "in charge"?
4. What facility was Carr in charge of? Is there more than one plausible answer?

THE CASE OF THE CHLORINE CLOUD

Mary Lou is a receptionist at Clean Tech, a small company that manufactures home cleaning products, including chlorine solutions. About 4,000 pounds of chlorine are regularly stored at the plant. At about 6:00 A.M. on Monday, an equipment malfunction allowed nearly 60 pounds of chlorine gas to escape, creating a thick, fog-like cloud in the area. Chlorine is classified as a hazardous substance, and the established RQ is 10 pounds.

When Mary Lou arrived for work at 7:30, she opened the door to the plant, smelled a strong chlorine odor, closed the door and left. Since she had forgotten to bring her cell phone to the office, she went to a nearby convenience store to call her boss. When she reached him at home, he told her to go back to the plant and keep other employees from entering.

Does Mary Lou have a duty to notify the authorities? Does her boss? Who is the person in charge? Would the answer be clearer if, in addition to telling Mary Lou to keep other employees out of the building, her boss had told her to go back into the plant and turn off the malfunctioning processing machine?

C. NOTIFICATION REQUIREMENTS

CERCLA requires persons in charge to immediately notify the National Response Center as soon as they know a reportable release has occurred[13] and, if the release is from a facility rather than a vessel, to notify appropriate local authorities. The standard governing when notice must be given requires two highly fact-specific inquiries. The threshold inquiry is when a person in charge knows a reportable release has occurred. Once that has been determined, the second inquiry is whether he or she has immediately given the required notification.

1. KNOWLEDGE

As is true in most other contexts we have considered, absolute certainty is not a condition precedent to finding knowledge that a spill has occurred. Instead, knowledge can be inferred from surrounding facts and circumstances.

A person in charge has actual knowledge of a release if he possesses information about an occurrence or event and the information "is an assurance of a fact or proposition founded on perception by the senses, or intuition."[14] In The Case of the Chlorine Cloud, could knowledge that chlorine had been released be imputed to Mary Lou or her boss? What facts are most relevant to this inquiry?

A person in charge has constructive knowledge of a release if he has knowledge of circumstances that would lead a prudent person, in the exercise of due diligence, to know a spill has occurred.[15] Suppose that in The Case of the Chlorine Cloud, the boss had told Mary Lou to take the day off and not to worry about the odor. After that, he turned on the television to watch the

---

[13]The National Response Center is a central clearinghouse for information about releases of hazardous substances that notifies other agencies to facilitate development of a response to such spills.

[14]In re Thoro Prod. Co., No. EPCRA VIII-90-04, 1992 WL 143993, at text accompanying n.8 (EPA May 19, 1992).

[15]*Id.* at text accompanying n.6 (EPA May 19, 1992).

early morning news. The lead report was about a possible cloud of chlorine gas that had emergency responders searching for the source of the leak in an area close to the plant. If the boss does nothing further, could he be charged with constructive knowledge? What facts are most relevant to this inquiry?

Certainty regarding the actual quantity of hazardous material that has been released is not required. Knowledge that the release is reportable can also be inferred from circumstances that would lead one to believe that the amount released equals or exceeds the RQ or from circumstances that would lead one to know, in the exercise of reasonable diligence, that an RQ had been released.

DISCUSSION QUESTIONS

1. The preceding discussion illustrates how knowledge of the chlorine release might be inferred. What facts would support an inference that Mary Lou and/or the boss knew a reportable quantity had been released? Are the standards for determining knowledge so inexact that they put the person in charge at risk of making the wrong judgment call about whether a reportable release has occurred?
2. If either Mary Lou or the boss had a duty to report, the duty arose "as soon as" they knew of the chlorine release. At what point in time could we say that one or both of them knew chlorine had been released?
3. To be reportable, a hazardous substance must be released. To establish the requisite knowledge, must the government prove that Mary Lou and her boss knew that chlorine is hazardous?[16]

THE CASE OF THE DECLINING DRUM COUNT

Burns operated a waste recycling and transportation business where he stored large drums of hazardous wastes. When he hired Michaels as the new plant manager, he told Michaels that one of his most important responsibilities was to "keep the drum count down" because he was forbidden under local law to have more than 1,300 drums of waste at the storage facility at any time.

---

[16]*Cf.* United States v. Buckley, 934 F.2d 84 (6th Cir. 1991).

From time to time when the facility was reaching its legal capacity for stored waste, Michaels occasionally followed the time honored tradition of some of his predecessors and dumped incoming waste directly onto the ground. Michaels thought that Burns approved because he frequently told his employees, "well, we got to keep this drum count down."

A receptionist who was not directly involved in this process had also overheard Burns tell subordinates that "a rainy day is a good day to get your drum count down."

On one occasion when Michaels had questioned what he should do with an incoming load of extremely toxic waste, Burns said, "I never had any problem with any of the other plant managers. Do I see a problem with you?"

On the occasion that led to Burns' prosecution under CERCLA, a truck driver who worked for the company delivered a 1,000-gallon truckload of waste that he had just picked up. Burns told him that he was going to need the truck again the next day to pick up another load of waste. The driver told Burns that there were no tanks or drums to pump the waste into and asked what to do with it. Burns asked, "Do I see a problem again?"

Later that day, the driver dumped the contents onto the ground without telling Burns how he solved the problem.

Did Burns have knowledge of the dumping? If so, was it actual or constructive knowledge?

Assuming Burns was a person in charge of the facility, he had a duty to notify federal authorities "as soon as" he had knowledge of the release. Assuming he can be charged with knowledge, when did he know the dumping had occurred?[17]

2. IMMEDIATE NOTICE

A person in charge has a duty to report as soon as he has knowledge of the release. The second, and intertwined, inquiry is whether the person in charge has fulfilled the requirement of "immediately" notifying the authorities as soon as he or she knows of the spill. Is it clear what "as soon as" and "immediately" mean in this context? Are these terms too

---

[17]*Cf.* United States v. Greer, 850 F.2d 1447 (11th Cir. 1988).

indeterminate to give a person in charge fair warning of what conduct is punishable?

THE CASE OF THE CHLORINE CLOUD: TAKE TWO

Building on the facts of The Case of the Chlorine Cloud, suppose the production manager is the first to arrive at 7:00 A.M. Upon entering the plant, he detects a stronger than usual chlorine odor, turns off the malfunctioning processing machine, and quickly leaves the building to call the boss. In this scenario the manager uses a cell phone to make the call once he is a safe distance from the plant. As it happens, the boss's cell phone is turned off, so the manager leaves a message and waits to hear back.

While he is waiting, the manager pulls out his laptop computer and sends an e-mail to his co-workers telling them not to come in this morning because production has been interrupted. When Mary Lou arrives at 7:30, the manager tells her not to enter the plant until the boss calls back.

The boss returns the manager's call at 8:00 A.M. After hearing the manager's concerns, the boss asks him to tell Mary Lou to go back into the building to retrieve some important contracts he left on her desk. The boss also tells the manager not to do anything until he arrives on the scene to check the situation out.

By the time the boss arrives at 8:45, a swarm of emergency vehicles are in the vicinity looking for the source of the leak. They have not associated the cloud with the plant because it has settled into a low lying area located some distance from the plant. Several hundred homes, an elementary school, and a number of businesses are located in the vicinity of the cloud, and the fire marshall has ordered several businesses to evacuate and told the superintendent to close the school for the day. In addition, several major commuter routes are cordoned off during the initial phase of the investigation.

After observing all of this activity, the manager turns on his car radio and hears local reporters describing the emergency du jour — a large cloud of what authorities suspect is chlorine gas from an unknown source. After hearing the report, the boss says "I guess we should call the NRC right away," and he immediately places the call.

Have CERCLA's notification requirements been satisfied? When and how did either the manager or the boss have knowledge that a release had occurred? That the release exceeded the RQ for chlorine? What do "as soon as" and "immediately" mean in this context?

3. THE CONSOLIDATED EDISON PROSECUTION

On August 19, 1989, the manhole on a Consolidated Edison steam pipe in Manhattan exploded, killing 3 people and injuring 24 others. The explosion shot scalding mud and debris 18 stories into the air, spraying apartment buildings in the Gramercy Park neighborhood with a layer of brown sludge as steam erupted in a thunderous roar. Four hours later, the geyser had finally subsided.

Con Ed officials knew within hours of the explosion that the pipe was not on a list of asbestos-free pipes, and thus should be assumed to be insulated with asbestos. The pipe was, indeed, lined with asbestos, and it was later determined that the explosion spewed at least 200 pounds of asbestos-contaminated debris into the neighborhood. Indeed, so much asbestos escaped that residents could see it caked on trees in the park.

Con Ed quickly tested the area for asbestos contamination, and by the next day it knew that six samples indicated the presence of asbestos. Still, the company told authorities that "all asbestos had been removed from the damaged area before the explosion as part of a continuing abatement program, and that in any case, tests from the blast area showed no asbestos."[18] Relying on Con Ed's tests and statements, city officials allowed residents back into their apartments, where they tracked contaminated debris into living areas and further increased their exposure.

Con Ed kept up the charade for four days, until residents of one of the affected buildings performed their own tests and confirmed that asbestos was present.

The incident led to criminal charges against Con Ed; Constantine Papakrasas, an assistant vice president in charge of the utility's steam operations division; and Philip McGivney, the division manager of steam construction. All three were charged with failure to comply with CERCLA's requirement that the utility immediately notify appropriate authorities that a release of a hazardous substance in an amount that equaled or exceeded the RQ for asbestos had occurred.

In announcing the indictment, U.S. Attorney Mary Jo White charged that "Con Ed had, and was aware of, records that the manhole where the explosion occurred contained over 200 pounds of asbestos" and was aware

---

[18]Matthew L. Wald, *Asbestos No Secret, Con Ed Says*, N.Y. TIMES, Dec. 18, 1993, § 1, at 26.

of "broad areas of contamination."[19]   The indictment accused Con Ed of trying to conceal the release in order to save the company the "significant expense of legally-mandated asbestos cleanup procedures."[20]

As we will see in Chapter 8, prosecutors often use conventional criminal statutes in environmental prosecutions, and the Con Ed case was no exception. In addition to the environmental violations, the indictment also charged the defendants with conspiracy to defraud the United States and with multiple counts of making false statements. The conspiracy count described Con Ed's steam pipe system, its internal procedures for handling steam emergencies, and the utility's failure to follow those procedures in the aftermath of the explosion. The indictment alleged that the defendants even failed to notify Con Ed's own internal departments, including its Central Information Group and its Environmental Affairs Division, which bore primary responsibility for dealing with steam incidents.

UNITED STATES V. CONSOLIDATED EDISON OF NEW YORK, INC. INDICTMENT

S1 93 Cr. 1063 (JSM) (S.D.N.Y. 1993)

* * *

II. Background of the Conspiracy
CON EDISON'S Steam System

4.   At all times relevant to this Indictment:

a.   CON EDISON, the defendant, maintained approximately 100 miles of underground steam pipes, which extended from the southern tip of Manhattan to 96th Street. Steam manholes located throughout Manhattan provided access to the underground piping.

b.   Piping in CON EDISON's steam system was covered with thermal insulation. The purpose of insulating the steam pipes was, in part, to reduce heat loss as steam travelled through the underground pipes, and thus to maximize the efficiency of the system.

---

[19]Jane Fritsch, *Con Ed Is Accused of 1989 Cover-up in Asbestos Blast*, N.Y. TIMES, Dec. 17, 1993, at A1.

[20]Indictment, United States v. Consol. Edison of New York, Inc., S1 93 Cr. 1063 (JSM), at 12 (S.D.N.Y. 1993). The indictment also charged them with failing to give required notification under the Emergency Planning and Community Right-to-Know Act of 1986.

c. CON EDISON maintained certain records from which it was able to, and from which it in fact did, determine whether or not sections of steam piping were installed with asbestos insulation. These records included maps of its underground steam pipes, known as "steam plates," and detailed drawings of the pipes as constructed, known as "loose leafs." Both types of documents reflected the date on which the piping depicted on them was installed. The date of installation was significant because during the period from approximately the 1920's through approximately 1974, asbestos-containing thermal insulation was installed on the steam pipes. Among the types of asbestos used for this purpose was amosite asbestos.

d. In or about the middle 1980's, CON EDISON embarked upon a program to abate, that is to remove, asbestos from the piping in its steam manholes. CON EDISON maintained, within its Steam Operations Division, a document known as an "asbestos free manhole log." The log listed all manholes known not to contain asbestos, either because the manhole had been abated, or because the manhole had been installed or rebuilt after 1974, when CON EDISON stopped installing asbestos insulation in its steam system. Piping contained in manholes not listed on the "asbestos free manhole log" was considered, by CON EDISON, to be asbestos insulated.

CON EDISON's Procedures for Handling Steam Emergencies

5. At all times relevant to this Indictment:

a. CON EDISON, the defendant, had written procedures which set forth the manner in which its officers and employees were to respond in the event of an emergency in the steam system which potentially could release asbestos into the environment.

b. The procedures governing the Steam Operations Division were contained in a document entitled "Handling and Control of Steam Incidents" as well as in CON EDISON's "Asbestos Management Manual." These procedures required CON EDISON personnel to assume that any debris resulting from a failure in the steam system contained asbestos, and to take certain precautions. Among other things, CON EDISON was required by these procedures to erect barricades to prevent pedestrian entry into the affected area, to post signs warning of asbestos danger, and to outfit workers entering the affected area with respirators and protective clothing.

c. CON EDISON's procedures further required that bulk debris be sampled and analyzed for the presence of asbestos. In accordance with government regulations, samples that contained greater than one percent asbestos would be deemed to be "positive." Positive samples would confirm the presumption that the debris was asbestos containing, and would require CON EDISON to remove the debris using proper asbestos abatement techniques.

d.   CON EDISON's procedures for "Handling and Control of Steam-Incidents" further required the management of the Steam Operations Division to communicate pertinent information regarding a possible asbestos release, including information regarding the asbestos test results, to CON EDISON's Central Information Group ("CIG"), for further dissemination of the information within the company.

e.   Among the divisions that CIG was required to notify regarding a possible asbestos release was CON EDISON's Environmental Affairs Division.   Upon receiving this information, the Environmental Affairs Division was charged with determining whether a report of an asbestos release to the NRC [National Response Center], as well as to state and local government agencies, was required, and with notifying CIG of its determination.   CIG, in turn, was charged with making any required notifications.

The Gramercy Park Explosion

6.   On Saturday, August 19, 1989, at approximately 6:30 P.M., piping in a steam manhole located on East 20th Street near Third Avenue, in the vicinity of Gramercy Park in Manhattan ("the Gramercy Park manhole"), exploded. The force of the explosion shattered the street, tore the roof from the manhole, stripped the pipes of their insulation, and spewed asbestos-containing debris from the manhole over the surrounding area.

7.   According to pertinent steam plates, loose leafs and other documents pertaining to the Gramercy Park manhole, the manhole and the piping in it had been installed during the period that CON EDISON, the defendant, insulated its steam pipes with asbestos-containing insulation. The Gramercy Park manhole was not listed on the "asbestos free manhole log," thus indicating that it was, at the time of the explosion, an asbestos-insulated manhole. Records being used by CON EDISON in connection with the repair of the Gramercy Park manhole following the explosion, together with other data then available to it, included information indicating that the insulation in the manhole contained approximately 200 pounds or more of asbestos.

8. On August 19 and 20, 1989, CON EDISON, the defendant, took twenty-one samples of the debris deposited in the area as a result of the explosion, and analyzed those samples in its chemical laboratory. Six of

those samples contained greater than one percent amosite asbestos and thus, under pertinent government regulations, were positive for amosite asbestos. These six positive samples established a zone of asbestos contamination that spread from the point of the explosion eastward to at least the middle of Third Avenue, and westward on East 20th Street toward Gramercy Park East. Three of these samples, taken on East 20th Street, contained between 10 percent and 30 percent amosite asbestos. The remaining fifteen samples taken by CON EDISON contained less than one percent asbestos. However, twelve of those "negative" samples contained detectible levels of amosite asbestos — a type of asbestos used in CON EDISON's steam system. CON EDISON did not sample further to determine how far the contamination had spread.

9.   Defendants CONSTANTINE J. PAPAKRASAS, a/k/a "Gus," and PHILIP B. McGIVNEY learned within several hours of the explosion, on August 19, 1989, that the Gramercy Park manhole was not listed on the "asbestos free manhole log." These defendants learned of the six positive test results, which confirmed the asbestos release, on Sunday, August 20, 1989.

10. During the period from on or about August 19, 1989 through on or about August 23, 1989, despite the facts known to the defendants and despite CON EDISON's own procedures, CON EDISON did not report that the Gramercy Park explosion had released more than a pound of asbestos into the environment to any federal, state or city government agency, to the media or to the public. CON EDISON informed an official of the EPA, in substance, that asbestos had been found in the area of the explosion, but that CON EDISON did not believe that the asbestos had come from the Gramercy Park manhole. Additionally, CON EDISON informed officials of the New York City Health Department and DEP that there was no asbestos in the manhole at the time of the explosion and that CON EDISON's sampling revealed that there was no significant asbestos contamination at Gramercy Park.

11. As a result of the defendants' failure to disclose the asbestos release, residents of buildings contaminated with CON EDISON's asbestos, who had previously been evacuated as a result of the explosion, returned to their homes; pedestrian and vehicular traffic was permitted in contaminated areas; and CON EDISON employees worked in contaminated areas without using respirators and clothing necessary to protect them from asbestos.

12. On or about August 23, 1989, a representative of the residents of 32 Gramercy Park South, a building which had been strewn with debris as a result of the explosion, informed the media that they had conducted tests and found asbestos inside their building.

13. On or about August 24, 1989, CON EDISON, the defendant, reported to the NRC by telephone that a steam main had exploded and that "follow-up testing" revealed that the material in a nearby building located at 32 Gramercy Park South contained asbestos. On that same day, in a written notification to the NRC, CON EDISON confirmed the report of asbestos at 32 Gramercy Park South, and stated that it had not been confirmed whether asbestos found in the building "came from the building or the steam pipe."

14. On or about August 24, 1989, CON EDISON, the defendant, notified the DEP that asbestos had been found at 32 Gramercy Park South, and stated that it had not been confirmed whether asbestos found in the building "came from the building or the steam pipe."

15. From on or about August 23 through on or about August 28, 1989, CON EDISON, the defendant, informed the media that it did not know the source of the asbestos found in the building located at 32 Gramercy Park South, that its August 20 test results were insignificant, and that the asbestos found in the building could have come either from the building, nearby construction debris, or CON EDISON's steam system.

16. After the Government and the public learned of the extensive asbestos contamination at Gramercy Park, CON EDISON, the defendant, paid over $90 million for an asbestos cleanup, to compensate residents, and for other expenditures related to the asbestos release.

III. The Conspiracy

17. From on or about August 19, 1989, up to and including on or about August 31, 1989, in the Southern District of New York and elsewhere, CON EDISON, CONSTANTINE J. PAPAKRASAS, a/k/a "Gus," and PHILIP B. McGIVNEY, the defendants, and others to the Grand Jury known and unknown, unlawfully, wilfully, and knowingly did combine, conspire, confederate, and agree together and with each other: (i) to defraud the United States and its departments and agencies in connection with the performance of lawful governmental functions; and (ii) to commit offenses against the United States, to wit, violations of Title 42, United States Code, Section 9603 and 11045(b)(4) and Title 18, United States Code, Section 1001.

Objects of the Conspiracy

18. It was a part and object of the conspiracy that CON EDISON, CONSTANTINE J. PAPAKRASAS, a/k/a "Gus," and PHILIP B.

McGIVNEY, the defendants, and others to the Grand Jury known and unknown, would and did seek to obstruct and hinder the federal government and its departments and agencies, including the NRC, EPA, and OSHA, from learning of the release into the environment of approximately 200 pounds or more of asbestos from the Gramercy Park manhole, in order to prevent the federal government from evaluating the risk to the public health, CON EDISON's employees, and the environment resulting from the release, and from directing appropriate containment, worker protection, and clean-up procedures, and thereby to enable CON EDISON, among other things, to avoid the significant expense of legally-mandated asbestos cleanup procedures.

19. It was further a part and object of the conspiracy that CON EDISON, CONSTANTINE J. PAPAKRASAS, a/k/a "Gus," and PHILIP B. McGIVNEY, the defendants, and others to the Grand Jury known and unknown, being in charge of a facility, to wit, the piping in CON EDISON's steam system, from which a hazardous substance, to wit, friable asbestos, had been released without a federal permit in a quantity greater than that determined pursuant [to] Title 42, United States Code, Section 9602, to wit, approximately 200 pounds or more, unlawfully, wilfully and knowingly would and did fail to notify immediately the appropriate agency of the United States Government, to wit, the NRC, as soon as they had knowledge of that release and would and did cause to be submitted, in a notification to the NRC, information which they knew to be false and misleading, in violation of Title 42, United States Code, section 9603.

20. It was further a part and object of the conspiracy that CON EDISON, CONSTANTINE J. PAPAKRASAS, a/k/a "Gus," and PHILIP B. McGIVNEY, the defendants, and others to the Grand Jury known and unknown, being the owners and operators of a facility, to wit, the piping in CON EDISON's steam system, at which a hazardous chemical was produced, used and stored, and from which a hazardous substance, to wit, friable asbestos, had been released in a quantity greater than that determined pursuant [to] Title 42, United States Code, Section 9602, to wit, approximately 200 pounds or more, unlawfully, wilfully and knowingly would and did fail to make the notification required by Title 42, United States Code, Section 11004 to the community emergency coordinator for the local emergency planning committee, the state emergency planning commission, or any of their respective designees, immediately after the release, in violation of Title 42, United States Code, Section 11045(b)(4).

21. It was further a part and object of the conspiracy that CON EDISON, CONSTANTINE J. PAPAKRASAS, a/k/a "Gus," and PHILIP B.

McGIVNEY, the defendants, and others to the Grand Jury known and unknown, in a matter within the jurisdiction of departments and agencies of the United States, to wit, the NRC and the EPA, unlawfully, wilfully and knowingly would and did falsify, conceal and cover up by trick, scheme and device a material fact, and cause to be made false, fictitious and fraudulent statements and representations, and make and use false writings and documents knowing the same to contain false, fictitious and fraudulent statements and entries, in violation of Title 18, United States Code, Section 1001.

Methods and Means of the Conspiracy

22. In order to carry out the above conspiracy to conceal the release of asbestos resulting from the explosion in the Gramercy Park manhole, and thereby to prevent city, state and federal government agencies from evaluating the public health risk and directing containment and clean-up procedures, the defendants and their co-conspirators used the following means, among others:

a. The defendants and their co-conspirators provided false, incomplete and misleading information to and withheld material facts from employees of the Environmental Affairs Division of CON EDISON, the defendant, which was investigating whether it was necessary to report to the NRC and other government agencies that asbestos had been released as a result of the explosion in the Gramercy Park manhole.

[The defendants and their co-conspirators also provided false, incomplete and misleading information to and withheld material facts from the Public Information Section of CON EDISON; from the Industrial Hygiene and Worker Safety Department of CON Edison; from CON EDISON employees working at the explosion site; and from city, state and federal agencies with regulatory authority over CON EDISON.]

e. The defendants and their co-conspirators failed to treat the debris as asbestos-containing; failed to establish a regulated area demarcated as an asbestos work area; failed to barricade the contaminated area; failed to post signs warning of asbestos danger; failed to abate the asbestos with special equipment and properly remove and dispose of it; failed to direct CON EDISON employees working in the contaminated area to use protective clothing, respirators and safety equipment; and failed to conduct personal monitoring of CON EDISON employees to ensure that they were not exposed to impermissibly high levels of asbestos.

The indictment alleged the conspiracy was carried out through falsification and concealment. Acts of concealment included failing to inform Con Ed's Central Information Group (CIG) that six samples of debris had tested positive for asbestos notwithstanding that CIG had earlier been told there was no asbestos in the first four samples that were tested; misrepresenting to those in charge of Con Ed's environmental and public relations departments and to various government agencies that it wasn't clear whether there had ever been asbestos in the manhole, but if there had been, it had been removed before the explosion; that the asbestos could have come from other sources, including a building or brake linings.[21]

Although Con Ed eventually spent around $90 million to clean up the asbestos and temporarily relocate affected residents, the utility's response to the indictment was a steadfast denial of involvement in any kind of cover up.

> In its statement, Con Ed said, "Given the extraordinary amount of media coverage of the incident and the fact that the company had full knowledge that government officials were carrying out their own independent asbestos tests, allegations of a cover-up are not credible."
>
> "It was quite well-known to concerned Con Edison employees and New York City police, fire and other government employees that both the New York City Dept. of Environmental Protection and Con Edison were testing for asbestos contamination immediately following the explosion. The [DEP] independently took four samples, all of which were negative. Con Edison took twenty-one samples, fifteen of which were negative, six positive," Con Ed added.
>
> The utility continued: "Con Edison, which has always accepted full responsibility for this devastating and unfortunate accident, shared the results of its asbestos tests with government officials as soon as the results became available.
>
> "Con Ed unequivocally believes that the charges are without merit and the company is confident that trial evidence will demonstrate the innocence of Con Edison and its two retired employees."[22]

DISCUSSION QUESTIONS

1. The indictment describes Con Ed's procedures for reporting environmental accidents. Does Con Ed's reporting policy shield the

---

[21]*Id.* at 16-18.

[22]*Grand Jury Indicts Con Ed, Two Workers of Fraud in Steam Asbestos Explosion*, UTIL. ENV'T REP., Dec. 24, 1993, at 1.

company from responsibility if individual employees deviate from normal operating procedures? Under what circumstances could Con Ed's CEO have been indicted for events stemming from the Gramercy Park explosion?

2. What purpose does CERCLA's notification requirement serve if, as in this case, state agencies are aware of the environmental accident and have already tested the area for contaminants?

3. Would Con Ed have been justified in relying on tests performed by the DEP?

4. In what sense were Papakrasas and McGivney persons in charge of a utility owned and operated by Con Ed?

5. When did Papakrasas and McGivney know that asbestos had been released? How and when did they know that an amount equal to or exceeding the RQ for asbestos had been released?

6. What was the facility from which the asbestos was released into the environment?

SENTENCING AND CORPORATE CULTURE

After five years of denials, Con Ed and Papakrasas entered guilty pleas in the Gramercy Park case. Charges were dropped against McGivney because a stroke had left him incompetent to stand trial. Papakrasas, who was not sentenced to any prison time because of poor health, was ordered to pay only a $5,000 fine, but Con Ed was ordered to pay the maximum fine — $2 million. At the sentencing hearing, the judge admonished that "there were people at Con Edison . . . who clearly knew and who should have been jumping up and down saying, 'there is asbestos there, we know it.' It was obvious that they didn't say it because they were intimidated from saying it, because they didn't think that was the corporate culture."[23]

To address Con Ed's culture of intimidation and its poor environmental compliance record, the judge also sentenced the utility to serve three years on probation under the supervision of a court-appointed monitor. The court order gave the monitor, Mitchell Bernard, extraordinary access to Con Ed and permitted him to review all of Con Ed's programs relating to legal compliance issues. Employees were instructed to contact Bernard if they knew of any violation of the law, and the court required that Bernard's phone number be posted at all of Con Ed's facilities. Bernard, in turn, was

---

[23] *The Front: Reddy Kilowatt: On Probation,* 18 MULTINATIONAL MONITOR 7 (Oct. 1997) [hereinafter *On Probation*].

responsible for investigating the calls and notifying law enforcement authorities of any violations.

The judge found this unusual step necessary because top executives at Con Ed had willfully ignored evidence that asbestos had been released. "There was a sense here at certain levels in this company that you better not tell the bad news," the judge said. "That is what I want to be sure has changed."[24] Because even a seven-figure fine could become just another cost of doing business for the $7 billion utility, the appointment of a special monitor was meant to "keep the sword of Damocles hanging over the company."[25]

Many of the monitor's reports reflected little or no change. In fact, they portrayed a picture of a few executives struggling to alter a deeply entrenched corporate culture. For example, Bernard's third report concluded with the observation that Con Ed was "expending a great deal of effort to develop and implement an effective program," but that its effort "exceeds its effect."[26]

> In his sixth report, released in June 1997, Bernard reports on a troubling incident of a Con Ed gas supervisor. The supervisor, working for the midnight shift, shuffled through a desk drawer for a stapler. He came across a thermostat containing mercury. He knew the thermostat should be stored in a drum designated for such waste. He packaged the thermostat, filled out the necessary paperwork and placed it in the appropriate storage drum.
>
> Believing he had not completed the form completely, he e-mailed his direct supervisor — a manager — telling him the story of the thermostat.
>
> Upon receiving the e-mail, the manager was perturbed. "We will probably read about this in the next monitor's report," he predicted.
>
> When the gas supervisor reported to work the next day, he found a shovel on his desk. "It had a tag bearing his name," Bernard wrote. The gas supervisor took the shovel to mean "bury him," and felt harassed.
>
> Bernard reported that "during my recent travels through the company, an unsettling number of employees continued to express a fear of reprisals if they report unwelcome news."
>
> "While the fear is especially intense at the lower end of the company hierarchy, it is not confined to this group," he reported. "Managers a rung

---

[24]James C. McKinley, Jr., *Con Edison Sentenced for Asbestos Cover-Up: 3 Years of Forced Monitoring for Hiding the Bad News*, N.Y. TIMES, Apr. 22, 1995, § 1, at 16.

[25]*Id.*

[26]*On Probation, supra* note 23.

or two below the officer level have expressed a fear of speaking up. Many employees said their fears will intensify once the probation ends."

"Retaliation occurs in an atmosphere that permits it," Bernard concluded. "I believe the chairman of the company was sincere when he told the court that 'intimidation and mistreatment in any way of anyone who reports an environmental problem will not be tolerated.' "

"Until that message is fully translated into vigilance at the local level, however, retaliation will continue to occur," Bernard wrote. Bernard said that he had come across six whistleblowers whose inquiries through the court-created hotline resulted in the most unflattering findings or significant discipline.[27]

Despite such troubling reports, Con Ed's probation was lifted in 1998 after the judge found the utility had made "genuine and significant strides toward developing and implementing" an environmental compliance program. Indeed, Con Ed's spokesman later conceded that the monitor's guidance had helped Con Ed focus on environmental concerns. "We have aggressively integrated environmental issues into the daily planning of our work, establishing environmental procedures, information systems, emergency response, system assessment, communications and compliance reports. . . . Our programs have evolved and strengthened, and we now have one of the leading environmental programs in the country."[28]

If the utility's initial response to a more recent steam pipe explosion is any indication, the judge seems to have been justified in his finding. On July 18, 2007, another Con Ed steam pipe exploded in New York City, this time just down the street from Grand Central Terminal. The explosion was powerful enough to create a crater approximately 35 feet by 40 feet and throw an 8-ton tow truck into the hole. Though the type and strength of the explosion were eerily similar to that of 1989, Con Ed's reaction could not have been more different.

Instead of denying the presence of asbestos for days, the company made a "nearly immediate" acknowledgment that asbestos from the blast might pose a danger.[29] Even before the area had been tested for asbestos, Con Ed's spokesman said that "[w]e always assume there's asbestos in a steam pipe, . . . so we are treating these materials set up by the rupture, including piping,

---

[27]*Id.* at 8.

[28]David W. Dunlap, *Memories of the '89 Blast Linger in Gramercy Park*, N.Y. TIMES, July 21, 2007, at B4.

[29]*Id.*

as if asbestos were in them."[30]   Although the city's Department of Environmental Protection found no asbestos in air samples, samples of debris showed traces of asbestos.

Unlike the 1989 clean up efforts, during which residents were allowed to enter their homes and track in asbestos-laden debris, immediately after the 2007 explosion police cordoned off several blocks around the blast as a "frozen zone" to restrict vehicular and pedestrian traffic.[31] This time around, those originally at the scene took heavy precautions against asbestos contamination. Firefighters wore breathing tanks on their backs, and as people who had been exposed to debris from the explosion flowed into a local hospital, they were stripped and quickly showered in a separate room before being examined. The day after the blast, the city's Office of Emergency Management announced that the steam was believed to contain asbestos, and it advised those caught in the geyser to discard their clothes and bathe carefully. Suffice it to say that if Con Ed had admitted at the outset that asbestos had been released in the Gramercy Park explosion, officials could have instituted some of the same procedures to protect emergency workers and residents from needless exposure to asbestos.

DISCUSSION QUESTIONS

1. Steam pipe explosions in New York City occur more often than one might expect. There have been more than a dozen in the last 20 years. But there is no suggestion that Con Ed was at fault (e.g., negligent) for the Gramercy Park explosion. If Con Ed was without fault, was criminal prosecution warranted?

2. We considered organizational liability briefly in Chapter 3. Under what theory could Con Ed be held criminally responsible? What is the rationale for prosecuting the company? Why wouldn't the government be satisfied to prosecute only Messrs. Papakrasas and McGivney?

3. The judge imposed a $2 million fine — the maximum — on Con Ed, a multi-billion dollar company. Does the fine serve the purpose of punishment? Of deterrence?

---

[30]James Barron, *An Explosion Rips Section of Midtown; Woman Dies*, N.Y. TIMES, July 19, 2007, at A1.

[31]Manny Fernandez, *Traffic Flows Again Near Site of Ruptured Steam Pipe*, N.Y. TIMES, July 22, 2007, at 23.

4. Con Ed ultimately paid almost $100 million in clean up costs. Is that a more effective penalty than the criminal fine?

5. The judge placed Con Ed on probation for three years and appointed a special monitor. What purpose does this part of the sentence serve?

6. It has been suggested that during the three-year probationary term, there was an effort to change Con Ed's corporate culture. What does this mean?

4. IMMUNITY

As is true under the Clean Water Act's notification provisions, the CERCLA duty to report releases of hazardous substances into the environment has obvious Fifth Amendment implications. As we saw in Illustration J in Chapter 4, the captain of a ship might be reluctant to report an oil spill when the ship runs aground because if he negligently caused the spill (he was intoxicated at the time), he would have committed a criminal violation of the Clean Water Act. That, in turn, leads to a personal dilemma. If he reports the spill, he will incriminate himself. If he doesn't report it, he commits an independent crime by failing to comply with the Clean Water Act's notification requirements. Thus, Congress provided immunity from prosecution for the person who is required to report, provided the information reported is truthful.

The same dilemma exists under CERCLA's notification provisions. The reportable release could well violate RCRA, the Clean Air Act, or the Clean Water Act, and the incriminating report would be made under legal compulsion. Congress addressed this issue in CERCLA by providing limited use immunity for a person in charge who is required to notify authorities of a reportable release. Under CERCLA, neither the contents of the notification given by the person in charge nor information that is derived from the notification can be used against the person giving the notice "in any criminal case, except a prosecution for perjury or for giving a false statement."[32]

Thus, if providing the required notice implicates the reporting party in a crime, that information may not be used against him in a criminal prosecution. But if the reporting party provides false information — say, by lying about the time when he learned about a release or about the nature or

---

[32]42 U.S.C. § 9603.

quantity of the substance that was released — then he remains subject to criminal prosecution under the federal perjury and false statements statutes.[33]

Notably, the statutory immunity extends only to criminal prosecutions based on the contents of the immunized notification. It does not protect the reporting party against use of the reported information in either civil or administrative proceedings.

Unlike immunity under the Clean Water Act, CERCLA's immunity provision does not distinguish between individuals and corporations. Thus, even though corporations have no Fifth Amendment privilege against self-incrimination, they are protected from any criminal prosecution based on truthful information the corporation reports pursuant to CERCLA's notification requirements.

---

[33]*See* 18 U.S.C. § 1001 (false statements); 18 U.S.C. § 1961 (perjury); 18 U.S.C. § 1963 (false declarations). *Cf.* United States v. Apfelbaum, 445 U.S. 115 (1980) (construing the federal use immunity statute, 18 U.S.C. § 6002, in the context of a perjury prosecution).

Liability under the perjury and false statements statutes will be considered in Chapter 8.

8

CONVENTIONAL CRIMINAL STATUTES

Conspiracy is the "darling of the modern prosecutor's nursery."[†]

The mail fraud statute is the federal government's "first line of defense" against fraudulent schemes.[††]

The principal focus of the prosecutions we have considered in previous chapters has been on substantive violations of the Clean Water Act, Clean Air Act, RCRA, and CERLA. That is not to say, however, that defendants who violate these statutes will necessarily be charged exclusively with environmental crimes. They often find themselves charged with collateral crimes defined in criminal statutes of general applicability. Thus, for example, a study of RCRA prosecutions brought in the first decade of the environmental criminal enforcement program found that roughly 45 percent of the prosecutions included a combination of environmental charges and charges brought under statutes of general applicability — principally the federal conspiracy, mail fraud, and false statements statutes — as shown in Table 1.

[†]Judge Learned Hand, United States Court of Appeals, Second Circuit.
[††]Chief Justice Warren Burger.

Table 1[1]

Title 18 Charging Patterns in RCRA Prosecutions
Fiscal Years 1983-1992

Title 18 Charges	Number of Cases	Percent
Conspiracy[2]	43	67%
False Statements	22	34%
Mail Fraud	7	10%
Other	9	14%

These Title 18 crimes[3] are almost always related to the environmental violations.

> They arise out of or are otherwise committed *because* of the environmental violation. [The] defendants filed false monitoring reports to cover up noncompliance with regulatory or permit requirements,[4] lied to environmental investigators to conceal violations or their role in committing them,[5] fraudulently billed business clients for promised services that were never performed,[6] made false bills of lading to deceive regulators or business associates about the nature of substances shipped or when the shipments occurred,[7] and falsely represented to grand juries that they had fully complied with subpoenaes.[8] In sum, the Title 18 crimes were almost invariably committed to facilitate successful evasion of environmental regulations.[9]

---

[1]Table 1 is adapted from Kathleen F. Brickey, *Charging Practices in Hazardous Waste Crime Prosecutions*, OHIO ST. L.J. 1077, 1107, 1112 (2001).

[2]Eleven cases (14 percent) charged both conspiracy and false statements violations.

[3]Because most conventional criminal statutes are codified in Title 18 of the United States Code, they are sometimes referred to as Title 18 crimes. — ED.

[4]*See, e.g.*, United States v. Brittain, 931 F.2d 1413 (10th Cir. 1991).

[5]*See, e.g.*, United States v. Blue Ridge Plating Co., 7 F.3d 226 No. 92-5441 1993 WL 358780 (4th Cir. Sept. 14, 1993) (unpublished table decision).

[6] *See, e.g.*, United States v. Eidson, 108 F.3d 1336 (11th Cir. 1997) (finding a scheme to defraud customers by falsely representing that wastewater would be properly disposed of).

[7]*See, e.g.*, United States v. Heuer, 4 F.3d 723 (9th Cir. 1993).

[8]*See, e.g.*, United States v. Asrar, 67 F.3d 309, Nos. 93-50610, 93-50623 1995 WL 579646 (9th Cir. Oct. 3, 1995) (unpublished table decision).

[9]Kathleen F. Brickey, *The Rhetoric of Environmental Crime: Culpability, Discretion, and Structural Reform*, 84 IOWA L. REV. 115, 139-140 (1998).

Thus, we pause to examine the use of these ancillary enforcement tools in environmental crime prosecutions.

A. CONSPIRACY

Judge Learned Hand once dubbed conspiracy the "darling of the modern prosecutor's nursery,"[10] and not without reason. Conspiracy doctrine plays a major role in federal criminal prosecutions,[11] including prosecutions that target environmental crime.

1. GENERAL PRINCIPLES

Conspiracy is an inchoate offense. It is an agreement between two or more parties to commit a crime. Like the law of attempt, conspiracy doctrine provides an independent basis for imposing liability for conduct that is preparatory to the commission of another crime. Yet conspiracy doctrine fixes liability at an earlier point in time. Participation in a conspiracy is punishable even if none of the conspirators actually commits or attempts to commit the other crime (the "object offense").

> **Illustration A:** Johnson and Jordan, officers of R & B chemicals, agree to dispose of untreated industrial wastewater by flushing it down the commode. Although R & B has a Clean Water Act permit to dispose of treated wastewater, introducing untreated wastewater into the sewer system violates the permit. Acting on an anonymous tip, federal investigators arrest Johnson and Jordan before they flush any of the wastewater down the commode.

> **Illustration B:** The same facts as in Illustration A, but with the following variation on the theme. Federal investigators don't receive the tip until after Johnson and Jordan have flushed hundreds of gallons of untreated wastewater down the commode.

---

[10]Harrison v. United States, 7 F.2d 259, 263 (2d Cir. 1925).

[11]The centrality of conspiracy doctrine in federal criminal law is partly a function of special procedural and evidentiary advantages the government enjoys, including liberal venue rules, a special exception to the hearsay rule, and the ability to jointly try members of the conspiracy. Prosecutors also benefit from a loose and rather inexact concept of what constitutes an agreement in this context.

What crime or crimes should Johnson and Jordan be charged with committing? In Illustration A, they could be charged with conspiracy to violate the Clean Water Act by failing to comply with the terms of the permit. They have agreed to commit a crime, but because the investigators intervened at an early stage of the game, Johnson and Jordan had not yet violated the Clean Water Act. In Illustration B, Johnson and Jordan could be charged both with conspiracy to violate and with violating the firm's CWA permit. Because the law treats conspiracy as an independent crime, it does not "merge" with the CWA violation. Thus, Johnson and Jordan could be convicted and punished both for conspiring to violate and for violating the CWA.

That brings us to the question of why conspiracies are (or should be) punishable as independent crimes. Since there was no environmental violation (and thus no actual harm) in Illustration A, why would a mere agreement to violate R & B's permit constitute a crime?

The rationale for punishing conspiracies revolves around a group danger theory. "[T]o unite, back of a criminal purpose, the strength, opportunities and resources of many is obviously more dangerous and more difficult to police than the efforts of a lone wrongdoer."[12] Thus, the argument runs, concerted criminal activity poses a greater threat to society than individual wrongdoing does.

Several assumptions are implicit in this rationale. First, concerted activity increases the probability that the conspirators will successfully achieve their criminal objective. It is assumed that Johnson and Jordan collectively are more likely to carry out the plan if they are acting in concert than if only one of them were acting alone. Second, collective actors are better equipped to pursue more ambitious or more complex goals. More resources, including sheer numbers of participants, make it possible to formulate and carry out more sophisticated or far-reaching plans. And third, even if a conspiracy begins with a relatively modest goal, the assumption is that, with an ongoing group already in place, the participants are more likely to expand their criminal objectives beyond the original goal.

---

[12]Krulewitch v. United States, 336 U.S. 440, 448-449 (1949).

DISCUSSION QUESTIONS

1. Does the stated rationale for punishing conspiracies adequately explain why, as in Illustration A, conduct that is merely preparatory to the commission of a crime should be separately punished? Are there additional reasons that would support this result?

2. Does the stated rationale adequately explain why a conspiracy does not merge into the completed offense when, as in Illustration B, the conspiratorial objective is successfully achieved? Why shouldn't it be enough that the government can prosecute Johnson and Jordan for the Clean Water Act violation? Does the rule that the conspiracy and its object offense do not merge unfairly give the government two bites at the apple?

3. Since the conspiracy and the object offense are related and may arise out of the same course of conduct, do we now have double jeopardy concerns?[13]

2. AGREEMENT

As noted above, conspiracy requires a plurality of parties. There can be no conspiracy absent proof of an agreement between two or more persons. Yet a conspiracy charge can be (and often is) relatively easy to prove, because the agreement need not be express or formal. It may be inferred from surrounding facts and circumstances such as concerted action among the alleged members of the group.

> **Illustration C:** Maureen, the president of Electroplating, Inc., asks Chris, the manager of M & O Transport, to haul a large load of hazardous waste from Electroplating's plant. Because Electroplating's business has fallen on hard times, Maureen tells Chris that Electroplating can't afford to "pay the freight" to have the waste disposed of at a licensed facility. Telling her that M & O will be happy to accommodate her needs, Chris quotes her an acceptable price for hauling the waste away. Once the deal is struck, Chris calls one of his drivers to arrange a pick up for the following day.

> **Illustration D:** Maureen e-mails Chris asking him to send a truck to pick up a load of hazardous waste and dispose of it at the local sanitary landfill.

---

[13]*Cf.* Blockburger v. United States, 284 U.S. 299 (1932). The *Blockburger* test is considered in Chapter 6.

The landfill is licensed to receive only ordinary household garbage. Chris never replies to the e-mail, but several days later an M & O Transport driver shows up at the Electroplating plant to pick up the load.

In Illustration C, even though Chris and Maureen may not have formalized the deal in writing or even sealed it with a handshake, they have an express agreement. Their objective — to dispose of hazardous waste at a facility that is not licensed to receive it — is a crime. And while the illegal objective has not yet been achieved (M & O has not yet picked up and disposed of the waste), the essence of the conspiracy is the agreement itself. Thus, there is ample evidence to establish a conspiracy between Chris and Maureen.

In Illustration D, there is no express agreement, but it would be reasonable to infer that Chris tacitly agreed to dispose of the waste at the landfill, an unlicensed facility. Absent additional unknown facts, there is no other plausible explanation for him to have sent the truck driver to the Electroplating plant the following day. Assuming Chris shares Maureen's intent to illegally dispose of the waste, there is a punishable conspiracy.

DISCUSSION QUESTIONS

1. Suppose that under the facts in Illustration C, Chris and Maureen are tried under a one count indictment for conspiring to illegally dispose of the waste at an unlicensed facility, in violation of RCRA. The jury returns a verdict finding Chris guilty and Maureen not guilty of conspiracy. Chris now argues that because the same jury that convicted him acquitted Maureen, the government failed to prove an essential element of the crime — an agreement between two parties. Can he prevail on the argument that the jury's inconsistent verdicts require reversal of his conviction?[14]

2. Implicit in Chris' argument is an assumption that the verdict acquitting Maureen of conspiracy is the "correct" verdict and that the verdict convicting him of the same crime is the "incorrect" one. Is this a logical (or supportable) assumption? Are there plausible explanations for the inconsistent verdicts?

3. Assume that Chris is correct in arguing that he was wrongfully convicted of conspiracy. Are there other ways to address the issue of wrongful

---

[14]*Cf.* United States v. Powell, 469 U.S. 57 (1984).

conviction besides throwing the conviction out simply because the jury returned inconsistent verdicts?

3. KNOWLEDGE AND INTENT

Even though the government can rely on circumstantial evidence like concerted action to prove an agreement, it cannot base its case on a theory of "guilt by association." One may innocently associate with others who, quite by happenstance, have conspired with one another. Thus, the prosecution must prove that each alleged conspirator knew the conspiracy existed and knowingly participated in it. But proof that the actor knew the full scope of the conspiracy or all of its details — or that he knew the identity and role of all of his fellow conspirators — is not required. Evidence that the actor knew the basic scope and general purpose of the conspiracy will suffice.

In addition to proving that the actor was a knowing participant, the government must also show intent to advance the conspiracy's unlawful goal.

Illustration E: Chris offers Maureen a deal she cannot refuse: he will haul away the hazardous waste from Electroplating's plant for a ridiculously low fee. Although Chris secretly intends to dump the waste in the woods, he does not tell Maureen where and how he plans to dispose of it. Obviously pleased with the offer Chris has made, Maureen does not ask what he plans to do with the waste. Instead, she thanks him and mails him a check for the fee.

DISCUSSION QUESTIONS

1. In Illustration E, Chris did not disclose his intention to dump the waste in the woods. Since Maureen did not know where and how he planned to dispose of the waste, can she successfully defend a conspiracy charge on the ground that she lacked the requisite knowledge and intent? What is the government's counter argument likely to be?
2. How, if at all, does intent to agree differ from intent to promote the object offense?

THE CASE OF THE SOLVENT-SATURATED SAWDUST

Hansen and Schmidt, both mid-level managers at PaintCo, decide to cut costs by having maintenance workers pour toxic chemical solvents into barrels of sawdust. When the solvents have been absorbed into the sawdust, the workers empty the barrels into a small dumpster containing PaintCo's ordinary garbage.

Hansen and Schmidt both know that: (1) the solvents are hazardous waste; (2) mixing the solvents with sawdust is improper; (3) Sanitary Trash Removal picks up PaintCo's trash from the dumpster twice a week and hauls it to the local landfill for disposal; and (4) the local landfill does not have a permit to receive hazardous waste.

Hansen knows the waste is highly toxic and can cause solvent poisoning if workers who handle it do not wear special protective gear. Hansen also knows that solvent poisoning can cause psycho-organic syndrome,[15] which can result in irreversible severe memory loss, serious psychiatric problems, and gross tremor. While Schmidt knows the solvents are toxic, he is unaware that special protective gear is needed to protect against solvent poisoning. Although the workers who handle the waste have neither asked for nor received any protective gear, none of them develops any symptoms of solvent poisoning.

DISCUSSION QUESTIONS

1. Have Hansen and Schmidt conspired to illegally transport hazardous waste?[16]
2. Have they conspired to illegally dispose of hazardous waste?[17]

---

[15]The Case of the Psycho-Organic Syndrome is considered in Chapter 6.
[16]The statute provides in relevant part:

Any person who —
    (1) knowingly transports or causes to be transported any hazardous
       waste . . . to a facility which does not have a permit . . .
[is guilty of a felony].

42 U.S.C. § 6928(d)(1).

[17]The statute provides in relevant part:

Any person who —
   . . .
    (2) knowingly treats, stores, or disposes of any hazardous waste . . . —
      (A) without having obtained a permit . . . or
      (B) in knowing violation of any material condition or requirement of

3. Have they conspired to illegally endanger the unprotected workers?[18]

4. OVERT ACT

There are a number of federal conspiracy statutes, many of which are directed at specific evils such as drug trafficking[19] and racketeering.[20] But for purposes of environmental crime prosecutions, the general federal conspiracy statute, 18 U.S.C. § 371, is by far the most important provision. Its prohibitions are relatively broad[21] and encompass conspiracies to violate any federal criminal law, including environmental laws that provide criminal penalties.

Apart from their relative degrees of subject matter specificity, federal conspiracy statutes are distinguishable from one another in that some require proof of an overt act while others do not.[22] The general conspiracy statute, § 371, is one that expressly requires an overt act in furtherance of the conspiratorial goal.

The overt act requirement is not particularly onerous, however. Although it must provide some objective evidence that the conspiracy is at work, the

---

> such permit . . .
> [is guilty of a felony].

42 U.S.C. § 6928(d)(2).

[18]The endangerment statute provides in relevant part:

> Any person who knowingly transports, treats, stores, disposes of, or exports any hazardous waste . . . who knows at that time that he thereby places another person in imminent danger of death or serious bodily injury [is guilty of a felony].

42 U.S.C. § 6928(e).

[19]*See, e.g.*, 21 U.S.C. § 846 (conspiracy to violate controlled substances act); 21 U.S.C. § 963 (conspiracy to import or export controlled substances).

[20]*See, e.g.*, 18 U.S.C. § 1962(d) (conspiracy to violate racketeering prohibitions in RICO statute).

[21]The general conspiracy statute prohibits conspiring to commit an offense against the United States or to defraud the United States. The distinctions between the "offense" clause and the "defraud" clause in § 371 are considered *infra*.

[22]The drug and racketeering conspiracy statutes cited in notes 19 & 20 do not expressly require an overt act. Consistent with the common law rule that the agreement is complete without proof of an overt act, the Supreme Court has ruled that if a conspiracy statute is silent on the point, no overt act is required. Salinas v. United States, 522 U.S. 52 (1997) (RICO conspiracy statute); United States v. Shabani, 513 U.S. 10 (1994) (drug conspiracy statute).

overt act need not be significant or even criminal. Thus, for example, in Illustration C when Chris picked up the phone to call the truck driver to arrange a pickup of the waste, he performed an overt act in furtherance of the conspiracy. Similarly, assuming the necessary knowledge and intent in Illustration E, Maureen's act of mailing the check for the transportation and disposal fee would satisfy the overt act requirement.

Because co-conspirators are deemed to be each other's agents, the overt act of one is attributable to all. Thus, the call between Chris and the truck driver (who is presumably not part of the conspiracy) would be enough to fix liability for both Chris and Maureen, as would Maureen's act of mailing the check to Chris — regardless of whether he knew it had been sent.

DISCUSSION QUESTIONS

1. What is the purpose of requiring an overt act? If facially innocent or innocuous conduct like making a telephone call or paying a service provider's fee can constitute an overt act, is this a meaningful prerequisite for criminal liability?
2. What rationale supports the rule that the overt act of one member of the conspiracy is attributable to all? In what sense can members of a conspiracy be considered agents of one another?
3. Suppose that in The Case of the Solvent-Laden Sawdust, Hansen and Schmidt had agreed to pour the solvent into the barrels of sawdust, which would violate the company's RCRA permit. But instead of recruiting others to perform the task, they decided to do it themselves. If Hansen and Schmidt are later charged with conspiracy to violate the permit and with the actual permit violation, should the government be allowed to rely on their act of pouring solvents into the sawdust as both the overt act needed to prove the conspiracy and as the conduct constituting the completed RCRA crime?

5. VICARIOUS LIABILITY

In addition to providing an independent basis for punishing conduct that is preparatory to the commission of another crime, conspiracy doctrine also provides a mechanism for imposing vicarious liability on a conspirator for substantive crimes committed by other members of the conspiracy.

PINKERTON V. UNITED STATES

328 U.S. 640 (1946)

Mr. Justice DOUGLAS delivered the opinion of the court.

[Daniel and Walter Pinkerton were convicted of one count of conspiracy to commit tax fraud and of six counts of tax fraud. Although there was no evidence that Daniel directly participated in the fraud, the evidence supported a finding that Walter had committed the fraud in furtherance of their unlawful agreement.]

... The question was submitted to the jury on the theory that each petitioner could be found guilty of the substantive offenses, if it was found at the time those offenses were committed petitioners were parties to an unlawful conspiracy and the substantive offenses charged were in fact committed in furtherance of it.[23]

Daniel relies on United States v. Sall, 116 F.2d 745. That case held that participation in the conspiracy was not itself enough to sustain a conviction for the substantive offense even though it was committed in furtherance of the conspiracy. The court held that, in addition to evidence that the offense was in fact committed in furtherance of the conspiracy, evidence of direct participation in the commission of the substantive offense or other evidence from which participation might fairly be inferred was necessary.

We take a different view. We have here a continuous conspiracy. There is here no evidence of the affirmative action on the part of Daniel which is necessary to establish his withdrawal from it. Hyde v. United States, 225 U.S. 347, 369. ... And so long as the partnership in crime continues, the partners act for each other in carrying it forward. It is settled that "an overt act of one partner may be the act of all without any new agreement specifically directed to that act." United States v. Kissel, 218 U.S. 601,

---

[23]The trial court charged: "... after you gentlemen have considered all the evidence in this case, if you are satisfied from the evidence beyond a reasonable doubt that at the time these particular substantive offenses were committed, that is, the offenses charged in the first ten counts of this indictment if you are satisfied from the evidence beyond a reasonable doubt that the two defendants were in an unlawful conspiracy, as I have heretofore defined unlawful conspiracy to you, then you would have a right, if you found that to be true to your satisfaction beyond a reasonable doubt, to convict each of these defendants on all these substantive counts, provided the acts referred to in the substantive counts were acts in furtherance of the unlawful conspiracy or object of the unlawful conspiracy, which you have found from the evidence existed." Daniel was not indicted as an aider or abettor, nor was his case submitted to the jury on that theory.

608. . . . The criminal intent to do the act is established by the formation of the conspiracy. . . . The unlawful agreement contemplated precisely what was done. It was formed for the purpose. The act done was in execution of the enterprise. The rule which holds responsible one who counsels, procures, or commands another to commit a crime is founded on the same principle. That principle is recognized in the law of conspiracy when the overt act of one partner in crime is attributable to all. An overt act is an essential ingredient of the crime of conspiracy under [18 U.S.C. § 371]. If that can be supplied by the act of one conspirator, we fail to see why the same or other acts in furtherance of the conspiracy are likewise not attributable to the others for the purpose of holding them responsible for the substantive offense.

A different case would arise if the substantive offense committed by one of the conspirators was not in fact done in furtherance of the conspiracy, did not fall within the scope of the unlawful project, or was merely a part of the ramifications of the plan which could not be reasonably foreseen as a necessary or natural consequence of the unlawful agreement. But as we read this record, that is not this case.

Affirmed.

[Opinion of RUTLEDGE, J., dissenting in part, omitted.]

DISCUSSION QUESTIONS

1. Is it clear what the scope of liability under the *Pinkerton* rule is? What is the underlying rationale supporting this species of liability?
2. Daniel was not indicted as an aider and abettor, and the jury was not instructed on an aiding and abetting theory. He was convicted of tax fraud only by virtue of evidence that he conspired with Walter. Could Daniel have been convicted as an aider and abettor?[24] Does *Pinkerton* liability differ from liability as an aider and abettor, or is liability under the two theories coextensive?
3. Daniel did not personally participate in the commission of the fraud. In fact, he was serving time in prison on unrelated charges. What, if anything, could he have done to avoid being vicariously liable for crimes committed by Walter?

---

[24]Aiding and abetting liability is considered in Chapter 2.

6. "OFFENSE" AND "DEFRAUD" CLAUSES

To be punishable under the general federal conspiracy statute, the conspiratorial objective must fall within one of two broad categories. First, it is unlawful to conspire to commit an offense against the United States. Simply put, under this prong of the statute, an agreement to violate any federal criminal statute is an agreement to commit a crime against the United States. Thus, for example, in Illustration A, Johnson and Jordan conspired to flush untreated wastewater down the commode. Since the conspiratorial objective was a criminal violation of the Clean Water Act, this is a conspiracy to commit an offense against the United States.

Second, it is unlawful to conspire to defraud the United States. In this context, the term "defraud" is not limited to financial fraud. Although the "defraud" clause would be violated by a scheme "to cheat the government out of property or money," it would also be violated if the conspiratorial objective was "to interfere with or to obstruct one of its lawful governmental functions by deceit, craft or trickery, or at least by means that are dishonest."[25]

> **Illustration F:** As part of the scheme to dispose of the untreated wastewater in Illustration A, Johnson and Jordan agree to cover up their unorthodox method of disposing of the waste by falsifying records they are required to maintain. They decide to record the disposal method as "discharge from pretreatment plant into Sandy Creek" in accordance with their CWA permit requirements.

Here, Johnson and Jordan's objective is to keep EPA at bay by depriving it of information it is entitled by law to receive. By lying about the waste disposal method, Johnson and Jordan have defrauded the agency by impeding its ability to carry out its regulatory mission.

Illustration F also raises another important question: what is the relationship between the offense clause and the defraud clause? The underlying facts in Illustration C begin with a plan to violate a Clean Water Act permit by improperly disposing of the wastewater, an apparent violation of the "offense" clause. The variation in Illustration F changes the focus to a plan to deprive EPA of accurate information about the disposal method, an apparent violation of the "defraud" clause. Is this a conspiracy to commit an offense against the United States, a conspiracy to defraud the United States,

---

[25]Hammerschmidt v. United States, 265 U.S. 182, 188 (1924).

or both?   If the agreement violates both prongs of the statute, is the government free to choose which clause it will charge Johnson and Jordan with violating?

The Fourth Circuit addressed these and other similar questions in United States v. Arch Trading Co.[26] In that case, Arch Trading was charged with conspiracy to commit an offense against the United States in connection with its installation of equipment it had supplied to a company owned by the Iraqi government. Although the equipment had been delivered before Iraq invaded Kuwait, the installation efforts occurred after the invasion and in violation of an executive order issued by President Bush. The executive order prohibited, inter alia, traveling to Iraq and dealing with the Iraqi government or its agents.

The court first held that violation of an executive order can constitute an offense under the "offense" clause of § 371, provided that Congress has authorized the executive order and has specified a criminal penalty for violating it. The court then turned to the relationship between the "offense" and "defraud" clauses of § 371.

> While Arch Trading's conduct could arguably have been charged also as a conspiracy "to defraud," the two prongs of § 371 are not mutually exclusive. Because of the broad interpretation which has been given the "defraud" clause, § 371's two clauses overlap considerably. . . .
>
> Because of this overlap, given conduct may be proscribed by both of the section's clauses. In such a situation, the fact that a particular course of conduct is chargeable under one clause does not render it immune from prosecution under the other. When both prongs of § 371 apply to the conduct with which a particular defendant is charged, the government enjoys considerable latitude in deciding how to proceed. *See* United States v. Jones, 976 F.2d 176, 183 (4th Cir. 1992) ("[F]aced with two equally applicable penal statutes, there is nothing wrong with the government's decision [absent an improper purpose] to prosecute under one and not the other"). Convictions under the "defraud" clause for conspiracies *to commit particular offenses* are commonly upheld. Conversely, convictions under the "offense" clause for conspiracy to engage in conduct which would defraud the United States are also proper. Many courts have even found it permissible to list both prongs of § 371 in a single indictment count rather than specifying whether the alleged conspiracy was one to defraud or one to commit an offense. . . .

---

[26]987 F.2d 1087 (4th Cir. 1993).

In short, the evidence in this case against Arch Trading would have supported conviction under either the "offense" or the "defraud" clause, and absent an improper motive, which is not alleged here, the government's choice of invoking the offense clause was an appropriate exercise of discretion.[27]

DISCUSSION QUESTIONS

1. In what sense can violating an executive order be equated with violating a statute? Under the reasoning in *Arch Trading*, are all violations of executive orders "offenses" for purposes of the conspiracy statute?
2. The court in *Arch Trading* said that absent an improper motive, the government is free to proceed at its discretion under either the offense clause or the defraud clause. What would constitute an improper prosecutorial motive?
3. What mental state is required to prove a conspiracy to commit an offense against the United States? Is it the same as the mental state required to prove a conspiracy to defraud the United States?
4. What is the difference between the scope of the "offense" and "defraud" clauses? Does the "defraud" clause reach agreements to engage in conduct that is not independently illegal (i.e., conduct that does not violate a separate criminal statute)?
5. Which of the following examples illustrates: (1) a conspiracy to defraud; (2) a conspiracy to commit an offense; (3) both; or (4) neither?
   a. The facts in Illustration F.
   b. Owens and Palmer ("the haulers"), who operate a hazardous waste hauling company, enter into a contract with Taylor, a hazardous waste generator, to transport and dispose of a tank of soil contaminated with a high concentration of PCBs. The contract provides that the haulers will transport the contaminated soil to a licensed facility, and the contract price is well within the normal range for properly performing the agreed upon service. Taylor provides the haulers a manifest that accurately describes the contents of the tank and designates the agreed upon licensed facility as the intended destination. Unbeknownst to Taylor, the haulers do not intend to deliver the contaminated soil to the designated facility. Instead, they intend to (and do) dump the soil in the woods. In

---

[27]*Arch Trading*, 987 F.2d at 1091-1092.

consequence, both the manifest and the records that EPA requires Taylor to maintain falsely represent that the soil has been properly disposed of at a licensed facility.

    c. Becker and Heller, the president and manager of an import certification laboratory that tests imported vehicles for compliance with EPA emission standards, file several thousand false vehicle emission reports certifying that noncomplying imported cars satisfy EPA standards.

6. If a conspiracy violates both the offense clause and the defraud clause of the statute, should the government charge the existence of a single conspiracy with alternative means for proving a prohibited conspiratorial objective? Or is it within the government's power to charge two separate conspiracy counts?

    To put this question in a more concrete context, assume the prosecutor wants to use the facts in Illustration A as the basis for charging Johnson and Jordan with conspiracy to commit a federal offense in Count 1 of an indictment. The prosecutor also wants to rely on the additional facts in Illustration F to support a separate charge of conspiracy to defraud the government in Count 2. If the government files a two count indictment and obtains convictions under each of the two counts, can it overcome a double jeopardy argument that the conspirators have been convicted twice for the same offense in violation of *Blockburger*?

7. The government's choice of which clause to proceed under can be a matter of considerable practical significance to the defendant, because most § 371 conspiracies are classified as felonies. The lone exception applies to a conspiracy to commit a federal crime that is classified as a misdemeanor. In this relatively rare situation, the punishment for the conspiracy can be no greater than the punishment for the underlying crime.

    Thus, for example, if an EPA employee embezzles $500 of the agency's funds, that constitutes a misdemeanor punishable by a year in prison and/or maximum fine of $100,000.[28] If the embezzlement had been the object of a conspiracy, the one year prison term and $100,000

---

[28] 18 U.S.C. § 641. The classification of the offense as a misdemeanor under § 641 is contingent on the amount of the theft. If the amount embezzled had exceeded $1,000, the theft would constitute a felony.

fine would also be the maximum punishment for the conspiracy if the conspiracy had been charged under the "offense" clause.

But as we have seen, the "offense" and "defraud" clauses are not mutually exclusive, and this hypothetical scenario could reasonably be characterized as a conspiracy to defraud the government of the embezzled funds. If charged under this theory, the conspiracy would be punishable as a felony. In situations like this, most courts give prosecutors wide latitude to charge the conspiracy under either clause, and a decision to charge under the defraud clause would elevate what would otherwise have been a misdemeanor prosecution to a felony case.

7. DURATION

Conspiracy is ordinarily a continuing offense. Its natural termination point is when the conspiratorial objective is achieved or all of the conspirators disavow its purpose. Individual members may terminate their participation in an ongoing conspiracy by withdrawing from it — i.e., by taking affirmative steps to disassociate themselves from the conspiracy and its criminal objectives. Although withdrawal does not extinguish the withdrawing member's liability for conspiracy or for crimes already committed in furtherance of its objective, it insulates the withdrawing party from liability for future crimes committed by fellow members of the conspiracy and causes the statute of limitations to begin to run on conspiracy charges that could be brought against him.

UNITED STATES V. JIMENEZ RECIO

537 U.S. 270 (2003)

Justice BREYER delivered the opinion of the Court.

We here consider the validity of a Ninth Circuit rule that a conspiracy ends automatically when the object of the conspiracy becomes impossible to achieve — when, for example, the Government frustrates a drug conspiracy's objective by seizing the drugs that its members have agreed to distribute. In our view, conspiracy law does not contain any such "automatic termination" rule. . . .

II

In *United States v. Cruz,* 127 F.3d 791 (9th Cir. 1997), the Ninth Circuit held that a conspiracy continues "'until there is affirmative evidence of abandonment, withdrawal, disavowal or defeat of the object of the conspiracy.'" The critical portion of this statement is the last segment, that a conspiracy ends once there has been "defeat of [its] object." The Circuit's holdings make clear that the phrase means that the conspiracy ends through "defeat" when the Government intervenes, making the conspiracy's goals impossible to achieve, even if the conspirators do not know that the Government has intervened and are totally unaware that the conspiracy is bound to fail. In our view, this statement of the law is incorrect. A conspiracy does not automatically terminate simply because the Government, unbeknownst to some of the conspirators, has "defeated" the conspiracy's "object."

Two basic considerations convince us that this is the proper view of the law. First, the Ninth Circuit's rule is inconsistent with our own understanding of basic conspiracy law. The Court has repeatedly said that the essence of a conspiracy is "an agreement to commit an unlawful act." That agreement is "a distinct evil," which "may exist and be punished whether or not the substantive crime ensues." The conspiracy poses a "threat to the public" over and above the threat of the commission of the relevant substantive crime — both because the "combination in crime makes more likely the commission of [other] crimes" and because it "decreases the probability that the individuals involved will depart from their path of criminality." Where police have frustrated a conspiracy's specific objective but conspirators (unaware of that fact) have neither abandoned the conspiracy nor withdrawn, these special conspiracy-related dangers remain. So too remains the essence of the conspiracy — the agreement to commit the crime. That being so, the Government's defeat of the conspiracy's objective will not necessarily and automatically terminate the conspiracy.

Second, the view we endorse today is the view of almost all courts and commentators but for the Ninth Circuit. . . . One treatise, after surveying lower court conspiracy decisions, has concluded that "impossibility of success is not a defense." 2 LaFave & Scott, Substantive Criminal Law § 6.5, at 85. . . .

In tracing the origins of the statement of conspiracy law upon which the *Cruz* panel relied, we have found a 1982 Ninth Circuit case, United States v. Bloch, 696 F.2d 1213, in which the court, referring to an earlier case, United States v. Krasn, 614 F.2d 1229 (9th Cir. 1980), changed the language of the traditional conspiracy termination rule. *Krasn* said that a conspiracy is "presumed to continue unless there is affirmative evidence that *the defendant* abandoned, withdrew from, or disavowed the conspiracy *or defeated its purpose.*" *Id.*, at 1236 (emphasis added). The *Bloch* panel changed the grammatical structure. It said that "a conspiracy is presumed to continue until *there is* . . . defeat of the purposes of the conspiracy." 696 F.2d at 1215 (emphasis added). Later Ninth Circuit cases apparently read the change to mean that a conspiracy terminates, not only when the *defendant* defeats its objective, but also when *someone else* defeats that objective, perhaps the police. . . . This history may help to explain the origin of the *Cruz* rule. But, since the Circuit's earlier cases nowhere give any reason for the critical change of language, they cannot help to justify it. . . .

[Opinion by STEVENS, J., concurring in part and dissenting in part, omitted.]

DISCUSSION QUESTION

1. What is the rationale for upholding convictions of would-be conspirators who joined an already defeated conspiracy? Does this stretch conspiracy law too far?

B. MAIL FRAUD

The mail fraud statute has long provided federal prosecutors a powerful tool to combat a multitude of frauds. Once described by Chief Justice Burger as the federal government's "first line of defense" against fraudulent schemes,[29] the mail fraud statute can be used to reach new and evolving forms of fraud long before Congress enacts specific legislation to combat them.[30] Thus, the statute has historically served as "a stopgap device"[31] to punish fraudulent conduct that may, but need not, constitute an independent crime. Indeed, the fraud itself need not be something that Congress can independently punish. The gist of the offense is the use of the mails to

---

[29]United States v. Maze, 414 U.S. 395, 405 (1974) (Burger, C.J., dissenting).

[30]Thus, for example, prosecutors invoked the mail fraud statute to reach fraudulent conduct such as loan-sharking, real estate swindles, securities fraud, and credit card fraud well before legislation that specifically targeted these types of fraud was enacted.

[31]*Maze*, 414 U.S. at 405.

further fraudulent activity. Thus, by virtue of its power to regulate the use of the United States mails, Congress can forbid using the mails to execute a fraudulent scheme "whether it can forbid the scheme or not."[32]

1. FRAUD

Although the mail fraud statute reaches three categories of schemes,[33] the prohibition against the use of the mails for the purpose of executing a scheme to defraud has become the primary enforcement tool. The broad proscription against using the mails to execute a scheme to defraud provides virtually open-ended liability, in part because the statute does not define the term "defraud." Nor have courts succeeded in providing concrete guidance. "To try to delimit 'fraud' by definition," as one court explained, "would tend to reward subtle and ingenious circumvention and is not done."[34] Thus, the mail fraud statute "condemns conduct which fails to match the reflection of moral uprightness, of fundamental honesty, fair play and right dealing in the general and business life of members of society."[35]

Notwithstanding that fraud is a fluid concept that courts have been unwilling to confine to a single definite meaning, a good working definition might be as follows: Fraud consists of an effort to gain an undue advantage or to bring about some harm through misrepresentation or breach of duty.

But not every deception rises to the level of fraud. Courts historically have assumed — and the Supreme Court more recently held[36] — that false or fraudulent representations or omissions must be material to constitute fraud under § 1341, even though the statute does not expressly require materiality. What, then, constitutes materiality in this context? Relying on

---

[32]Badders v. United States, 240 U.S. 391, 393 (1916). Thus, for example, schemes involving the mailing of fraudulent state tax returns are within the reach of the statute, even though Congress lacks jurisdiction over state tax matters. United States v. Mirabile, 503 F.2d 1005 (8th Cir. 1974).

[33]The statute prohibits the use of the mails to: (1) execute a scheme or artifice to defraud; (2) obtain money or property by false or fraudulent pretenses; or (3) sell, exchange, distribute, or procure for unlawful use counterfeit coins, securities, or other articles. 18 U.S.C. § 1341.

[34]Foshay v. United States, 68 F.2d 205, 211 (8th Cir. 1933). Cf. Weiss v. United States, 122 F.2d 675, 681 (5th Cir. 1941) (the term "fraud" simply "needs no definition").

[35]Blachly v. United States, 380 F.2d 665, 671 (5th Cir. 1967). Not surprisingly, the breadth and elasticity of the concept of fraud in this context has prompted criticism that the mail fraud statute places too much power in the prosecutor's hands.

[36]See Neder v. United States, 527 U.S. 1 (1999).

the Restatement (Second) of Torts, the Supreme Court in Neder v. United States adopted this definition of materiality. A statement is material if:

> (a) a reasonable man would attach importance to its existence or nonexistence in determining his choice of action in the transaction in question; or
>
> (b) the maker of the representation knows or has reason to know that its recipient regards or is likely to regard the matter as important in determining his choice of action, although a reasonable man would not so regard it.[37]

Simply put, to be material, a misrepresentation or omission must relate to the heart of the bargain. It cannot be mere window dressing.

Hand in glove with the materiality requirement is the additional overlay of intent to defraud. An inadvertent misstatement of a material fact would not, without more, constitute fraud, even though it might mislead or deceive. The misstatement must be "reasonably calculated to deceive persons of ordinary prudence and comprehension."[38]

Yet while fraud is the central concern, no actual harm or injury need be shown. "To hold otherwise would lead to the illogical result that the legality of a defendant's conduct would depend on his fortuitous choice of a gullible victim."[39]

THE CASE OF THE 100 MILE LIMIT

Adam and Eve were, respectively, the comptroller and "sludge coordinator" for Anchor Marine Transport. Anchor contracted with a number of municipalities to transport raw sewage sludge by barge for disposal at sea. Until 1987, federal regulations allowed disposal of the waste as close as 10 miles from shore. In 1987, a change in the law required the disposal site to be 100 miles from shore. In consequence, the disposal costs for Anchor's municipal customers increased by two to four times the original disposal fee. After the change in regulation, Anchor routinely engaged in "short dumping" — i.e., disposing of sewage sludge far short of the 100-mile limit. To conceal its illegal dumping, Anchor also falsified billing-related

---

[37]*Id.* at 22 n.5 (quoting Restatement (Second) of Torts § 538 (1976)).

[38]United States v. Hawkey, 148 F.3d 920, 924 (8th Cir. 1998) (quoting United States v. Coyle, 63 F.3d 1239, 1243 (3d Cir. 1995)).

[39]United States v. Pollack, 534 F.2d 964, 971 (D.C. Cir. 1976).

records. Adam and Eve participated in the deceptive billing practices, and all bills were sent through the mail.

After being told they would be charged with mail fraud, Anchor, Adam, and Eve argued that while their conduct might have violated ocean dumping rules, they did not commit mail fraud. They maintained that they had no intent to harm because the municipalities received what they bargained for — sludge removal — and that it was irrelevant to the municipalities where their sewage was disposed of. As the prosecutor, how would you respond? Does this scheme amount to mail fraud?[40]

DISCUSSION QUESTIONS

1. Would it make a difference if Anchor did not charge its municipal customers any more than it had in the past?
2. Does it matter whether the municipalities were concerned about environmental compliance? What if the illegal disposal could result in regulatory fines for the municipalities or in loss of environmental licenses?
3. Under what theory could Anchor be held criminally liable for violating the ocean dumping rule?

a. Money or Property

Courts historically have treated the concept of fraud under the mail fraud statute as highly elastic. Indeed, in many jurisdictions a theory known as the intangible rights doctrine flourished for years. This doctrine applied to situations in which the government alleged that the defendant had deprived another person or entity of the intangible right to receive the defendant's honest and loyal services. In the public sector, the intangible rights doctrine was invoked to reach various forms of public corruption in which public officials engaged in self-dealing at the expense of their constituents' right to honest government[41] or honest elections.[42] In the private sector, those who breached fiduciary duties to their employers, clients, or unions were often prosecuted under the intangible rights doctrine.[43]

---

[40]*Cf.* United States v. Frank, 156 F.3d 332 (2d Cir. 1997).
[41]*See, e.g.*, United States v. Holzer, 816 F.2d 304 (7th Cir. 1987).
[42]*See, e.g.*, United States v. Girdner, 754 F.2d 877 (10th Cir. 1985).
[43]*See, e.g.*, United States v. George, 477 F.2d 508 (7th Cir. 1973).

In 1987, the Supreme Court brought this theory of prosecution to an abrupt end in McNally v. United States.[44] *McNally* was a public corruption case in which the government alleged that a state political party chairman had breached a fiduciary duty not to use public office for private gain.[45] The Supreme Court reversed, holding that the mail fraud statute is limited to schemes involving the deprivation of money or property and cannot be stretched to reach deprivation of intangible rights such as the right to have the state's affairs conducted honestly. Since it was neither alleged nor shown that the scheme in *McNally* was directed toward deprivation of a property right, the government's case could not be sustained.

To reach this conclusion, the majority construed two clauses written in the disjunctive as if "or" meant "and." The Court conceded that because the statute criminalizes schemes "to defraud" *or* "for obtaining money or property by means of false or fraudulent pretenses, representations, or promises:"

> it is arguable that they are to be construed independently and that the money-or-property requirement of the latter phrase does not limit schemes to defraud to those aimed at causing deprivation of money or property. This is the approach that has been taken by each of the Courts of Appeals that has addressed the issue: schemes to defraud include those designed to deprive individuals, the people or the government of intangible rights, such as the right to have public officials perform their duties honestly.
>
> As the Court long ago stated, however, the words "to defraud" commonly refer "to wronging one in his property rights by dishonest methods or schemes," and "usually signify the deprivation of something of value by trick, deceit, chicane or overreaching." . . . As we see it, adding the second phrase simply made it unmistakable that the statute reached false promises and misrepresentations as to the future as well as other frauds involving money or property. . . .
>
> . . . Rather than construe the statute in a manner that leaves its outer boundaries ambiguous and involves the Federal Government in setting standards of disclosure and good government for local and state officials, we read 1341 as limited in scope to the protection of property rights.[46]

---

[44]483 U.S. 350 (1987).

[45]Although the party chairman was not, technically speaking, a public official, he had been given what was tantamount to absolute authority to select the insurance carrier that would receive a lucrative contract to provide state workers' compensation coverage. The government argued that this was sufficient to impose a fiduciary duty on the chairman not to personally benefit from the selection process.

[46]483 U.S. at 359.

In a stinging dissent, Justice Stevens took his colleagues on the Court to task. Up until now, he wrote, it had been widely accepted that the statute has three separate prohibitions, each of which is independent. The statute expressly prohibits use of the mails for the purpose of executing "*any*" scheme to defraud "*or*" for obtaining money or property by false or fraudulent pretenses. By reading "or" out of the crucial part of the provision, the majority treated the second clause as nothing more than an elaboration of the means by which the first clause could be violated. He continued, "I am at a loss to understand the source or justification for this holding. Certainly no canon of statutory construction requires us to ignore the plain language of the provision."[47]

DISCUSSION QUESTION

1. The Court acknowledged that every circuit court that had considered the issue had recognized the intangible rights theory of mail fraud, but it categorically rejected that theory of liability. Why would the majority stake out the position that the "or" that appears between the first and second clauses makes it "arguable" that they are independent? Is Justice Stevens correct in asserting that the majority has simply ignored the plain language of the statute to reach this result?

b. Intangible Property

Although the Court's unexpected ruling in *McNally* clearly foreclosed further prosecutions under the intangible rights doctrine, it created uncertainty about what other potential ramifications the decision might have. Thus, for example, while the Court imposed a money or property requirement on prosecutions brought under the "scheme to defraud" clause of the statute, it had no occasion to consider the question of what qualifies as property. To the relief of many, the Court seized an early opportunity to begin clarifying the contours of *McNally* the following Term in Carpenter v. United States.[48]

In *Carpenter*, R. Foster Winans, a financial columnist for the *Wall Street Journal*, misappropriated the contents of some of his influential "Heard on

---

[47]*Id.* at 365.
[48]484 U.S. 19 (1987).

the Street" columns by sharing them with friends before the articles were published. Since the market often responded to information published in the column, Winans conferred (and intended to confer) a market advantage on his friends, who bought or sold stock on the basis of the unpublished columns.

As Winans well knew, prepublication disclosure of the contents of the column violated the *Journal*'s longstanding confidentiality policy.

The government's theory was that Winans' misappropriation of the *Journal*'s confidential information amounted to defrauding it of an intangible property right and thus was not at cross purposes with the ruling in *McNally*. The Supreme Court agreed.

> We held in *McNally* that the mail fraud statute does not reach "schemes to defraud citizens of their intangible rights to honest and impartial government" and that the statute is "limited in scope to the protection of property rights." Petitioners argue that the *Journal*'s interest in prepublication confidentiality for the "Heard" columns is no more than an intangible consideration outside the reach of § 1341; nor does that law, it is urged, protect against mere injury to reputation. This is not a case like *McNally*, however. The *Journal*, as Winans' employer, was defrauded of much more than its contractual right to his honest and faithful service, an interest too ethereal in itself to fall within the protection of the mail fraud statute, which "had its origin in the desire to protect individual property rights." Here, the object of the scheme was to take the *Journal*'s confidential business information—the publication schedule and contents of the "Heard" column—and its intangible nature does not make it any less "property" protected by the mail and wire fraud statutes. *McNally* did not limit the scope of § 1341 to tangible as distinguished from intangible property rights.[49]

DISCUSSION QUESTIONS

1. What is the difference between an intangible "property right" and a mere "intangible right?" How does the right infringed in *Carpenter* differ from the right allegedly infringed in *McNally*?
2. Winans' disclosure of confidential information before it was published breached his contract with the *Wall Street Journal*. What elevates the

---

[49]*Id.* at 25.

disclosure beyond a mere breach of contract to an infringement of a property interest?

3. The *Wall Street Journal* did not suffer any economic harm as a result of Winans' prepublication disclosure of the contents of his columns. Should the lack of tangible harm be relevant to a determination whether fraud has occurred?

c. Licenses

Although *Carpenter* resolved an important issue by ruling that a deprivation of intangible property is within the range of harms contemplated by the mail fraud statute, the Court still did not resolve the root question of what property is. This proved to be a particularly daunting question in the context of categorizing intangibles like licenses and permits.

The Court undertook the task of providing some clarity on this point in Cleveland v. United States.[50]   In *Cleveland*, the defendant and his confederates had applied for and received a license from the State of Louisiana to operate video poker machines at truck stops the defendant owned. The basis for the prosecution was that the defendant's license application fraudulently concealed and misrepresented potentially disqualifying information about his fitness to operate a gambling business. As the theory of the prosecution was that the defendants fraudulently obtained the video poker license, the question before the Court was whether the State had been defrauded into parting with "property" when it issued the license.

Although the Court recognized that Louisiana has a substantial interest in controlling who operated gambling businesses, "the State's core concern is *regulatory*"[51] and Louisiana's licensing procedures and fitness requirements were characteristic of "a typical regulatory program."

> It licenses, subject to certain conditions, engagement in pursuits that private actors may not undertake without official authorization. In this regard, it resembles other licensing schemes long characterized by this Court as exercises of state police powers.[52]

---

[50]531 U.S. 12 (2000).

[51]*Id.* at 20.

[52]*Id.* at 21. The State's "intangible rights of allocation, exclusion, and control amount to no more and no less than Louisiana's sovereign power to regulate." *Id.* at 23.

The government argued that Louisiana's substantial economic stake in the operation of video poker machines distinguished this case from the run of the mill regulatory scheme. The licensing scheme created a significant revenue stream for the State. For truck stop licenses, the revenue the State expected to receive included:

- a $10,000 application processing fee;
- a $1,000 renewal application fee;
- a $2,000 annual fee;
- a $1,000 device operation fee; and
- 32.5 percent of the net revenue from each video poker machine.

In *Cleveland*, even though the State's share of the defendant's operating revenue was more than $1.2 million between 1993 and 1995,[53] the Court was unpersuaded by the government's argument.

> It is hardly evident . . . why these tolls should make video poker licenses "property" in the hands of the State. The State receives the lion's share of its expected revenue not while the licenses remain in its own hands, but only after they have been issued to licensees. Licenses pre-issuance do not generate an ongoing stream of revenue. At most, they entitle the State to collect a processing fee from applicants for new licenses. Were an entitlement of this order sufficient to establish a state property right, one could scarcely avoid the conclusion that States have property rights in any license or permit requiring an upfront fee, including drivers' licenses, medical licenses, and fishing and hunting licenses. Such licenses, as the Government itself concedes, are "purely regulatory."[54]

The Government argued in the alternative that even if video poker licenses were not property in the hands of the State, they were property in the hands of the licensee, who thus *obtained* property through the fraud. But while the Court recognized that it is possible that holders of video poker licenses may have a property interest in their licenses,"[55] the holding in

---

[53]It was undisputed that Louisiana received the full amount of revenue it was entitled to receive from the defendant.

[54]*Id.* at 22.

[55]   Notwithstanding the State's declaration that "any license issued or renewed . . . is not property of a protected interest under the constitutions of either the United States or the state of Louisiana," La. Rev. Stat. Ann. § 27:301 (D) (West Supp. 2000), "the question whether a state-law right

McNally made it clear that "the mail fraud statute . . . had its origin in the desire to protect individual property rights, and any benefit which the Government derives from the statute must be limited to *the Government's interests as property holder.*"[56]

DISCUSSION QUESTIONS

1. Since the state has an economic interest in the video poker operations that it licenses, why don't its economic expectations constitute a property right?
2. Is it clear why the *Wall Street Journal*'s right to control the timing of the release of confidential business information is property while Louisiana's right to control who receives potentially lucrative state-issued video poker licenses is not?
3. Does the decision in *Cleveland* clarify what status a video poker license has in the hands of the licensee? Does the issued license constitute "property"?

THE CASE OF THE PERGOLA PERMIT

Jones and his nephew Miller agreed to buy a 19-acre dumpsite (the Pergola Dumpsite) from Freedman for $1 million. The sale was contingent on the successful transfer of the site's existing dumpsite permit to the purchasers. The applicable environmental regulations provided that the permit was transferable only on approval, by the state's Department of Environmental Enforcement (DEE), of the transferee's suitability to operate the dumpsite. DEE's administration of the permit program was subject to periodic EPA review, and its authority to administer the program could be revoked if EPA determined that DEE failed to follow EPA-approved standards and procedures, or that unqualified individuals or firms were otherwise obtaining permits.

---

constitutes 'property' or 'rights to property' is a matter of federal law," Dyre v. United States, 528 U.S. 49, 58 (1999). In some contexts, we have held that individuals have constitutionally protected property interests in state-issued licenses essential to pursuing an occupation or livelihood. *See, e.g.*, Bell v. Burson, 402 U.S. 535, 539 (1971) (driver's license). *Id.* at 25 n.4.

[56]*Id.* at 25-26 (quoting *McNally*, 483 U.S. at 359 n.8) (emphasis added by the Court).

Jones and Miller had operated three other dumpsites in the state and had a history of serious environmental violations that had resulted in DEE's closing two of the sites and ordering cleanup of the third (the Hawk Point site) at Jones' and Miller's expense. Thus, it was highly unlikely that DEE would approve the transfer of the Pergola Dumpsite permit to either of them. That being true, Jones and Miller enlisted Taylor, their longtime lawyer, to do the following: (1) incorporate a business under the name of Hauler's Haven; (2) name two front men, Parker and Peabody, as principals in the business; (3) structure the purchase and sale agreement to make Hauler's Haven appear to be the beneficial owner of the dumpsite; (4) to identify Hauler's Haven, Parker, and Peabody as the prospective owners and operators of the Pergola Dumpsite in the application to transfer the dumpsite permit; and (5) take any other necessary steps to conceal Jones' and Miller's connection with the corporation and the dumpsite.

After papering the deal to make it look as though Jones and Miller had no connection with either the company or the dumpsite, Taylor mailed the permit application to DEE. Seeing that the application appeared to be in good order, DEE approved the transfer of the permit to Hauler's Haven. Jones and Miller, of course, fully intended to operate the dumpsite themselves after paying the front men handsomely for their services.

Although the Pergola Dumpsite permit allowed only construction and demolition debris to be disposed of at the site, Jones and Miller intended to dispose of solid chemical waste in addition to construction debris, in clear violation of the permit's terms and conditions.

DISCUSSION QUESTIONS

1. Assuming arguendo the mailing requirement has been satisfied, have Jones and Miller violated § 1341 by fraudulently inducing DEE to transfer the Pergola permit to Hauler's Haven? Does it matter that DEE would not have issued the permit if it had known the true facts?
2. Assuming arguendo that Jones and Miller violated § 1341, has Taylor also committed mail fraud?
3. Suppose that Freedman would have refused to sell Jones and Miller the property and transfer the permit if he had known they planned to illegally dispose of chemical waste at the Pergola Dumpsite. Would that provide the government a plausible alternative theory or theories of mail fraud?
4. Suppose the chemical waste Jones and Miller planned to dispose of at the Pergola Dumpsite came from the Hawk Point cleanup site. Jones and

Miller had decided in advance that once they had cleaned up the Hawk Point site by transferring the chemical waste to the Pergola site, they would abandon the Pergola site and flee the country. Since the newly contaminated Pergola site would have to be cleaned up, and Jones and Miller would be beyond EPA's jurisdiction, EPA would have to bear the cost of the cleanup. Is this relevant to the determination whether Jones and Miller committed mail fraud?

5. Do the facts warrant charging Jones and Miller with conspiracy to defraud the government under § 371 on the ground that they planned to fraudulently obtain the Pergola permit?

d. Intangible Rights

As noted above, the Court in *McNally* invalidated the intangible rights theory of mail fraud. Congress responded the following year by enacting a statute, 18 U.S.C. § 1346, that reinvigorated the intangible rights theory in a somewhat altered form. Section 1346 provides that for purposes of the mail fraud statute,[57] "the term 'scheme or artifice to defraud' includes a scheme or artifice to deprive another of the intangible right of honest services."

Although there is evidence that some members of Congress intended to overturn *McNally* and reinstate pre-*McNally* case law, there is no statutory definition of "the intangible right of honest services" and scant legislative history to guide the courts in construing this language. Thus, courts have adopted divergent views on a number of questions, including whether it is appropriate to invoke pre-*McNally* case law in construing § 1346, whether the corrupted individual must act for personal gain, whether the dishonesty must violate a state law duty or a collateral criminal law, and so on down the road.

Although it was unclear whether courts would rule that the statute applies to both public and private sector frauds, the consensus now seems to be that it does. In United States v. Czubinski,[58] the First Circuit addressed the components of honest services fraud in the context of public corruption.

> We recently had the opportunity to discuss, at some length, the proper application of the section 1346 honest services amendment to the wrongful acts of public officials. *See Sawyer*, 85 F.3d at 722-26. . . . First, as a

---

[57]As well as for companion statutes such as the bank and wire fraud statutes.
[58]106 F.3d 1069 (1st Cir. 1997).

general matter, we noted in *Sawyer* that although the right to honest services "eludes easy definition," honest services convictions of public officials typically involve serious corruption, such as embezzlement of public funds, bribery of public officials, or the failure of public decision-makers to disclose certain conflicts of interest. Second, we cautioned that "the broad scope of the mail fraud statute, however, does not encompass every instance of official misconduct that results in the official's personal gain." Third, and most importantly, *Sawyer* holds that the government must not merely indicate wrongdoing by a public official, but must also demonstrate that the wrongdoing at issue is intended to prevent or call into question the proper or impartial performance of that public servant's official duties.

A few years later in United States v. DeVegter,[59] the Eleventh Circuit fleshed out the distinction between honest services fraud in the public and private sectors. The court divided public sector honest services fraud into two different categories. "First, 'a public official owes a fiduciary duty to the public, and misuse of his office for private gain is a fraud.' "[60] "Second, 'an individual without formal office may be held to be a public fiduciary if others rely on him because of a special relationship with the government and he in fact makes governmental decisions.' "[61] The court then went on to say:

> On the other hand, such a strict duty of loyalty ordinarily is not part of private sector relationships. Most private sector interactions do not involve duties of, or rights to, the "honest services" of either party. Relationships may be accompanied by obligations of good faith and fair dealing, even in arms-length transactions. These and similar duties are quite unlike, however, the duty of loyalty and fidelity to purpose required of public officials. For example, "[e]mployee loyalty is not an end in itself, it is a means to obtain and preserve pecuniary benefits for the employer. An employee's undisclosed conflict of interest does not by itself necessarily pose the threat of economic harm to the employer." United States v. Lemire, 720 F.2d 1327, 1336 (D.C. Cir. 1983). . . . Therefore, for a private sector defendant to have violated the victim's right to honest services, it is not enough to prove the defendant's breach of loyalty alone. Rather, as is always true in a breach of loyalty by a public official, the breach of loyalty by a private sector defendant must in each case contravene — by inherently harming — the purpose of the parties' relationship.

---

[59]198 F.3d 1324 (11th Cir. 2000).
[60]*Id.* at 1328 n.3 (quoting *McNally*, 483 U.S. at 355).
[61]*Id.*

. . . "The prosecution must prove that the employee intended to breach a fiduciary duty, and that the employee foresaw or reasonably should have foreseen that his employer might suffer an economic harm as a result of the breach." United States v. Frost, 125 F.3d 346, 368 (6th Cir. 1997).

DISCUSSION QUESTIONS

1. Assuming arguendo that the mailing element would otherwise be satisfied, which of the following public sector scenarios would violate prohibition against honest services fraud?
   a. Niles applies for a Clean Water Act permit to discharge pre-treated industrial wastewater into a river. Jan, the EPA official who reviews the application, informs Niles that the proposed pre-treatment plan is inadequate and that the permit will be denied. Niles offers to give Jan $1,000 in the hope that she can "see her way clear" to grant the permit.
   b. When Niles applies for the permit, Jan tells him that the office has an unusually large backlog of applications and that it will be about two months before his is processed. Fearing that he would have to shut down his plant if approval were to be delayed that long, Niles offers her $1,000 to expedite the review of his application.
   c. Niles believes his competitor has been discharging untreated wastewater into the river and that the competitor has been recently cited and fined for violating its Clean Water Act permit. Niles wants to know the details of the competitor's compliance problems so he can advertise his own company's "clean" environmental record compared with the competitor's record as a polluter. To confirm the details, Niles calls Jan and persuades her to share enforcement information contained in the competitor's file. Information sharing is strictly forbidden by EPA rules.[62]
   d. Suppose that in "c" above, Jan refuses to give Niles information about the competitor's enforcement record because it is against the rules. But Niles' request has peaked Jan's curiosity because the competitor is a high-profile business that actively promotes itself as an environmentally responsible company. After she tells Niles that she can't share the enforcement information, Jan satisfies her own curiosity by browsing confidential EPA computer files. Although she

---

[62]*Cf.* United States v. Czubinski, 106 F.3d 1069 (1st Cir. 1997).

has a valid password, EPA employees are allowed to access confidential files only in the course of carrying out their official responsibilities.[63]

2. Assuming arguendo the mailing element would otherwise be satisfied, which of the following private sector scenarios would violate the prohibition against honest services fraud?

   a. Jasper, the transportation manager for a large chemical manufacturer, has sole responsibility for contracting with licensed truckers to transport chemical waste to safe disposal sites. Company guidelines allow truckers to earn as much as a 10 percent profit for each tanker truckload of waste they transport to a proper disposal site. Although competition for waste hauling contracts is brisk, Jasper enters into what amounts to an exclusive dealing arrangement with Tucker Trucking. Jasper agrees to give Tucker the exclusive right to transport the chemical waste and to receive a 10 percent profit for each tanker truckload of waste if Tucker will pay Jasper a 2 percent kickback. Tucker's transportation services are satisfactory in all respects.[64]

   b. Carbide Company was a manufacturer whose operations produced vast amounts of wastewater containing zinc. Bella, an administrative assistant to the manager of Carbide's wastewater treatment plant, believed that tests the company performed to check wastewater for excess levels of zinc had been manipulated. On several occasions she overheard the manager tell subordinates that the reported test results showed unacceptably high levels of zinc and that he was going to discard the report. On these occasions she also heard him encourage the subordinates to dilute wastewater samples with tap water to reduce the concentration of zinc to permissible levels, and to backdate the new report. The backdated reports would, of course, falsely represent that the treatment plant was in compliance with its Clean Water Act permit.

   Although it was Bella's responsibility to shred the original reports and keep the backdated reports on file, Bella decided to document these irregularities by: (1) keeping the discarded test results; (2) making personal copies of the corresponding backdated reports; and (3) keeping a detailed log of what she saw and heard. When she thought she had enough evidence to document the manager's

---

[63]*Id.*

[64]*Cf.* United States v. George, 477 F.2d 508 (7th Cir. 1973).

misconduct, she mailed the documents to the regional EPA office. Company rules strictly forbade employees from copying, removing, or disclosing the contents of documents relating to environmental compliance.

3. Would any of the scenarios in Questions 1 and 2 support a charge of conspiracy to defraud the United States?

4. Could any of the scenarios in Questions 1 and 2 plausibly be cast as a scheme to deprive the defrauded party of money or property?

2. USE OF THE MAILS

Use of the mails in furtherance of a scheme to defraud is the heart of § 1341. Yet the mailing element need not be central to the scheme to defraud. As long as it is "incident to an essential part of the scheme," that is enough.[65] This is a fact-specific inquiry that can lead to a finding of liability even when the mailing seems remote from the fraud.

The use of the mails must be "for the purpose of executing" the fraudulent scheme, but established case law equates the "for the purpose of" language with using the mails "in furtherance of" the scheme to defraud. Although the statutory language and its established judicial gloss seem to suggest a conscious decision to use the mails to promote the fraud, the use of the mails may be in furtherance of the fraudulent scheme even though it is not expressly contemplated as part of the plan or its execution. Any reasonably foreseeable use of the mails will suffice.

Thus, while the perpetrator's personal use of the mails will satisfy this requirement, mailings by the victim or even a third party will also suffice if they are a foreseeable consequence of the scheme. Nor is it required that the mailing contain any fraudulent misrepresentations. The mailed material may be wholly innocuous.

Illustration G: In a variation on The Case of the 100 Mile Limit, Adam and Eve routinely mailed monthly bills to the municipalities with which Anchor Marine was under contract. The bills described the service Anchor Marine had provided as "ocean disposal of sewage sludge at a minimum of 100 miles from shore" and calculated the fee accordingly. Contrary to the statements in the bills, however, Anchor Marine had engaged in short dumping by disposing of the sludge only 10 miles from shore.

---

[65]Pereira v. United States, 347 U.S. 1, 8 (1954).

Illustration H: In a variation on the facts in Illustration G, when the Ocean Dumping Law was changed to require dumping beyond the 100 mile limit, Adam and Eve (on behalf of Anchor Marine) and the city of Greenleaf negotiated new contract terms, including a revised fee schedule that reflected the higher costs Anchor would incur if it transported the sludge an additional 90 miles. At the conclusion of their discussion, Greenleaf's lawyer said she would draft an amendment to the contract that incorporated the new terms, including the revised fee schedule. Soon after that, she mailed the contract amendments to Adam and Eve.

In Illustration G, the mailings were clearly in furtherance of the fraud. The false bills were sent by Anchor Marine (the perpetrator) to the municipalities (the victims of the fraud) for the purpose of collecting higher disposal fees under false pretenses. The mailing of the fraudulent bills was clearly part of the scheme as it was envisioned by Anchor's agents.

In Illustration H, the mailing was initiated by the city's lawyer, an innocent third party acting on behalf of the city, which was one of Anchor Marine's victims. Assuming that Adam and Eve did not intend to transport the sludge beyond the old ten mile limit, the mailing of the contract amendment was in furtherance of the fraudulent scheme even though they may not have anticipated this particular mailing. The amendment memorialized the city's fraudulently induced agreement to pay higher fees for the same service it received under the original fee schedule, and it was foreseeable that the amended contract and other related documents would be delivered by mail.

To be in furtherance of the fraudulent scheme, the use of the mails must not have occurred after the scheme has reached fruition. But mailings that occur after the perpetrator of the fraud has received everything he expects to get from the victims can satisfy this element if the mailed communications are designed to postpone discovery of the fraud by lulling the victims into a false sense of security. That said, however, the difference between post-fraud communications and lulling letters is not always a bright-line distinction.

Illustration I: Suppose Anchor Marine's owners collect all outstanding fees from the municipalities and secretly decide to abandon the business and leave the country. After transferring all of Anchor Marine's liquid assets to an offshore account, they mail a stack of letters to the municipalities while en route to an offshore island. The letters thank the cities for their business and cite serious unexpected health problems as the reason they were suddenly going out of business.

Is it clear that the mailings occurred after the fraud came to fruition? Or could they be deemed lulling letters that are part of the fraud?

DISCUSSION QUESTIONS

1. Does the mail fraud statute punish schemes to defraud, the use of the mails, or both?
2. If a court should determine that the statute punishes the use of the mails rather than the fraudulent scheme, what would the practical significance of that determination be? Would the same number of crimes have been committed in Illustrations G and H?
3. Why are "lulling letters" deemed to be "in furtherance of a scheme to defraud?" If Anchor Marine had received all of the money it expected to get from the municipalities *before* it sent the letters in Illustration I, why wouldn't that be dispositive of the question whether the mailings came *after* the culmination of the scheme?

3. JURISDICTION

First enacted in 1872, the mail fraud statute historically required the use of the United States Postal System to execute a scheme to defraud. The use of the mails requirement provided Congress a convenient jurisdictional hook to bring the statute's prohibitions within the growing body of federal criminal law only because Congress has the power to regulate the postal system.

But as modern means of communication and transportation evolved, modern means of avoiding liability under the mail fraud statute kept pace. Thus, for example, with the advent of new and increasingly popular modes of delivery, the use of carriers offering express delivery services began to eclipse the use of the mails and foretold the potential obsolescence of the mail fraud statute as an effective prosecutorial tool.

To avoid that inevitability, in 1994 Congress amended the mail fraud statute to extend its reach to the use of "any private or commercial interstate carrier" to execute a scheme or artifice to defraud. Thus, although the crime is still officially called mail fraud, the statute now also applies to cases in which carriers like Federal Express and UPS are used in furtherance of the scheme. Notably, the 1994 amendment provided a second jurisdictional hook for federal regulation, this time through exercise of congressional power to regulate interstate commerce.

4. WIRE FRAUD

Although the wire fraud statute is a newer entrant into the field (it was enacted in 1952), its prohibitions closely parallel those found in the mail fraud statute.[66] The wire fraud statute, 18 U.S.C. § 1343, prohibits transmitting or causing the transmission of material via interstate wire, radio, or television communication for the purpose of executing a scheme to defraud.

Like the 1994 amendment to the mail fraud statute, the wire fraud statute relies on congressional power to regulate under the Commerce Clause. Thus, the wire fraud statute requires interstate transmissions in furtherance of the fraud. But because the focus is on interstate *transmissions*, the wire fraud statute (like the mail fraud statute) can reach frauds that are otherwise intrastate.

> **Illustration J:** Assume the facts in Illustration I with the following stipulations. Anchor Marine's principal office is located in the city of Greenleaf, and Adam and Eve work at the Greenleaf office. Thus, all of the contract negotiations occur in the city lawyer's office. But rather than mailing the amended contract to Adam and Eve, the lawyer sends the draft contract via e-mail.

Under what circumstances would the e-mail communication bring Anchor's scheme within the reach of the wire fraud statute? If the e-mail was communicated via satellite or other mode of transmission that routed the communication out of and then back into the state where the parties are located, that will suffice. And, importantly, it is not necessary for anyone to have known or foreseen that the transmission would travel interstate.[67] All that is required is that the use of a wire transmission was foreseeable.

---

[66]Thus, the rule that statutes that are in pari materia — i.e., statutes that are on the same subject or matter — should be given parallel construction applies. The practical consequence here is that principles articulated in cases decided under one of the statutes are equally applicable to cases arising under the other.

[67]United States v. Bryant, 766 F.2d 253 (8th Cir. 1985) (telegrams defendants sent from Kansas City, Missouri, to Bridgeton, Missouri, were routed electronically through a Western Union installation in Middletown, Virginia).

DISCUSSION QUESTION

1. The indictment against W.R. Grace for the asbestos contamination of Libby, Montana charged Grace and several of the individual defendants with two counts of wire fraud. Count V of the indictment alleged that Grace had entered into an agreement to sell property that was contaminated with tremolite asbestos without disclosing the associated health risks. As part of the sales transaction Grace sent, via an interstate wire transmission, a letter of intent that described Grace's plan for cleaning the property up and disclosing the compensation the purchasers would receive. If the letter of intent truthfully described the cleanup plan and the compensation, does Count V contain sufficient allegations of fraud to sustain a wire fraud charge?

C. FALSE STATEMENTS

The federal false statements statute, 18 U.S.C. § 1001, often provides the government an alternative theory for reaching misconduct that may be collateral to another offense. It is a versatile prosecutorial tool that punishes making or using unsworn false statements or writings that are within the jurisdiction of the executive, legislative, or judicial branch of the federal government.

1. JURISDICTION

Although there are dozens of other federal criminal statutes — including environmental statutes[68] — that punish making false statements, § 1001 is the most versatile among them, partly because of its broad jurisdictional language. Most of the other false statements provisions are applicable only in particularized contexts. Thus, for example, separate statutes punish making false statements to the Federal Trade Commission,[69] the Securities and Exchange Commission,[70] the Department of Agriculture,[71] the Secretary

---

[68]*See, e.g.*, 42 U.S.C. § 7413(c)(2) (Clean Air Act provision prohibiting, inter alia, making false material statements or omitting material information from required records, reports, or documents).

[69]18 U.S.C. § 50.

[70]15 U.S.C. § 77yyy.

[71]18 U.S.C. § 1026.

of Commerce,[72] the Environmental Protection Agency,[73] and myriad other departments, agencies, and officials — often in connection with specific types of transactions.

Section 1001, in contrast, is generic. It reaches false statements in *any* matter "within the jurisdiction of" any of the three coordinate branches of the federal government. This distinction highlights the primacy of the statute's jurisdictional element, which the Supreme Court has construed broadly.

In United States v. Rodgers,[74] for example, the defendant enlisted the services of the FBI and the Secret Service to find his wife, who had left him. The problem was that he lied about the reason for her unknown whereabouts, falsely telling the FBI that she had been kidnapped and the Secret Service that she was involved in a plot to kill the President. Those lies led to an indictment charging him with two counts of making false statements.

Rodgers moved to dismiss, arguing that the investigations conducted at his behest were not matters within the jurisdiction of the FBI and the Secret Service for purposes of § 1001. The trial court granted the motion, and the Eighth Circuit affirmed. Relying on prior Eight Circuit precedent,[75] the court ruled that the term "jurisdiction" included the "power to make monetary awards, grant governmental privileges, or promulgate binding administrative and regulative determinations," but excluded "the mere authority to conduct an investigation."[76] Since the FBI and Secret Service "had no power to adjudicate rights, establish binding regulations, compel the action or finally dispose of the problem giving rise to the inquiry,"[77] the investigations of the alleged kidnapping and assassination plot were not matters "within the jurisdiction of" either agency.

Finding this reading of § 1001 "unduly strained,"[78] the Supreme Court reversed.

> "Jurisdiction" is not defined in the statute. We therefore "start with the assumption that the legislative purpose is expressed by the ordinary meaning of the words used." Richards v. United States, 369 U.S. 1, 9 (1962). The most natural, nontechnical reading of the statutory language is that it covers

---

[72] 19 U.S.C. § 1919.
[73] 33 U.S.C. § 1319(c)(4) (CWA); 42 U.S.C. § 7413(c)(2) (CAA).
[74] 466 U.S. 475 (1984).
[75] Friedman v. United States, 374 F.2d 363, 367 (8th Cir. 1967).
[76] *Id.*
[77] *Id.* at 368.
[78] *Rodgers*, 466 U.S. at 479.

all matters confided to the authority of an agency or department. Thus, Webster's Third New International Dictionary 1227 (1976) broadly defines "jurisdiction" as, among other things, "the limits or territory within which any particular power may be exercised: sphere of authority." A department or agency has jurisdiction, in this sense, when it has the power to exercise authority in a particular situation. *See* United States v. Adler, *supra*, at 922 ("the word 'jurisdiction' as used in the statute must mean simply the power to act upon information when it is received"). Understood in this way, the phrase "within the jurisdiction" merely differentiates the official, authorized functions of an agency or department from matters peripheral to the business of that body.[79]

Although the Court acknowledged that in other contexts, the term "jurisdiction" often has "a narrower, more technical meaning[]" than authority to act in the matter at hand,[80] all of the Court's prior decisions construing § 1001 had embraced an inclusive rather than restrictive reading of the jurisdictional language. Since the FBI and the Secret Service both had statutory authority to conduct the investigations that Rodgers' false crime reports had precipitated and the reports had perverted the authorized functions of both agencies by sending them on a wild goose chase, the Court concluded that there is "valid legislative interest in protecting the integrity of [such] official inquiries," an interest clearly embraced in, and furthered by, the broad language of § 1001.[81]

Although the jurisdictional language in § 1001 extended to false statements in any matter within the jurisdiction of "any department or agency" of the United States when *Rodgers* was decided, the Court later held in Hubbard v. United States[82] that § 1001 did not apply to false statements made in judicial proceedings, because the judicial branch did not qualify as a "department" or "agency." A year after *Hubbard* was handed down, Congress amended § 1001 to broaden the jurisdictional language to specifically include the executive, legislative, and judicial branches of the federal government. But as we shall soon see, Congress carved out notable exceptions to the statute's applicability to legislative and judicial matters.

---

[79]*Id.* at 479.
[80]*Id.* at 480.
[81]*Id.* at 481-482.
[82]514 U.S. 695 (1995).

a. Executive Branch

UNITED STATES V. WRIGHT

988 F.2d 1036 (10th Cir. 1993)

ANDERSON, Circuit Judge. . . .

Background

During the period 1987-1989, Mr. Wright was the superintendent and manager of a water treatment plant and distribution system at Lake Tenkiller, near Vian, Oklahoma. As part of his managerial duties he prepared and filed with the Sequoyah County (Oklahoma) Health Department monthly operating reports containing data on the suspended particulate matter (turbidity) in the water at his plant. These reports were false in that they purported to show information on turbidity from water samples when, in fact, no samples were analyzed or taken.

The reports, sampling, analytical, and record keeping requirements resulting in the type of data in question are required by federal regulations promulgated by the EPA pursuant to its authority and responsibility under the Act. The regulations require, among other things, daily monitoring of turbidity and submission to the state of monthly reports of the daily values within 10 days of the end of the month.

The Act permits a state to apply to the Administrator of the EPA for primary enforcement responsibility over drinking water standards. On March 30, 1977, the Administrator approved Oklahoma's application for primary enforcement responsibility and Oklahoma had that authority during the period in question. Within the State of Oklahoma, responsibility for enforcing drinking water standards has been given to the Department of Health, which provided the forms which Mr. Wright filled out and filed with the County Health Department. The County Health Department forwards filed forms to the State Health Department.

A federal grand jury indicted Mr. Wright on January 9, 1992, charging him with seven counts of violating 18 U.S.C. § 1001 by making false written statements in a matter within the jurisdiction of the EPA. After the district court denied his motion to dismiss the indictment on jurisdictional grounds, Mr. Wright entered into a plea agreement with the government pursuant to which he pled guilty to three counts of violating 18 U.S.C. § 1001, reserving his right to appeal the denial of his motion.

As part of the plea agreement, the parties stipulated that . . . all of the monthly reports he prepared concerning water turbidity were submitted by him to the Sequoyah County Health Department, and not to the EPA or any other federal agency or department.

The parties also stipulated that if a named responsible official of the EPA testified he would state that the EPA: (1) conducts annual evaluations of the Oklahoma public water system program under the Act; (2) makes semiannual visits to the Oklahoma State Department of Health to review the state public water system; (3) conducts biannual audits of the state program, during which operational reports are randomly selected for review; and (4) makes annual grants to the Oklahoma Department of Health which have ranged from approximately $500,000 to $700,000 since 1987. In addition, it was stipulated that such annual financial grants are dependent, in part, on the outcome of EPA's evaluation of the state public water program. The district court and the parties have treated these recitations as established facts, as do we.

Discussion

. . .

The parties agree that "jurisdiction," as it is used in section 1001, is to be defined broadly. "The most natural, nontechnical reading of the statutory language is that it covers all matters confided to the authority of an agency or department." United States v. Rogers, 466 U.S. 475, 479 (1984). . . .

The false statement need not be made directly to the federal agency to be within its jurisdiction. *See* United States v. Wolf, 645 F.2d 23, 25 (10th Cir. 1981). . . .

Mr. Wright asserts that a writing does not fall within the jurisdiction of an agency unless there is a "direct relationship" between the writing and an authorized function of the agency. He then contends that there was no direct relationship between the reports he submitted and a function of the EPA "[b]ecause the EPA had surrendered primary authority for enforcement of Safe Drinking Water Act standards to the State of Oklahoma," and because he filed the report with the state, not the EPA. We disagree.

Regardless of the standard employed, the false turbidity data filed by Mr. Wright fell within the jurisdiction of the EPA. A grant of primary authority is not a grant of exclusive authority. Congress passed the Act " 'to assure that water supply systems serving the public meet minimum national standards for the protection of public health.' " Montgomery County v.

Environmental Protection Agency, 662 F.2d 1040, 1041 (4th Cir. 1981). The Act requires the Administrator to promulgate maximum contaminant level goals and national primary drinking water regulations. The regulations relating to the collection and reporting of turbidity data, described above, were promulgated pursuant to that charge and authority. The EPA retains the authority, in the discharge of its duties under the Act, to enforce its regulations; and, turbidity data clearly concern an authorized function of the EPA.

Furthermore, in this situation, the EPA is actively involved in assuring state compliance with national safe water standards. It audits, reviews, and evaluates the state of Oklahoma's program, including an inspection of the monthly reports of the type involved in this case. Such reports, therefore, directly implicate the ongoing function and mission of the agency. In addition, the Act *expressly* authorizes the EPA to take enforcement actions in states having primary enforcement authority.

Finally, EPA's funding of the Oklahoma public water program is conditioned, in part, on the results of its annual evaluations of that program. This court is in accord with other circuits which have found that a state agency's use of federal funds, standing alone, is generally sufficient to establish jurisdiction under section 1001. *Suggs*, 755 F.2d at 1542; *see also Wolf*, 645 F.2d at 25 ("[w]e are in accord" with cases finding the jurisdictional requirement of section 1001 to be met when the "federal government acted as a supervisor of disbursement or was to reimburse the defrauded non-federal agency"); *Baker*, 626 F.2d at 514 n.5 ("[T]he necessary link between deception of the non-federal agency and effect on the federal agency is provided by the federal agency's retention of 'the ultimate authority to see that the federal funds are properly spent.'").

Conclusion

For the reasons stated, we agree with the district court's denial of Wright's motion to dismiss the indictment, and we affirm the judgment of conviction.

DISCUSSION QUESTIONS

1. How important is it that EPA performed periodic evaluations of the Oklahoma program? Would it make a difference if the EPA had

discretionary authority to evaluate the program, but did not exercise its power to do so?

2. What if the forms that Wright filled out were kept on file at the water treatment plant where he worked instead of being filed with the Sequoyah County Health Department? Would that affect the outcome?

3. What policy considerations support imposing liability where the false statements at issue are not made directly to a federal agency, as in *Rodgers*?

4. The court in *Wright* said it agreed with other circuits that have found that a state agency's use of federal funds is ordinarily enough to establish jurisdiction under § 1001. What are the implications of that reading of the statute?

In Chapter 7 we considered some legal and practical consequences of the explosion of a Consolidated Edison steam pipe in Gramercy Park, including the indictment of Con Ed and two of its executives for violating notification requirements imposed by CERCLA and the Emergency Planning and Community Right-to-Know Act (EPCRA). In addition to being charged with failing to notify authorities that asbestos had been released, the defendants were also charged with five counts of making false statements in violation of § 1001.

UNITED STATES V. CONSOLIDATED EDISON OF NEW YORK, INC.
INDICTMENT

S1 93 Cr. 1063 (JSM) (S.D.N.Y. 1993)

. . .

Count Four

. . .

29. On or about August 20, 1989, in the Southern District of New York and elsewhere, CON EDISON and CONSTANTINE J. PAPAKRASAS, a/k/a "Gus," the defendants, and others to the Grand Jury known and unknown, in a matter within the jurisdiction of a department and agency of the United States, to wit, the EPA, unlawfully, wilfully and knowingly falsified, concealed and covered up by trick, scheme and device a material fact, and caused false, fictitious and fraudulent statements and

representations to be made, to wit, the defendant CONSTANTINE J. PAPAKRASAS, a/k/a "Gus," falsely informed the New York City Department of Health, which was attempting to determine whether the explosion of the Gramercy Park manhole resulted in asbestos contamination, in substance, that there was no asbestos in the manhole at the time of the explosion.

(Title 18, United States Code, Sections 1001 and 2.)

Count Five

. . .

31. From on or about August 19, 1989 up to and including on or about August 23, 1989, . . . CON EDISON, CONSTANTINE J. PAPAKRASAS, a/k/a "Gus," and PHILIP B. McGIVNEY, the defendants, . . . in a matter within the jurisdiction of a department and agency of the United States, to wit, the EPA, unlawfully, wilfully and knowingly falsified, concealed and covered up by trick, scheme, and device a material fact, and caused false, fictitious and fraudulent statements and representations to be made, to wit, by withholding material facts from and misleading employees of the Environmental Affairs Division of CON EDISON, the defendants and others caused CON EDISON to falsely inform the EPA, in substance, that CON EDISON did not believe that the asbestos found in its sampling had come from the explosion in the Gramercy Park manhole.

(Title 18, United States Code, Sections 1001 and 2.)

Count Six

. . .

33. On or about August 24, 1989, . . . the defendants, . . . in a matter within the jurisdiction of departments and agencies of the United States, to wit, the NRC and the EPA, unlawfully, wilfully and knowingly falsified, concealed and covered up by trick, scheme, and device, a material fact, and caused false, fictitious and fraudulent statements and representations to be made, to wit, after asbestos was discovered within a building located at 32 Gramercy Park South, the defendants and others caused a report to be made to the NRC which falsely suggested that CON EDISON did not have sufficient information to make a report to the NRC before August 23, 1989.

(Title 18, United States Code, Sections 1001 and 2.)

Count Seven

. . .

35. On or about August 24, 1989, . . . CON EDISON, . . . in a matter within the jurisdiction of . . . the National Response Center ("NRC") and the EPA, unlawfully, wilfully and knowingly falsified, concealed and covered up by trick, scheme, and device, a material fact, and caused false, fictitious and fraudulent statements and representations to be made, and made and used a false writing and document knowing the same to contain a false, fictitious and fraudulent statement and entry, to wit, after asbestos was discovered within a building located at 32 Gramercy Park South, CON EDISON made a report to the NRC which falsely stated that it had not been confirmed whether asbestos discovered in the building on August 23, 1989 had come from the building or CON EDISON's steam pipe.

(Title 18, United States Code, Sections 1001 and 2.)

Count Eight

. . .

37. On or about August 24, 1989, . . . CON EDISON, . . . in a matter within the jurisdiction of . . . the EPA, unlawfully, wilfully and knowingly falsified, concealed and covered up by trick, scheme, and device, a material fact, and caused false, fictitious and fraudulent statements and representations to be made, and made and used a false writing and document knowing the same to contain a false, fictitious and fraudulent statement and entry, to wit, after asbestos was discovered within a building located at 32 Gramercy Park South, the defendant made a report to the [Department of Environmental Protection] which falsely stated that it had not been confirmed whether asbestos discovered in the building on August 23, 1989 had come from the building or CON EDISON's steam pipe.

(Title 18, United States Code, Sections 1001 and 2.)

UNITED STATES V. CONSOLIDATED EDISON OF NEW YORK, INC.
OPINION

1994 WL 414407 (S.D.N.Y. 1994)

JOHN S. MARTIN, JR., District Judge. . . .

Papakrasas is charged in Count Four with making a false statement in a matter within the jurisdiction of the United States in violation of Title 18, United States Code § 1001 in that he "falsely informed the New York City Department of Health . . . that there was no asbestos in the manhole at the time of the explosion." Defendant claims that this statement to a New York City official was not a statement made in a matter within the jurisdiction of an agency of the United States. The Government contends that it was because the release of asbestos into the atmosphere was a matter within the jurisdiction of the Environmental Protection Agency.

The legal principals controlling on this motion were clearly set forth in the Second Circuit in United States v. Davis, 8 F.3d 923, 929 (2d Cir. 1993), where the Court stated

> [T]here is no requirement that a false statement be made *to* the federal agency; it must only have been made in *'any* matter *within the jurisdiction of any department [or] agency of the United States'*. . . .

> * * *

> A federal department or agency has jurisdiction within the meaning of 18 U.S.C. § 1001 'when it has the power' to exercise authority in a particular situation as distinguished from 'matters peripheral to the business of that body.' United States v. Rodgers, 466 U.S. 475, 479 (1984). In situations in which a federal agency is overseeing a state agency, it is the mere existence of the federal agency's supervisory authority that is important to determining the jurisdiction.

In this case, the Environmental Protection Agency clearly had supervisory authority over the state agency with respect to a potentially hazardous release of asbestos into the atmosphere. The Comprehensive Environmental Response Compensation and Liability Act of 1980 ("CERCLA") was enacted to address problems of pollution caused by hazardous substances such as asbestos "by creating a comprehensive and uniform system of notification, emergency governmental response, enforcement and liability." United States v. Carr, 880 F.2d 1550, 1552 (2d

Cir. 1989).   Acting pursuant to CERCLA, the EPA administrator promulgated the National Contingency Plan ("NCP") to provide coordinated responses to the release of hazardous substances. Under the NCP in effect at the time of the explosion, a federal on-scene coordinator is designated to coordinate the Government's response to the release of a hazardous substance and is to coordinate efforts with appropriate state and local response agencies. Provisions of CERCLA were supplemented in 1986 with the adoption of the Superfund Amendments and Reauthorization Act of 1986, which included the Emergency Planning and Community Right-to-Know Act ("EPCRA"). EPCRA established planning and notification requirements concerning the presence of hazardous chemicals and requires owners and operators of facilities to notify state and local emergency planning authorities of releases of materials such as asbestos. Although the defendants argue that EPCRA did not apply to Con Edison's facility at issue in the present case, the Court at oral argument rejected that contention.

Given the fact that the NCP designates the EPA as the federal on-scene coordinator for hazardous substance releases in Manhattan, and recognizes the role to be played by state and local public safety officials who are anticipated to be the first government representatives on the scene of a potential environmental incident, Mr. Papakrasas' statements to the Department of Health official was clearly a matter within the jurisdiction of the United States. A knowingly false statement to the local Department of Health official would, therefore, constitute a violation of Title 18, United States Code § 1001. . . .

So ordered.

DISCUSSION QUESTIONS

1. The Con Ed indictment included five false statements charges relating to Con Ed's response to the steam pipe explosion. How do the theories underlying each of the five counts differ?
2. Is the nexus between the false statement and agency jurisdiction stronger or weaker in *Wright* than in the false statements counts in *Con Ed*?
3. The Double Jeopardy Clause of the Fifth Amendment prohibits punishing an individual twice for the same offense. When we considered the *Blockburger* test for double jeopardy in Chapter 6, the focus was on whether convictions based on charges brought under different statutes amounted to convictions for the same offense.

In *Con Ed*, we have five counts brought under the same statute. This puts the question in a somewhat different light — i.e., whether the indictment is multiplicitous. "A multiplicitous indictment . . . is one that charges in separate counts two or more crimes, when in fact and law, only one crime has been committed."[83] Is the Con Ed indictment subject to challenge on the ground that it is multiplicitous?

4. W.R. Grace, whose misdeeds in Libby, Montana were explored in Chapter 5, had earlier run afoul of the false statements statute in conjunction with the contamination of drinking water wells in Woburn, Massachusetts. You may already be familiar with the underlying facts of the story, which are famously told in Jonathon Harr's *A Civil Action*.

Briefly, the government accused Grace of lying to EPA officials about a hazardous chemical it used at a plant in Woburn, not far from the contaminated wells. Grace pled guilty in 1988 to one count of making false statements in violation of § 1001. As part of the plea agreement, the government dropped a second charge that Grace had concealed its dumping of hazardous waste behind the plant. Grace was fined $10,000 — which at that time was the maximum authorized under the statute — but neglected to pay it for a period of ten years. The case was prosecuted under § 1001 because the misconduct was not then punishable under RCRA.

Two years earlier, Grace reportedly had paid $8 million to settle a civil suit brought by leukemia victims and their families who claimed their illnesses were caused by drinking and otherwise being exposed to the contaminated well water.

b. Legislative Branch

Before Congress amended the false statements statute in 1996, § 1001 did not expressly address whether Congress or an arm of Congress would qualify as a "department or agency" of the United States. The Supreme Court removed the uncertainty in United States v. Bramblett[84] a decade before the statute was amended. The issue in *Bramblett* was whether the disbursing office of the House of Representatives was a department or agency under § 1001. The Court rejected the argument that § 1001 applied only to the executive branch of government, concluding that the statute called for an

---

[83]United States v. Harris, 79 F.3d 223, 231 (2d Cir. 1996).
[84]348 U.S. 503 (1955).

unrestricted interpretation of the term "department" to fully achieve its purposes. Thus, the Court in *Bramblett* found that § 1001 applied to the executive, legislative, and judicial branches of government.

Although it might be tempting to conclude that the 1996 amendment codified the holding in *Bramblett*, the amended statute contains an important qualification.

> (c) With respect to any matter within the jurisdiction of the legislative branch, [§ 1001] shall apply only to –
>> (1) administrative matters, including a claim for payment, a matter related to the procurement of property or services, personnel or employment practices, or support services, or a document required by law, rule, or regulation to be submitted to the Congress or any office or officers within the legislative branch; or
>> (2) any investigation or review, conducted pursuant to the authority of any committee, subcommittee, commission or office of the Congress, consistent with applicable rules of the House or Senate.

THE CASE OF THE SENATE SUBCOMMITTEE HEARING

Suppose the events surrounding Con Ed's steam pipe explosion unfold as follows. The steam pipe explodes and spews asbestos in Gramercy Park, but Con Ed falsely denies there was asbestos in the pipe. Two weeks later, Con Ed admits there was asbestos and that the explosion had spread asbestos debris throughout the area, including in and around residences where homeowners had prematurely been told it was safe to return. An outraged congressman who represents the district where the explosion occurred calls for hearings into the cause of the explosion and Con Ed's response to it. Six weeks later, a subcommittee hearing is convened to look into the matter and to consider whether stiffer penalties should be enacted for failure to comply with CERCLA's notification requirements.

Did Con Ed make a false statement within the jurisdiction of the legislative branch when it falsely denied there was asbestos in the pipe?[85]

---

[85] *Cf.* United States v. Pickett, 353 F.3d 62 (D.C. Cir. 2004).

c. Judicial Branch

When the Court ruled in *Bramblett* that the pre-amendment version of § 1001 applied to the legislative branch, it rejected the argument that the statute applies only to false statements made to the executive branch. Notably, however, it ruled (perhaps gratuitously) that the word "department" referred to "the executive, legislative and *judicial* branches of Government."[86]

The reference to the judicial branch spawned a flurry of cases testing the limits of the statute's reach into the workings of the courts. This litigation eventually led to a circuit split on the question whether § 1001 was applicable only when a court was exercising an "administrative" or "housekeeping" function, or whether it applied to trial tactics and statements made when the court was exercising a "judicial" function such as conducting a hearing or trial.[87] As we have seen, some three decades later the Supreme Court overruled *Bramblett* in *Hubbard,* holding that § 1001 did not extend to the judicial branch of government.

The 1996 amendment to § 1001, enacted scarcely a year after *Hubbard* was decided, expressly included the judicial branch within the jurisdictional clause. But as with its treatment of the legislative branch, the amendment included a significant judicial branch qualification. By its express terms, § 1001 "does not apply to a party to a judicial proceeding, or that party's counsel, for statements, representations, writings or documents submitted by such party or counsel to a judge or magistrate in that proceeding."

DISCUSSION QUESTIONS

1. Why would Congress limit the application of § 1001 in the context of judicial proceedings?
2. Under the 1996 amendment, what kinds of representations and documents would be shielded by the limitation on statements made in the context of judicial proceedings? Suppose, for example, that before his sentencing hearing, the defendant in *Wright* had forged a letter addressed to the court that purported to be from his supervisor at the water treatment plant. Although the supervisor had fired him when the indictment was handed

---

[86]*Bramblett*, 348 U.S. at 509 (emphasis added).

[87]The D.C. Circuit took the lead in advocating an administrative/judicial function distinction in Morgan v. United States, 309 F.2d 234 (D.C. Cir. 1962).

down, the forged letter made Wright sound like a saint. It praised Wright's honesty and integrity, falsely stated that Wright was the sole support for his aged and infirm mother, and falsely represented that if the court did not imprison him, Wright could continue working at the plant and providing support for his mother.

If Wright submits the forged letter to the court, has he violated the false statements statute?[88]

2. FALSE STATEMENT

a. Misrepresentation

Section 1001 reaches a broad array of statements. It reaches "any materially false, fictitious, or fraudulent statements or representations."[89] It does not matter whether the statements are oral or written, or whether they are volunteered or legally required. And while the misrepresentations may relate to past or present facts, the statute also encompasses statements relating to future intent. Thus, a promise may constitute a statement, but a prediction that proves to be wrong will not, without more.

Although an affirmative misrepresentation of fact is sufficient, it is not a necessary condition for imposing liability. An omission or failure to speak may also be deemed a statement if there is a duty to disclose. Similarly, nondisclosure may also violate the statute if the actor has made an affirmative statement that was true at the time it was made, but later became false because of changed circumstances.

> **Illustration K:** An environmental compliance manager at an industrial wastewater treatment plant is required to fill out periodic reports on changes in turbidity. The EPA form includes the following: "Please note increases in turbidity that exceed turbidity levels on date of last report by more than 2%." The manager fills in "N/A" in the space for the answer.

> **Illustration L:** The same facts as in Illustration K, but with the following variation. The manager leaves the space provided for the answer blank.

> **Illustration M:** A city successfully applies for federal funds to underwrite part of the cost of upgrading its sewage treatment plant. The city continues

---

[88]*Cf.* United States v. McNeil, 362 F.3d 570 (9th Cir. 2004).
[89]18 U.S.C. § 1001(a)(2).

to receive the funds without disclosing that environmental engineers have determined that the planned upgrade is not technologically feasible.

The manager in Illustration K has made an affirmative statement. By writing "N/A" in the blank space, he has affirmatively represented that the question is not applicable. In Illustration L, the manager's failure to respond to the question by leaving the space for the answer blank could be found to impliedly represent that the question is not applicable or that he has no relevant information to supply.

And in Illustration M, the city's original application for funding represents that the funds will be used to upgrade the sewage treatment plant. Once this is no longer true and the upgrade plans have been scrapped, the city has a duty to disclose the changed circumstances because they would disqualify it from continuing to receive the funds.

Until the late 1980s, there was a split of authority on the question whether an "exculpatory no" constituted a statement under § 1001. The underlying concern related partly to whether a simple "no" in response to a question propounded by a government investigator was a statement. But the real driving force behind the "exculpatory no" defense was a strong concern that in this context, the statute came "uncomfortably close" to implicating the Fifth Amendment privilege against self-incrimination.[90] Although most jurisdictions ultimately came to recognize an "exculpatory no" exception, stated rationales and often complex multi-part tests for when the exception would apply varied markedly from circuit to circuit.

The Supreme Court broke the logjam in 1997 in Brogan v. United States.[91] In *Brogan*, the Court held that the plain language of the statute leaves no room for an exculpatory no exception. Because a simple false denial in response to a question can hide the truth as effectively as a more elaborate falsehood, recognition of a judicially created exculpatory no exception could defeat the goal of the statute.

The Court also rejected the argument that basing liability on an exculpatory no violates the privilege against self-incrimination. A person who is being questioned by the police can choose to answer truthfully or remain silent, but there is no constitutional right to lie.

---

[90]United States v. Lambert, 501 F.2d 943, 946 n.4 (5th Cir. 1974).
[91]522 U.S. 398 (1998).

Notwithstanding the Court's clarification of the scope of § 1001, Justice Department policy counsels prosecutors to make cautious use of the statute in the exculpatory no context.

> It is the Department's policy not to charge a § 1001 violation in situations in which a suspect, during an investigation, merely denies guilt in response to questioning by the government. This policy is to be narrowly construed, however; affirmative, discursive and voluntary statements to Federal criminal investigators would not fall within the policy. Further, certain false responses to questions propounded for administrative purposes (e.g., statements to border or United States Immigration and Naturalization Service agents during routine inquiries) are also prosecutable, as are untruthful "no's" when the defendant initiated contact with the government in order to obtain a benefit.[92]

DISCUSSION QUESTIONS

1. In what sense might it be said that, absent an "exculpatory no" exception, the false statements statute comes "uncomfortably close" to the privilege against self-incrimination? Was the Court in *Brogan* too quick to dismiss the Fifth Amendment concerns that prompted many lower courts to recognize an "exculpatory no" defense?
2. The Justice Department policy distinguishes mere denials of guilt and "affirmative, discursive and voluntary" statements. What is the difference between the two types of statements? And in what sense is the policy using the term "voluntary?"

b. Concealment

Concealment is an alternative way to violate § 1001. Conduct through which the actor "falsifies, conceals, or covers up" a material fact "by any trick, scheme, or device" is punishable if the jurisdictional requirement is satisfied.[93] Yet while this form of deception is defined in a separate prong of the statute, it is often difficult to draw clear cut distinctions between falsification and concealment.

---

[92]U.S.A.M. § 9-42.160.
[93]18 U.S.C. § 1001(a)(1).

Illustration N: A chemical manufacturer ships dangerous chemicals under a bill of lading that identifies the contents of the shipment as distilled water.

Illustration O: The manufacturer's environmental engineer maintains files that understate the turbidity of water discharged from the company's wastewater treatment plant.

In both Illustrations there is an element of falsification. The bill of lading in Illustration N misrepresents the contents of the shipment, and the turbidity files in Illustration O falsify the quantity of pollutants discharged from the plant. But in each illustration, the falsification of one fact serves to conceal another. Similarly, nondisclosure — which can constitute an implied misrepresentation where there is a duty to disclose — also conceals what the actor has failed to reveal.

It is unlikely that Congress intended these distinct theories of liability to be interchangeable in the ordinary course of events. Thus, one might argue that, to violate the concealment prong of the statute, the misrepresentations in Illustrations N and O need the additional element of an affirmative act of concealment "by trick, scheme, or device." Unfortunately, there is little case law guidance on what the phrase "trick, scheme, or device" means.

THE CASE OF THE LEVEL SEVEN SCRUB

Suppose the engineer in Illustration O kept two sets of turbidity files. The files that understated the level of pollutants in the wastewater were stored in a file cabinet in his office. The turbidity files that accurately recorded unacceptable levels of pollutants in the wastewater were stored on the hard drive of his laptop.

A year after he began keeping the double set of files, the president of the company sent a memo to all employees informing them that a grand jury had begun a criminal investigation of the company's environmental compliance. The memo also alerted them to the possibility that the U.S. Attorney might obtain a search warrant to find and seize potentially incriminating evidence from the plant.

Alarmed by this development, the engineer hired a computer expert at Geeks Unlimited to do a "level seven" scrub of the computer hard drive, a procedure that would make it virtually impossible for anyone to restore the deleted information. When the FBI executed the search warrant and discovered the clean hard drive, the engineer explained that he had it scrubbed to get rid of a computer virus. "I don't believe you," the agent replied. "This isn't how you remove a computer virus. It's how the CIA covers its tracks. You scrubbed the hard drive because you were afraid the feds were on the way with a search warrant, didn't you?" "I did not!" the engineer shot back.

DISCUSSION QUESTIONS

1. What part or parts of the engineer's conduct violated the concealment prong of § 1001? What part or parts violated the misrepresentation prong?
2. What is the purpose of having separate concealment and misrepresentation prongs in § 1001?

c. Falsity

When a § 1001 prosecution is based on misrepresentation, the government must prove that the statement was false at the time it was made. Although a false statements conviction cannot be premised on a statement that is fundamentally ambiguous, that principle does not preclude a conviction simply because the statement is susceptible of different interpretations. A fundamental ambiguity exists only when persons of ordinary intelligence cannot understand the statement. If a statement is subject to more than one plausible interpretation but is not fundamentally ambiguous, the government bears the burden of negating "any reasonable interpretation" that would make it factually true.[94]

d. Materiality

Both prongs of § 1001 contain a materiality requirement. The statute prohibits the concealment of material facts and the making of materially false representations. A statement is material if it has the capacity or natural tendency to influence a governmental action or decision. Although this is "a fairly low bar for the government to meet,"[95] this does not mean that it is *no* bar. At minimum, the government must prove "how the false statement in question was capable of influencing federal functioning."[96] And in this

---

[94]United States v. Stephenson, 895 F.2d 867, 873-874 (2d Cir. 1990).
[95]United States v. White, 270 F.3d 356, 365 (6th Cir. 2001).
[96]*Id.*

context, the focus of the inquiry is the statement's intrinsic capacity to influence rather than its actual effect.

DISCUSSION QUESTIONS

1. What is the purpose of the materiality requirement? Does a definition of materiality that imposes a "low" hurdle for the government accomplish that objective?
2. Does "material" mean something different than "relevant"?
3. What kinds of statements would not be material under this definition? Suppose that in The Case of the Level Seven Scrub, when the engineer had called Geeks Unlimited, he told the expert he wanted the hard drive scrubbed "to CIA standards" so none of the data could be restored. Unbeknownst to the engineer, his phone was wiretapped and the FBI recorded the conversation. When the FBI agent appeared in the engineer's office to question him, the engineer told the agent that he hired Geeks Unlimited to remove a virus. When the agent challenged this explanation, the engineer strenuously denied that his purpose was to destroy data. If the agent already knew the engineer was lying, would the engineer's false statements be material?

3. MENTAL STATE

To violate § 1001, the actor must "knowingly and willfully" conceal a material fact or make a materially false statement. At a minimum, this requires proof of knowledge of the falsity. But for a time it was unclear whether the government must also prove knowledge that the falsehood was a matter within the jurisdiction of a governmental entity.

The Supreme Court addressed this question in United States v. Yermian[97] and held that knowledge of the jurisdictional requirement was not an element of the offense. As in other contexts, the Court found the jurisdictional requirement served merely "to identify the factor that makes the false statement an appropriate subject for federal concern."[98] But while the Court's holding made it clear that no "actual" knowledge of agency jurisdiction need be shown, it left open the possibility that some lesser standard of culpability

---

[97]468 U.S. 63 (1984).
[98]*Id.* at 68.

might be required.[99] Although the high Court has yet to revisit the issue, the general consensus is that no culpable mental state is required with respect to the jurisdictional element.

DISCUSSION QUESTIONS

1. Suppose the Geeks "expert" who came to clean the hard drive in The Case of the Level Seven Scrub was actually an undercover FBI agent. When the "expert" expressed some skepticism about why the engineer wanted the hard drive wiped clean, the engineer insisted that the computer had been repeatedly plagued by an insidious virus and that he was sure this was the only way to remove it. The engineer knew, of course, that there was no virus, but had no way of knowing that the "expert" was an FBI agent. Has the engineer violated § 1001?

2. Given the low threshold for proof of materiality and the lack of a culpability requirement for the jurisdictional element, does § 1001 create a trap for the unwary? Does it raise the specter of punishing ostensibly innocent conduct?

4. PREEMPTION

UNITED STATES V. SHAW

150 Fed. App'x. 863 (10th Cir. 2005)

O'BRIEN, Circuit Judge. . . .

[Shaw was convicted of violating § 1001 by engaging in a scheme to falsify or conceal the presence of asbestos at a refinery. On appeal, he argued that the court lacked subject matter jurisdiction under § 1001 because a provision in the Clean Air Act, 42 U.S.C. § 7413(c), provided the exclusive vehicle for prosecuting him for falsifying a form required by the CAA.]

---

[99]The trial court had instructed the jury that to convict, it must find the defendant "knew or should have known" the false statements were within federal agency jurisdiction. Since the government failed to object to the reasonably foreseeable language, the Supreme Court found it unnecessary to consider whether the government must prove the defendant should have known the statement was within federal agency jurisdiction. *Id.* at 75 n.14.

1. Subject Matter Jurisdiction

The CAA contains a provision entitled "Federal Enforcement." *See* 42 U.S.C. § 7413. Within that provision is a subsection entitled "Criminal penalties" which states in relevant part:

> (2) Any person who knowingly —
>   (A) makes any false material statement, representation, or certification in, or omits material information from, or knowingly alters, conceals, or fails to file or maintain any notice, application, record, report, plan, or other document required pursuant to this chapter to be either filed or maintained (whether with respect to the requirements imposed by the Administrator or by a State);
> . . .
> shall, upon conviction, be punished by a fine pursuant to Title 18, or by imprisonment for not more than 2 years, or both. . . .

42 U.S.C. § 7413(c)(2)(A).

Shaw contends [that] § 7413(e)(2)(A) is the sole and exclusive means by which the Government may prosecute the making [of] a false statement to the EPA in violation of the CAA. Thus, he argues the district court lacked subject matter jurisdiction over his prosecution under 18 U.S.C. § 1001. Shaw also maintains that because § 7413(c)(2)(A) and § 1001 proscribe the same conduct, the specific statute, trumps § 1001, the general statute, unless Congressional intent demonstrates the general statute is to control. He asserts the language of § 7413(c)(2)(A) and the legislative history of the two statutes indicate Congress intended § 7413(c)(2)(A) to trump § 1001. Lastly, to the extent there is any ambiguity as to which statute controls, Shaw contends the rule of lenity requires application of § 7413(c)(2)(A) because its penalty provision maximizes punishment at two years as opposed to five years under § 1001.

The Government maintains § 1001(a)(1) and § 7413(c)(2)(A) are two separate statutes which criminalize different behavior — the former criminalizes a scheme to conceal a material fact from the Government and the latter prohibits the making of a false statement within a document required to be filed by the EPA. It argues it was not required to choose one statute over the other and Shaw's conduct (knowingly and willfully submitting false and fraudulent representations to the EPA over a lengthy period of time) was prohibited by § 1001(a)(1). The Government further contends that because § 1001(a)(1) is not ambiguous, the rule of lenity is inapplicable.

Shaw's jurisdictional argument is without merit. It is well settled that "when an act violates more than one criminal statute, the Government may prosecute[] under either so long as it does not discriminate against any class of defendants." United States v. Batchelder, 442 U.S. 114, 123-24 (1979) ("Whether to prosecute and what charge to file or bring before a grand jury are decisions that generally rest in the prosecutor's discretion."). This is true even when one statute provides a harsher penalty. . . .

We addressed a similar issue in United States v. Wiles, 102 F.3d 1043 (10th Cir. 1996). There, the defendant was charged with making a false statement to the Securit[ies] and Exchange Commission (SEC) under 18 U.S.C. § 1001. On appeal, he alleged that Congress intended the Government to prosecute the making of a false statement to the SEC under 15 U.S.C. § 78ff, a specific provision in the Securities Exchange Act of 1934 which criminalizes the willful making of a false or misleading statement to the SEC. Thus, the defendant argued that the making of a false statement to the SEC could not support a conviction under § 1001. We rejected this argument, holding: "Without any express indication that Congress intended otherwise, we . . . conclude that both § 78ff and § 1001 proscribe the making of false statements to the SEC, and the government may prosecute such conduct under either statute." *See also* United States v. Radetsky, 535 F.2d 556, 567-68 (10th Cir. 1976) (rejecting argument that the defendant should have been prosecuted under specific statute criminalizing the making of false statements in connection with medicare claims rather than § 1001 because there was no evidence of an intent to make the specific statute a substitute for any part of § 1001).

The same reasoning applies here. Despite Shaw's attempt to persuade us otherwise, we fail to discern from either the language of the CAA or its legislative history any Congressional intent to foreclose prosecutions under § 1001 where § 7413(c)(2)(A) may also apply. Without such intent, we defer to the Government's prosecutorial discretion. Moreover, the Government alleged Shaw engaged in a scheme to conceal the presence of asbestos. Section 7413(c)(2)(A) of the CAA does not proscribe such conduct. Consequently, charging Shaw under § 1001(a)(1), which does prohibit such conduct was proper. . . .

Shaw's conviction is Affirmed. . . .

DISCUSSION QUESTION

1. Why wouldn't Congress want a specific statute that is tailored to fit the particular circumstances of a case to trump a more general statute that covers the same conduct? If Congress wanted the specific statute to preempt the general statute, what would it have to do to ensure that result?

5. PERJURY

Perjury and false statements violations share some obvious similarities. Most notable among them is that both offenses involve some form of lying. Unlike false statements violations, however, perjury is limited to untrue statements made under oath.[100]   And perjury ordinarily occurs in an adversarial setting, where opposing counsel have the opportunity to probe and prod to get at the truth.[101]

In contrast, violations of the false statements statute typically involve misrepresentations made to undermine the government's information gathering process. This form of mischief often occurs in settings where there is no active interplay between the agency propounding the questions and the person providing the answers — e.g., questions that appear on a standard printed form. Given the government's need to rely on the accuracy of information provided on standard forms, some jurisdictions permit § 1001

---

[100]The principal statutes are 18 U.S.C. § 1621 (Perjury) and 18 U.S.C. § 1623 (False Declarations). Both apply to sworn false statements made before federal courts and grand juries. But the statutes differ in three notable respects: (1) the perjury statute applies to a broader range of proceedings; (2) the perjury statute contains more rigorous proof requirements on the issue of falsity; and (3) the false declarations statute provides a limited defense of recantation.

[101]While the false declarations statute is limited to sworn falsehoods made before federal courts and grand juries, the perjury statute extends to sworn false statements made within the jurisdiction of any tribunal that is authorized by federal law to administer oaths. Thus, in addition to judicial proceedings, the perjury statute applies to false statements made under oath before such tribunals as congressional committees and administrative agencies. The perjury statute also applies to "any declaration, certificate, verification, or statement under penalty of perjury," 18 U.S.C. § 1621(2), which would include attestations on printed forms like income tax returns.

violations to be based on literally true but unresponsive answers to the questions.[102]

D. OBSTRUCTION OF JUSTICE

As is true with false statements, a panoply of criminal laws may be used to reach conduct designed to cover up wrongdoing in order to avoid criminal prosecution, administrative sanctions, or civil liability.[103]   Although the obstruction of justice statutes protect participants in judicial and administrative proceedings from the use of force, intimidation, or corrupt means to influence them in the discharge of their duties, in the context of environmental crime, the most common focus is on the part of the statute that protects the integrity of judicial and administrative decision-making processes.

The principal statutory tools have historically been 18 U.S.C. § 1503, which applies to civil and criminal judicial proceedings; 18 U.S.C. § 1505, which applies to administrative agency and congressional proceedings; and 18 U.S.C. § 1510, which applies to federal criminal investigations.   More recent enactments have altered the traditional role of these statutes and created new offenses that include witness tampering,[104] evidence tampering (particularly destruction, alteration and concealment of documents)[105] and retaliating against witnesses or informants, including corporate whistleblowers.[106]

1. SECTIONS 1503 AND 1505

The traditional obstruction of justice statute, 18 U.S.C. § 1503, prohibits specific acts such as threatening jurors and officers of the court. For our purposes, however, the heart of the statute is the omnibus clause, which

---

[102]Perjury prosecutions cannot be based on misleading but unresponsive answers. Bronston v. United States, 409 U.S. 352 (1973).

[103]These cover-up crimes include a number of provisions found in environmental statutes. *See, e.g.*, 42 U.S.C. § 7413(c)(2) (Clean Air Act provision prohibiting, inter alia, altering or concealing any required record or document, or tampering with any required monitoring device).

[104]18 U.S.C. § 1512.

[105]18 U.S.C. § 1519.

[106]18 U.S.C. § 1513.

forbids corruptly endeavoring "to influence, obstruct, or impede, the due administration of justice."

Courts have interpreted this clause to require that a judicial proceeding actually be pending for the statute to apply. In the context of criminal cases, this requirement could be satisfied by a prosecutor's convening of a grand jury or filing of an indictment or information. In the rare instance in which the statute is applied to misconduct that occurs in a civil case,[107] the proceeding would begin, and thus be pending, when the complaint is filed. Knowledge (or reasonable grounds to believe) that a proceeding is pending is required.

The element that distinguishes lawful from unlawful conduct under the omnibus clause is the requirement that the conduct be undertaken corruptly. Yet "corruptly" is a word of many meanings. In this context, corruptly can mean undertaken with an improper or evil motive[108] or with intent to obstruct.[109]

The omnibus clause in § 1503 "is essentially a catch-all provision which generally prohibits conduct that interferes with the due administration of justice."[110] As such, it predictably reaches a broad array of wrongs, including hiding, altering, or destroying evidence; instructing others to withhold evidence; secluding a witness; refusing to testify before a grand jury after receiving a grant of immunity; and filing bogus motions to sabotage a grand jury investigation. Perjury, standing alone, is not an obstruction of justice.[111]

Since the omnibus clause is directed toward corrupt "endeavors," an attempt to impede need not be successful to be punishable. The omnibus clause punishes *any* effort to do what the statute forbids, provided that the conduct has "at least a reasonable tendency" to corrupt a legal proceeding.[112] Thus, for example, one who tries to bribe a witness to destroy subpoenaed

---

[107]*See, e.g.*, United States v. Lundwall, 1 F. Supp. 2d 249 (S.D.N.Y. 1998) (destruction of documents during discovery stage of civil racial discrimination suit against Texaco).

[108]United States v. Collis, 128 F.3d 313, 318 (6th Cir. 1997).

[109]United States v. Russell, 234 F.3d 404, 407 (8th Cir. 2000). *But see* United States v. Neiswender, 590 F.2d 1269, 1273-1274 (4th Cir. 1979) (adopting a reasonably foreseeable rule).

[110]United States v. Thomas, 916 F.2d 647, 650 n.3 (11th Cir. 1990).

[111]United States v. Griffin, 589 F.2d 200, 204-205 (5th Cir. 1979) (recognizing that while perjury distorts the truth, it does not, without more, impede or block the due administration of justice). *But cf.* United States v. Sharpe, 193 F.3d 852, 865 (5th Cir. 1999) (perjured testimony that has the "natural and probable effect" of impeding the administration of justice can constitute obstruction under § 1503 if the witness has the requisite intent to impede).

[112]United States v. Harris, 558 F.2d 366, 369 (7th Cir. 1977).

documents violates the statute, even if the witness declines the bribe and produces the documents.

A companion provision, 18 U.S.C. § 1505, prohibits corruptly endeavoring "to influence, obstruct, or impede the due and proper administration of the law under which any pending proceeding is being had before any department or agency of the United States."[113] In this context, courts have construed the pending proceeding requirement broadly to include both an agency's investigative and administrative functions, provided that the agency has adjudicative or rulemaking powers. Thus, when EPA opens an informal inquiry into a company's compliance with its environmental permit, a proceeding is pending for purposes of § 1505.

Unlike § 1503, which provides no guidance on what the term "corruptly" means, a limited definition of "corruptly" as that term is used in § 1505 is provided in a companion provision.

> (b) As used in section 1505, the term "corruptly" means acting with an improper purpose, personally or by influencing another, including making a false or misleading statement, or withholding, concealing, altering, or destroying a document or other information.[114]

DISCUSSION QUESTIONS

1. What is the reason for criminalizing the types of conduct that fall within the prohibitions of §§ 1503 and 1505?
2. Which of the cases, case studies, and illustrations considered in earlier sections of this chapter involve conduct that would violate § 1503 or § 1505?

a. The W.R. Grace Prosecution

In addition to the charges relating more directly to the asbestos contamination of Libby, Montana,[115] the W.R. Grace indictment included four counts charging Grace and one of the individual defendants with obstruction of justice. The indictment alleged that they violated § 1505 by:

---

[113]Section 1505 also applies to congressional inquiries and investigations conducted in accordance with "the due and proper exercise of the power of inquiry." The inquiry may be conducted by either House of Congress or a congressional committee or joint committee.

[114]18 U.S.C. § 1515(b).

[115]*See supra* Chapter 5.

- providing false and misleading information to EPA by representing that the vermiculite concentrate had less than 1 percent tremolite asbestos and that the asbestos contamination problems at the mine had been resolved (Count VII);
- providing false and misleading information in the company's response to an EPA CERCLA request for information by representing that Grace did not provide vermiculite to the general public; that mine employees did not have asbestos dust on their clothes when they left the mine; that Grace had provided vermiculite tailings for the high school running track, when it had also provided it for the junior high running track and the elementary school ice skating rink; that Grace "took actions to treat the roadway to the mine to minimize dust created by vehicular traffic," when it had in fact used vermiculite mill tailings to build, surface, and sand the road; and that Grace failed to tell EPA about air and environmental media sampling studies and results (Count VIII);
- denying the EPA Emergency Response Team access to three contaminated property sites (Count IX); and
- providing false and misleading information to EPA by representing that the vermiculite did not pose a risk to human health or the environment (Count X).[116]

DISCUSSION QUESTIONS

1. Is there a pending proceeding for purposes of § 1505?
2. Are the allegations in Counts VII-X sufficient to sustain a finding that the defendants acted corruptly for purposes of § 1505?
3. Could the conduct described in Counts VII-X have been prosecuted as obstruction of justice under § 1503?
4. The indictment charged the defendants with one count of conspiracy (in violation of § 371), three counts of knowing endangerment (in violation of the Clean Air Act), and two counts of wire fraud (in violation of § 1343). What is gained by adding four obstruction of justice charges to the mix? Is this a case of prosecutorial piling on?
5. Could the conduct described in some or all of the obstruction of justice counts have been prosecuted under the false statements statute? If so, why would the government charge violations of § 1505 instead?
6. If some of the conduct described in the obstruction of justice counts in the indictment could have been prosecuted as false statements violations,

---

[116]Grace was the only defendant charged in Count X.

could the government have brought charges under both statutes without implicating double jeopardy concerns?

2. SECTION 1512

Section 1512 is worth briefly mentioning because it expands liability to situations in which there is no pending judicial or administrative proceedings. It proscribes various forms of interference that are undertaken with *intent* to improperly obstruct or influence an official proceeding, but the statute explicitly provides that no official proceeding needs to be pending or about to be instituted at the time the conduct occurs.[117] Thus, one who acts in anticipation of a grand jury or other judicial proceeding, an agency investigation, or a congressional inquiry[118] may violate the statute, even if the anticipated proceeding is never initiated.

Section 1512 is stunning in its breadth. Its prohibitions include corruptly persuading or attempting to persuade another, or engaging in misleading conduct toward another, with intent to influence testimony, to cause evidence or witnesses to be unavailable, or to hinder communication to federal law enforcement officers (e.g., FBI agents) of information about the possible commission of a federal crime; to corruptly alter, destroy, or conceal physical evidence to impair its integrity or availability in an official proceeding or to "otherwise" obstruct or impede an official proceeding; and to intentionally harass another to interfere with anyone's participation in an official proceeding or investigation.

3. ENVIRONMENTAL STATUTES

A number of environmental statutes contain criminal provisions that overlap the prohibitions in more traditional obstruction of justice statutes. Consider, for example, the following Clean Air Act provision.

(2) Any person who knowingly —
    (A) . . . alters, conceals, or fails to file or maintain any notice, application, record, report, plan, or other document required pursuant to this Act . . .; [or]
    . . .

---

[117] 18 U.S.C. § 1512(f)(1).
[118] The term "official proceeding" is defined in 18 U.S.C. § 1515(a)(1).

(C) falsifies, tampers with, renders inaccurate, or fails to install any
monitoring device or method required to be maintained or followed
under this Act . . .
[is guilty of a felony].[119]

As we have seen, alteration, concealment, falsification, and tampering are
clearly within the range of acts prohibited by Title 18 obstruction of justice
statutes considered above.

DISCUSSION QUESTION

1. Given the similarity of the prohibitions in the obstruction of justice and
   Clean Air Act provisions, what factors would guide a prosecutor's
   decision whether to charge a Clean Air Act violation or to charge
   obstruction of justice? What are the salient differences between the CAA
   and Title 18 obstruction offenses?

---

[119]42 U.S.C. § 7413(c)(2).

9

ENFORCEMENT

[T]he good sense of prosecutors, the wise guidance of trial judges, and the ultimate judgment of juries must be trusted.[†]

Under the prosecutorial discretion approach, which could be called the "Al Capone" model, prosecutors are blindly trusted to exploit the full sweep of the criminal law only against those who are truly culpable and not against the morally innocent who only technically fall within the terms of the criminal prohibition. This approach [allows prosecutors] to obtain conviction based on relatively little evidence of actual culpability.[††]

[R]ather than portraying environmental prosecutors as loose cannons, it would be more accurate to state that centralized decision-making and multi-level review of prospective criminal cases [impose] real constraints on discretion and autonomy and [guard] against arbitrary action.[†††]

[†]Justice Felix Frankfurter.
[††]Professor Richard J. Lazarus.
[†††]Professor Kathleen F. Brickey.

The term "environmental enforcement" has historically been synonymous with civil enforcement. To be sure, nuisance law played an occasional role in the prosecution of polluters whose activities affected the public at large. In the early nineteenth century, for example, the city of Albany was successfully prosecuted for allowing the Hudson River to become "foul, filled and choked up with mud, rubbish, and dead carcasses of animals."[1] In another nineteenth century nuisance prosecution, the owner of a hog rendering business was charged with maintaining excessive quantities of putrid carcasses that emitted "noxious odors and gases" and deprived surrounding communities of the "enjoyment of the air, free from unnecessary pollution."[2] While these examples vividly illustrate why a mechanism for state intervention was sorely needed, nuisance prosecutions had relatively limited utility as an environmental enforcement tool.

Around the turn of the century Congress enacted the Refuse Act,[3] one of the earliest federal water pollution statutes. Although the Act was one of the first to provide criminal penalties for activities that produced pollution,[4] its criminal enforcement scheme was weak and prosecutions were few and far between.

It was not until the advent of modern environmental statutes in the 1970s and 1980s that Congress came to recognize the important role that meaningful criminal penalties could play in environmental enforcement. In consequence, lawmakers cautiously began to add felony provisions to key anti-pollution laws.

Although the emergence of criminal enforcement authority initially spawned inter- and intra-agency squabbling at the Justice Department and EPA, the Justice Department's fledgling criminal enforcement program achieved a remarkable degree of success in a relatively short period of time. And as one might expect, improved relations between EPA and Justice Department officials facilitated the development of a methodical approach to criminal enforcement issues gradually over time.

But as systematic criminal enforcement strategies began to emerge, major policy considerations inevitably came to the fore. How would EPA and the

---

[1]People v. Corporation of Albany, 11 Wend. 539, 543 (N.Y. Sup. Ct. 1834).

[2]Seacord v. State, 13 N.E. 194, 201 (Ill. 1887).

[3]33 U.S.C. § 407. The statute is also known as the Rivers and Harbors Act.

[4]*See, e.g.,* Dollar Steamship Co. v. United States, 101 F.2d 638 (9th Cir. 1939) (prosecution for throwing garbage from a ship into the Honolulu Harbor); United States v. Alaska S. Packing Co. (*In re* La Merced), 84 F.2d 444 (9th Cir. 1936) (prosecution for discharging oil from a vessel into Lake Union in Seattle).

Justice Department decide which violations to criminally investigate? Once an investigation was underway, what criteria would they use to determine which cases were worthy of criminal prosecution? And what role would prosecutorial discretion play in the larger scheme of things? These and other pivotal criminal enforcement issues are the core concern of this chapter.

A. ENFORCEMENT AUTHORITY

1. INVESTIGATION

The Environmental Protection Agency has no criminal enforcement authority. All environmental crime prosecutions are brought by a United States Attorney's office and/or the Environmental Crimes Section of the Justice Department. That said, EPA often plays a pivotal role in the process because most environmental crime prosecutions begin with an investigation by EPA, sometimes with the assistance of the FBI.[5]

Although various environmental statutes confer specific investigative powers on EPA, they are not necessarily full or exclusive statements of the agency's authority. In Dow Chemical Co. v. United States, for example, EPA enforcement officials had inspected — with Dow's consent — two power plants at a Dow facility in Midland, Michigan. The officials later requested permission to conduct a second inspection, but Dow denied their request. Without informing Dow or obtaining an administrative search warrant, EPA then hired a commercial aerial photographer to take pictures of the facility. Although the perimeters of Dow's 2,000 acre compound were elaborately secured to prevent public view of the premises from the ground, some of the manufacturing equipment and conduits were not under cover and thus could be seen from the air.

When Dow learned about the flight, it sued to enjoin EPA from taking or using aerial photographs of its facility, arguing that the use of aerial observation and photography exceeded the agency's statutory investigative authority. The Supreme Court disagreed.

> Congress has vested in EPA certain investigatory and enforcement authority, without spelling out precisely how this authority was to be exercised in all the myriad circumstances that might arise in monitoring

---

[5]Other agencies such as the Corps of Engineers or the Bureau of Land Management may also initiate environmental investigations or assist EPA in conducting its own.

matters relating to clean air and water standards. When Congress invests an agency with enforcement and investigatory authority, it is not necessary to identify explicitly each and every technique that may be used in the course of executing the statutory mission. Aerial observation authority, for example, is not usually expressly extended to police for traffic control, but it could hardly be thought necessary for a legislative body to tell police that aerial observation could be employed for traffic control of a metropolitan area, or to expressly authorize police to send messages to ground highway patrols that a particular over-the-road truck was traveling in excess of 55 miles per hour. Common sense and ordinary human experience teach that traffic violators are apprehended by observation.

Regulatory or enforcement authority generally carries with it all the modes of inquiry and investigation traditionally employed or useful to execute the authority granted. Environmental standards such as clean air and clean water cannot be enforced only in libraries and laboratories, helpful as those institutions may be.

[T]he Clean Air Act provides that "upon presentation of . . . credentials," EPA has a "right of entry to, upon, or through any premises." Dow argues this limited grant of authority to enter does not authorize any aerial observation. In particular, Dow argues that unannounced aerial observation deprives Dow of its right to be informed that an inspection will be made or has occurred, and its right to claim confidentiality of the information contained in the places to be photographed, as provided in 42 U.S.C. §§ 7414(a) and (c). It is not claimed that EPA has disclosed any of the photographs outside the agency.

Section [7414(a)], however, appears to expand, not restrict, EPA's general powers to investigate. Nor is there any suggestion in the statute that the powers conferred by this section are intended to be exclusive. There is no claim that EPA is prohibited from taking photographs from a ground-level location accessible to the general public. EPA, as a regulatory and enforcement agency, needs no explicit statutory provision to employ methods of observation commonly available to the public at large: we hold that the use of aerial observation and photography is within EPA's statutory authority.[6]

In addition to finding that EPA has implied authority to use aerial photography as an investigative tool, the Court in *Dow Chemical* ruled that aerial photography of Dow's plant within navigable air space was not a warrantless search prohibited by the Fourth Amendment. But *Dow Chemical* did not provide an occasion for the Court to consider whether EPA is

---

[6]Dow Chemical v. United States, 476 U.S. 227, 233-235 (1986).

authorized to obtain an ex parte warrant to conduct an administrative search. That issue arose several years later in an action for injunctive and declaratory relief under the Toxic Substances Control Act (TSCA).

The suit was filed by Boliden Metech, Inc., which operated a plant that reclaimed precious metals. Out of concern that PCBs might be escaping into the ground and a nearby river, a state investigator obtained samples of material from the plant without Boliden's consent. The material was suppressed at an administrative hearing because the hearing officer found that taking the samples without first obtaining consent constituted a warrantless search that violated the Fourth Amendment.

When Boliden's employees later denied an EPA request to conduct sampling tests at the plant, EPA filed an ex parte application for an administrative search warrant to enter and inspect the premises. After the warrant was issued and executed, Boliden filed suit to have the search declared illegal, challenging, inter alia, EPA's authority to obtain ex parte warrants. The trial court ruled in favor of EPA, holding that the agency had implied authority under TSCA to obtain such warrants.

A. Warrant Authority

Under the "inspections and subpoenas" section of TSCA, representatives of the EPA "may inspect any establishment, facility, or other premises in which chemical substances or mixtures are manufactured, processed, stored, or held before or after their distribution." 15 U.S.C. § 2610. [Section] 2610 further provides that an inspection may be made "upon the presentation of appropriate credentials and of a written notice to the owner. . . ." *Id.* While this inspection section does not dictate what steps the EPA is to take to gain entry to a facility if access is denied, it seems logical to believe that Congress intended to authorize the EPA to take reasonable steps, such as obtaining a warrant, to fulfill its inspection obligation. Obtaining an inspection warrant is in keeping with the Congressional policy underlying TSCA which seeks to provide adequate authority to regulate hazardous chemicals. In short, by granting the EPA the authority to enter and inspect under 15 U.S.C. § 2610, Congress implicitly gave that body the power to use reasonable means, such as an administrative search warrant, to carry out the inspections.

Where, as here, Congress has given the EPA the right of entry, it would frustrate the will of Congress to deny the EPA the ability to obtain a warrant to compel entry, if the targeted owner refuses to consent. In See v. City of Seattle, 387 U.S. 541 (1967), the Supreme Court held that "administrative entry, without consent, upon the portions of commercial premises which are not open to the public may only be compelled through prosecution or physical force within the framework of a warrant procedure." *Id.* at 545. Thus, a statute which authorizes non-consensual, warrantless entry would be unconstitutional. Since Congress promulgated TSCA ten years after the Supreme Court's decision in *See*, it is reasonable to assume that in granting "administrative entry," Congress necessarily granted the EPA the ability to compel access "through prosecution or physical force within the framework of a warrant procedure.". . .

B. Ex Parte Warrant

Boliden maintains that an ex parte warrant is improper under TSCA because it denies Boliden the opportunity to be heard on whether there are grounds to issue the warrant. Boliden contends that its involvement prior to the issuance of an inspection warrant is necessary not only to protect its privacy interests, but also to give it the opportunity to influence the types of investigative procedures that will be authorized for use by the EPA. Since the Supreme Court has affirmed the right of an administrative agency to obtain an ex parte warrant in a similar situation, the Court is not persuaded by Boliden's arguments. Marshall v. Barlow's, Inc., 436 U.S. at 316-20.

In the first place, requiring the EPA to engage in an adversary proceeding in order to gain access to toxic substance facilities after entry has been denied by the facility's owner would deny the EPA the element of surprise. The advance warning of an inspection would allow the owner to correct any transgressions of TSCA before the EPA could detect them, and then return to business as usual after the inspection is complete. Moreover, a business subject to an EPA search has the opportunity to challenge the grounds underlying the search warrant at any subsequent administrative proceeding, which is in turn subject to judicial review before a United States Court of Appeals. Finally, requiring an adversary proceeding to determine which types of inspection techniques are permissible under TSCA would force a magistrate to make determinations outside his field of expertise, and compel the judiciary to trespass in that sphere of power traditionally left to the other branches of government. . . .

Boliden argues that a pre-search adversary proceeding is necessary so that the Court can determine what types of investigative techniques are justified. However, the judiciary is without expertise as to what scientific techniques are best suited for detecting PCBs in various types of chemical facilities. It is beyond the province of the courts to direct the EPA in the proper manner of conducting its day to day operations. Instead, it is sufficient for an impartial magistrate, when issuing an ex parte administrative search warrant, to specify that only "reasonable" inspection methods may be employed in the course of an investigation pursuant to a warrant. Should the EPA act unreasonably or in bad faith in performing its functions under the warrant, the target of the search has the opportunity to raise such transgressions in the course of any subsequent administrative proceeding and before a United States Court of Appeals. Thus a target company's privacy interests are adequately protected without forcing a district court to do violence to the separation of powers doctrine by unnecessarily enmeshing itself in the nuts and bolts operation of an administrative agency. . . .[7]

The court thus held that EPA has implicit statutory authority to seek ex parte warrants during the course of an investigation.

2. CASE SELECTION

Since the early 1990s, EPA has had an enforcement policy that provides specific guidance for assessing which violations warrant criminal investigation and which should remain on the civil enforcement side. A 1990 memorandum to regional administrators (the Strock Memorandum), provided the first official EPA policy statement on criminal case selection.[8] Criteria to be considered in making this determination included such factors as: (1) a history of repeated violations; (2) deliberate wrongdoing; (3) falsifying or withholding information in cases where other aggravating circumstances were present; (4) tampering with pollution control or monitoring devices; and (5) facts indicating the existence of potential environmental harm. The 1990 policy was supplemented in 1994 by a document known as the Devaney Memorandum, which provided additional guidance on factors that should be considered in determining whether a criminal investigation is warranted.

---

[7]Boliden Metech, Inc. v. United States, 695 F. Supp. 77, 80-83 (D.R.I. 1988).

[8]Memorandum from Assistant Administrator James Strock, Office of Enforcement and Compliance Assurance, U.S. Environmental Protection Agency, to the Regional Administrators (Dec. 3, 1990).

ENVIRONMENTAL PROTECTION AGENCY, MEMORANDUM:
THE EXERCISE OF INVESTIGATIVE DISCRETION

SUBJECT: The Exercise of Investigative Discretion
FROM: Earl E. Devaney, Director
            Office of Criminal Enforcement
TO: All EPA Employees Working in or in Support of the Criminal
            Enforcement Program

* * *

II. Legislative Intent Regarding Case Selection

The criminal provisions of the environmental laws are the most powerful enforcement tools available to EPA. Congressional intent underlying the environmental criminal provisions is unequivocal: criminal enforcement authority should target the most significant and egregious violators.

The Pollution Prosecution Act of 1990 recognized the importance of a strong national environmental criminal enforcement program and mandates additional resources necessary for the criminal program to fulfill its statutory mission. The sponsors of the Act recognized that EPA had long been in the posture of reacting to serious violations only after harm was done, primarily due to limited resources. Senator Joseph I. Lieberman (Conn.), one of the co-sponsors of the Act, explained that as a result of limited resources, ". . . few cases are the product of reasoned or targeted focus on suspected wrongdoing." He also expressed his hope that with the Act's provision of additional Special Agents, ". . . EPA would be able to bring cases that would have greater deterrent value than those currently being brought."

Further illustrative of Congressional intent that the most serious of violations should be addressed by criminal enforcement authority is the legislative history concerning the enhanced criminal provisions of RCRA:

> [The criminal provisions were] intended to prevent abuses of the permit system by those who obtain and then knowingly disregard them. It [RCRA sec. 3008(d)] is not aimed at punishing minor or technical variations from permit regulations or conditions if the facility operator is acting responsibly. The Department of Justice has exercised its prosecutorial discretion responsibly under similar provisions in other statutes and the conferees assume that, in light of the upgrading of the penalties from misdemeanor to

felony, similar care will be used in deciding when a particular permit violation may warrant criminal prosecution under this Act. H.R. Conf. Rep. No. 1444, 96th Cong., 2d Sess. 37, reprinted in 1980 U.S. Code Cong. & Admin. News 5036.

While EPA has doubled its Special Agent corps since passage of the Pollution Prosecution Act, and has achieved a presence in nearly all federal judicial districts, it is unlikely that OCE will ever be large enough in size to fully defeat the ever-expanding universe of environmental crime. Rather, OCE must maximize its presence and impact through discerning case [] selection, and then proceed with investigations that advance EPA's overall goal of regulatory compliance and punishing criminal wrongdoing.

III. Case Selection Process

The case selection process is designed to identify misconduct worthy of criminal investigation. The case selection process is not an effort to establish legal sufficiency for prosecution. Rather, the process by which potential cases are analyzed under the case selection criteria will serve as an affirmative indication that OCE has purposefully directed its investigative resources toward deserving cases.

This is not to suggest that all cases meeting the case selection criteria will proceed to prosecution. Indeed, the exercise of investigative discretion must be clearly distinguished from the exercise of prosecutorial discretion. The employment of OCE's investigative discretion to dedicate its investigative authority is, however, a critical precursor to the prosecutorial discretion later exercised by the Department of Justice.

At the conclusion of the case selection process, OCE should be able to articulate the basis of its decision to pursue a criminal investigation, based on the case selection criteria. Conversely, cases that do not ultimately meet the criteria to proceed criminally should be systematically referred back to the Agency's civil enforcement office for appropriate administrative or civil judicial action, or to a state or local prosecutor.

IV. Case Selection Criteria

The criminal case selection process will be guided by two general measures — significant environmental harm and culpable conduct.

A. Significant Environmental Harm

The measure of significant environmental harm should be broadly construed to include the presence of actual harm, as well as the threat of significant harm, to the environment or human health. The following factors serve as indicators that a potential case will meet the measure of significant environmental harm.

Factor 1. *Actual* harm will be demonstrated by an illegal discharge, release or emission that has an identifiable and significant harmful impact on human health or the environment. This measure will generally be self-evident at the time of case selection.

Factor 2. The *threat* of significant harm to the environment or human health may be demonstrated by an actual or threatened discharge, release or emission. This factor may not be as readily evident, and must be assessed in light of all the facts available at the time of case selection.

Factor 3. Failure to report an actual discharge, release or emission within the context of Factors 1 or 2 will serve as an additional factor favoring criminal investigation. While the failure to report, alone, may be a criminal violation, our investigative resources should generally be targeted toward those cases in which the failure to report is coupled with actual or threatened environmental harm.

Factor 4. When certain illegal conduct appears to represent a trend or common attitude within the regulated community, criminal investigation may provide a significant deterrent effect incommensurate with its singular environmental impact. While the single violation being considered may have a relatively insignificant impact on human health or the environment, such violations, if multiplied by the numbers in a cross-section of the regulated community, would result in significant environmental harm.

B. Culpable Conduct

The measure of culpable conduct is not *necessarily* an assessment of criminal intent, particularly since criminal intent will not always be readily evident at the time of case selection. Culpable conduct, however, may be indicated at the time of case selection by several factors.

Factor 1. History of repeated violations

While a history of repeated violations is not a prerequisite to a criminal investigation, a potential target's compliance record should always be carefully examined. When repeated enforcement activities or actions, whether by EPA, or other federal, state and local enforcement authorities, have failed to bring a violator into compliance, criminal investigation may be warranted. Clearly, a history of repeated violations will enhance the government's capacity to prove that a violator was aware of environmental regulatory requirements, had actual notice of violations and then acted in deliberate disregard of those requirements.

Factor 2. Deliberate misconduct resulting in violation

Although the environmental statutes do not require proof of specific intent, evidence, either direct or circumstantial, that a violation was deliberate will be a major factor indicating that criminal investigation is warranted.

Factor 3. Concealment of misconduct or falsification of required records

In the arena of self-reporting, EPA must be able to rely on data received from the regulated community. If submitted data are false, EPA is prevented from effectively carrying out its mandate. Accordingly, conduct indicating the falsification of data will always serve as the basis for serious consideration to proceed with a criminal investigation.

Factor 4. Tampering with monitoring or control equipment

The overt act of tampering with monitoring or control equipment leads to the certain production of false data that appears to be otherwise accurate. The consequent submission of false data threatens the basic integrity of EPA's data and, in turn, the scientific validity of EPA's regulatory decisions. Such an assault on the regulatory infrastructure calls for the enforcement leverage of criminal investigation.

Factor 5. Business operation of pollution-related activities without a permit, license, manifest or other required documentation

Many of the laws and regulations within EPA's jurisdiction focus on inherently dangerous and strictly regulated business operations. EPA's criminal enforcement resources should clearly pursue those violators who choose to ignore environmental regulatory requirements altogether and operate completely outside of EPA's regulatory scheme.

V. Additional Considerations When Investigating Corporations

While the factors under measures IV. A and B, above, apply equally to both individual and corporate targets, several additional considerations should be taken into account when the potential target is a corporation.

In a criminal environmental investigation, OCE should always investigate individual employees and their corporate employers who may be culpable. A corporation is, by law, responsible for the criminal act of its officers and employees who act within the scope of their employment and in furtherance of the purposes of the corporation. Whether the corporate officer or employee personally commits the act, or directs, aids, or counsels other employees to do so is inconsequential to the issue of corporate culpability.

Corporate culpability may also be indicated when a company performs an environmental compliance or management audit, and then knowingly fails to promptly remedy the noncompliance and correct any harm done. On the other hand, EPA policy strongly encourages self-monitoring, self-disclosure, and self-correction. When self-auditing has been conducted (followed up by prompt remediation of the noncompliance and any resulting harm) and full, complete disclosure has occurred, the company's constructive activities should be considered as mitigating factors in EPA's exercise of investigative discretion. Therefore, a violation that is voluntarily revealed and fully and promptly remedied as part of a corporation's systematic and comprehensive self-evaluation program generally will not be a candidate for the expenditure of scarce criminal investigative resources. . . .

B. PROSECUTORIAL DISCRETION

Prosecutorial discretion is a magnet for criticism of environmental criminal enforcement. Critics claim that reliance on prosecutorial discretion to weed out cases that would be inappropriate targets for criminal enforcement invites uncertainty and is likely to lead to abusive prosecutions. But published Justice Department policies and criteria for initiating and declining criminal prosecutions provide concrete guidance on the exercise of prosecutorial discretion. That being true, these guidelines provide a logical starting point for evaluating claims that prosecutorial discretion is an unnecessary evil to be avoided at all costs.

1. JUSTICE DEPARTMENT POLICY

DEPARTMENT OF JUSTICE, UNITED STATES ATTORNEYS MANUAL:
PRINCIPLES OF FEDERAL PROSECUTION

9-27.001 Preface

These principles of Federal prosecution provide to Federal prosecutors a statement of sound prosecutorial policies and practices for particularly important areas of their work. As such, it should promote the reasoned exercise of prosecutorial authority and contribute to the fair, evenhanded administration of the Federal criminal laws.

The manner in which Federal prosecutors exercise their decision-making authority has far-reaching implications, both in terms of justice and effectiveness in law enforcement and in terms of the consequences for individual citizens. A determination to prosecute represents a policy judgment that the fundamental interests of society require the application of the criminal laws to a particular set of circumstances — recognizing both that serious violations of Federal law must be prosecuted, and that prosecution entails profound consequences for the accused and the family of the accused whether or not a conviction ultimately results. Other prosecutorial decisions can be equally significant. Decisions, for example, regarding the specific charges to be brought, or concerning plea dispositions, effectively determine the range of sanctions that may be imposed for criminal conduct. The rare decision to consent to pleas of nolo contendere may affect the success of related civil suits for recovery of damages. Also, the government's position during the sentencing process will help assure that the court imposes a sentence consistent with the Sentencing Reform Act.

These principles of Federal prosecution have been designed to assist in structuring the decision-making process of attorneys for the government. For the most part, they have been cast in general terms with a view to providing guidance rather than to mandating results. The intent is to assure regularity without regimentation, to prevent unwarranted disparity without sacrificing necessary flexibility.

The availability of this statement of principles to Federal law enforcement officials and to the public serves two important purposes: ensuring the fair and effective exercise of prosecutorial responsibility by attorneys for the government, and promoting confidence on the part of the public and individual defendants that important prosecutorial decisions will be made rationally and objectively on the merits of each case. The Principles provide convenient reference points for the process of making prosecutorial decisions; they facilitate the task of training new attorneys in the proper discharge of their duties; they contribute to more effective management of the government's limited prosecutorial resources by promoting greater consistency among the prosecutorial activities of all United States Attorney's offices and between their activities and the Department's law enforcement priorities; they make possible better coordination of investigative and prosecutorial activity by enhancing the understanding of investigating departments and agencies of the considerations underlying prosecutorial decisions by the Department; and they inform the public of the careful process by which prosecutorial decisions are made. . . .

9-27.110 Purpose

A. The principles of Federal prosecution set forth herein are intended to promote the reasoned exercise of prosecutorial discretion by attorneys for the government with respect to:

1. Initiating and declining prosecution;
2. Selecting charges;
3. Entering into plea agreements;
4. Opposing offers to plead nolo contendere;
5. Entering into non-prosecution agreements in return for cooperation; and
6. Participating in sentencing.

B. Comment. Under the Federal criminal justice system, the prosecutor has wide latitude in determining when, whom, how, and even whether to prosecute for apparent violations of Federal criminal law. The prosecutor's broad discretion in such areas as initiating or foregoing prosecutions, selecting or recommending specific charges, and terminating prosecutions by accepting guilty pleas has been recognized on numerous occasions by the courts. This discretion exists by virtue of his/her status as a member of the Executive Branch, which is charged under the Constitution with ensuring that the laws of the United States be "faithfully executed." U.S. Const. Art. § 3.

Since Federal prosecutors have great latitude in making crucial decisions concerning enforcement of a nationwide system of criminal justice, it is desirable, in the interest of the fair and effective administration of justice in the Federal system, that all Federal prosecutors be guided by a general statement of principles that summarizes appropriate considerations to be weighed, and desirable practices to be followed, in discharging their prosecutorial responsibilities. . . .

9-27.230 Initiating and Declining Charges — Substantial Federal Interest

A. In determining whether prosecution should be declined because no substantial Federal interest would be served by prosecution, the attorney for the government should weigh all relevant considerations, including:

1. Federal law enforcement priorities;
2. The nature and seriousness of the offense;
3. The deterrent effect of prosecution;
4. The person's culpability in connection with the offense;
5. The person's history with respect to criminal activity;
6. The person's willingness to cooperate in the investigation or prosecution of others; and
7. The probable sentence or other consequences if the person is convicted.

B. Comment. USAM 9-27.230 lists factors that may be relevant in determining whether prosecution should be declined because no substantial Federal interest would be served by prosecution in a case in which the person is believed to have committed a Federal offense and the admissible evidence is expected to be sufficient to obtain and sustain a conviction. The list of relevant considerations is not intended to be all-inclusive. Obviously, not all of the factors will be applicable to every case, and in any particular case one factor may deserve more weight than it might in another case. . . .

2. Nature and Seriousness of Offense. It is important that limited Federal resources not be wasted in prosecuting inconsequential cases or cases in which the violation is only technical. Thus, in determining whether a substantial Federal interest exists that requires prosecution, the attorney for the government should consider the nature and seriousness of the offense involved. A number of factors may be relevant. One factor that is obviously of primary importance is the actual or potential impact of the offense on the community and on the victim.

... In assessing the seriousness of the offense in these terms, the prosecutor may properly weigh such questions as whether the violation is technical or relatively inconsequential in nature and what the public attitude is toward prosecution under the circumstances of the case. ...

3. Deterrent Effect of Prosecution. Deterrence of criminal conduct, whether it be criminal activity generally or a specific type of criminal conduct, is one of the primary goals of the criminal law. This purpose should be kept in mind, particularly when deciding whether a prosecution is warranted for an offense that appears to be relatively minor; some offenses, although seemingly not of great importance by themselves, if commonly committed would have a substantial cumulative impact on the community.

4. The Person's Culpability. Although the prosecutor has sufficient evidence of guilt, it is nevertheless appropriate for him/her to give consideration to the degree of the person's culpability in connection with the offenses, both in the abstract and in comparison with any others involved in the offense. If for example, the person was a relatively minor participant in a criminal enterprise conducted by others, or his/her motive was worthy, and no other circumstances require prosecution, the prosecutor might reasonably conclude that some course other than prosecution would be appropriate.

9-27.300 Selecting Charges — Charging Most Serious Offenses

A. Except as [otherwise] provided ..., once the decision to prosecute has been made, the attorney for the government should charge, or should recommend that the grand jury charge, the most serious offense that is consistent with the nature of the defendant's conduct, and that is likely to result in a sustainable conviction. If mandatory minimum sentences are also involved, their effect must be considered, keeping in mind the fact that a mandatory minimum is statutory and generally overrules a guideline. The "most serious" offense is generally that which yields the highest range under the sentencing guidelines. ...

B. Comment. Once it has been determined to initiate prosecution, either by filing a complaint or an information, or by seeking an indictment from the grand jury, the attorney for the government must determine what charges to file or recommend. When the conduct in question consists of a single criminal act, or when there is only one applicable statute, this is not a difficult task. Typically, however, a defendant will have committed more than one criminal act and his/her conduct may be prosecuted under more than one statute. Moreover, selection of charges may be complicated further by the fact that different statutes have different proof requirements and provide substantially different penalties. In such cases, considerable care is required to ensure selection of the proper charge or charges. In addition to reviewing the concerns that prompted the decision to prosecute in the first instance, particular attention should be given to the need to ensure that the prosecution will be both fair and effective.

In addition to generally applicable guidelines on initiating and declining criminal prosecutions, the Justice Department has also issued guidelines that address the exercise of prosecutorial discretion in the specific context of environmental crimes.

DEPARTMENT OF JUSTICE, FACTORS IN DECISIONS IN CRIMINAL PROSECUTIONS FOR ENVIRONMENTAL VIOLATIONS

I. Introduction

It is the policy of the Department of Justice to encourage self-auditing, self-policing and voluntary disclosure of environmental violations by the regulated community by indicating that these activities are viewed as mitigating factors in the Department's exercise of criminal environmental enforcement discretion. This document is intended to describe the factors that the Department of Justice considers in deciding whether to bring a criminal prosecution for a violation of an environmental statute, so that such prosecutions do not create a disincentive to or undermine the goal of encouraging critical self-auditing, self-policing, and voluntary disclosure. It is designed to give federal prosecutors direction concerning the exercise of prosecutorial discretion in environmental criminal cases and to ensure that such discretion is exercised consistently nationwide. It is also intended to give the regulated community a sense of how the federal government exercises its criminal prosecutorial discretion with respect to such factors as the defendant's voluntary disclosure of violations, cooperation with the government in investigating the violations, use of environmental audits and other procedures to ensure compliance with all applicable environmental laws and regulations, and use of measures to remedy expeditiously and completely any violations and the harms caused thereby.

This guidance and the examples contained herein provide a framework for the determination of whether a particular case presents the type of circumstances in which lenience would be appropriate.

II. Factors to be Considered

Where the law and evidence would otherwise be sufficient for prosecution, the attorney for the Department should consider the factors contained herein, to the extent they are applicable, along with any other relevant factors, in determining whether and how to prosecute. It must be emphasized that these are examples of the types of factors which could be relevant. They do not constitute a definitive recipe or checklist of requirements. They merely illustrate some of the types of information which is relevant to our exercise of prosecutorial discretion.

It is unlikely that any one factor will be dispositive in any given case. All relevant factors are considered and given the weight deemed appropriate in the particular case.

A. Voluntary Disclosure

The attorney for the Department should consider whether the person[9] made a voluntary, timely and complete disclosure of the matter under investigation. Consideration should be given to whether the person came forward promptly after discovering the noncompliance, and to the quantity and quality of information provided. Particular consideration should be given to whether the disclosure substantially aided the government's investigatory process, and whether it occurred before a law enforcement or regulatory authority (federal, state or local authority) had already obtained knowledge regarding noncompliance. A disclosure is not considered to be "voluntary" if that disclosure is already specifically required by law, regulation, or permit.[10]

---

[9]As used in this document, the terms "person" and "violator" are intended to refer to business and nonprofit entities as well as individuals.

[10]For example, any person in charge of a vessel or of an on shore facility or an offshore facility is required to notify the appropriate agency of the United States Government of any discharge of oil or a hazardous substance into or upon *inter alia* the navigable waters of the United States. 33 U.S.C. § 1321(b)(5).

B. Cooperation

The attorney for the Department should consider the degree and timeliness of cooperation by the person. Full and prompt cooperation is essential, whether in the context of a voluntary disclosure or after the government has independently learned of a violation. Consideration should be given to the violator's willingness to make all relevant information (including the complete results of any internal or external investigation and the names of all potential witnesses) available to government investigators and prosecutors. Consideration should also be given to the extent and quality of the violator's assistance to the government's investigation.

C. Preventive Measures and Compliance Programs

The attorney for the Department should consider the existence and scope of any regularized, intensive, and comprehensive environmental compliance program; such a program may include an environmental compliance or management audit. Particular consideration should be given to whether the compliance or audit program includes sufficient measures to identify and prevent future noncompliance, and whether the program was adopted in good faith in a timely manner.

Compliance programs may vary but the following questions should be asked in evaluating any program: Was there a strong institutional policy to comply with all environmental requirements? Had safeguards beyond those required by existing law been developed and implemented to prevent noncompliance from occurring? Were there regular procedures, including internal or external compliance and management audits, to evaluate, detect, prevent and remedy circumstances like those that led to the noncompliance? . . . Was environmental compliance a standard by which employee and corporate departmental performance was judged?

D. Additional Factors Which May [Be] Relevant

1. Pervasiveness of Noncompliance

Pervasive noncompliance may indicate systemic or repeated participation in or condonation of criminal behavior. It may also indicate the lack of a meaningful compliance program. In evaluating this factor, the attorney for the Department should consider, among other things, the number and level of employees participating in the unlawful activities and the obviousness, seriousness, duration, history, and frequency of noncompliance.

2. Internal Disciplinary Action

Effective internal disciplinary action is crucial to any compliance program. The attorney for the Department should consider whether there was an effective system of discipline for employees who violated company environmental compliance policies. Did the disciplinary system establish an awareness in other employees that unlawful conduct would not be condoned?

3. Subsequent Compliance Efforts

The attorney for the Department should consider the extent of any efforts to remedy any ongoing noncompliance. The promptness and completeness of any action taken to remove the source of the noncompliance and to lessen the environmental harm resulting from the noncompliance should be considered. Considerable weight should be given to prompt, good-faith efforts to reach environmental compliance agreements with federal or state authorities, or both.   Full compliance with such agreements should be a factor in any decision whether to prosecute.

---

2. CRITIQUES

Critics of the environmental criminal enforcement program find the practice of giving prosecutors wide latitude to determine what and whom to prosecute highly problematic.

> By criminalizing far more conduct than it would expect to be the subject of criminal enforcement, Congress has, in effect, delegated all of the line-drawing issues to the executive branch without providing any guidance on how that discretion should be exercised. No doubt there are public policy areas in which such open-ended delegations are workable, probably because the legislative branch is willing to trust the executive branch's implementation and because there is otherwise some shared understanding between and within those branches regarding how that discretion should be exercised.   When, however, neither such trust nor such a shared understanding exists, an open-ended delegation can be a recipe for disaster,

especially when public health concerns are likely to trigger substantial public scrutiny and second guessing.[11]

Embedded in this skeptical view of criminal enforcement is the perception that environmental criminal law is plagued by overbreadth (with a subtle hint of vagueness), minimal culpability requirements, and broad discretionary powers that rest almost entirely in the prosecutor's hands.

RICHARD J. LAZARUS, MEETING THE DEMANDS OF INTEGRATION IN THE EVOLUTION OF ENVIRONMENTAL LAW: REFORMING ENVIRONMENTAL CRIMINAL LAW

83 Geo. L.J. 2407, 2487-2490 (1995)

. . . Under the prosecutorial discretion approach, which could be called the "Al Capone" model, prosecutors are blindly trusted to exploit the full sweep of the criminal law only against those who are truly culpable and not against the morally innocent who only technically fall within the terms of the criminal prohibition.[12]   This approach has the advantage of allowing prosecutors, once they have identified the "truly culpable" actors, to obtain conviction based on relatively little evidence of actual culpability. Higher conviction rates are thereby obtained.

There are, however, great disadvantages to this delegation model. First, there is a very real cost to criminalizing conduct of a far wider scope than society plans to subject to criminal sanction. Even assuming that prosecutors can exercise their prosecutorial discretion in a manner that successfully distinguishes between the "truly culpable" and the "morally innocent" better than the legislature can in the first instance, it remains that both types of conduct are made criminal under the law. Accordingly, many individuals must live in fear of possible criminal prosecution and depend on governmental goodwill to maintain their freedom. Deterrence is achieved, but at a price — the demoralization felt by the many individuals vulnerable to prosecution. The demoralization problem is especially acute when environmental pollution is the basis of the underlying offense because many

---

[11]Richard J. Lazarus, *Assimilating Environmental Protection into Legal Rules and the Problem with Environmental Crime*, 27 LOY. L.A. L. REV. 867, 884 (1994).

[12]*See, e.g.*, United States v. Dotterweich, 320 U.S. 284, 285 (1943) ("In such matters the good sense of prosecutors, the wise guidance of trial judges, and the ultimate judgment of juries must be trusted.").

legitimate, unavoidable activities are among those subject to possible prosecution.

There is also good reason to question both the ability of prosecutors to draw the necessary distinctions, as well as the accuracy of the threshold assumption that prosecutors are better equipped than legislators to decide the policy question of who warrants criminal incarceration.

There is nothing scientific about the exercise of prosecutorial discretion. It is necessarily based on highly subjective, impressionistic determinations. "'Discretion' raises the specter of inconsistency, arbitrary treatment, bias, and corruption." The danger that such prosecutorial abuse will occur is considerable. "Little in the background, training, self-selection, or general outlook of prosecutors suggests that they are best equipped to make whatever diagnostic and rehabilitative judgments may be involved. . . ." [T]his is especially so in environmental law where there is a separation of environmental policy and criminal law expertise between EPA and the United States Attorney Offices. There is certainly no reason to assume that federal prosecutors working on environmental cases are somehow magically immune from abusive prosecutorial practices that otherwise occur.

Finally, the current prosecutor-delegation model suffers from an even more fundamental problem, at least as applied to environmental criminal law. The volatility of the politics surrounding environmental law is too destabilizing and potentially destructive. The mere perception of prosecutorial abuse in environmental law, regardless of whether that perception is true, is sufficient to destroy what might otherwise be an effective program, including the careers of those prosecutors swept into the resulting controversy. A pathological cycle of controversy has long plagued environmental law and its implementation, largely as a result of the high level of distrust between different branches of government and the regulated and environmental communities.

The delegation of sweeping prosecutorial discretion cannot survive easily within such a politically charged environment. Effective delegation of this authority requires some mutual understanding between branches of government regarding the exercise of this authority and the bare modicum of trustworthiness necessary to handle those inevitable occasions when problems arise.

The environmental crime context has proven to be an exceedingly difficult area for nurturing such mutual understandings. Criminal prosecutors are protective of their jurisdiction and independence. They do not even regard EPA as their client, as Justice Department lawyers do in the civil context. In the criminal arena, the United States is the client. This further separation of perspectives makes it that much less likely that the policymakers at EPA and the criminal prosecutors will work well together to create a coherent program, let alone educate congressional overseers regarding their efforts.

With the benefit of hindsight, it seems quite clear that the effect of congressional delegation of sweeping discretion in environmental criminal prosecution was equivalent to setting two trains in motion toward each other on a single track.   Policy decisions had to be made, and . . . they were inevitably made on an ad hoc basis. Lack of trust, coupled with an absence of clear policy guidance and explication, accelerated the claims of abuse of prosecutorial authority.

———————

In contrast with the "train wreck" scenario that Professor Lazarus portrays, I view the prosecutorial discretion model through a far less critical lens.

KATHLEEN F. BRICKEY, THE RHETORIC OF ENVIRONMENTAL CRIME: CULPABILITY, DISCRETION, AND STRUCTURAL REFORM

84 Iowa L. Rev. 115, 126-131 (1998)

. . . Notwithstanding that the decision whether to prosecute or decline prosecution is necessarily a discretionary call, many critics find the existence of discretion troubling. For them, prosecutorial discretion "raises issues of fairness associated with the predictability of criminal investigation of the many cases that fall far short of the clarity of a midnight dumper." Because prosecutors have "unfettered discretion" to prosecute even unavoidable technical violations, the argument runs, the decision to pursue any given case may be made at the prosecutor's "whim." The current system "blindly trusts" prosecutors to make discrete judgments about blameworthiness and moral innocence and "to exploit the full sweep of the criminal law" only when confronted with clear evidence of moral culpability. But critics maintain that environmental prosecutors appear to pursue increasingly expansive theories of prosecution "arbitrarily and without oversight." . . .

Like other branches of statutory law, much of federal criminal law is flawed by imperfect draftsmanship. That being true, prosecutorial discretion is essential to fair and efficient criminal enforcement decisions. As a counterpoint to critics' portrayal of prosecutorial discretion as a tool for widening the net of criminal enforcement efforts, I would pose it as a necessary mechanism for screening out marginal cases. Federal law requires, for example, that "except as otherwise provided by law, each United States attorney, within his district, shall . . . prosecute for *all* offenses against the United States."[13] While this could be cited as a model of drafting clarity that admits no exceptions to its commands, justice and limited resources require that it be tempered by judicious exercise of criminal enforcement power. Literally construed, this statutory mandate would not only be impossible to fully execute, it would provoke a storm of criticism that would echo the very complaints that animate criminal enforcement critics. To enforce more than three thousand federal criminal laws for every nominal violation, no matter how trivial, would invoke the full power of the criminal law against not only the culpable but against the morally innocent as well. It would also make an enormous percentage of the population vulnerable to prosecution and the consequent demoralization that overdeterrence can cause, particularly where the underlying offense arises out of otherwise legitimate activity. Without prosecutorial discretion to cull out marginal cases and set enforcement priorities, the "criminal justice" system would (deservedly) fall into disrepute and collapse under its own weight.

Although the subtext of the [critiques] conjures up images of federal environmental prosecutors as unguided missiles, it clearly overstates the case. Decisions to prosecute environmental violations are scrutinized under extensive procedures designed to winnow out all but the most egregious violations. Before the Environmental Protection Agency (EPA) refers a violation for criminal prosecution, the case goes through a five-step screening process to determine whether it meets formal criteria for criminal referral. Once it is referred to the Department of Justice (DOJ), which has its own formalized criminal enforcement criteria, the case is subject to additional levels of scrutiny. According to Michael Penders,[14] "there is no area of criminal law enforcement where a violation receives more administrative review and scrutiny from prosecutors." A congressional committee's staff echoed Mr. Penders' comment when it concluded that DOJ's "centralized 'veto authority' over cases referred for criminal prosecution is not only 'unusual,' but that it 'gives Main Justice far more power over environmental cases than it has over most other types of criminal prosecution.'"

---

[13]28 U.S.C. § 547(1) (1994) (emphasis added).

[14]Michael Penders served as Special Counsel with the United States Environmental Protection Agency's Office of Criminal Enforcement, Forensics, and Training, and also served as Special Assistant to the EPA Assistant Administrator for Enforcement. — ED.

Thus, rather than portraying environmental prosecutors as loose cannons, it would be more accurate to state that centralized decision-making and multi-level review of prospective criminal cases [impose] real constraints on discretion and autonomy and [guard] against arbitrary action. . . .

———————

The heightened levels of administrative scrutiny that precede decisions to charge environmental crimes suggest that there is *more* certainty — not less — about what conduct will be prosecuted. But critics of the criminal enforcement regime find little comfort in this observation. Instead, they promote a variety of "fixes" to prevent uncertainty and abuse despite the lack of empirical support for the underlying premise that the current system is seriously flawed.

> Consider the claim that the existence of prosecutorial discretion will lead to prosecution of more environmental cases than is warranted because the culpability standards and burden of proof requirements for environmental crimes are low. Assuming arguendo the validity of the stated premises, the conclusion might make intuitive sense. But available data suggest just the opposite. The percentage of environmental cases that are prosecuted following completed criminal investigations is disproportionately *lower*, not higher, than the norm in other criminal matters. Overall, about two-thirds of offenses investigated by United States Attorneys ripen into actual prosecutions. In contrast, only half of the environmental cases they investigate culminate in a decision to prosecute. While these figures are not precisely comparable due to methodological differences in reporting the data, it seems likely that the comparison actually *understates* the declination rate for environmental cases, because environmental prosecutions characteristically involve multiple defendants.[15] Thus, it appears that prosecutorial discretion is a tool that, contrary to critics' concerns, effectively narrows the universe of environmental violations subject to criminal prosecution.

———————

[15]A GAO study reported an average of 2.2 defendants per environmental prosecution between 1988 and 1993. In federal criminal prosecutions generally, the average number of defendants per prosecution is 1.4. Since Justice Department figures reflect the total percentage of individual *defendants* the Department investigated but declined to prosecute, and GAO figures reflect the percentage of environmental *cases* (regardless of the number of defendants per case) the Department declined to prosecute, the GAO study's declination rate probably understates the difference since it is not adjusted to reflect the presumably greater number of environmental defendants who were investigated but not prosecuted.

The critiques also surmise that low culpability and evidentiary thresholds will enable prosecutors to achieve higher conviction rates. In fact, prosecutors do achieve somewhat higher conviction rates for environmental crimes. . . . But empirical confirmation of higher conviction rates in environmental prosecutions is a far cry from establishing a causal relationship between allegedly low culpability or proof standards and successful outcomes. A higher conviction rate would be consistent with what we know about relative declination rates, for example. If prosecutors are more selective in deciding which environmental cases to prosecute, it is likely that they require a higher threshold to proceed. Simply put, they prosecute what they believe are strong cases and winnow out the rest.[16]

Notwithstanding multiple layers of formal screening designed to bring predictability and consistency to the selection of cases for criminal prosecution, critics of the prosecutorial discretion model posit that continued distrust of the criminal enforcement program has been fueled by suspicion that political influence plays a role in the decision to prosecute. That perception was reinforced by a series of controversial judgment calls in the late 1980s about several "obviously" meritorious cases the Justice Department declined to prosecute.[17] The contested decisions resulted in rare public clashes between line prosecutors and criminal enforcement policy makers, and by the time Congress convened what were destined to be contentious oversight hearings, the atmosphere was rife with accusations of political interference with prosecutorial decision making.

While the accusations from the political left have probably been the loudest, voices on the right have also made their share of accusations. These latter claims have long focused on the federal wetlands program,[18] and, in recent years, they have found great political momentum

---

[16]Kathleen F. Brickey, *The Rhetoric of Environmental Crime: Culpability, Discretion, and Structural Reform*, 84 IOWA L. REV. 115, 133-135 (1998).

[17]*See generally* JONATHAN TURLEY, CRIMINAL ENVIRONMENTAL PROSECUTION BY THE UNITED STATES DEPARTMENT OF JUSTICE — PRELIMINARY REPORT (1992).

[18]*See* Tom Bethell, *Property and Tyranny*, AM. SPECTATOR, Aug. 1994, at 16 (critique of wetlands enforcement); Paul D. Kamenar, *The Truth: There Are Not Environmental Crimes*, CAL. LAW., Aug. 1993, at 89 (arguing that many environmental violations would be more appropriately addressed by civil or administrative remedies); H. Jane Lehman, *Trials and Tribulations of Landowners*, L.A. TIMES, Oct. 18, 1992, at K2 (reporting on enigmatic enforcement of wetlands regulations); *Maryland Wetlands Conviction Stirring Heated Debate*, WASH. POST, Feb. 20, 1993, at F6 (same); *Review & Outlook — Property Busters*, WALL ST. J., Jan. 11, 1990, at A14 (same); *see also Review & Outlook — The Ellen Pardon*,

in attacks on the federal endangered species program. The claim is that the Justice Department has overreached and prosecuted morally innocent conduct.[19]

Allegations of prosecutorial overreaching in the wetlands criminal enforcement program quickly gained political traction. But despite the heated rhetoric, the accusations lacked empirical support. Indeed, the wetlands criminal enforcement record suggests remarkable prosecutorial restraint.

KATHLEEN F. BRICKEY, WETLANDS REFORM AND THE CRIMINAL ENFORCEMENT RECORD: A CAUTIONARY TALE

76 Wash. U. L.Q. 71, 76-84 (1998)

. . . Despite estimates that suggest a high level of criminal enforcement activity, a look at the enforcement record reveals surprisingly few wetlands prosecutions to date. An exhaustive search of available sources of information revealed only twenty criminal prosecutions for wetlands violations. And as the following discussion demonstrates, these violations share remarkably similar traits that reveal vulnerable fault lines in current criticisms of the wetlands enforcement program.

. . . In the nineteen wetlands prosecutions for which there is sufficient information to classify the defendants, eleven defendants were corporate entities or partnerships that developed wetlands commercially. Eight of the twenty individual defendants were officers of those corporations who had operational responsibility for the development. Nine of the remaining defendants were contractors, commercial developers or professional engineers.[20] Thus, with three exceptions, all of the defendants were

---

WALL ST. J., Jan. 15, 1993, at A10 (arguing against wetlands convictions based on a lack of political consensus about environmental crimes); *Review & Outlook — EPA's Most Wanted*, WALL ST. J., Nov. 18, 1992, at A16 (concluding that wetlands enforcement has "gotten out of hand").

[19]Richard J. Lazarus, *Meeting the Demands of Integration in the Evolution of Environmental Law: Reforming Environmental Criminal Law*, 83 GEO. L.J. 2407, 2490 (1995).

[20]One of the engineers, James Brackenrich, was a former state senator who chaired the senate's committee on natural resources. Brackenrich had been fined twice before for storing chemicals in a leaking tank and allowing raw sewage from one of his businesses to leak into a limestone cavern.

experienced in some facet of commercial real estate development and were (or should have been) knowledgeable about restrictions on developing sites containing wetlands.

William Ellen exemplifies this profile. Ellen operated a business that specialized in the design of, and acquisition of permits for, construction projects involving wetlands and subaqueous areas.[21] He had a bachelor of science and engineering degree and had been a staff environmental engineer with a state agency. While holding that position, he had responsibility for reviewing the regulation of wetlands projects. He later formed his own company to specialize in the design of wetlands construction projects. As project supervisor for [a] commercial hunting preserve development, Ellen was directly responsible for acquiring environmental permits and complying with state and federal environmental regulations. Yet despite his extensive experience, specific project responsibilities and knowledge that the development site contained wetlands, Ellen failed to obtain a single permit.

Of the three defendants whose profiles differed from those described above, two . . . were business owners who developed property containing wetlands for the purpose of maintaining or expanding their businesses. Thus, with one lone exception, all of the cases revolved around developing wetlands for commercial purposes. . . .

The inference that commercial purpose or economic motive is relevant in deciding whether to prosecute wetlands violators is consistent with the record in [Marinus] Van Leuzen's case.[22] Although some officials involved in the decisionmaking process disagreed about whether his violation should be treated as a criminal or civil matter, one factor that militated against criminal prosecution was the belief that the case was too small to be worth prosecuting. The Assistant United States Attorney to whom the matter was assigned urged caution in selecting the first wetlands case for criminal prosecution in her district. Observing that past practice had been to rely on civil remedies for wetlands violations, she noted that guidelines for deciding whether to pursue a case civilly or criminally were needed to avoid the appearance of being "arbitrary or unfair." Those sentiments also had been echoed by an Assistant Attorney General who recommended forbearance in bringing criminal charges in wetlands cases until prosecutors found " 'a worthy subject — i.e., a developer.' "

---

[21]*See* United States v. Ellen, 961 F.2d 462, 463 (4th Cir. 1992).

[22]Van Leuzen illegally developed wetlands to enhance his enjoyment of his waterfront lot. High-level Justice Department discussions culminated in a decision not to prosecute him. — ED.

Thus, it seems safe to say that the wetlands criminal enforcement program is aimed primarily at commercial actors who seek to profit from their violations. The perception that the government singles out the unsophisticated "little guy" for wetlands prosecutions is simply not true.

The offense profiles of the cases in the data base provide even more striking evidence of why they were considered appropriate targets for prosecution. They demonstrate that defendants were selected for criminal prosecution when there was strong evidence not only of culpability in a legal or technical sense, but of actual awareness of wrongdoing as well. Defendants in five cases hired (and sometimes fired) one or more professional consultants who warned them that the property contained wetlands and could not legally be developed without approval from the Corps [of Engineers]. More telling still, defendants in a dozen cases had received one or more verbal warnings from regulators that the development was illegal. And in ten of the cases, the defendants ignored one or more written cease and desist orders directing them to stop further development immediately.

Several of these cases distinguish themselves from the rest of the pack. In one, a defendant who received cease and desist orders attempted to bribe an official to unlawfully issue a permit. In another, the putative defendant filed suit to enjoin the government's criminal investigation. In two others, the defendants' probation was revoked because they continued to develop wetlands illegally without a permit. But the grand prize goes to the defendant in United States v. Bieri. Bieri, a contractor, filled in the same site three different times after restoring it twice on orders from the Corps. Worse still, Bieri flaunted his lawbreaking to gain a competitive edge. In his discussions with potential customers, Bieri exaggerated the amount of time it takes to obtain a permit and said that he could finish the job sooner because he would not delay a project to apply for one.

The unsung examples are legion, but let us return to the sung heroes of the wetlands reform movement. Once again, William Ellen fits the profile. Ellen hired a civil engineer who told him that the project site contained wetlands and that a permit was required. Four to five months later, Corps officials toured the property with Ellen and pointed out which areas were wetlands. On a follow-up visit, Corps officials actually marked off the wetlands area by tying survey ribbons on trees and bushes. Yet despite these and other unmistakable warnings, Ellen refused to stop the work because of contractual deadlines.

And what about John Pozsgai, the small businessman who was simply trying to realize the American dream of owning and developing his own land? Was he unfairly singled out for prosecution? Heed the rest of this cautionary tale. Before he purchased the fourteen-acre tract, Pozsgai hired an engineering firm to determine whether the land was suitable for expansion of his truck repair business. The engineering consultant advised him by letter that it was not. The entire site constituted wetlands and could not be developed without a permit from the Corps. While he was still considering purchasing the site, a Corps of Engineers biologist also informed him that he could not fill the land without a permit. As negotiations to buy the property continued, Pozsgai hired a second engineering consultant to evaluate the site, was again told that the property was wetlands and was again warned that any site preparation would require prior approval from the Corps. Ever the optimist, Pozsgai hired yet a third engineering consultant, who confirmed that the tract was protected wetlands. After receiving the three consultants' reports and the notice from the Corps, Pozsgai turned adversity into advantage by renegotiating the purchase price downward by $32,000 — and then began filling in the site.

Following this negotiating coup, Corps of Engineers officials repeatedly warned Pozsgai that he was violating the law. Yet despite the warnings, which included at least two cease and desist letters, Pozsgai relentlessly filled in the land. Even after the United States Attorney filed a civil action and obtained a temporary restraining order ("TRO") against him, Pozsgai remained undeterred. Two days after the issuance of the TRO, a video camera installed by the EPA on nearby property recorded the dumping of twenty-five truckloads of debris onto the land and showed Pozsgai operating a bulldozer to level the fill. Shortly thereafter, the court held Pozsgai in contempt.

Like their counterparts in other wetlands prosecutions then, Pozsgai's and Ellen's violations were neither casual nor inadvertent. They were committed in flagrant disregard of clearly stated rules of the game.

The trait of flagrant disregard of authority becomes manifest in other offense characteristics as well. Many wetlands violations that resulted in criminal prosecution were aggravated by acts of misrepresentation, concealment and obstruction. Defendants lied to the Corps of Engineers about wetlands on property they were developing. They falsely promised regulators that they would come into compliance, but at the same time instructed their workers to proceed apace. They lied to purchasers of property about the nature of the work being performed and the regulated status of the property, and erected physical barriers to conceal illegal construction activity from public view. One defendant even threatened his environmental consultant, ordering him to destroy an unfavorable report on the status of the property and not to communicate the contents to regulatory authorities. Although in this particular regard Ellen and Pozsgai were not the worst of the lot, their crimes were compounded by acts of misrepresentation and concealment as well. . . .

What lessons can be learned from this cautionary tale? . . .

First, it is abundantly clear that criminal prosecution for wetlands violations is the exception rather than the rule. Public relations campaigns notwithstanding to the contrary, the criminal enforcement record reflects sometimes remarkable restraint. The details of the record reveal that the decision to prosecute normally follows repeated efforts by Corps and other officials to obtain compliance through persistent but relatively informal administrative steps over a substantial period of time. Criminal prosecution seems to be viewed as a measure of last, rather than first, resort. Stated differently, the criminal enforcement record is consistent with highly selective enforcement decisions that reserve criminal prosecution for the rare (but aggravated) case.

A second lesson flows from the first. The case studies reveal recurring patterns of flagrant and repeated violations committed under circumstances that leave no room for doubt about the violator's culpability. The decision to prosecute more often than not follows repeated civil and administrative efforts to bring the violator into compliance. Thus, no matter how technical or complex wetlands regulations may be, criminal liability for wetlands violations is not a trap for the unwary. The criminal wetlands cases are (or should become) notorious for the wealth of evidence of actual culpability. The defendants had all been warned that they were violating the law. Nonetheless, they all chose to ignore the warnings, and in many instances took affirmative steps to cover their tracks. The picture that emerges is one of a cast of characters who are, on the whole, an uncommonly colorful lot. Defiant, deceitful and largely unrepentant, their violations bespeak disdain for regulatory authority rather than a failure to comprehend arcane and technical regulations. They obstinately refused to conform their conduct to the law.

A third and related lesson is that those who are prosecuted for wetlands violations are scarcely unsophisticated innocents. On the contrary, they are almost exclusively knowledgeable economic actors. They are businesses and experienced businessmen whose economic stake can provide a powerful incentive to ignore wetlands regulations that could delay, impede or even prevent a lucrative commercial development. They seem to view the possibility of a civil fine or restoration order and the minimal risk of criminal prosecution as costs of doing business — nothing more, nothing less.

C. CRIMINAL ENFORCEMENT RECORD

Between 1970 and 1980, only 25 criminal environmental prosecutions occurred at the federal level.[23] But between 1983 and 1993, the government obtained 911 environmental crime indictments and 686 guilty pleas and convictions.[24] During the same period, Congress repeatedly added new criminal provisions to the major environmental statutes, upgraded most misdemeanor violations to felonies, and generally provided more severe penalties for environmental crimes. Several factors seem to have contributed to the increased emphasis on criminal enforcement.[25]

First, most of the key environmental statutes were relatively new in the 1970s. It may well be that courts, regulators, and the regulated community needed time to become fully acquainted with these complex regulatory schemes before the government embarked on a course of vigorous criminal enforcement.

Second, the enactment of CERCLA and the addition of felony penalties to RCRA provided greater impetus for the government to pursue hazardous waste prosecutions.

Third, with the establishment of the Office of Criminal Enforcement at EPA and of the Environmental Crimes Section in the Justice Department, the government began to develop expertise in investigating and prosecuting environmental cases. The creation of these new units facilitated cooperation between EPA and Justice and made criminal investigation and prosecution of environmental violations far less cumbersome.

Although the increase was relatively gradual until the mid-1990s, the number of criminal referrals EPA made to the Justice Department rose from 31 in 1984 to 256 in 2001.[26] At the same time, the number of defendants

---

[23] Habicht, *The Federal Perspective on Environmental Criminal Enforcement: How to Remain on the Civil Side*, 17 ELR 10478, 10479 (Dec. 1987).

[24] *National Enforcement Investigations Center Summary of Environmental Criminal Prosecutions, reprinted in* 2 C. HARRIS, R. MARSHALL & P. CAVANAUGH, ENVIRONMENTAL CRIMES, Appendix F (1992).

[25] The factors discussed in the text are derived from Habicht, *supra* note 23, at 10479-10480.

[26] Arnold W. Reitze, Jr., *Criminal Enforcement of Pollution Control Laws*, 9 ENVTL. LAW. 1, 11 (2002). The number of criminal referrals during this period peaked at 278 in 1997.

charged rose from 36 in 1984 to 372 in 2001.[27] Annual EPA enforcement data through 2007 indicate a downward trend in the overall number of defendants charged.[28]

1. CHARGING PRACTICES

Criminal enforcement priorities initially developed along two different but complementary lines. On the one hand, prosecutors gave high priority to prosecuting those who operated completely out of the system (e.g., midnight dumpers who had no permits). On the other hand, prosecutors gave enforcement priority to those who purportedly operated within the system but misrepresented or concealed the nature or extent or their regulated activities (e.g., permit holders who filed EPA reports that falsely represented the holders had complied with conditions contained in their permits).

While criminal cases have been brought under all of the major environmental statutes, Clean Water Act and RCRA violations are by far the most commonly prosecuted environmental crimes. In 1997, for example, more than half of all environmental crime prosecutions were brought under the Clean Water Act, and nearly 30 percent were hazardous waste prosecutions brought under RCRA.

---

[27]*Id.*

[28]The EPA data also indicate a downward trend in the number of criminal investigations initiated over the last five years. Detailed criminal and civil enforcement data are available in annual EPA reports on enforcement and compliance results, which can be accessed at http://www.epa.gov/compliance/data/results/annual/index.html.

TABLE 1
DEFENDANTS CHARGED BY STATUTE[29]

OFFENSE	1992	1994	1995	1996	1997	1998	2000
CLEAN WATER ACT	51	52	88	97	108	119	90
CLEAN AIR ACT	6	19	36	40	31	51	39
RCRA	38	31	34	37	59	58	25
CERCLA	9	11	15	4	4	0	4
TSCA	11	6	6	12	6	3	0
REFUSE ACT	6	0	—	5	—	2	2
OTHER[30]	23	8	43	5	1	0	0

It is not uncommon for violations of more than one environmental statute to be charged in these prosecutions. A comprehensive study of the first decade of RCRA prosecutions found that the government filed charges under multiple environmental statutes in more than 40 percent of RCRA cases, and that violations of CERCLA and the Clean Water Act were most frequently charged in tandem with RCRA violations. Upon reflection, this charging pattern should come as no surprise.

The prevalence of combined charges under RCRA and CERCLA may be explained by their complementary regulatory schemes. While RCRA regulates hazardous waste management practices, CERCLA regulates the release of "hazardous substances" — a term that includes RCRA hazardous wastes — into the environment. CERCLA imposes a duty on responsible parties to notify authorities when a "reportable quantity" of hazardous substances is released into the environment. The following example illustrates how the statutes work in tandem. The manager of a waste treatment facility dumps hazardous waste onto the ground without a permit. The dumping constitutes illegal disposal of the waste in violation of RCRA. If the amount of waste is a reportable quantity, the release of the

---

[29] Adapted from Bureau of Justice Statistics, Special Report: Federal Enforcement of Environmental Laws, 1997, at 5 [hereinafter BJS Special Report], and Reitze, *supra* note 26, at 15.

[30] Excludes prosecutions under the Prevention of Pollution From Ships Act and under wildlife protection statutes.

waste into the environment triggers a CERCLA duty to notify authorities. Failure to report the release is a felony under CERCLA. Thus, the illegal disposal charge (RCRA) dovetails with the failure to notify charge (CERCLA), and both violations could logically arise in a single prosecution.[31]

Similarly, it is not uncommon for prosecutors to bring hybrid environmental prosecutions that combine environmental charges with charges brought under conventional criminal statutes — primarily Title 18 crimes.[32] Although the RCRA study found that Title 18 charges were brought under nearly 20 different criminal statutes,[33] violations of the conspiracy and false statements statutes were by far the most commonly charged. Conspiracy charges were included in nearly 70 percent of RCRA prosecutions in which Title 18 violations were alleged, and false statements charges were brought in nearly 35 percent of the cases.[34] Fourteen percent of hybrid RCRA prosecutions alleged both conspiracy and false statements violations.

These charging practices reveal significant information about the dynamics of the underlying environmental crimes. Conspiracy doctrine requires proof of multiple criminal actors and conventional criminal intent. The false statements statute requires proof that the actor lied to the government to deceive or conceal.[35] Thus, these defendants are scarcely the "innocents at risk" portrayed by criminal enforcement critics. Instead of involving a single isolated act, these prosecutions are based on a course of conduct that violates multiple criminal laws.

---

[31]Kathleen F. Brickey, *Charging Practices in Hazardous Waste Crime Prosecutions*, 62 Ohio St. L.J. 1077, 1109-1112 (2001) [hereinafter Brickey, *RCRA Charging Practices*].

[32]*See supra* Chapter 8.

[33]Although the next most prevalent charge was mail fraud, other charges included false claims violations (18 U.S.C. § 287), perjury (18 U.S.C. §§ 1621, 1623), bank fraud (18 U.S.C. § 1344), RICO violations (18 U.S.C. § 1962), and obstruction of justice (18 U.S.C. §§ 1503, 1510, 1512).

[34]Brickey, *RCRA Charging Practices*, *supra* note 31, at 1106-1109. The conspiracy charges were brought under 18 U.S.C. § 371, and false statements charges were brought under the general federal false statements statute, 18 U.S.C. §1001. *See supra* Chapter 8.

[35]The RCRA study revealed that in prosecutions brought under the false statements statute, the defendants lied on industrial waste questionnaires, falsely claimed they were exempt from EPA regulations, lied about how they generated and stored hazardous industrial wastes, and misrepresented that hazardous wastes had been incinerated. Brickey, *RCRA Charging Practices*, *supra* note 31, at 1112-1113.

An analysis of the occupational status of individual defendants in the RCRA study is also telling. A high percentage of those who were prosecuted were corporate owners, officers, and managers who had substantial authority and operational responsibility.[36] They were not, in the main, low-level subordinates who were just "following orders" from above. And, in addition, recent studies suggest that about 15 percent of all defendants charged with environmental crimes are organizations.[37]

2. OUTCOMES

As is true in the context of prosecutions brought under criminal statutes of general applicability, a high percentage of environmental prosecutions result in convictions. In 1997, 85 percent of the defendants who were prosecuted for environmental crimes were convicted, and — as is typical in federal prosecutions — approximately 90 percent of the convictions were obtained through guilty pleas.

Sentences imposed on environmental defendants tend to be at the low end of the scale, however. First, far fewer environmental defendants are sentenced to prison than defendants who are convicted of other categories of crimes. While roughly 80 percent of all defendants convicted of federal crimes are sent to prison, between 1995 and 2001 only about 35 percent of environmental defendants received prison terms.[38]

Second, the length of prison sentences imposed in environmental prosecutions tends to be shorter than average. Nearly 60 percent of environmental defendants who were sentenced to prison between 1995 and 2001 received sentences of one year or less,[39] in contrast with only about 25 percent of all defendants sentenced to prison during that time.[40] On the high end of the scale, a very small number of environmental defendants were sentenced to a term of more than six years,[41] while more than a fifth of all defendants who were sentenced to prison received sentences that long.[42]

---

[36]Brickey, *RCRA Charging Practices, supra* note 31, at 1123-1128.

[37]*See* BJS Special Report, *supra* note 29, at 4. In the RCRA study, the percentage of corporate defendants was considerably higher.

[38]Michael M. O'Hear, *Sentencing the Green-Collar Offender: Punishment, Culpability, and Environmental Crime*, 95 J. CRIM. L. & CRIMINOLOGY 133, 205, Table 1 (2004).

[39]*Id.* at 206, Table 2.

[40]*Id.* at 207, Table 3.

[41]About 2%.

[42]*Id.* at 206-207, Tables 2 & 3.

About 20 percent of environmental defendants who were sentenced to prison terms received sentences of 1-2 years, about 10 percent were sentenced to serve 2-4 years, and roughly 5 percent were ordered to serve terms of 4-6 years.[43] On average, these sentences were shorter than sentences imposed on defendants convicted of other types of crimes.[44]

Approximately two thirds of environmental defendants were sentenced to pay a fine, either as the exclusive criminal penalty or in combination with a sentence of imprisonment and/or probation.[45]

But the entry of a criminal conviction and imposition of a sentence may not be the end of the road. In addition to the attendant adverse publicity and potentially ruinous private civil suits, other collateral statutory and administrative consequences — some of which are mandatory — may flow from the fact of conviction.

Thus, for example, convictions under the Clean Water and Clean Air Acts may result in automatic administrative penalties that bar convicted individual and organizational defendants from contracting with federal agencies.[46] Such bans remain in effect until EPA certifies that the condition that led to the conviction has been corrected. For some violations, EPA also has authority to ban performance of government contracts at related facilities that may have had no involvement in the violation. Thus, a conviction based on conduct that occurs at only one of many facilities that are under common ownership or control can affect the ability of the entire organization to obtain or perform lucrative government contracts.

And then there is the prospect of parallel civil and criminal government investigations and proceedings. As a general matter, EPA and the Justice Department have concurrent civil environmental enforcement authority that may be exercised contemporaneously with a criminal investigation and prosecution. To compound the problem further, there is the additional prospect of state and local enforcement actions — both civil and criminal — based on the conduct that gave rise to the federal criminal

---

[43]*Id.* at 206, Table 2.

[44]The comparisons for all defendants who were sentenced to serve prison terms during the same period are as follows: about 18% of the defendants were sentenced to serve 1-2 years, 20% were sentenced to 2-4 year terms, and nearly 14% were sentenced to serve 4-6 years of imprisonment. *Id.* at 207, Table 3.

[45]BJS Special Report, *supra* note 29, at 5.

[46]33 U.S.C. § 1368(a) (Clean Water Act); 42 U.S.C. § 7606(a) (Clean Air Act). The bar applies if the contract is to be performed at the facility that gave rise to the conviction and the facility is run by the convicted individual or organization.

charges. Thus, the opening of an EPA or Justice Department criminal investigation may well be only the tip of the iceberg.

TABLE OF CASES

Principal cases appear in italics.

TABLE OF STATUTES

FEDERAL STATUTES

United States Code

GLOSSARY OF ACRONYMS

ACOE	Army Corps of Engineers
CAA	Clean Air Act
CEO	Chief Executive Officer
CERCLA	Comprehensive Environmental Response, Compensation, and Liability Act
CWA	Clean Water Act
DEP	Department of Environmental Protection
DOJ	Department of Justice
EPA	Environmental Protection Agency
EPCRA	Emergency Planning and Community Right-to-Know Act
FBI	Federal Bureau of Investigation
FDA	Food and Drug Administration
FFDCA	Federal Food, Drug, and Cosmetic Act
GAO	Government Accountability Office
MSHA	Mine Safety and Health Administration
NCP	National Contingency Plan
NESHAPs	National Emissions Standards for Hazardous Air Pollutants
NPDES	National Pollutant Discharge Elimination System
NRC	National Response Center
OCE	Office of Criminal Enforcement (EPA)
OSHA	Occupational Safety and Health Act
POTW	Publicly Owned Treatment Works
RCRA	Resource Conservation and Recovery Act
RQ	Reportable Quantity
SIPs	State Implementation Plans
SWANCC	Solid Waste Agency of Northern Cook County
TRO	Temporary Restraining Order
TSCA	Toxic Substances Control Act
TSD	Treatment, Storage, and Disposal Facility
WWTP	Wastewater Treatment Plant

INDEX